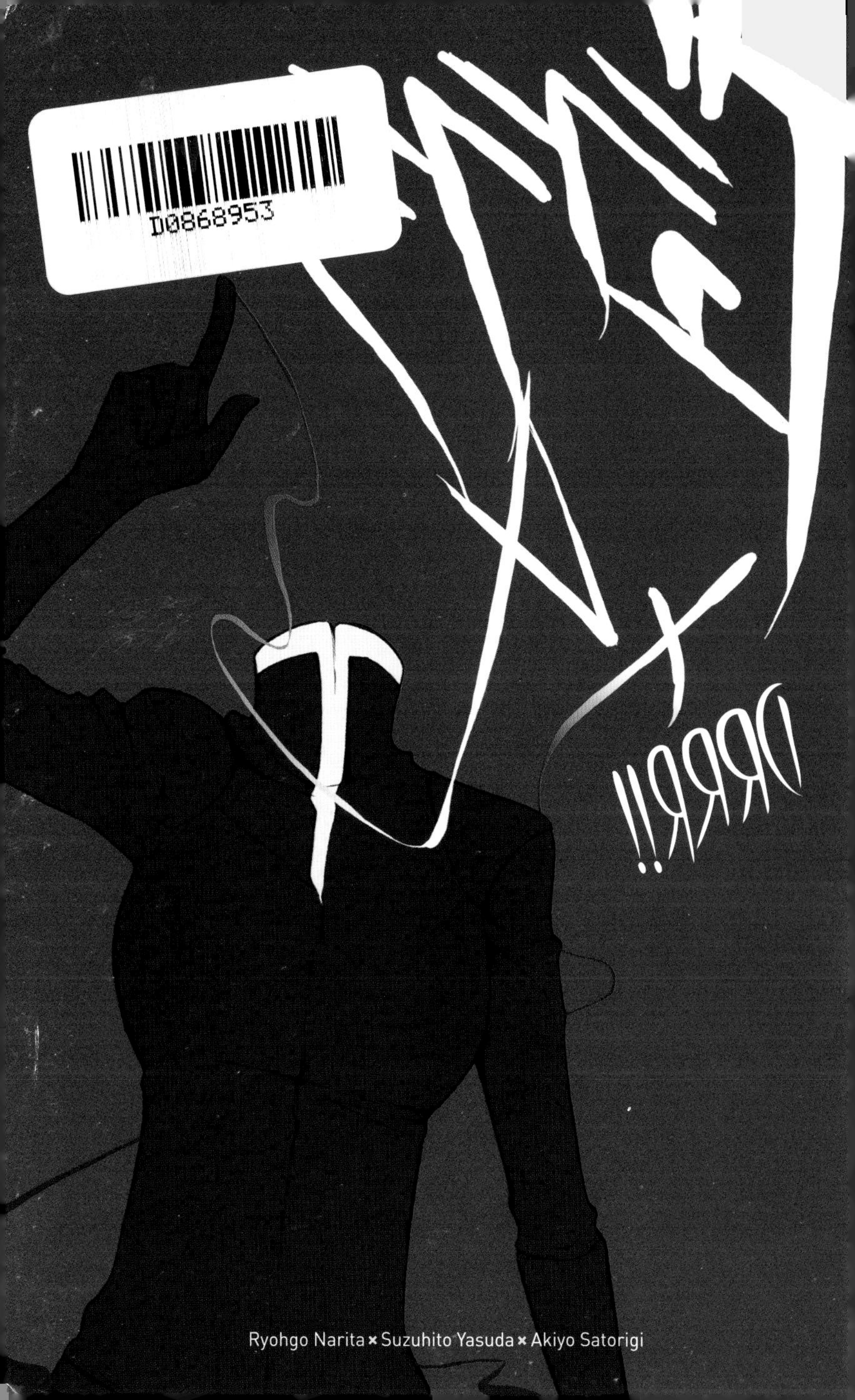
DRRR!!

Ryohgo Narita × Suzuhito Yasuda × Akiyo Satorigi

Contents

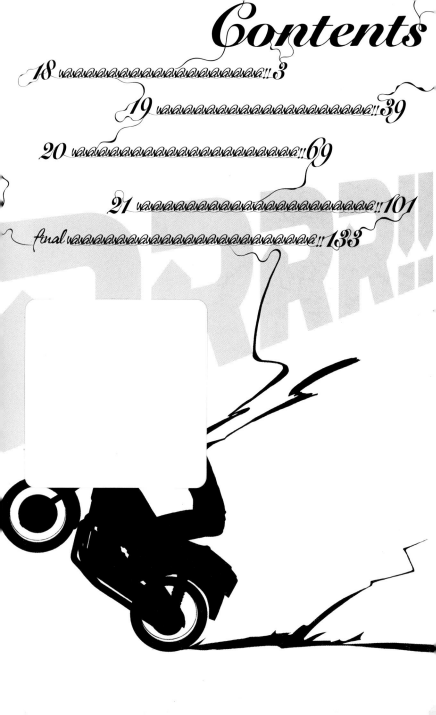

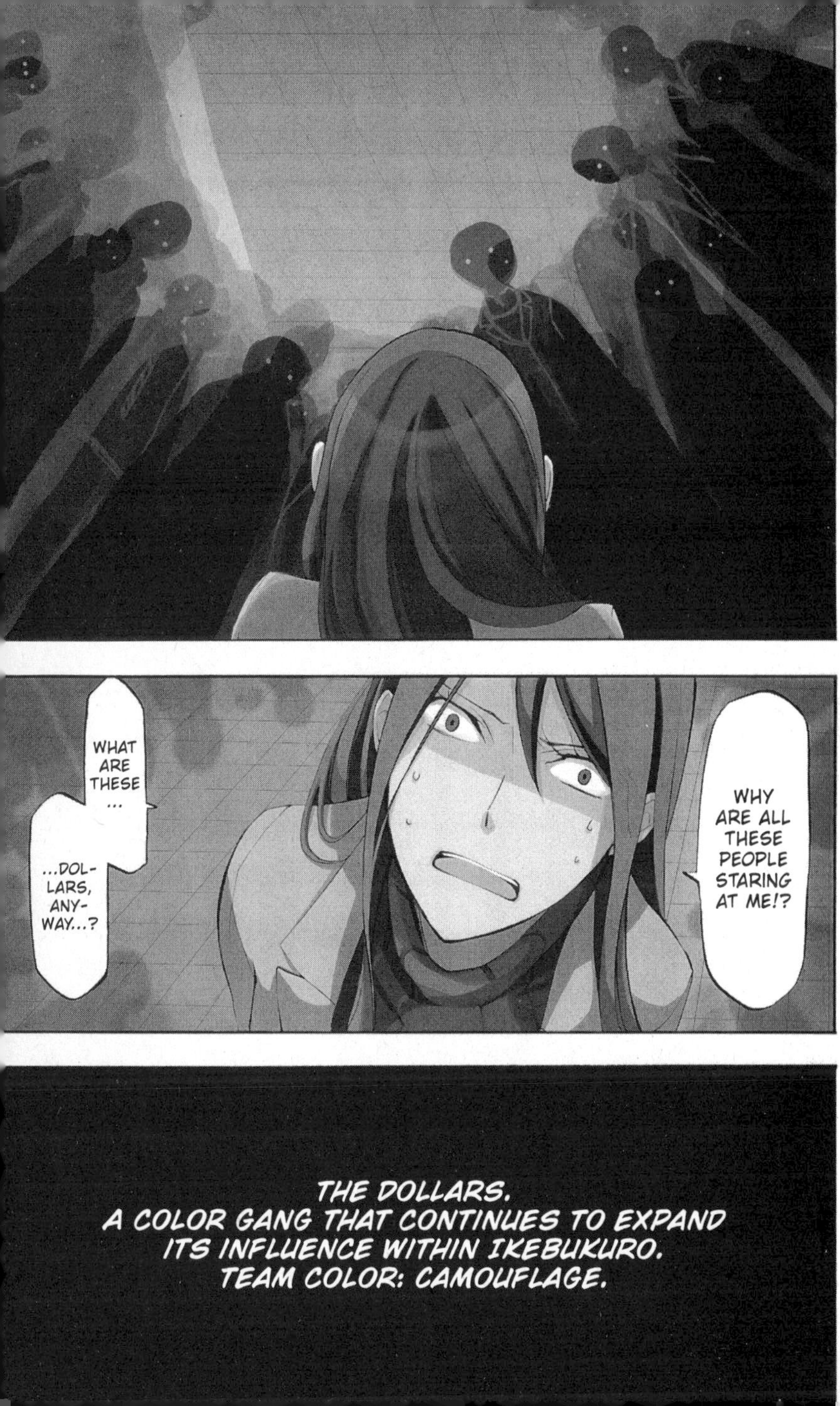
WHY ARE ALL THESE PEOPLE STARING AT ME!?
WHAT ARE THESE...
...DOL-LARS, ANY-WAY...?
THE DOLLARS.
A COLOR GANG THAT CONTINUES TO EXPAND ITS INFLUENCE WITHIN IKEBUKURO.
TEAM COLOR: CAMOUFLAGE.

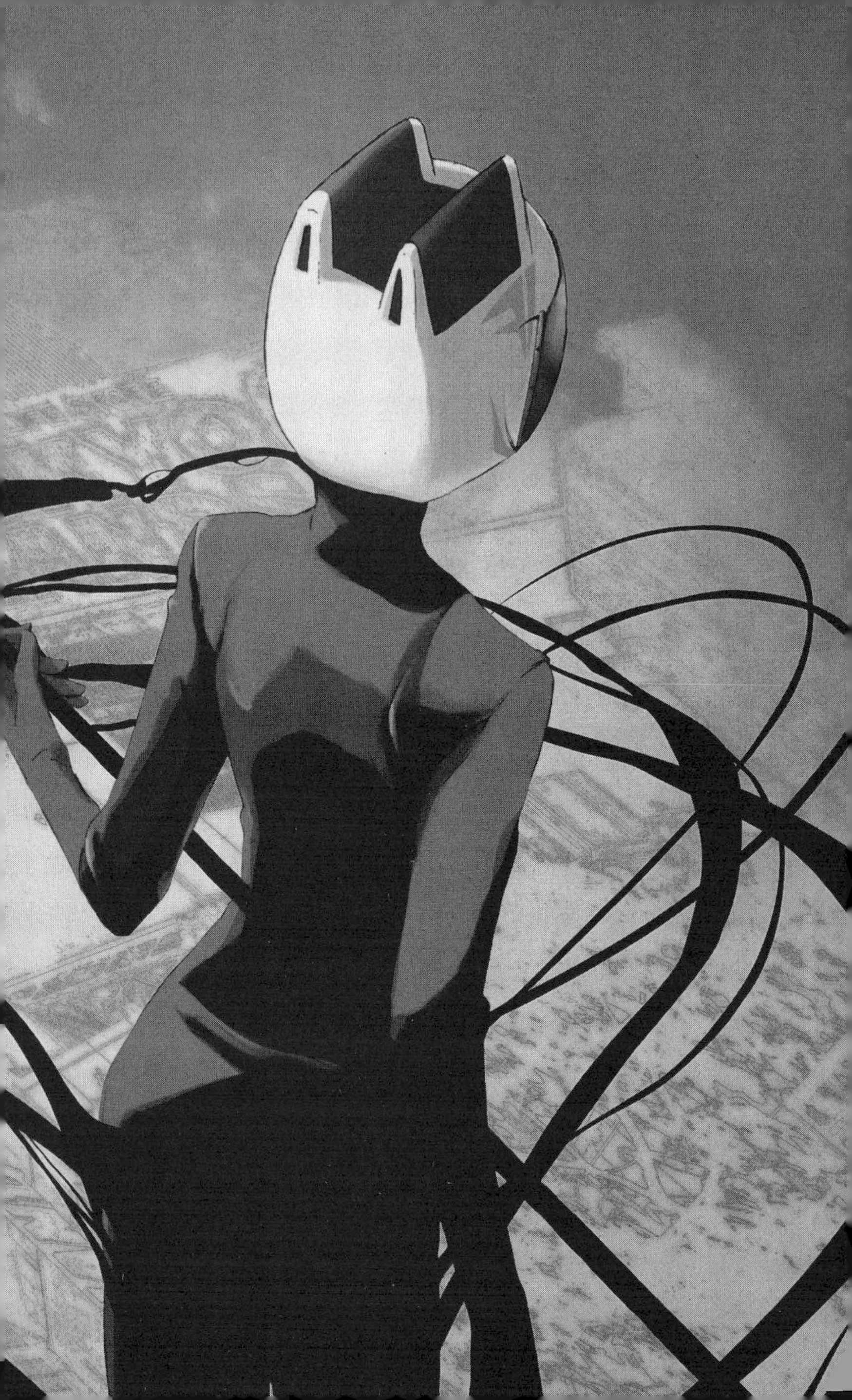

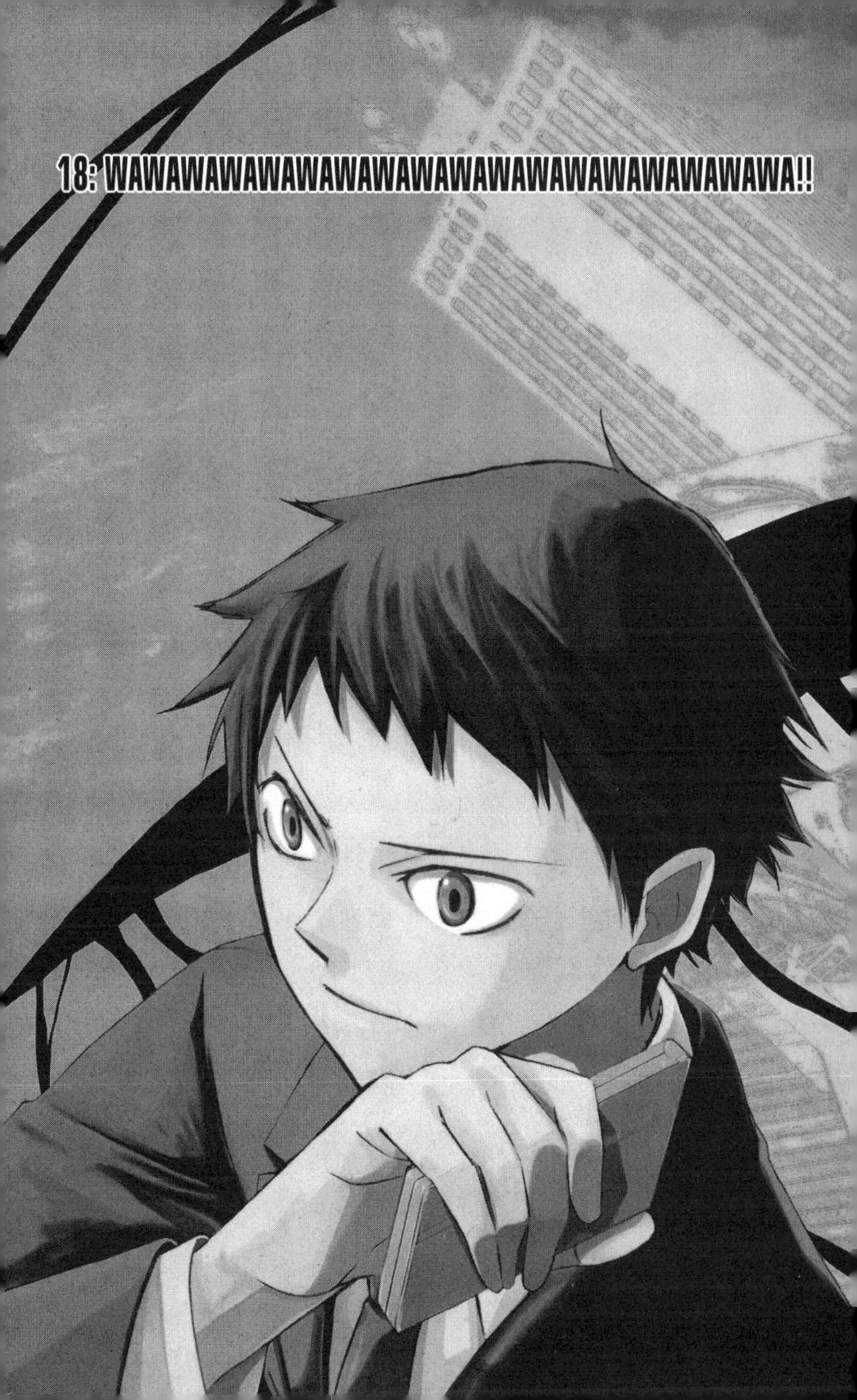
18: WAWAWAWAWAWAWAWAWAWAWAWAWAWAWAWAWAWAWAWA!!

DRRR!!

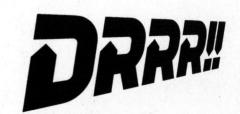

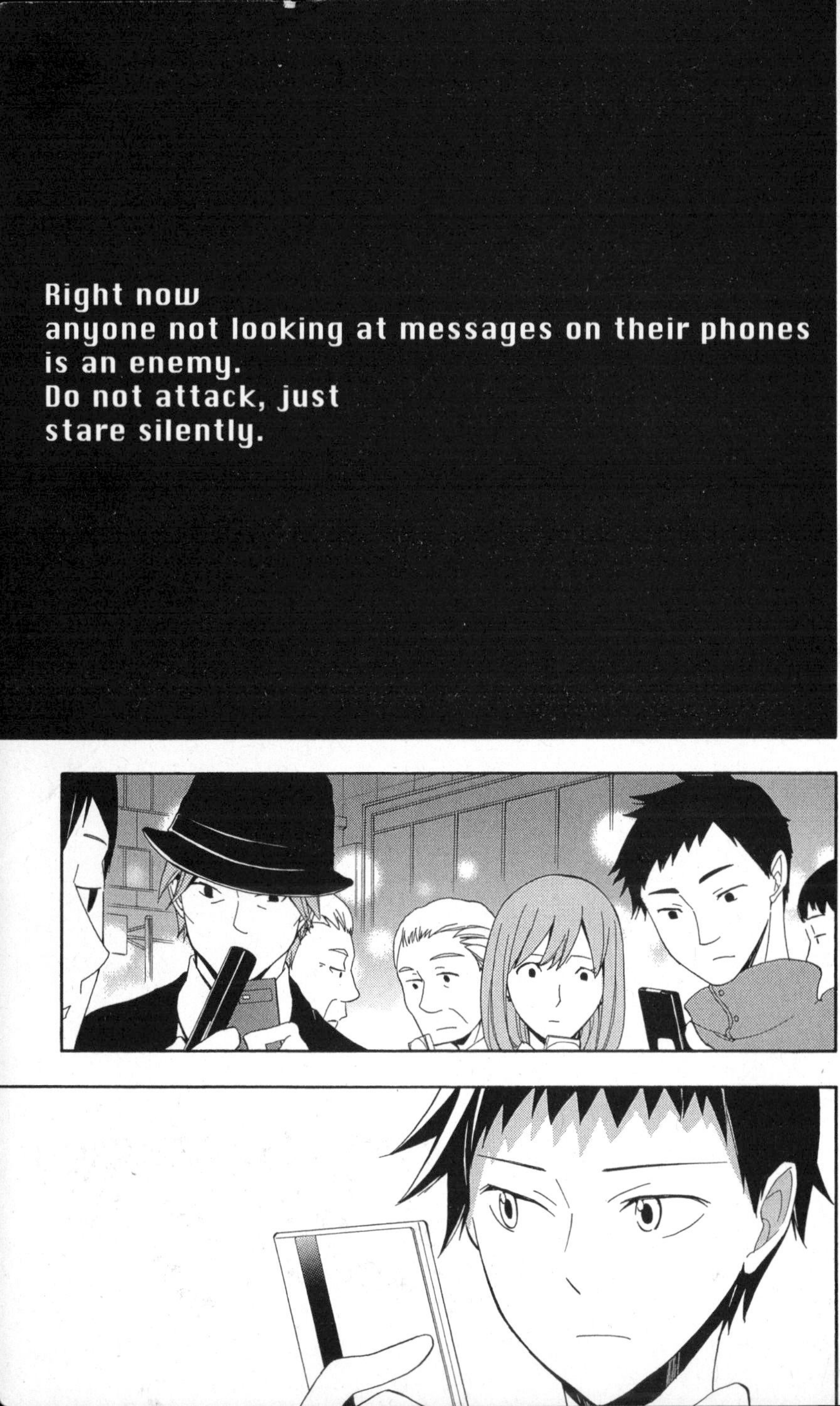
Right now
anyone not looking at messages on their phones
is an enemy.
Do not attack, just
stare silently.

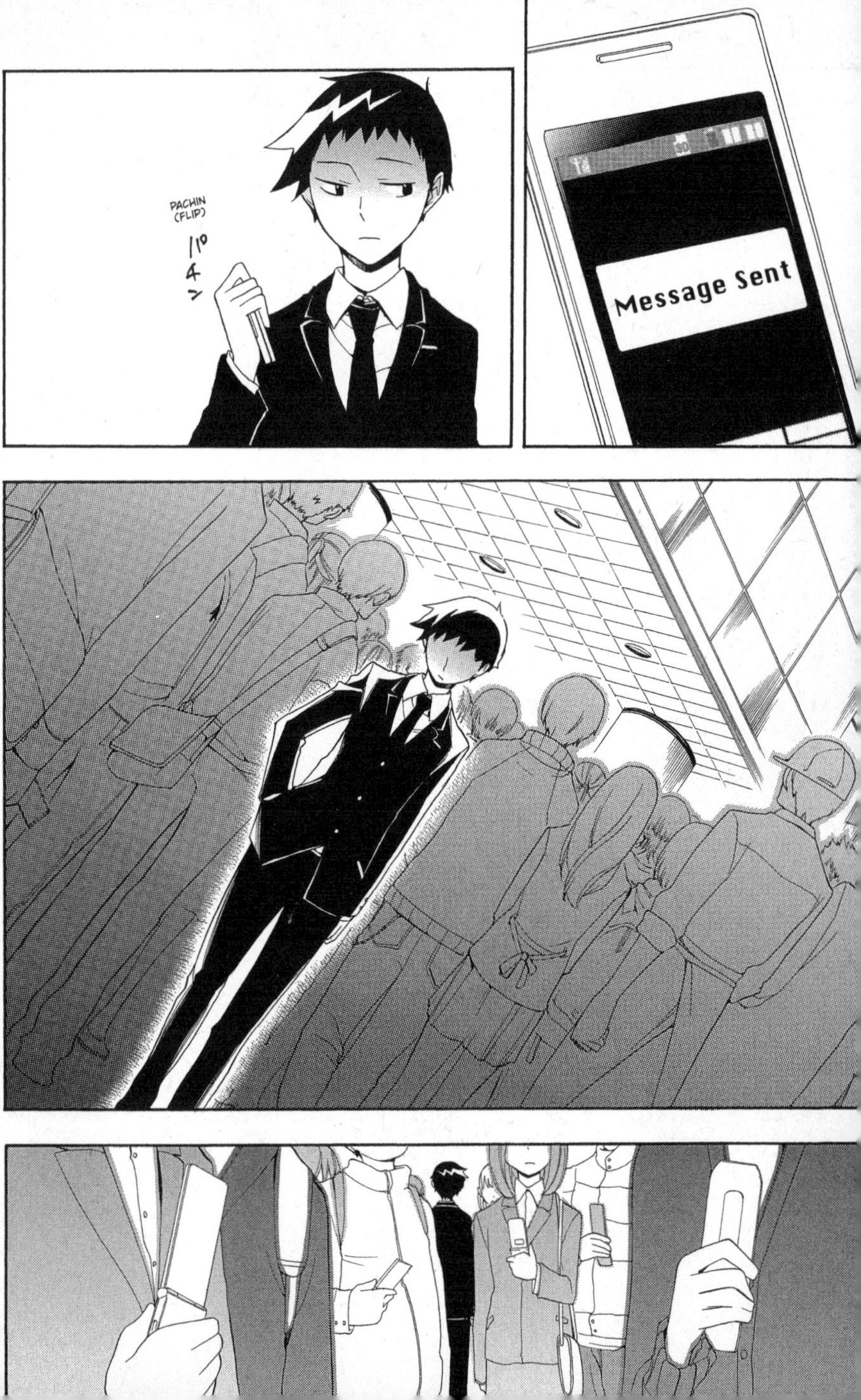
Message Sent
パチン
PACHIN (FLIP)

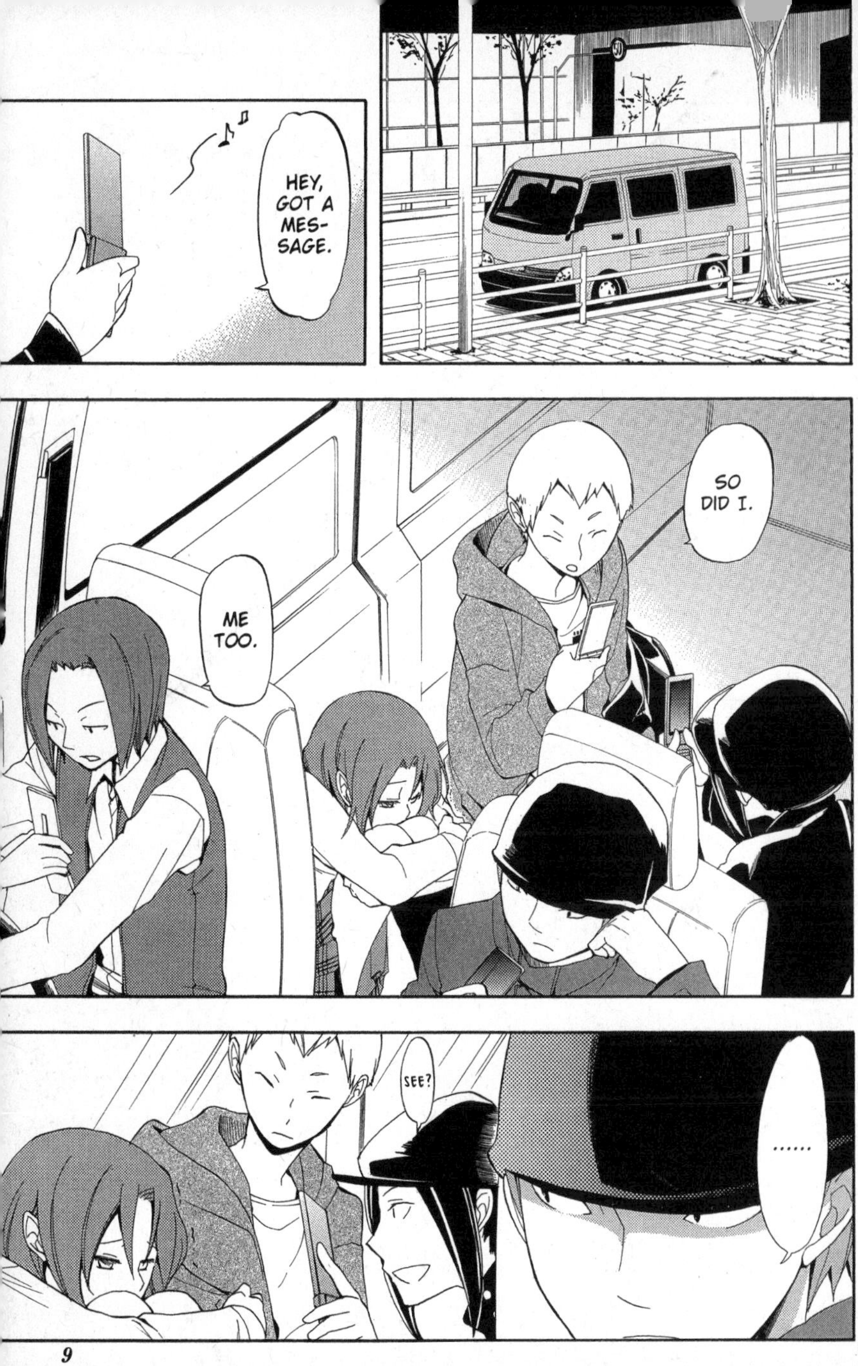

HEY, GOT A MES-SAGE.
SO DID I.
ME TOO.
......
SEE?

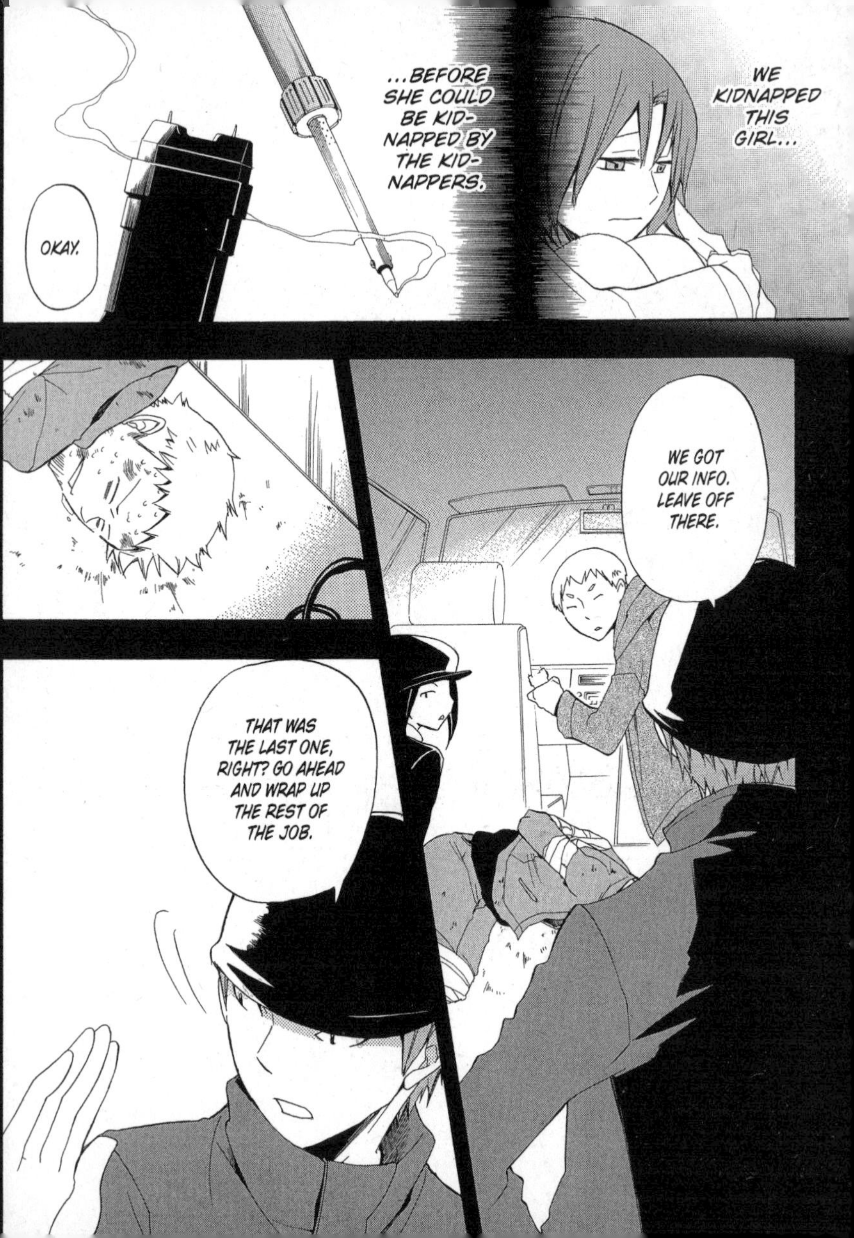
WE KIDNAPPED THIS GIRL...
...BEFORE SHE COULD BE KID-NAPPED BY THE KID-NAPPERS.
OKAY.
WE GOT OUR INFO. LEAVE OFF THERE.
THAT WAS THE LAST ONE, RIGHT? GO AHEAD AND WRAP UP THE REST OF THE JOB.

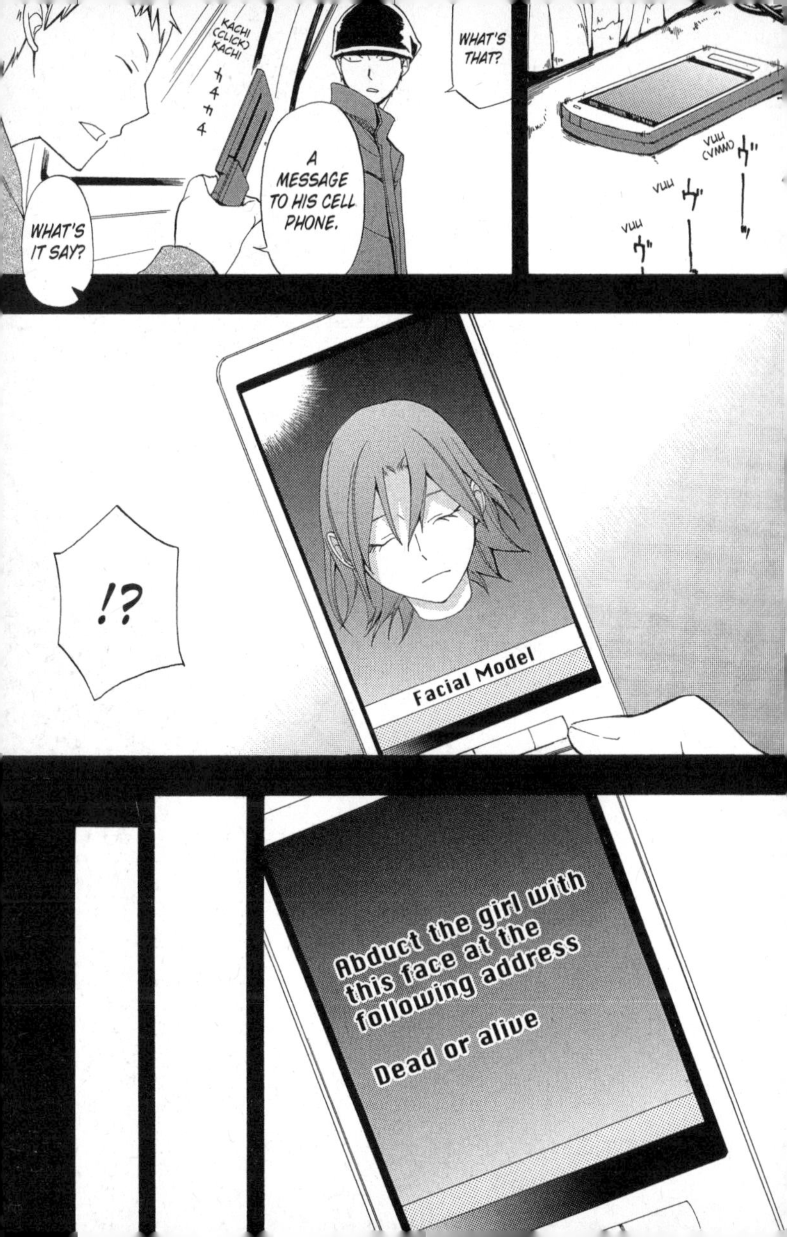
VUU (VMM)
VUU
VUU
WHAT'S THAT?
KACHI (CLICK) KACHI
A MESSAGE TO HIS CELL PHONE.
WHAT'S IT SAY?
!?
Facial Model
Abduct the girl with this face at the following address
Dead or alive

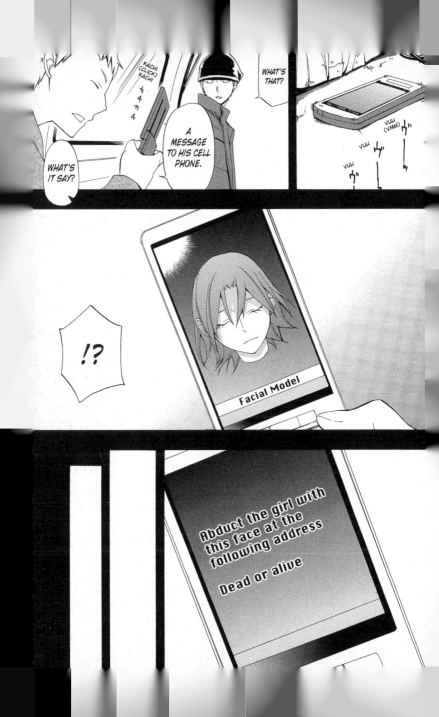

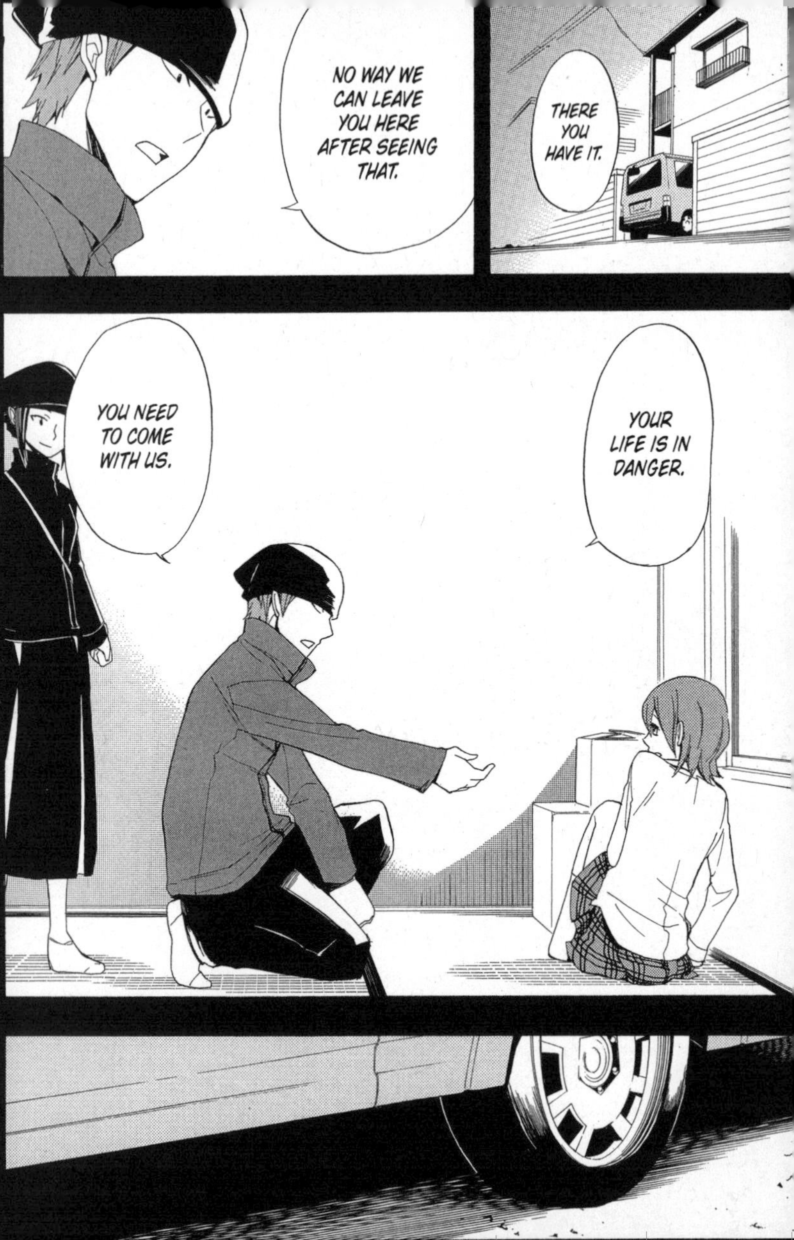
THERE YOU HAVE IT.
NO WAY WE CAN LEAVE YOU HERE AFTER SEEING THAT.
YOUR LIFE IS IN DANGER.
YOU NEED TO COME WITH US.

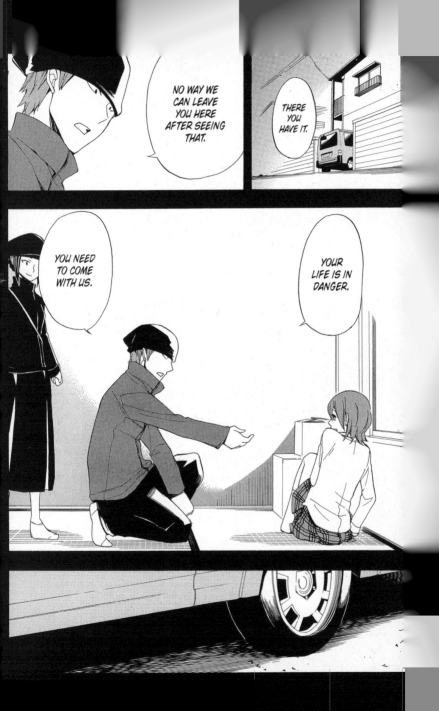

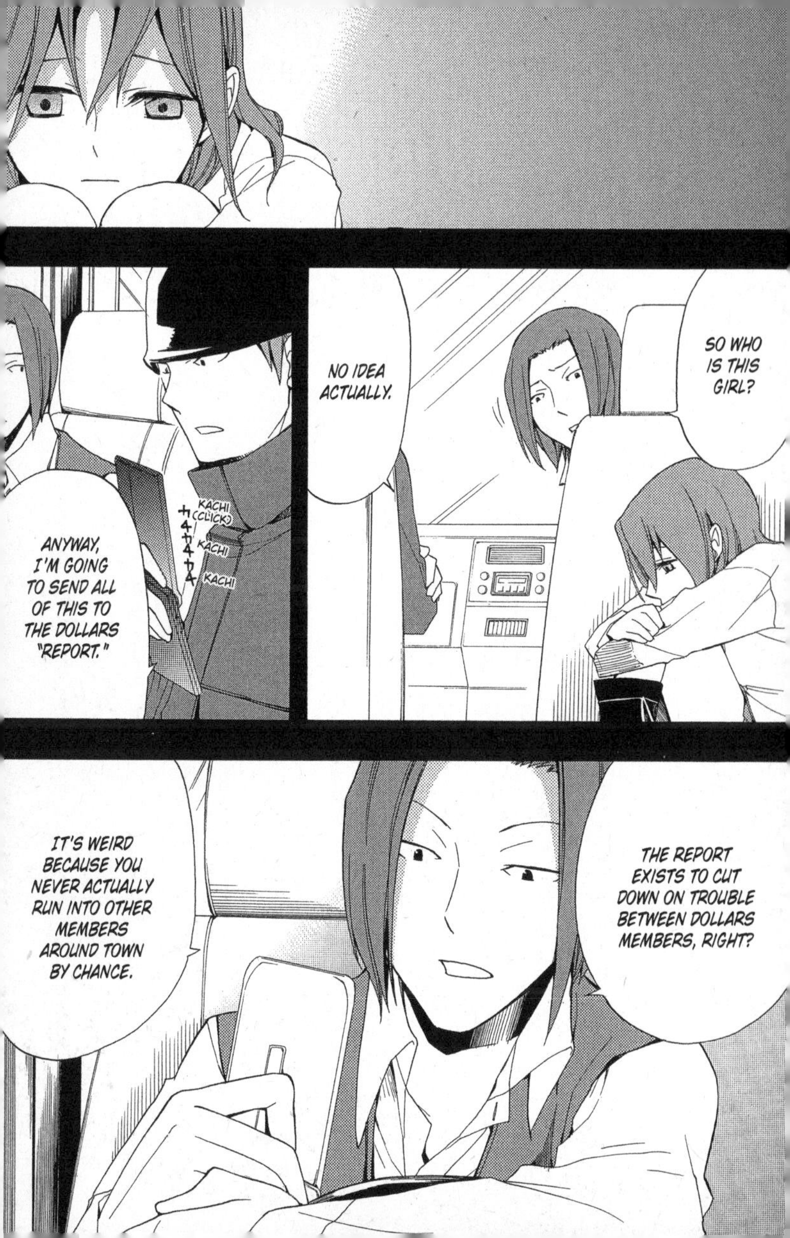
SO WHO IS THIS GIRL?
NO IDEA ACTUALLY.
カチカチカチ
KACHI (CLICK)
KACHI
KACHI
ANYWAY, I'M GOING TO SEND ALL OF THIS TO THE DOLLARS "REPORT."
THE REPORT EXISTS TO CUT DOWN ON TROUBLE BETWEEN DOLLARS MEMBERS, RIGHT?
IT'S WEIRD BECAUSE YOU NEVER ACTUALLY RUN INTO OTHER MEMBERS AROUND TOWN BY CHANCE.

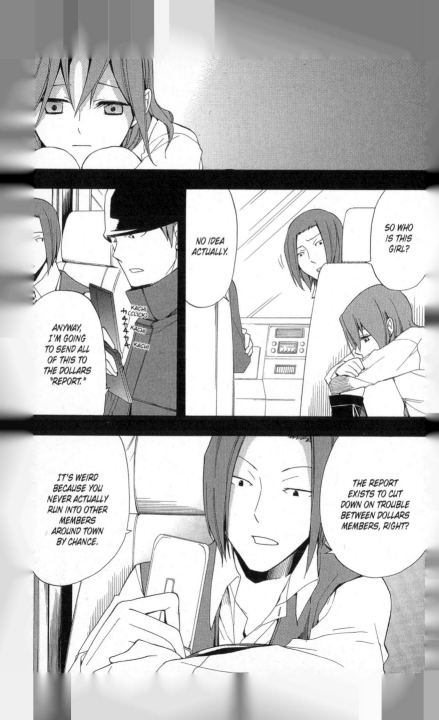

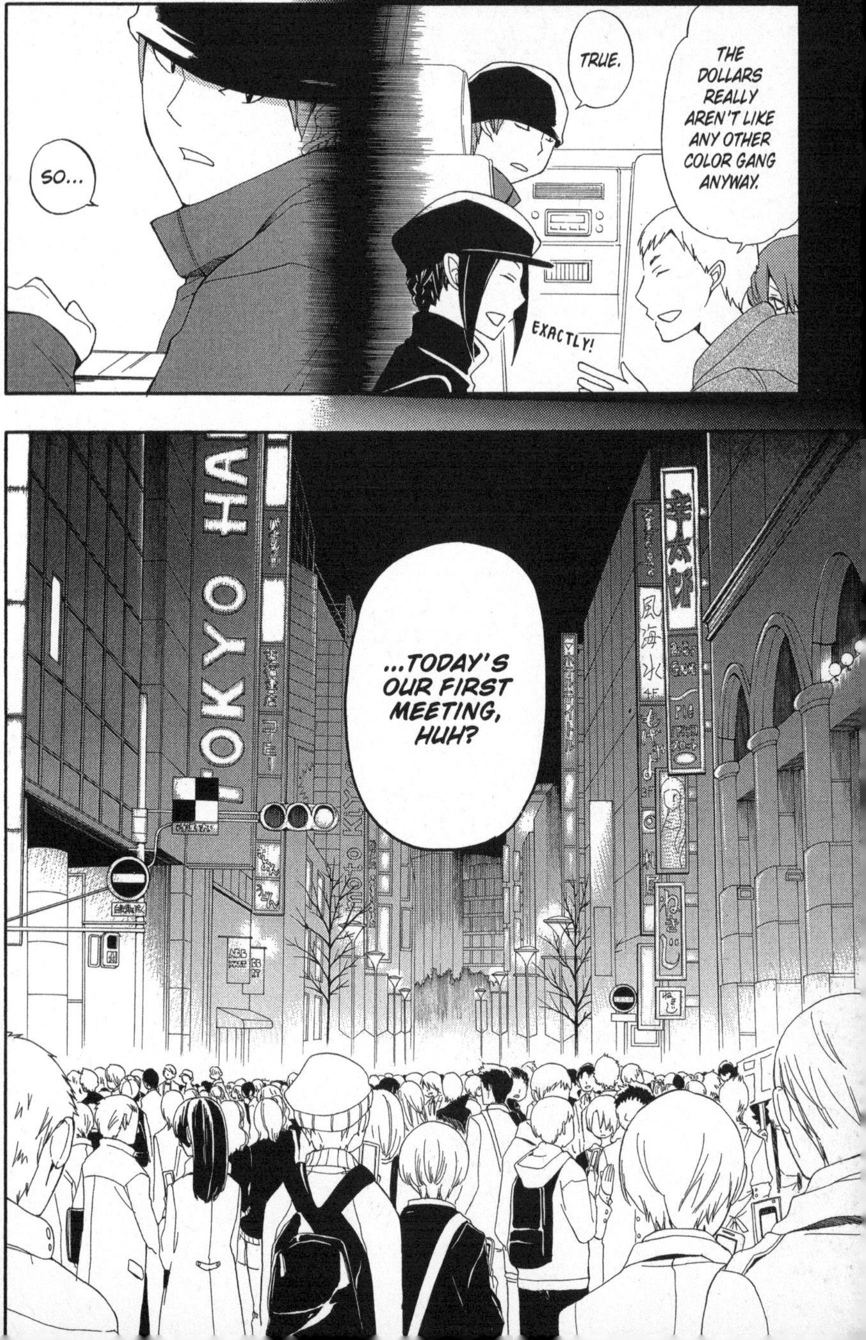
THE DOLLARS REALLY AREN'T LIKE ANY OTHER COLOR GANG ANYWAY.
TRUE.
EXACTLY!
SO...
TOKYO HA
...TODAY'S OUR FIRST MEETING, HUH?

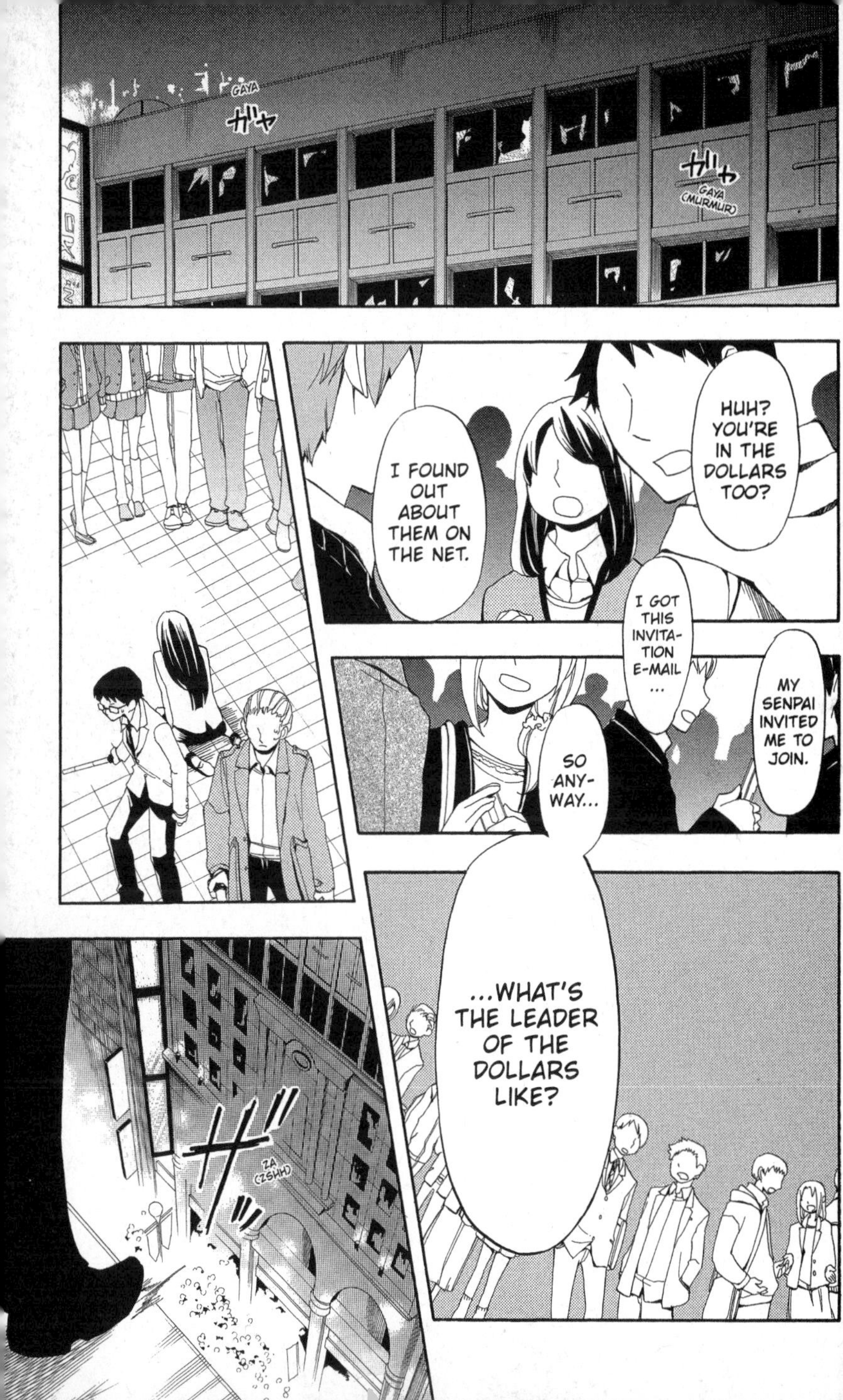
GAYA
ガヤ
ガヤ
GAYA (MURMUR)
HUH? YOU'RE IN THE DOLLARS TOO?
I FOUND OUT ABOUT THEM ON THE NET.
MY SENPAI INVITED ME TO JOIN.
I GOT THIS INVITATION E-MAIL...
SO ANYWAY...
...WHAT'S THE LEADER OF THE DOLLARS LIKE?
ザ
ZA (ZSHH)

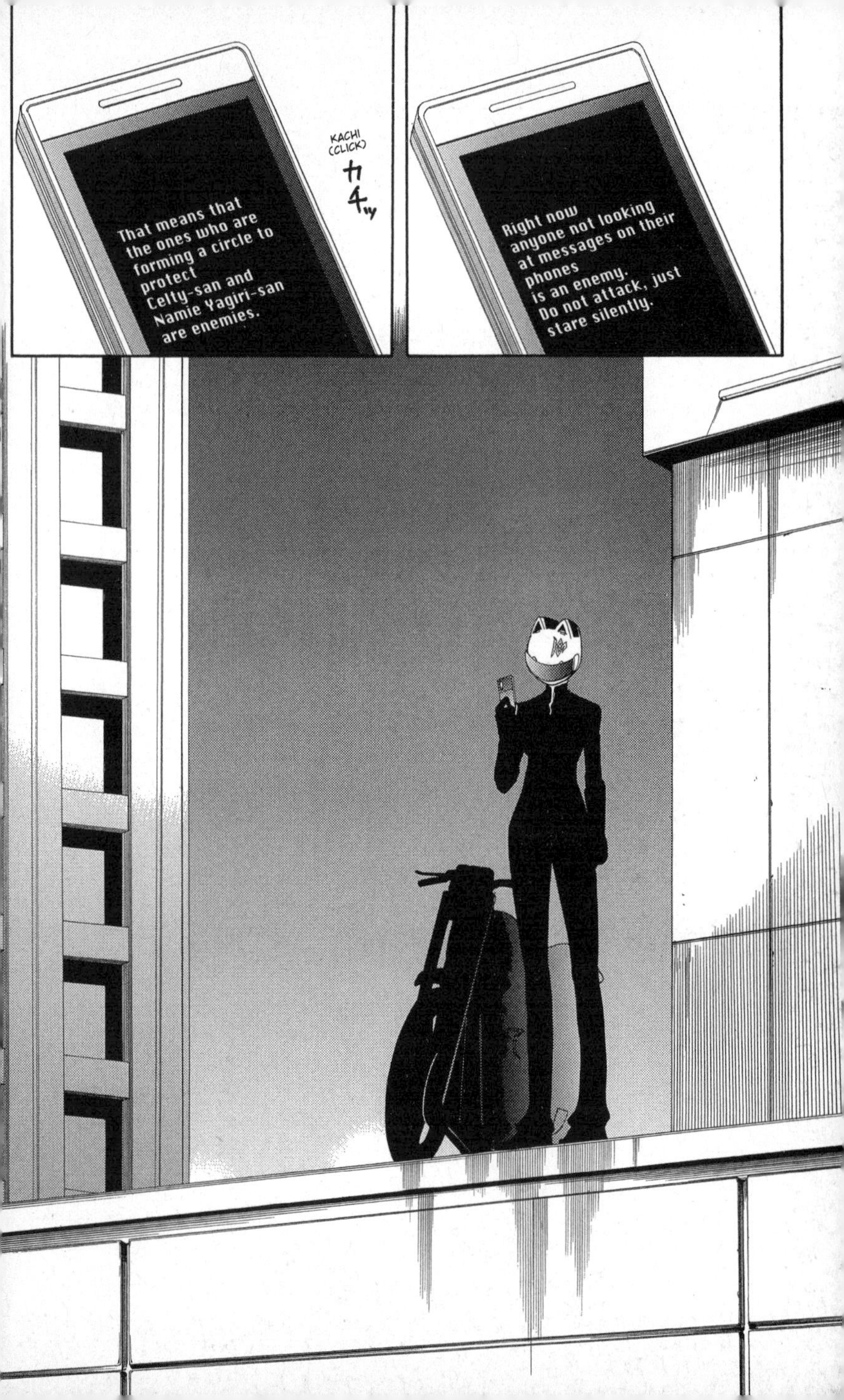
Right now
anyone not looking
at messages on their
phones
is an enemy.
Do not attack, just
stare silently.
KACHI
(CLICK)
カチッ
That means that
the ones who are
forming a circle to
protect
Celty-san and
Namie Yagiri-san
are enemies.

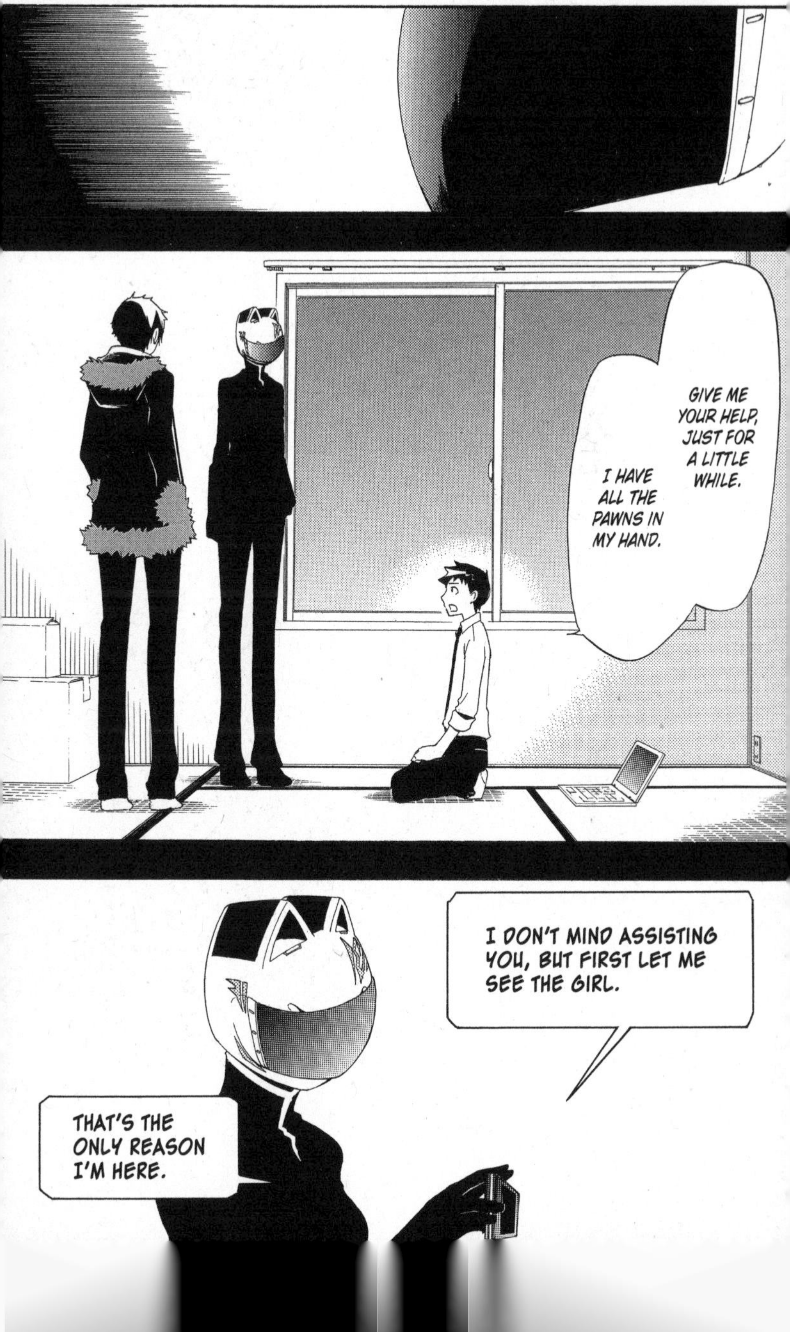
GIVE ME YOUR HELP, JUST FOR A LITTLE WHILE.
I HAVE ALL THE PAWNS IN MY HAND.
I DON'T MIND ASSISTING YOU, BUT FIRST LET ME SEE THE GIRL.
THAT'S THE ONLY REASON I'M HERE.

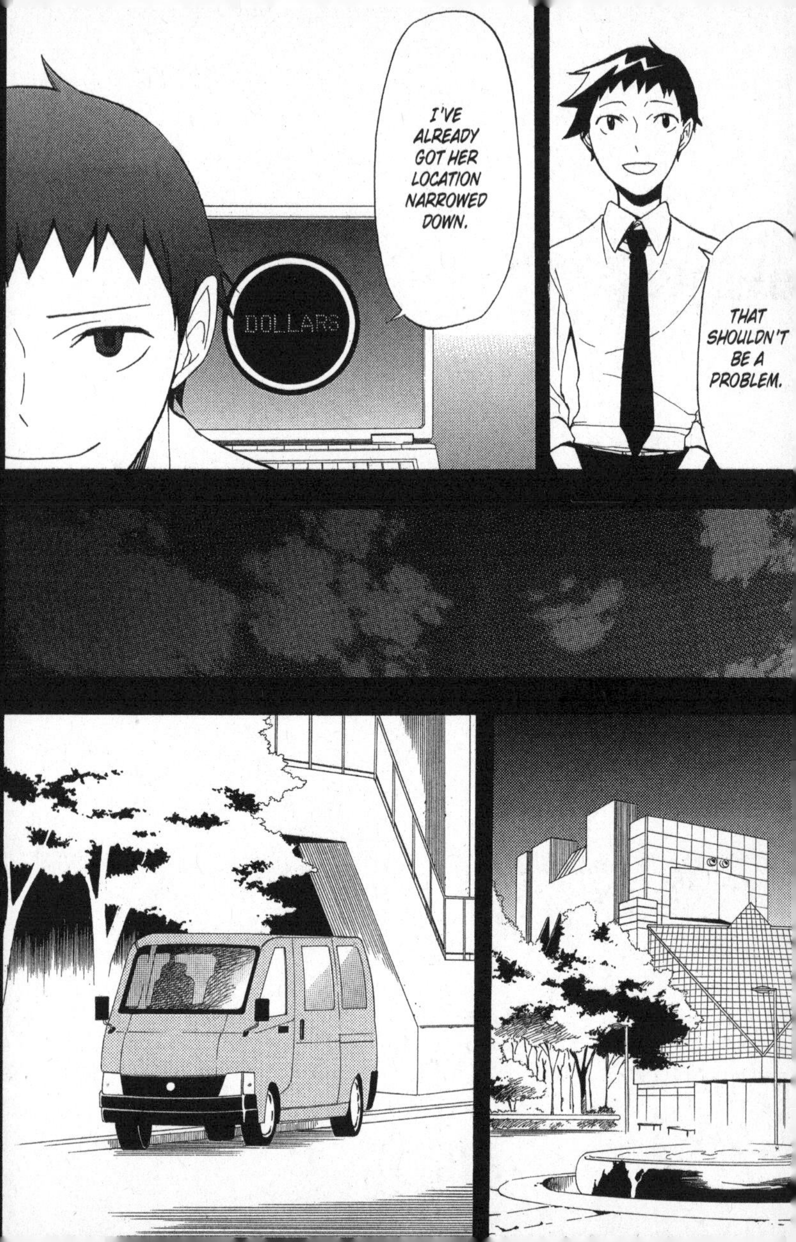
THAT SHOULDN'T BE A PROBLEM.
I'VE ALREADY GOT HER LOCATION NARROWED DOWN.
DOLLARS

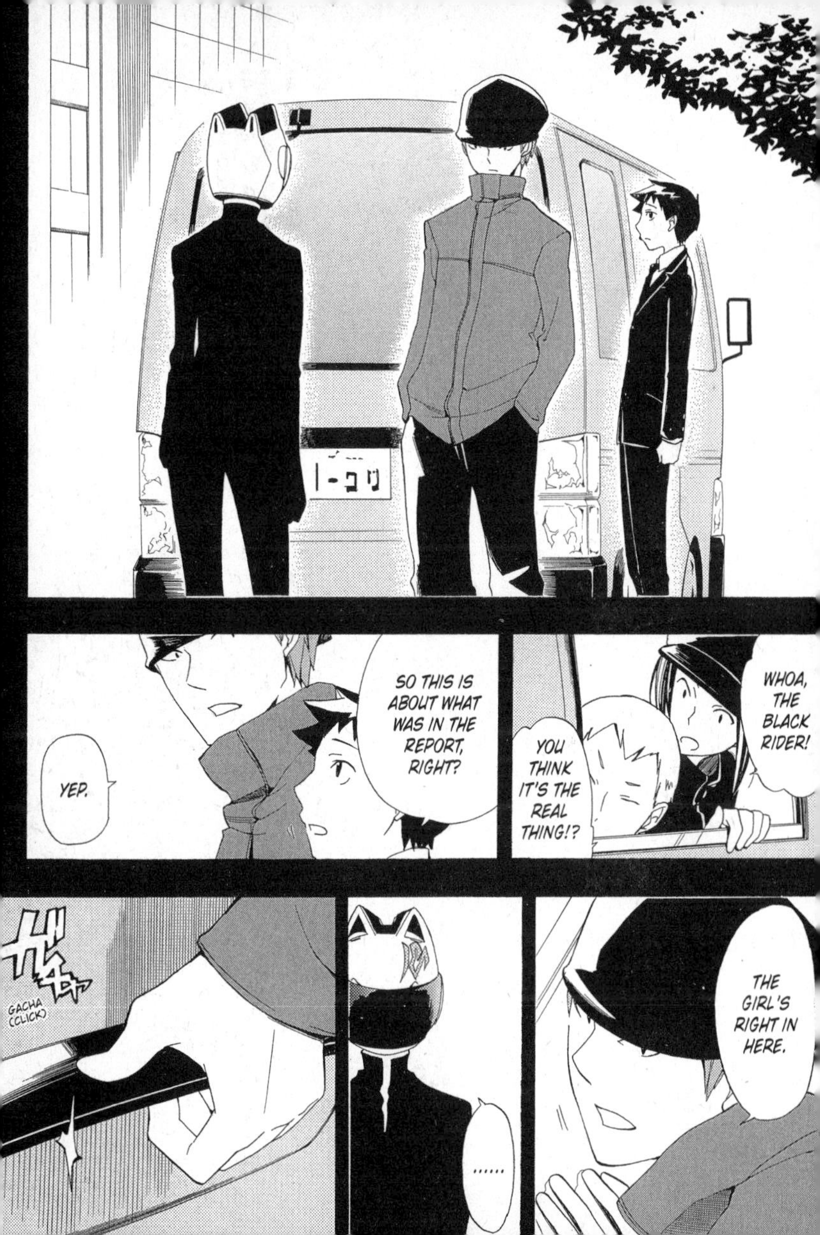
WHOA, THE BLACK RIDER!
YOU THINK IT'S THE REAL THING!?
SO THIS IS ABOUT WHAT WAS IN THE REPORT, RIGHT?
YEP.
THE GIRL'S RIGHT IN HERE.
......
ガチャ
GACHA (CLICK)

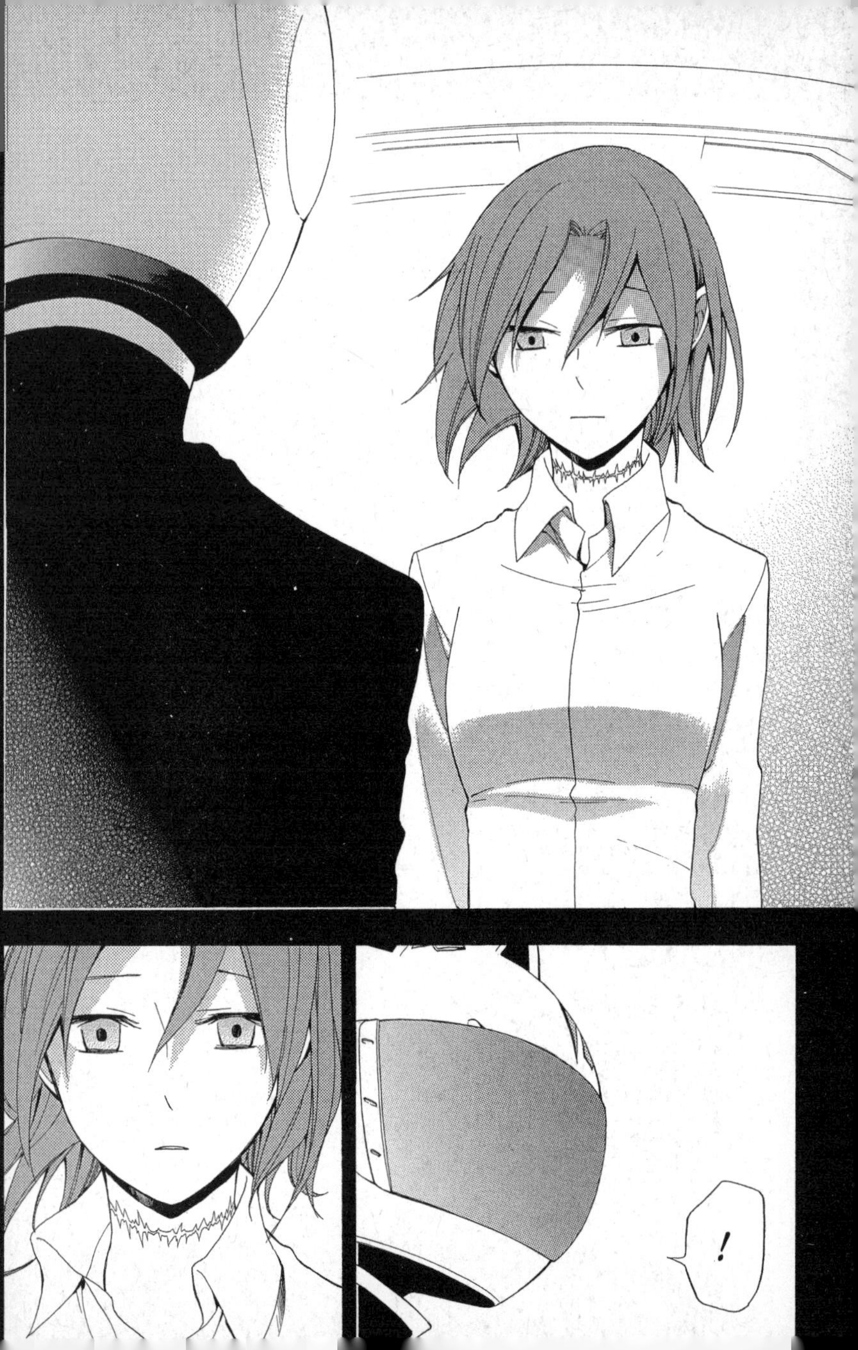
!

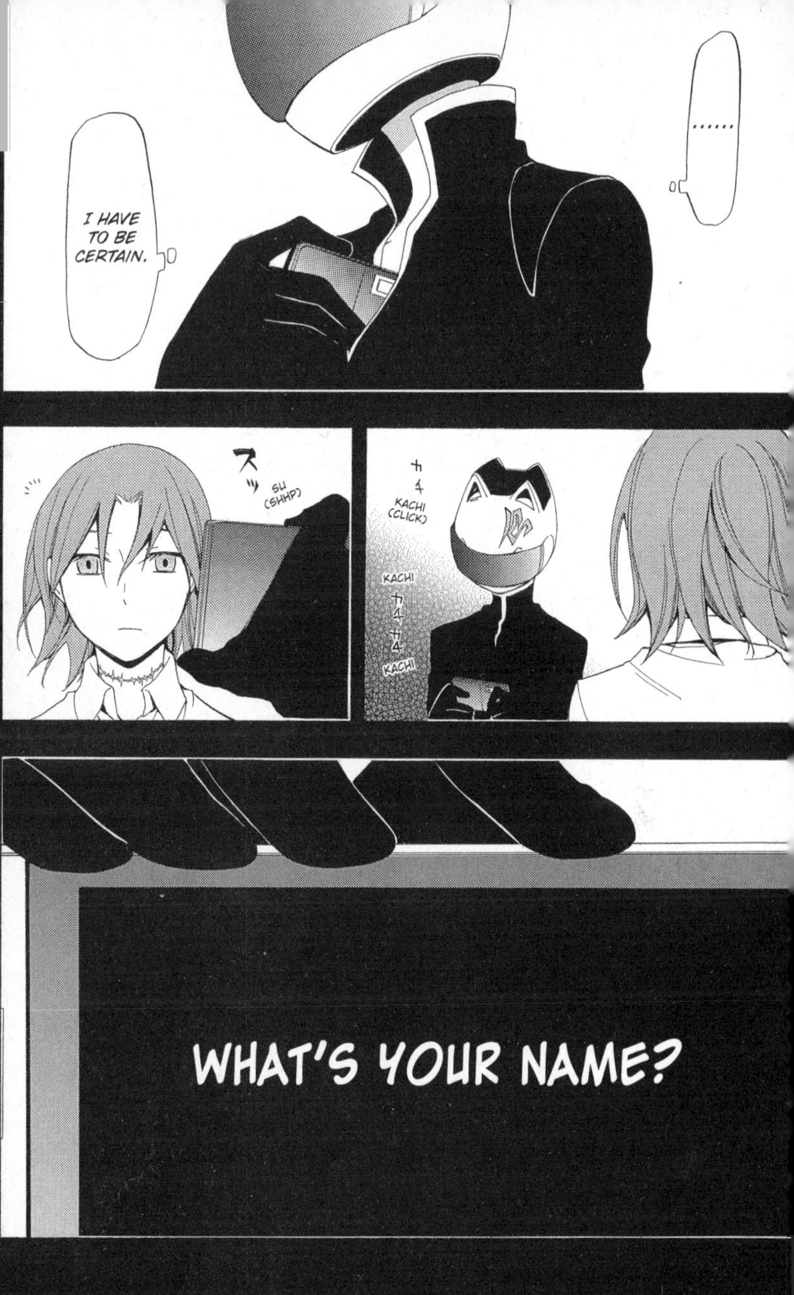

......
I HAVE TO BE CERTAIN.
カチ
KACHI (CLICK)
KACHI
カチ カチ
KACHI
スッ
SU (SHHP)
WHAT'S YOUR NAME?

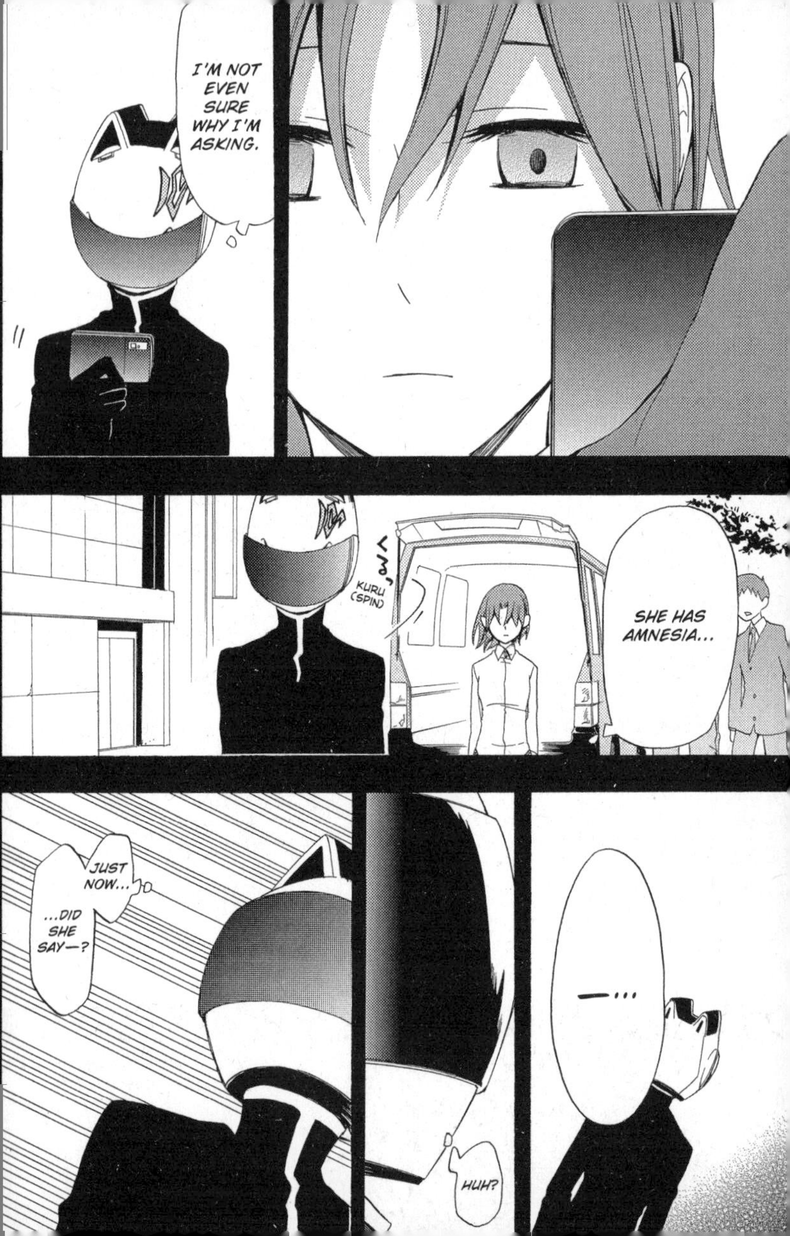
I'M NOT EVEN SURE WHY I'M ASKING.
SHE HAS AMNESIA...
KURU (SPIN)
—...
HUH?
JUST NOW...
...DID SHE SAY—?

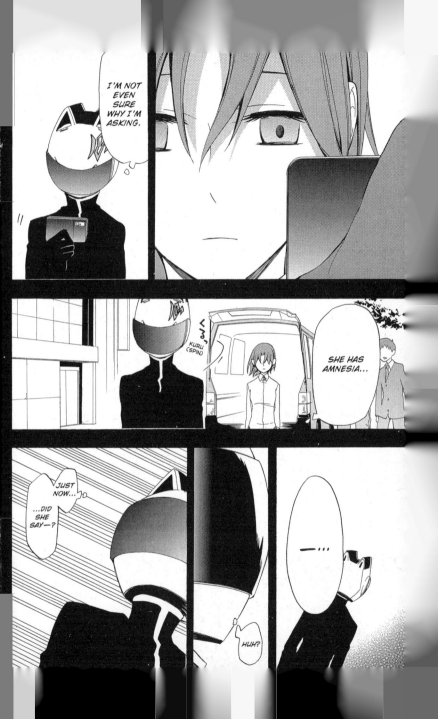

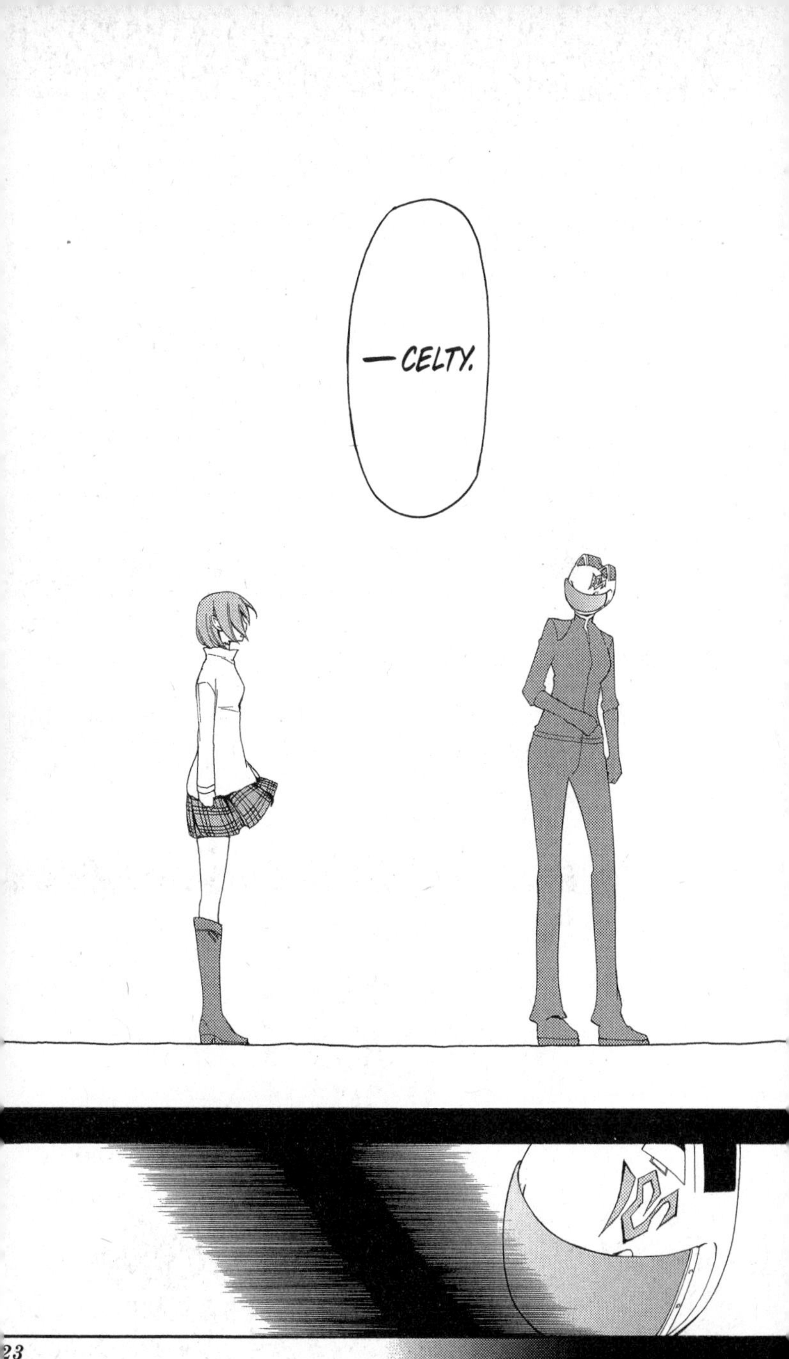
—CELTY.

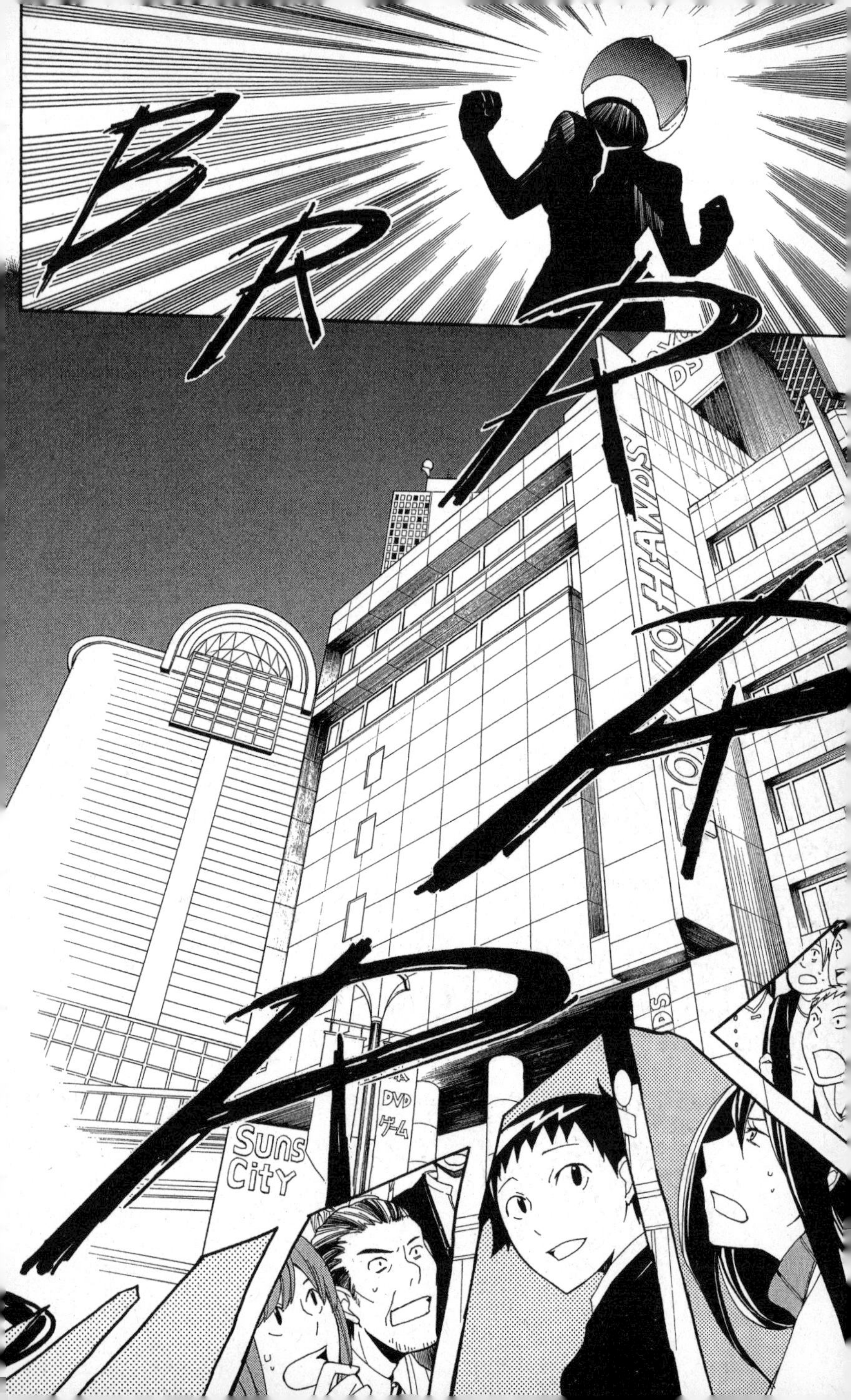
HANDS
DVD
ゲーム
Suns City

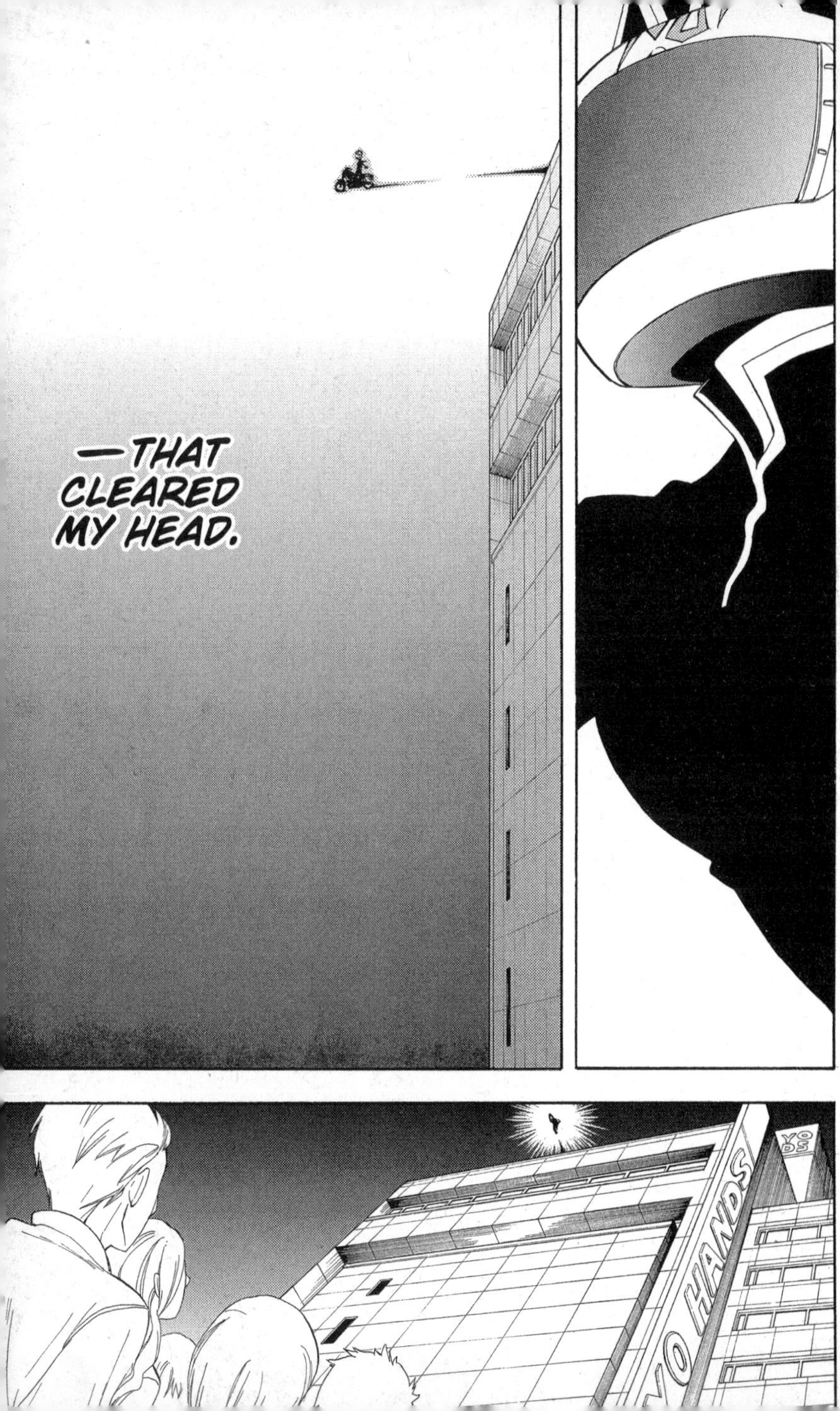
—THAT CLEARED MY HEAD.

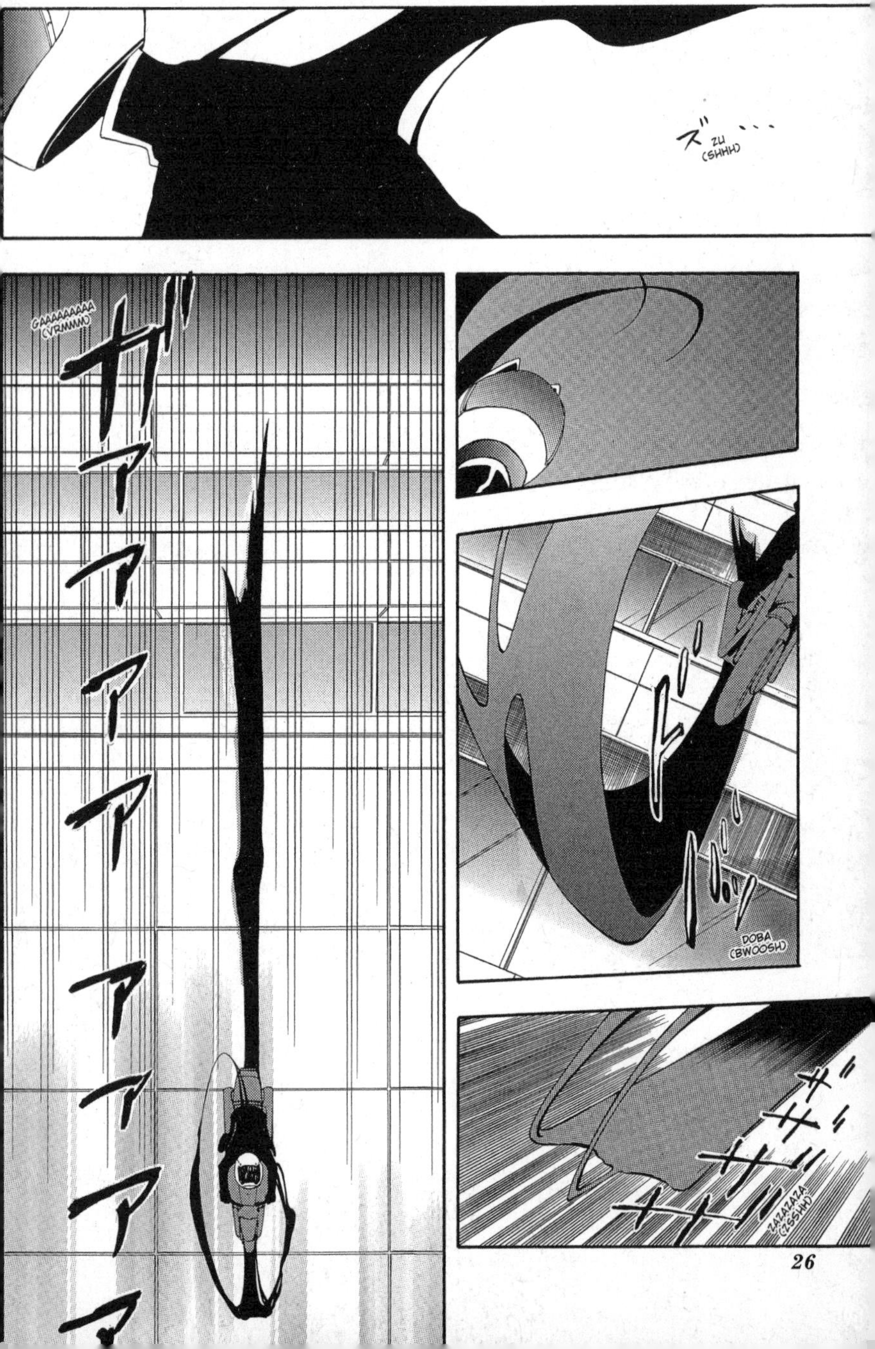
ズ ZU
(SHHH)
ドバッ DOBA
(BWOOSH)
ザザザザ ZAZAZAZA
(ZSSHH)
ガアアアアアアアア GAAAAAAAAA
(VRMMM)

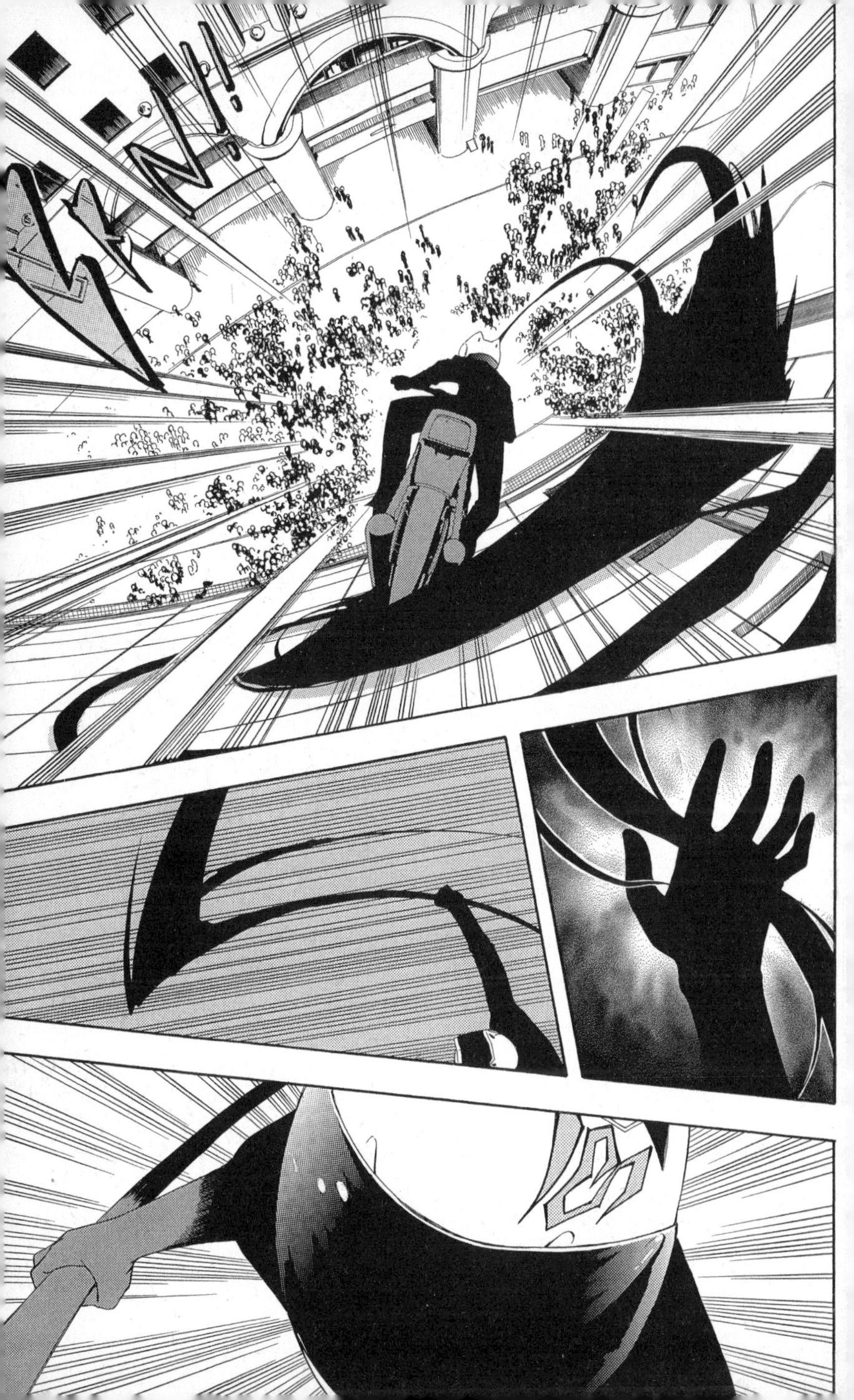
WN!!

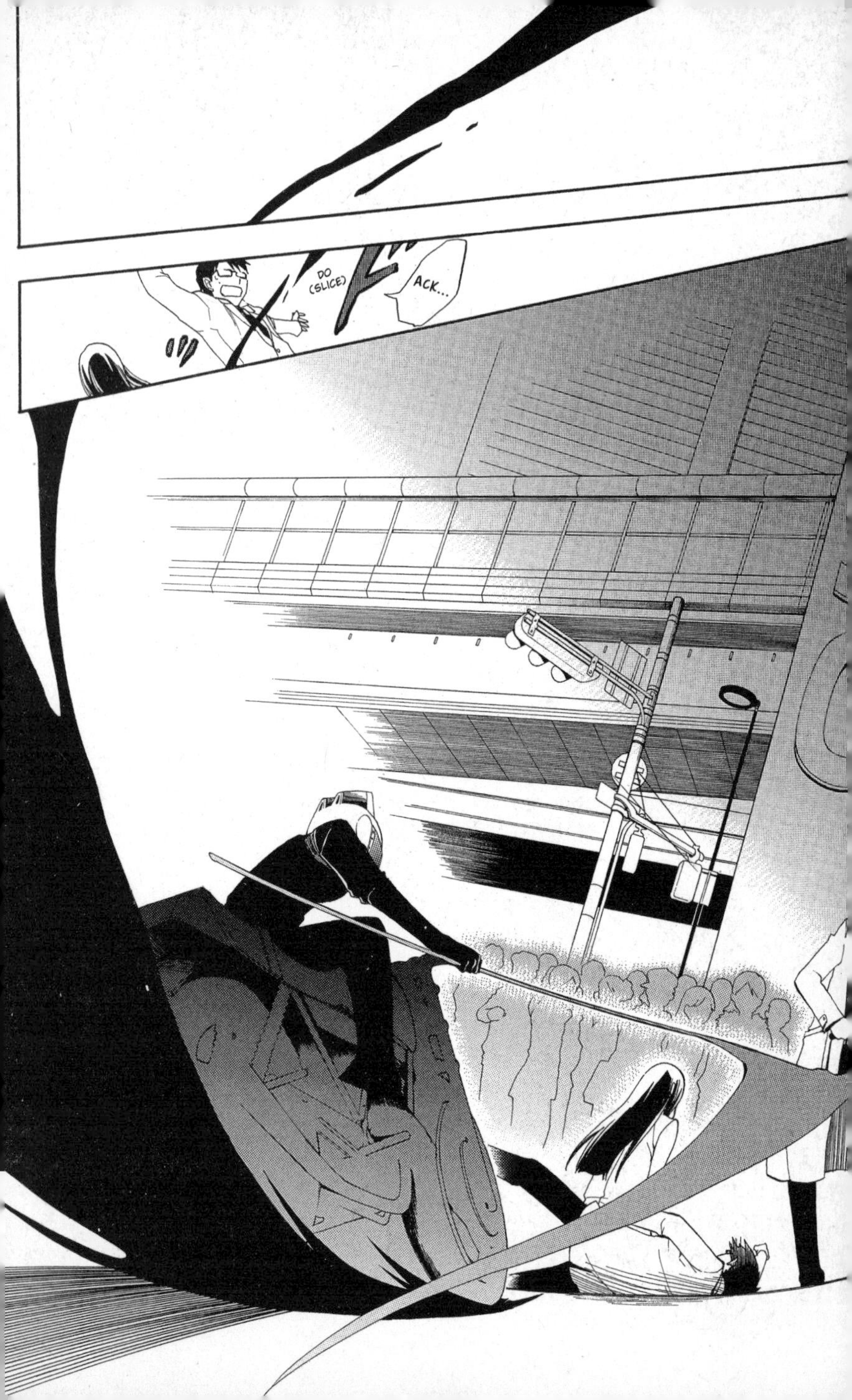
ACK...
DO (SLICE)

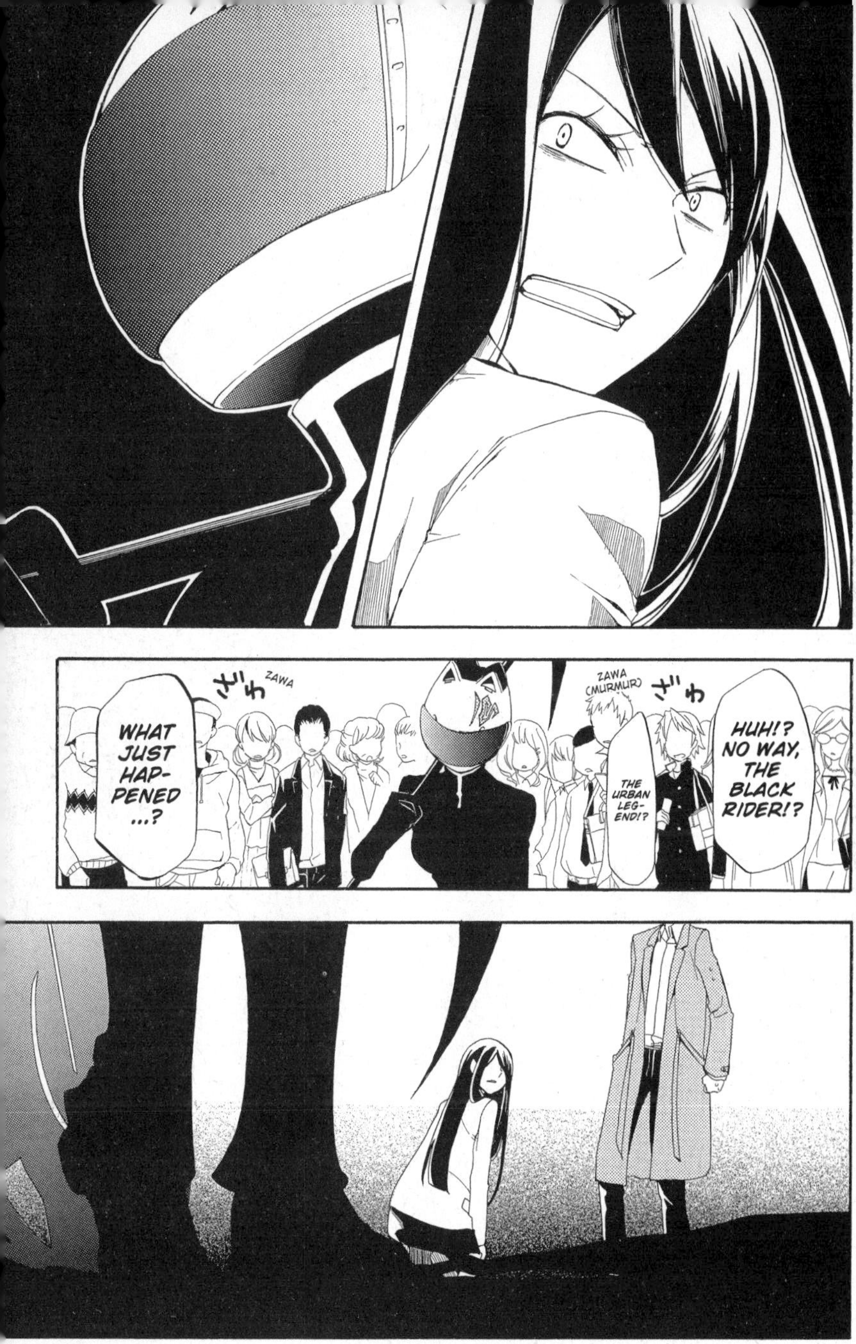
ZAWA (MURMUR)
ざわ
HUH!? NO WAY, THE BLACK RIDER!?
THE URBAN LEG-END!?
ざわ
ZAWA
WHAT JUST HAP-PENED ...?

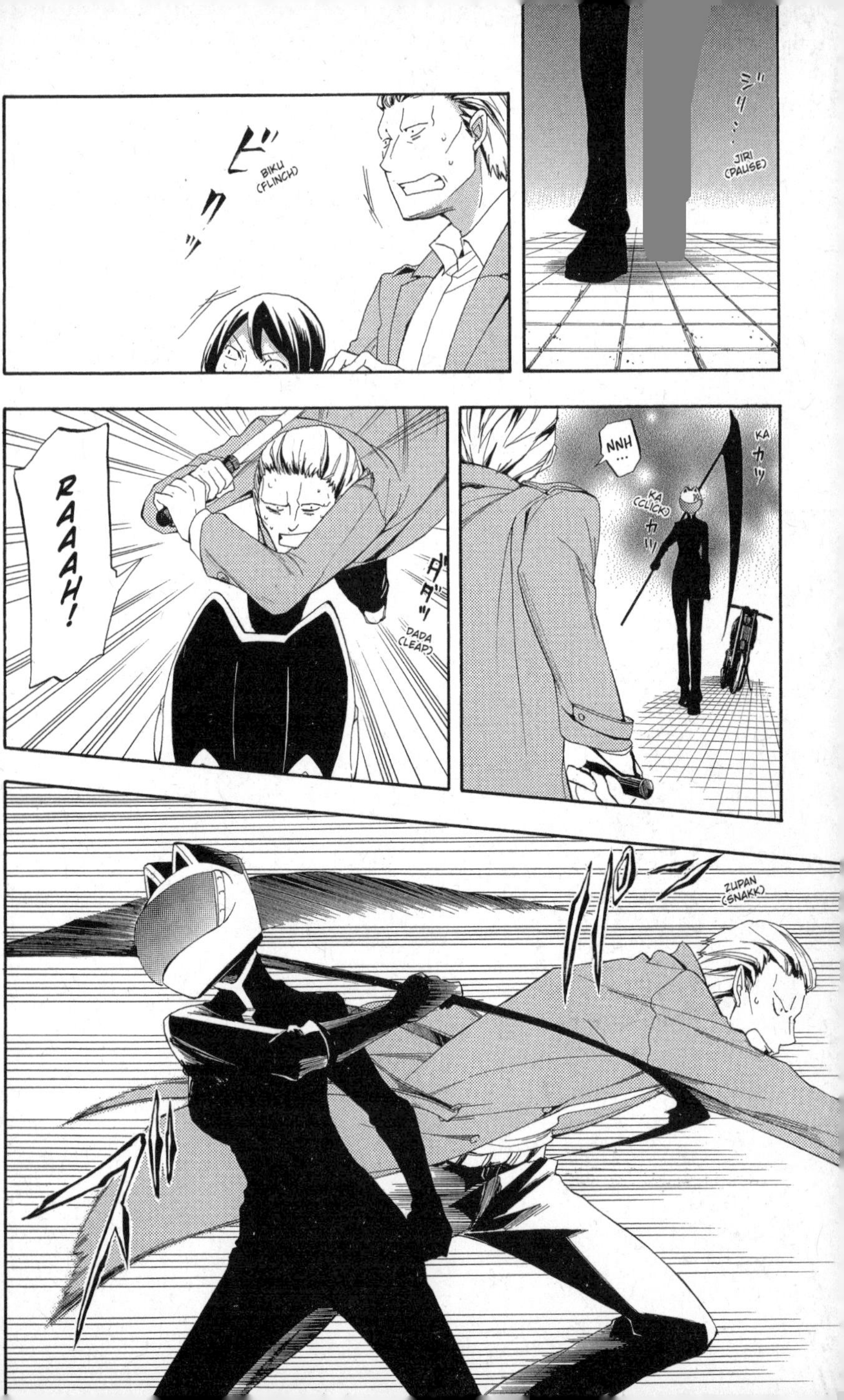
JIRI
(PAUSE)
BIKU
(FLINCH)
NNH ...
KA
KA
(CLICK)
RAAAH!
DADA
(LEAP)
ZUPAN
(SNAKK)

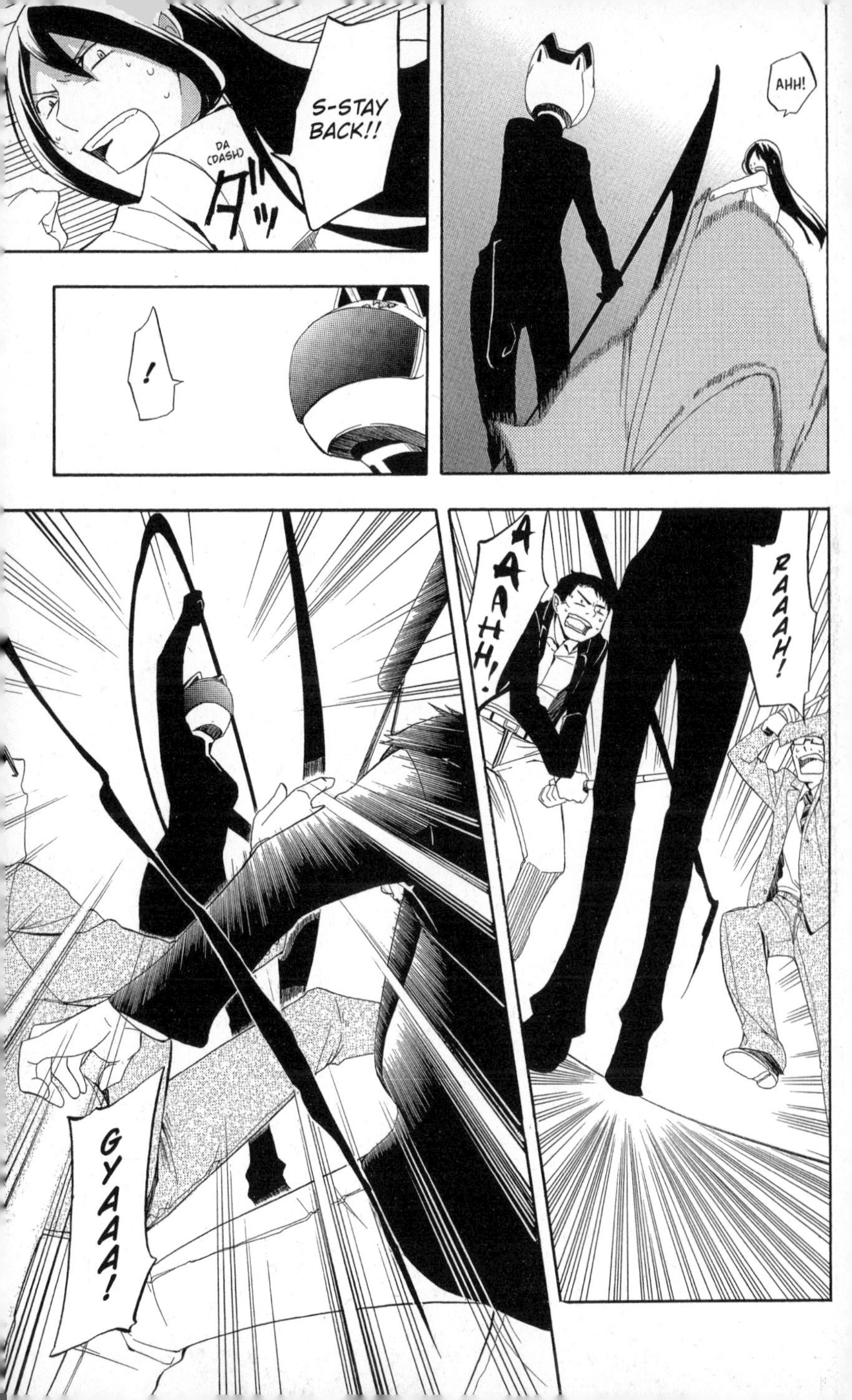
AHH!
S-STAY BACK!!
DA (DASH)
!
RAAAAH!
AAAHH!
GYAAAA!

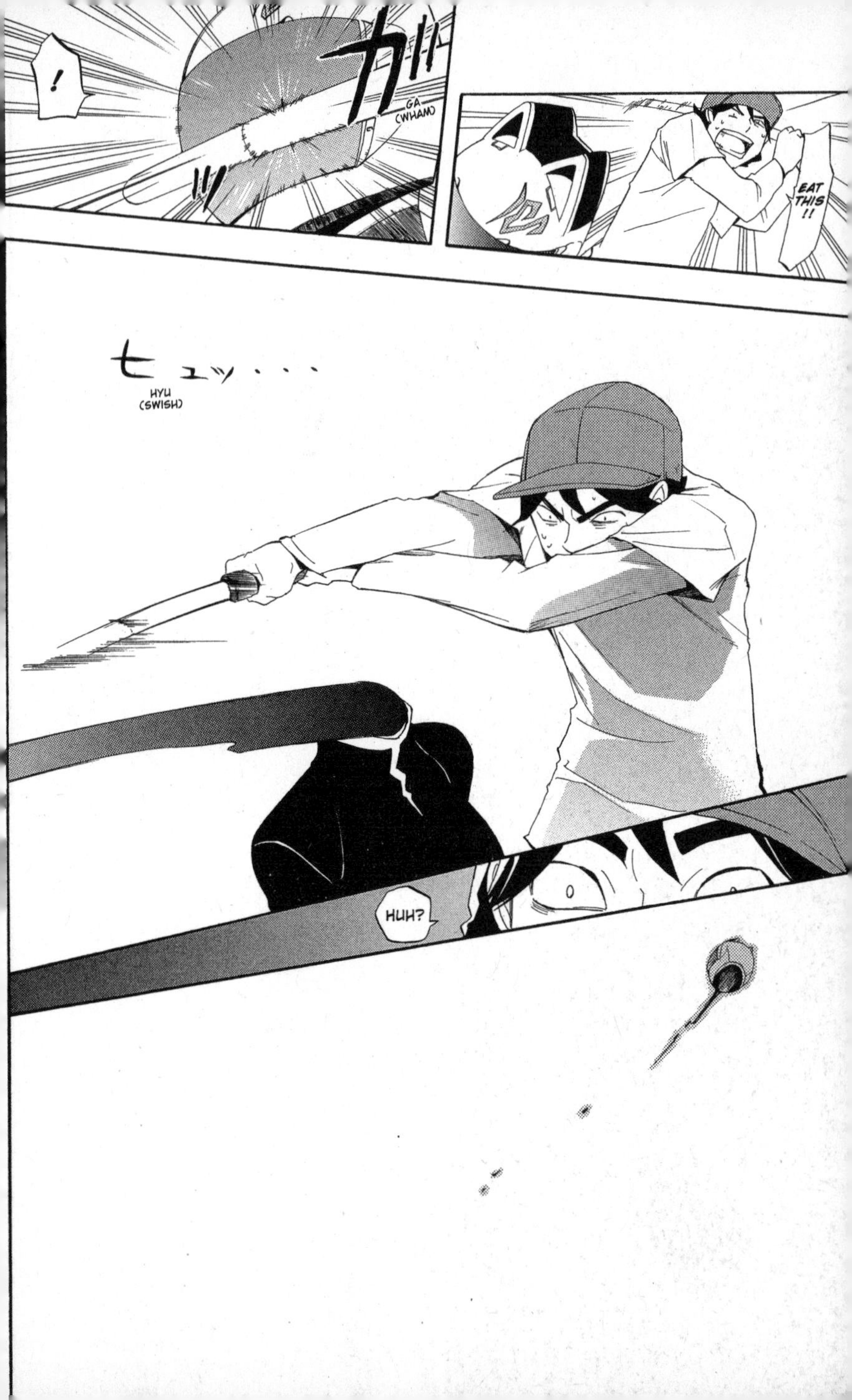
EAT THIS !!
!
カッ
GA (WHAM)
ヒュッ・・・
HYU (SWISH)
HUH?

KORORORORORORO
(ROLL)

KO
(THUNK)

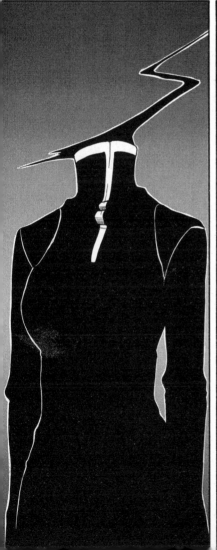

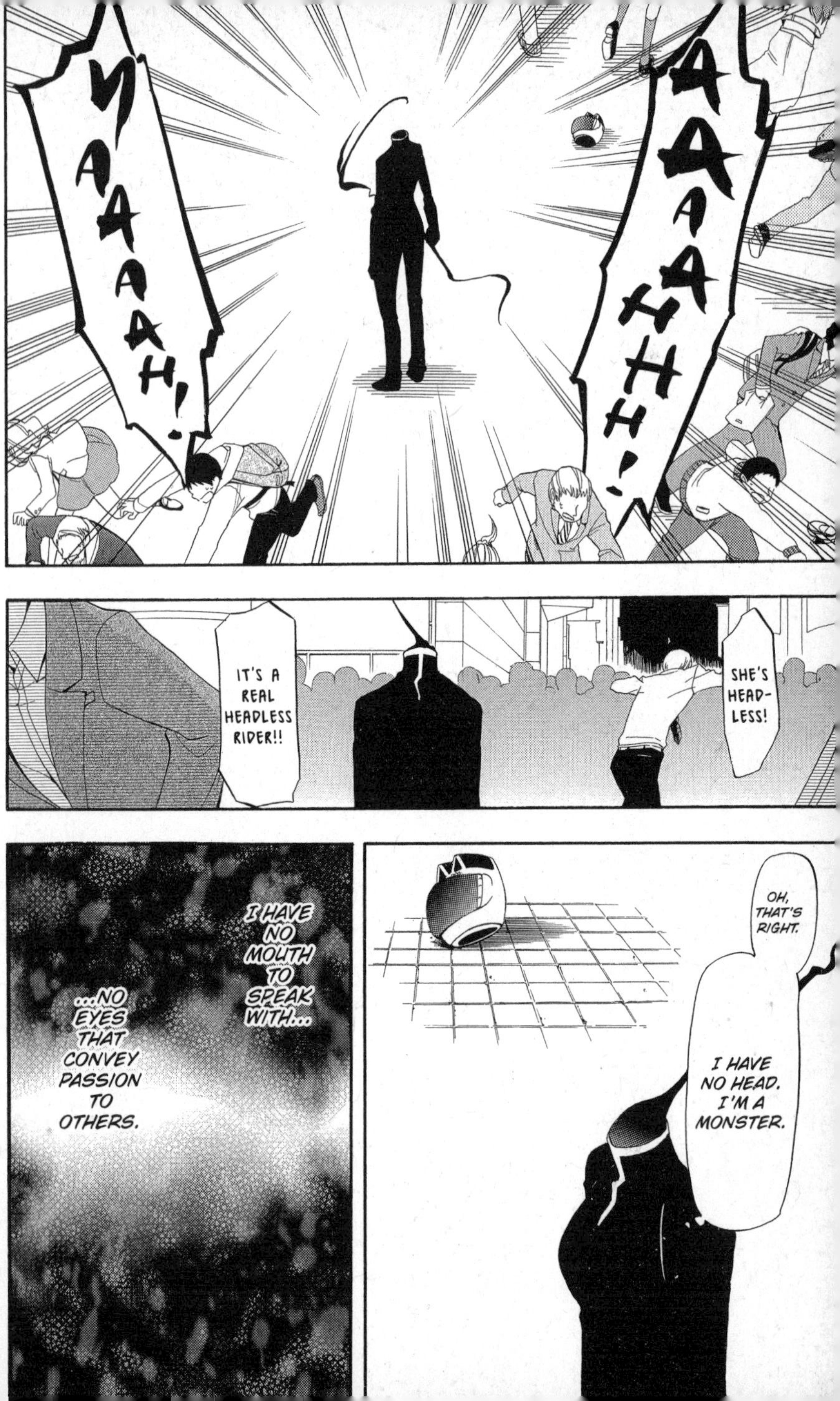
AAAAHHH!
YAAAAH!
SHE'S HEAD-LESS!
IT'S A REAL HEADLESS RIDER!!
OH, THAT'S RIGHT.
I HAVE NO HEAD. I'M A MONSTER.
I HAVE NO MOUTH TO SPEAK WITH...
...NO EYES THAT CONVEY PASSION TO OTHERS.

BUT
SO
WHAT?

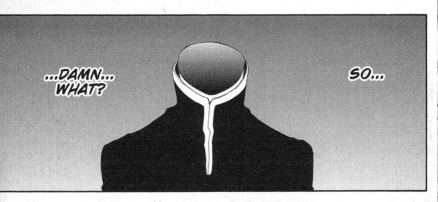

...DAMN...
WHAT?

SO...

I'M
RIGHT
HERE.

I AM
HERE,
AND I
EXIST.

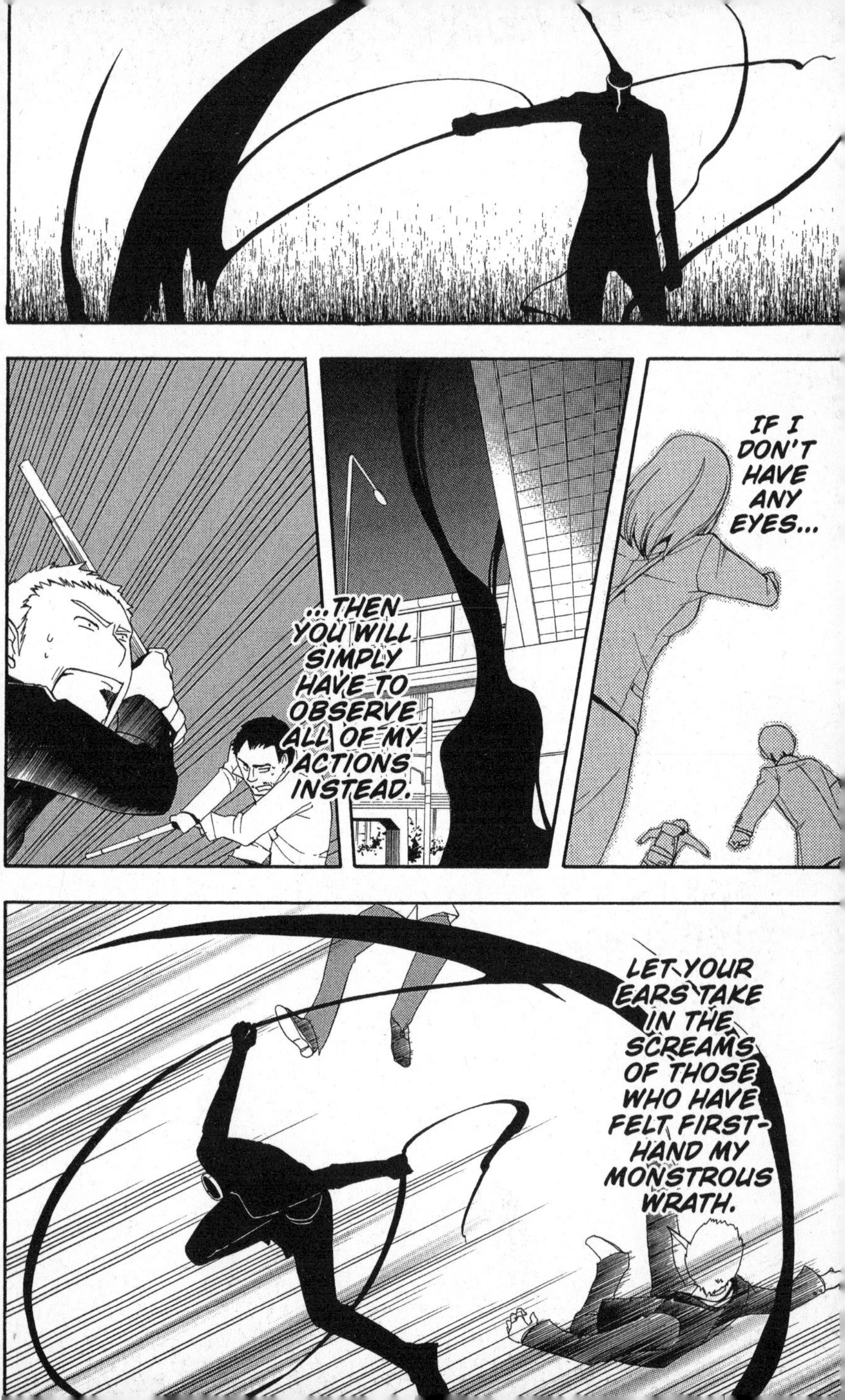
IF I DON'T HAVE ANY EYES...
...THEN YOU WILL SIMPLY HAVE TO OBSERVE ALL OF MY ACTIONS INSTEAD.
LET YOUR EARS TAKE IN THE SCREAMS OF THOSE WHO HAVE FELT FIRST-HAND MY MONSTROUS WRATH.

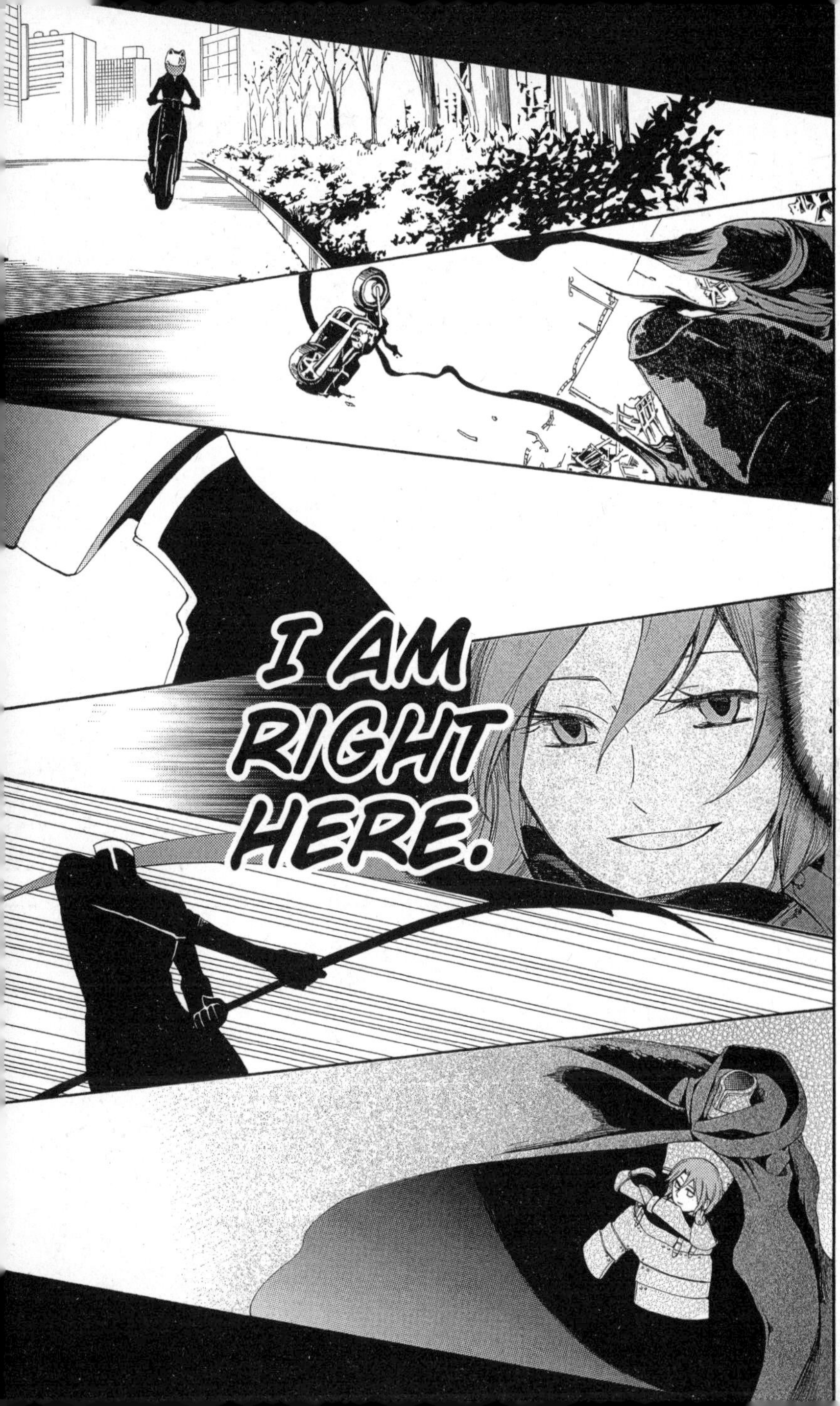
I AM RIGHT HERE.

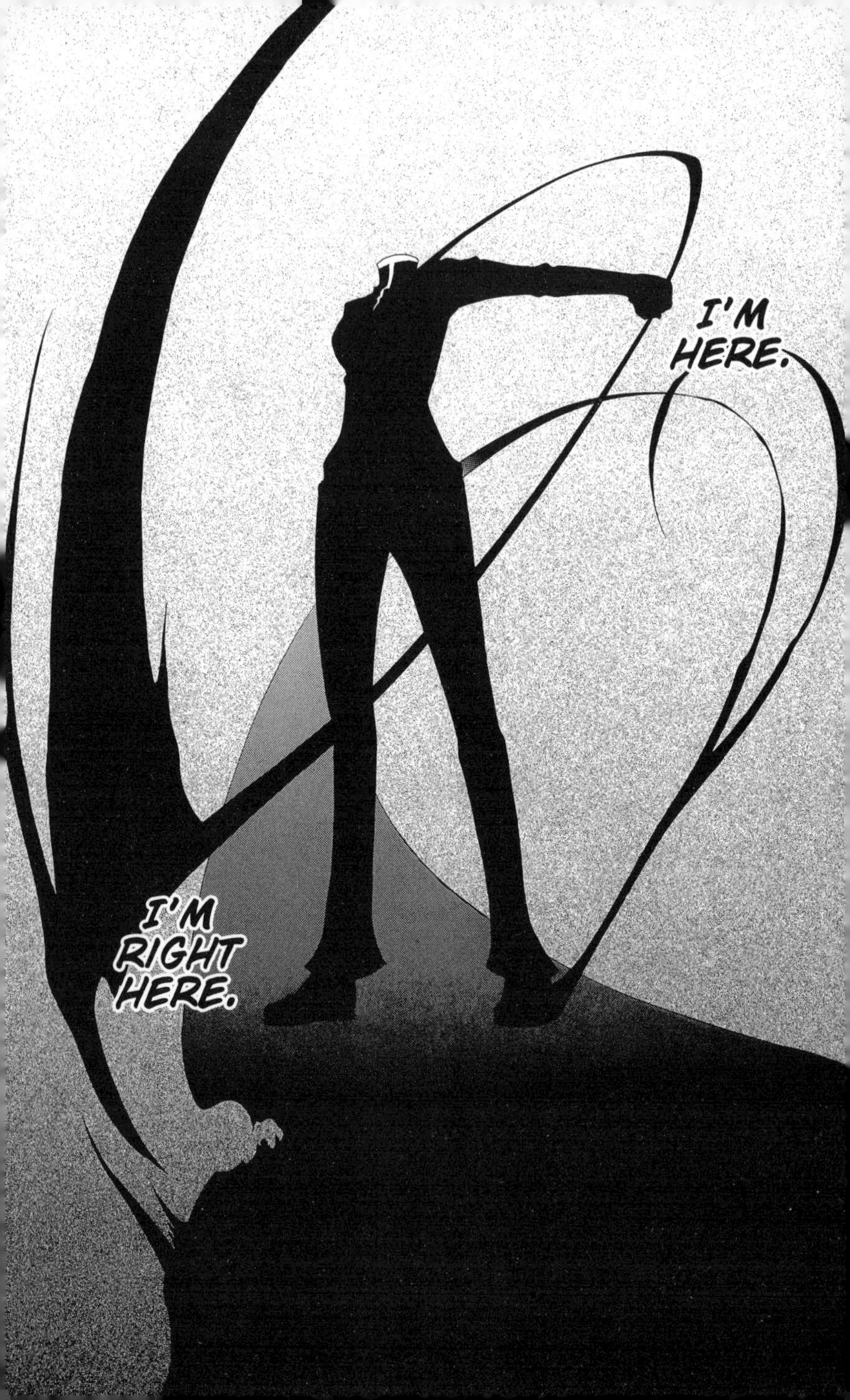
I'M HERE.
I'M RIGHT HERE.

19: WAWAWAWAWAWAWAWAWAWAWAWAWAWAWAWAWAWAWAWAWA!!

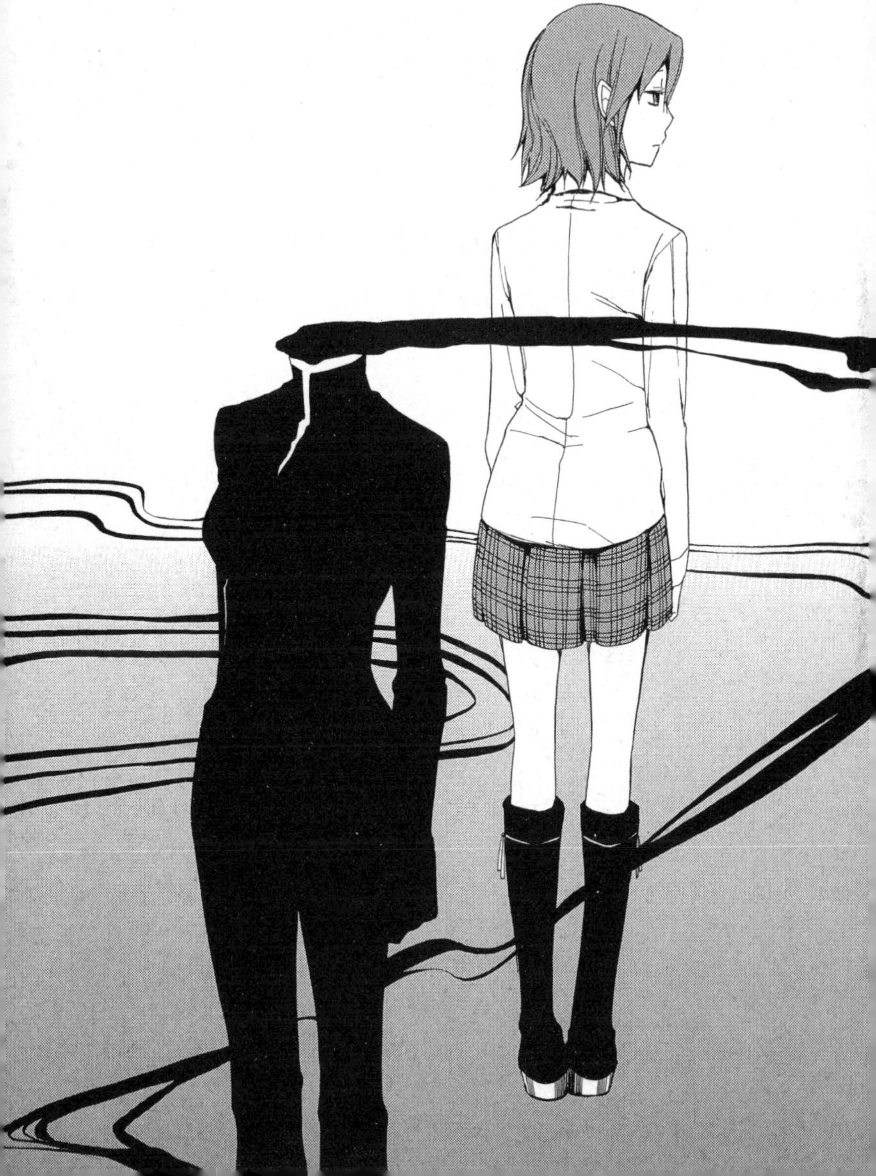

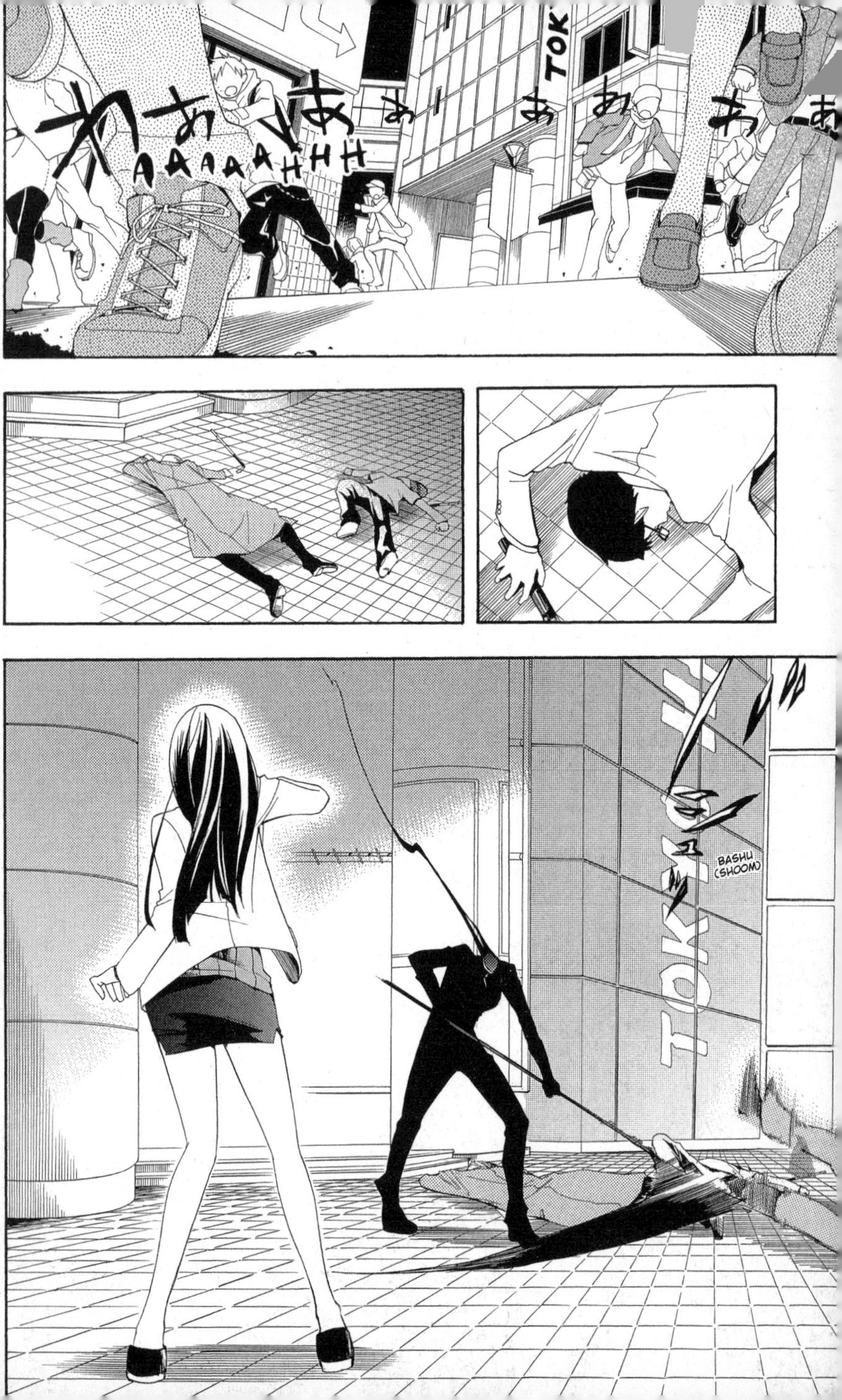
TOK
AAAAAHHH
BASHU
(SHOOM)
TOK

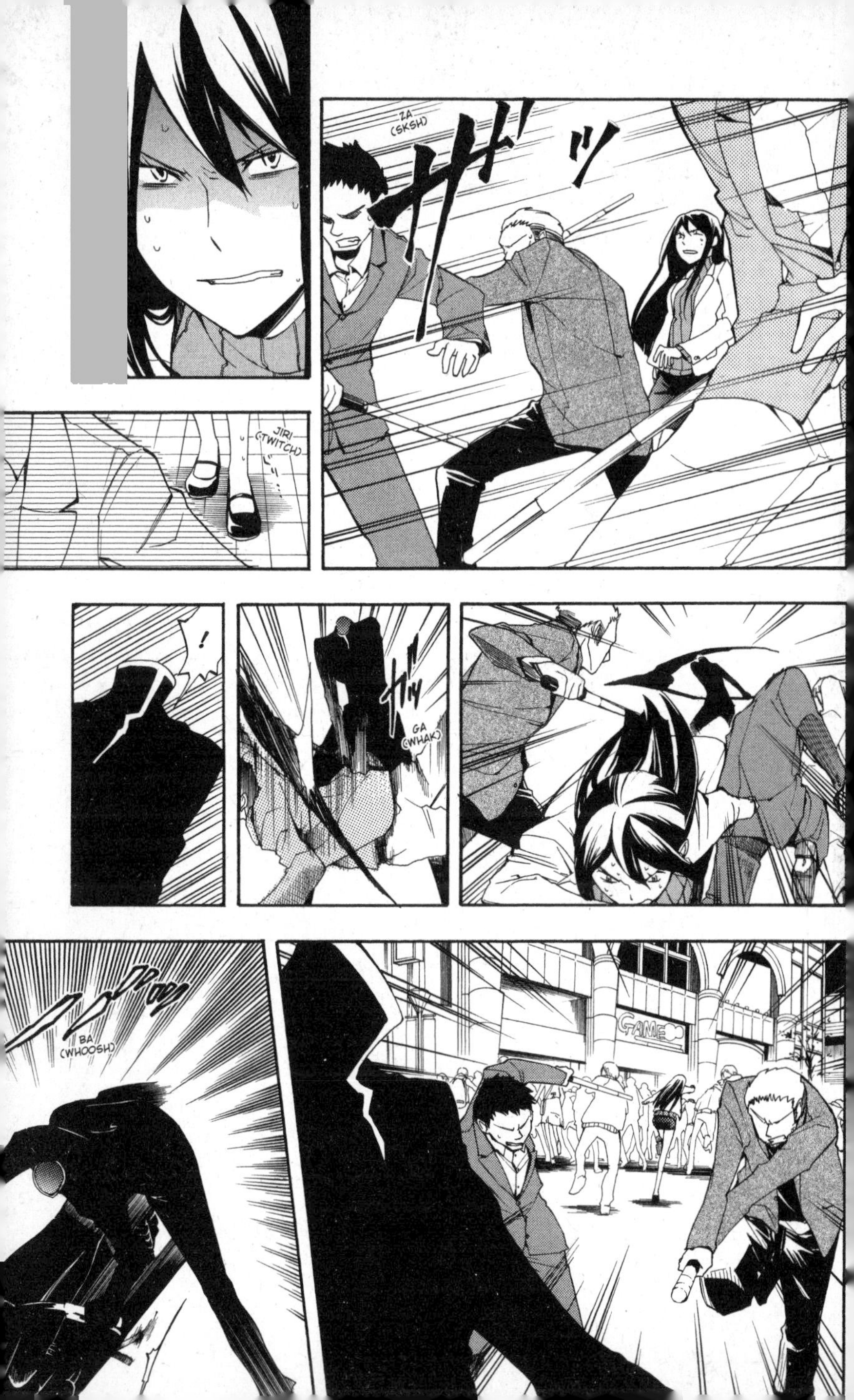
ZA
(SKSH)
ザザッ
JIRI
(TWITCH)
GA
(WHAK)
!
GAME
BA
(WHOOSH)

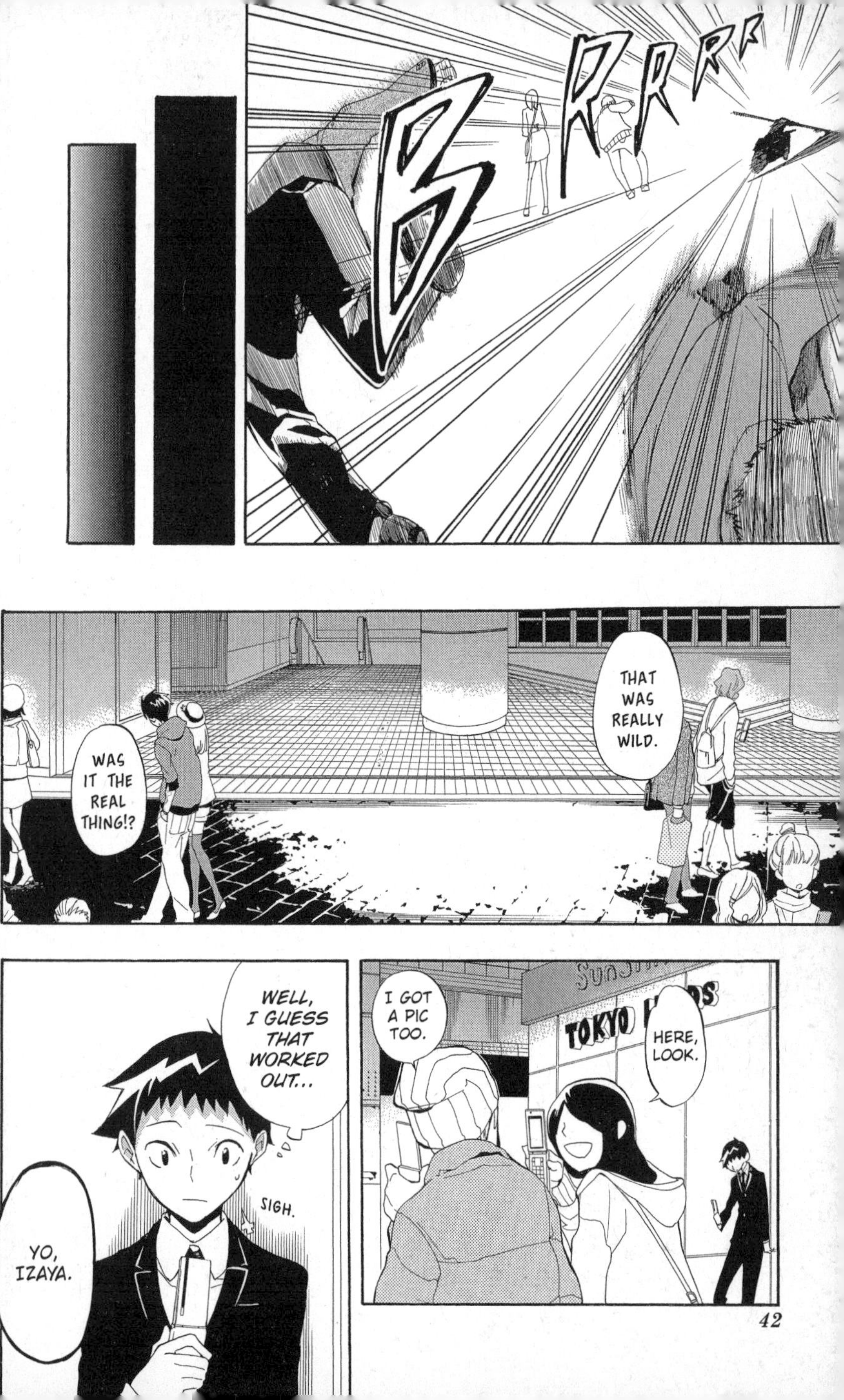
BRRRR
THAT WAS REALLY WILD.
WAS IT THE REAL THING!?
HERE, LOOK.
I GOT A PIC TOO.
WELL, I GUESS THAT WORKED OUT...
SIGH.
YO, IZAYA.

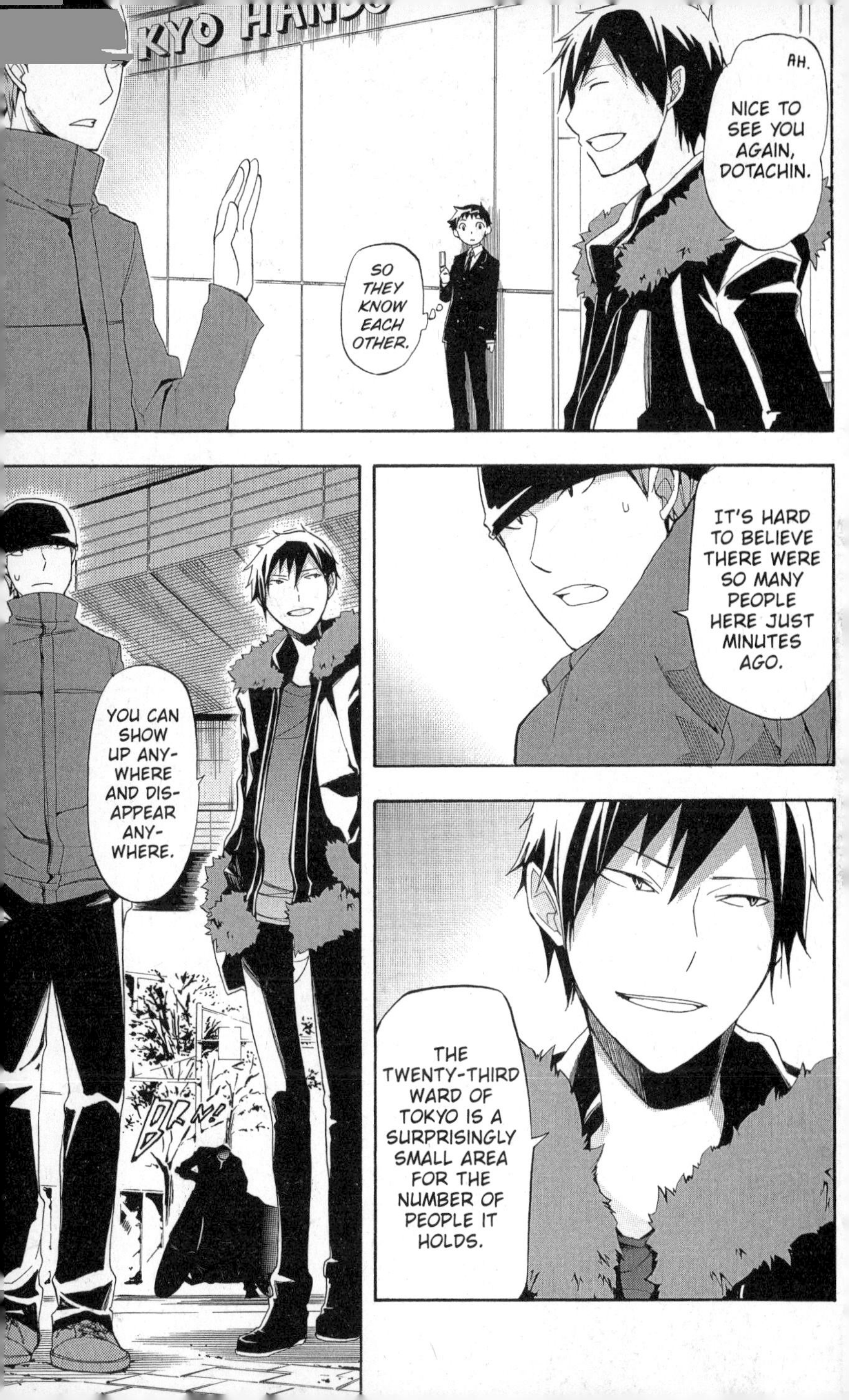
AH.
NICE TO SEE YOU AGAIN, DOTACHIN.
SO THEY KNOW EACH OTHER.
IT'S HARD TO BELIEVE THERE WERE SO MANY PEOPLE HERE JUST MINUTES AGO.
THE TWENTY-THIRD WARD OF TOKYO IS A SURPRISINGLY SMALL AREA FOR THE NUMBER OF PEOPLE IT HOLDS.
YOU CAN SHOW UP ANY-WHERE AND DIS-APPEAR ANY-WHERE.

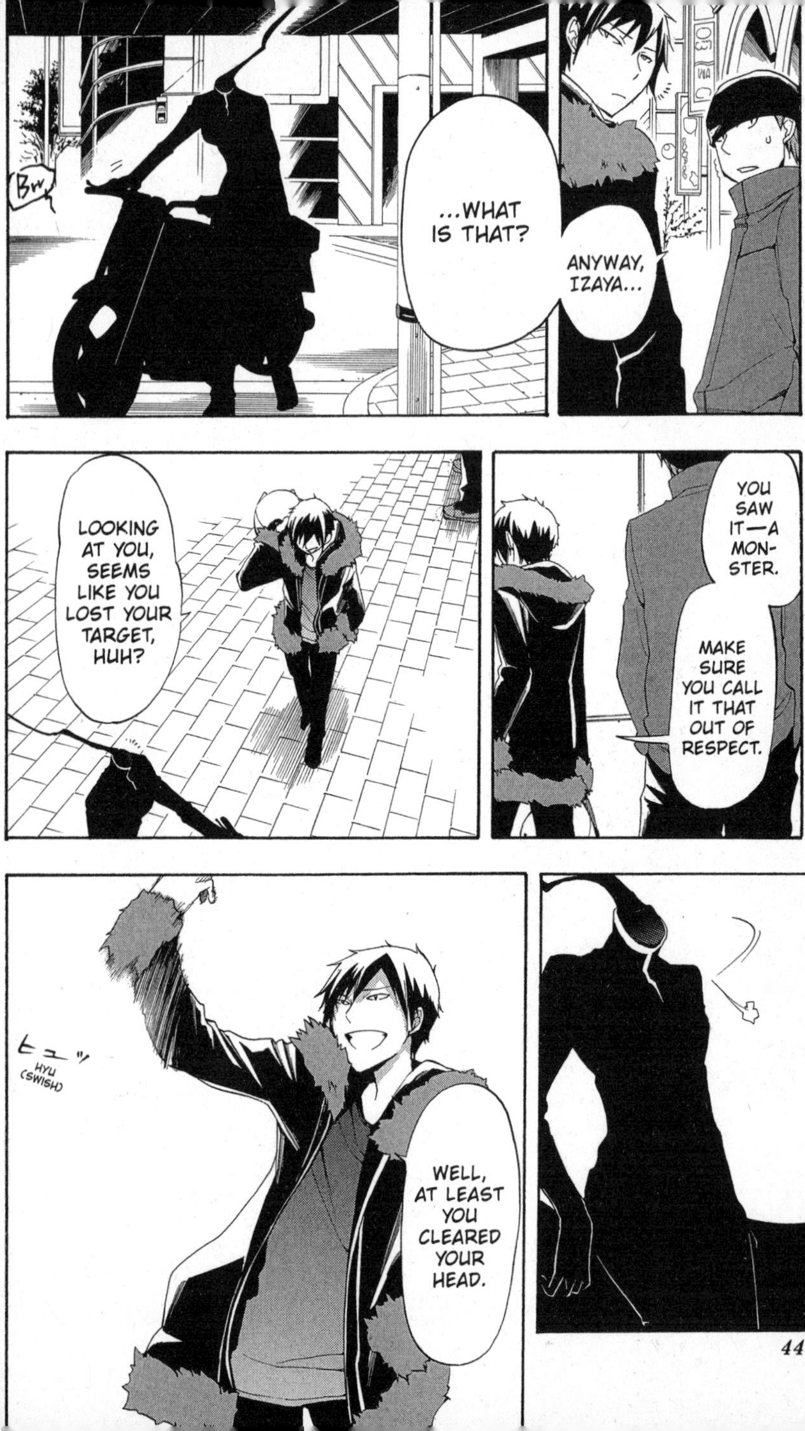
...WHAT IS THAT?
ANYWAY, IZAYA...
Brr
YOU SAW IT—A MONSTER.
MAKE SURE YOU CALL IT THAT OUT OF RESPECT.
LOOKING AT YOU, SEEMS LIKE YOU LOST YOUR TARGET, HUH?
ヒュッ
HYU (SWISH)
WELL, AT LEAST YOU CLEARED YOUR HEAD.

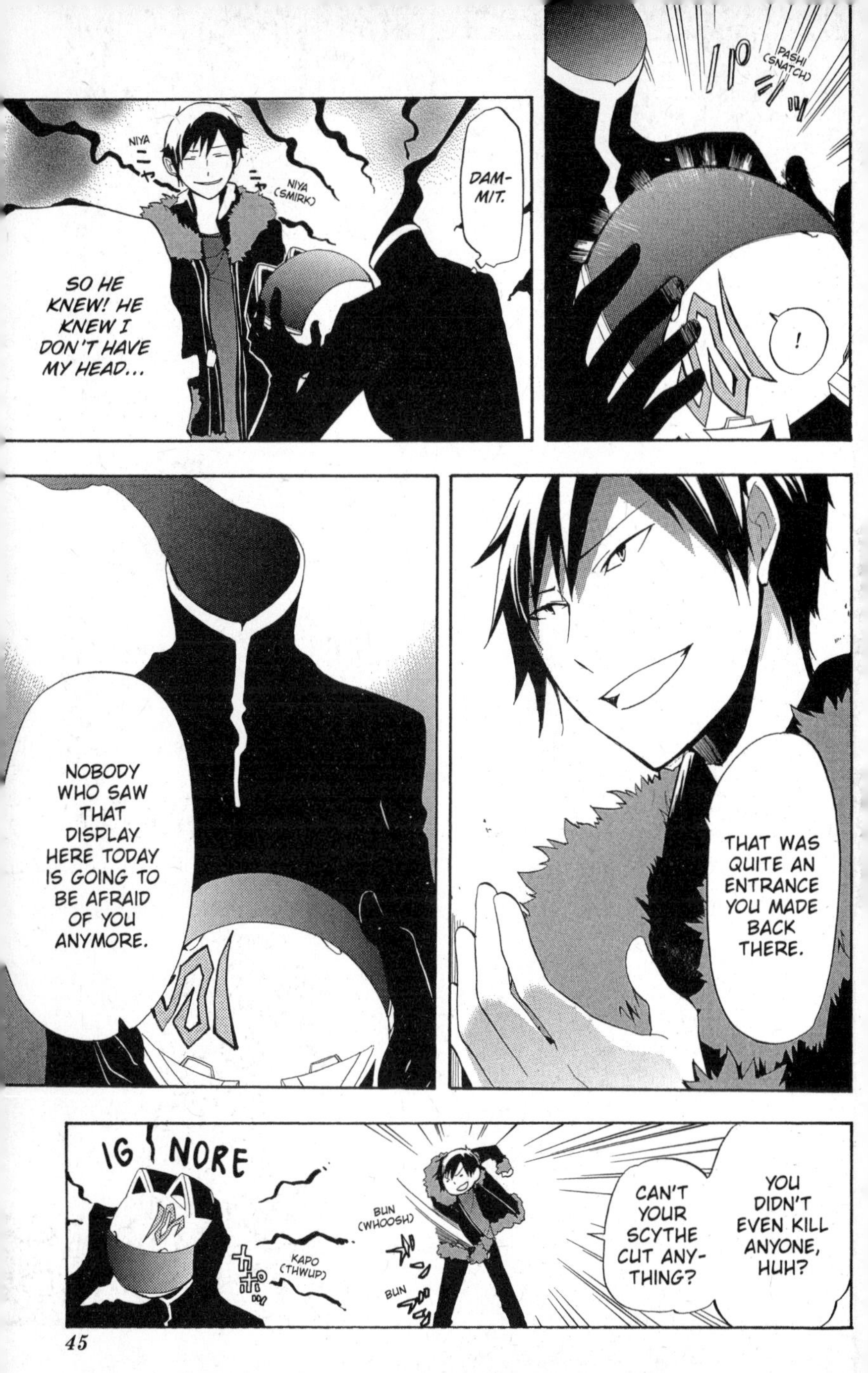
PASHI (SNATCH)
!
DAM-MIT.
NIYA (SMIRK)
NIYA
SO HE KNEW! HE KNEW I DON'T HAVE MY HEAD...
THAT WAS QUITE AN ENTRANCE YOU MADE BACK THERE.
NOBODY WHO SAW THAT DISPLAY HERE TODAY IS GOING TO BE AFRAID OF YOU ANYMORE.
YOU DIDN'T EVEN KILL ANYONE, HUH?
CAN'T YOUR SCYTHE CUT ANY-THING?
BUN (WHOOSH)
BUN
KAPO (THWUP)
IG NORE

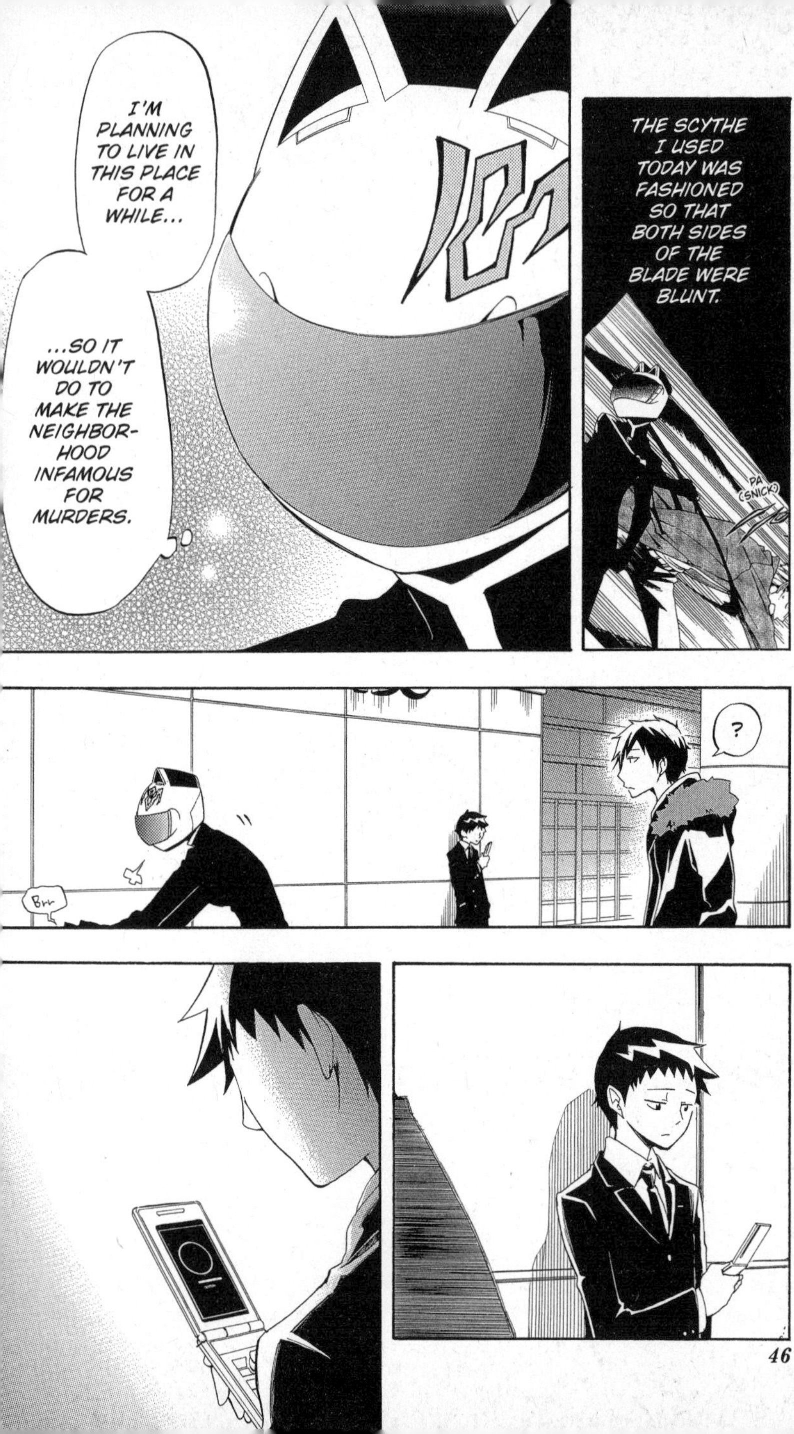
THE SCYTHE I USED TODAY WAS FASHIONED SO THAT BOTH SIDES OF THE BLADE WERE BLUNT.
PA (SNICK)
I'M PLANNING TO LIVE IN THIS PLACE FOR A WHILE...
...SO IT WOULDN'T DO TO MAKE THE NEIGHBOR-HOOD INFAMOUS FOR MURDERS.
?
Brr

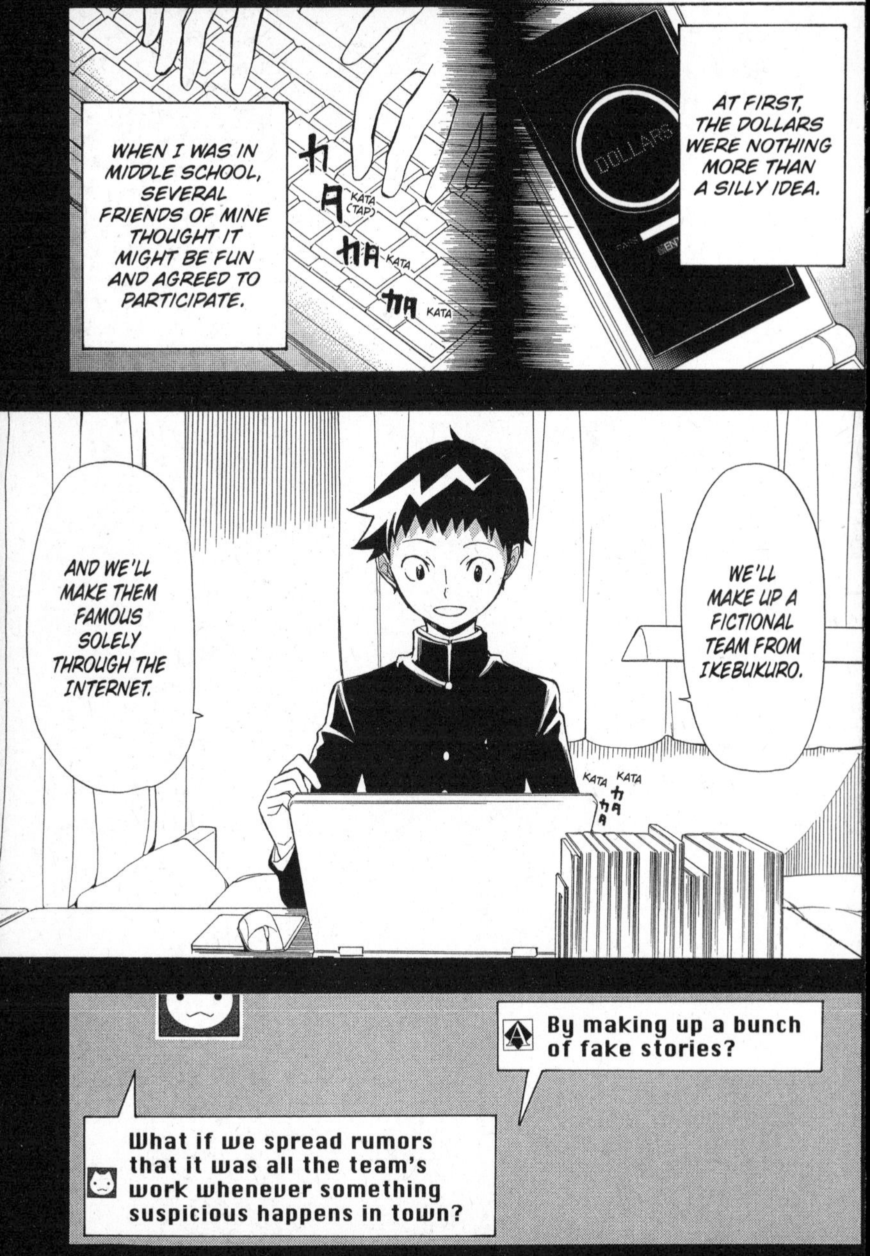
DOLLARS
AT FIRST, THE DOLLARS WERE NOTHING MORE THAN A SILLY IDEA.
WHEN I WAS IN MIDDLE SCHOOL, SEVERAL FRIENDS OF MINE THOUGHT IT MIGHT BE FUN AND AGREED TO PARTICIPATE.
カタ KATA (TAP)
カタ KATA
カタ KATA
WE'LL MAKE UP A FICTIONAL TEAM FROM IKEBUKURO.
AND WE'LL MAKE THEM FAMOUS SOLELY THROUGH THE INTERNET.
KATA KATA カタ
By making up a bunch of fake stories?
What if we spread rumors that it was all the team's work whenever something suspicious happens in town?

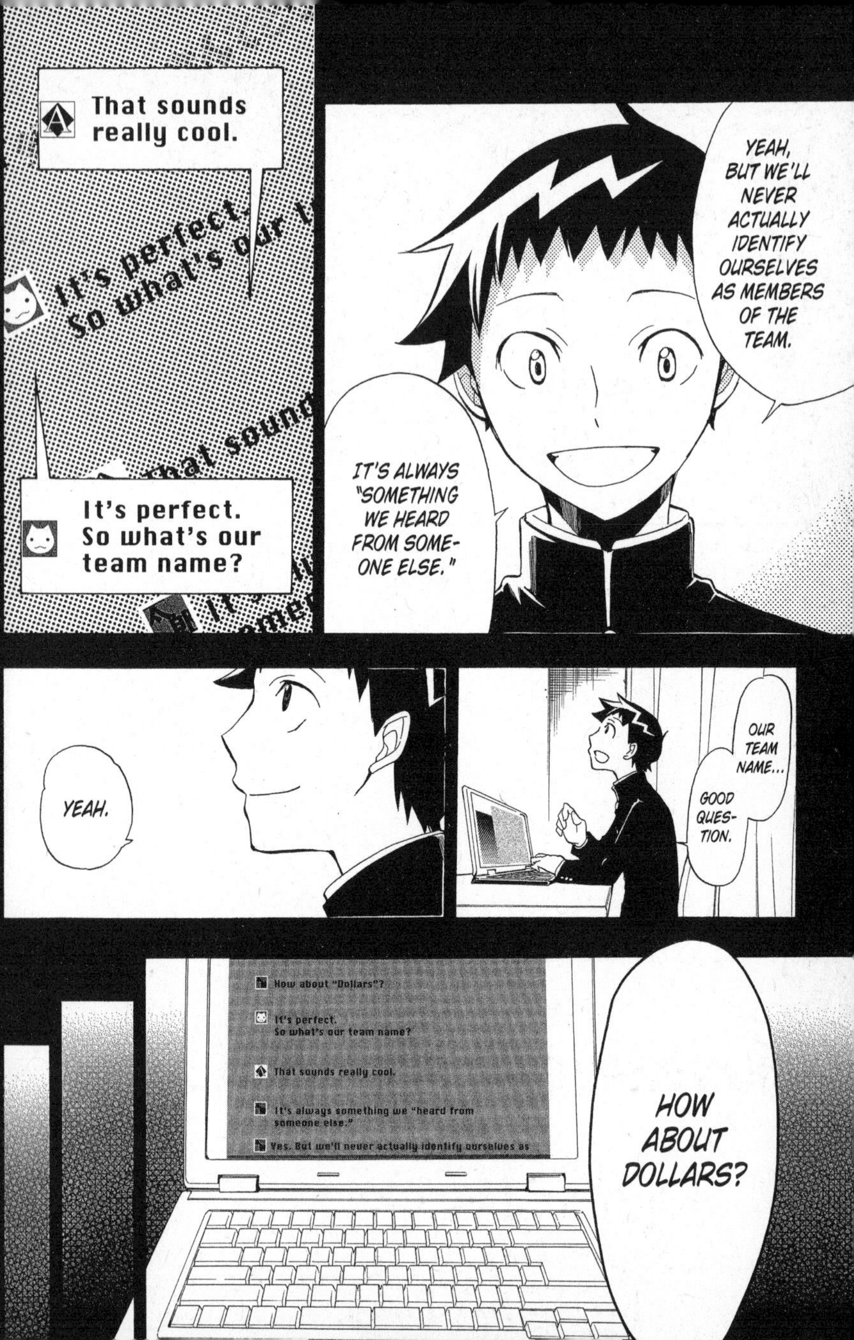
YEAH, BUT WE'LL NEVER ACTUALLY IDENTIFY OURSELVES AS MEMBERS OF THE TEAM.
IT'S ALWAYS "SOMETHING WE HEARD FROM SOME-ONE ELSE."
That sounds really cool.
It's perfect. So what's our team name?
OUR TEAM NAME...
GOOD QUES-TION.
YEAH.
HOW ABOUT DOLLARS?
How about "Dollars"?
It's perfect.
So what's our team name?
That sounds really cool.
It's always something we "heard from someone else."
Yes. But we'll never actually identify ourselves as

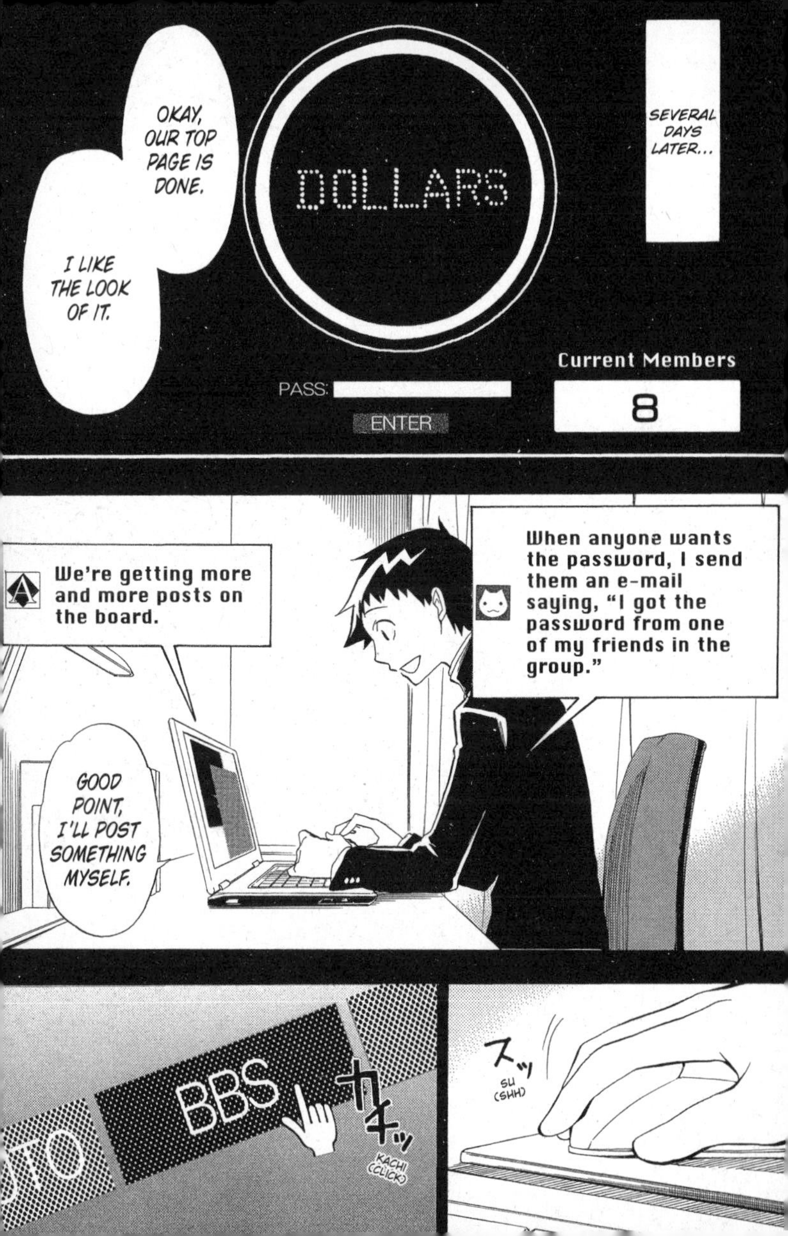
SEVERAL DAYS LATER...
DOLLARS
Current Members
8
PASS:
ENTER
OKAY, OUR TOP PAGE IS DONE.
I LIKE THE LOOK OF IT.
When anyone wants the password, I send them an e-mail saying, "I got the password from one of my friends in the group."
We're getting more and more posts on the board.
GOOD POINT, I'LL POST SOMETHING MYSELF.
スッ
SU (SHH)
BBS
カチッ
KACHI (CLICK)

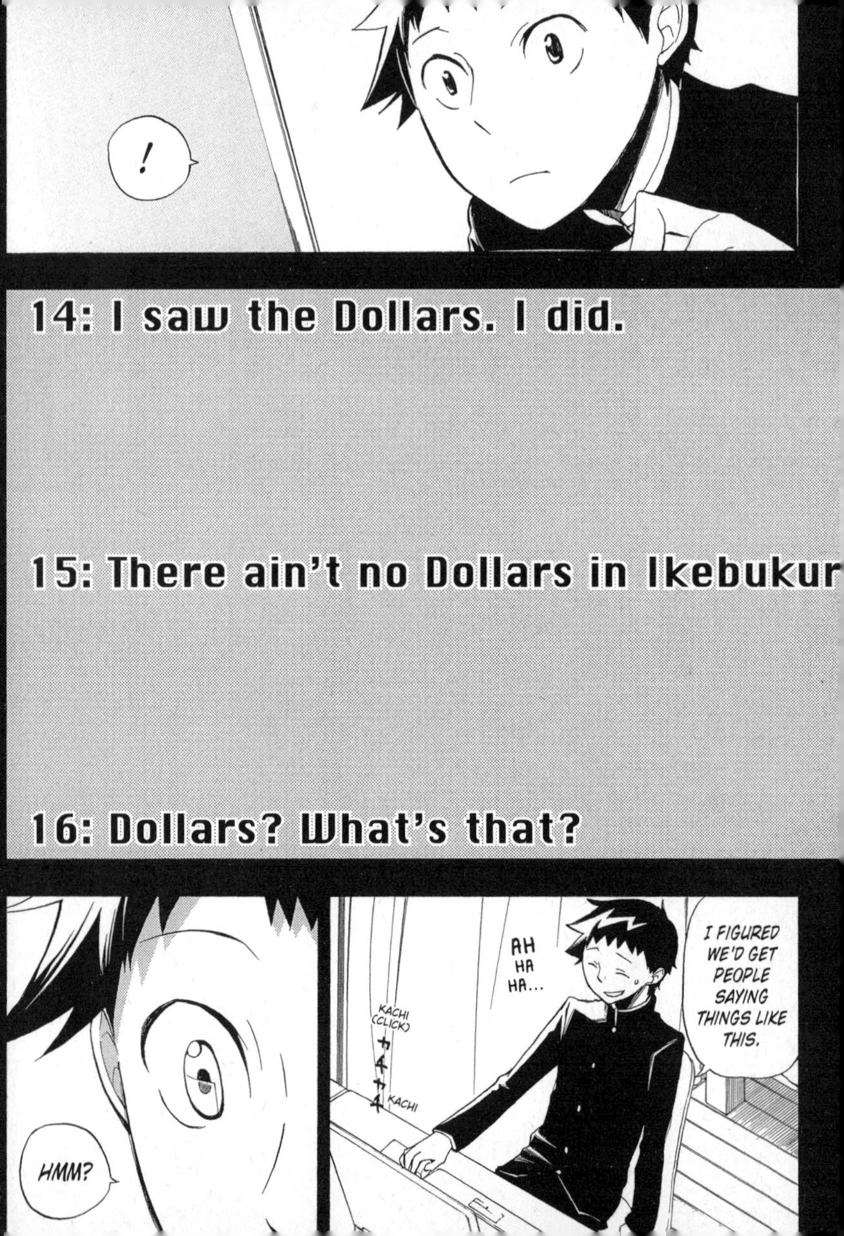
!
14: I saw the Dollars. I did.
15: There ain't no Dollars in Ikebukur
16: Dollars? What's that?
I FIGURED WE'D GET PEOPLE SAYING THINGS LIKE THIS.
AH HA HA...
KACHI (CLICK)
KACHI
HMM?

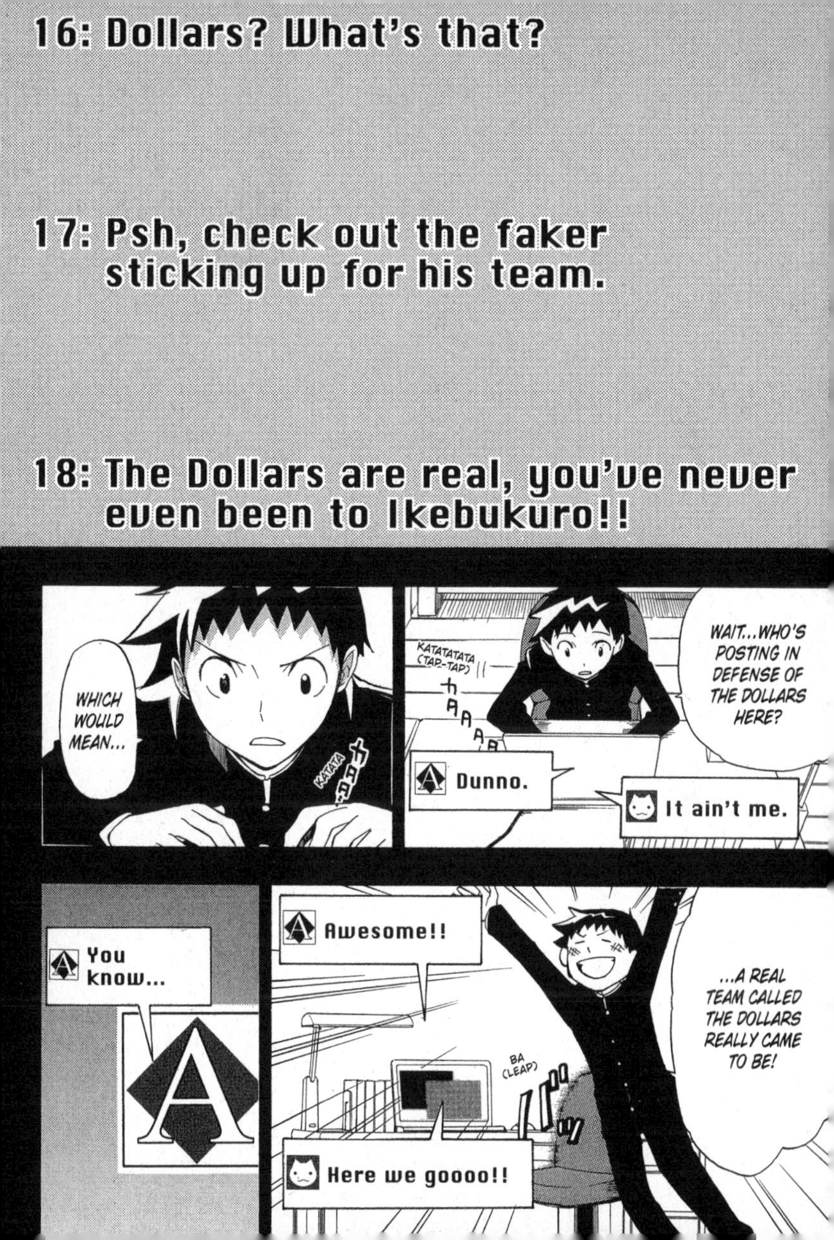
16: Dollars? What's that?
17: Psh, check out the faker sticking up for his team.
18: The Dollars are real, you've never even been to Ikebukuro!!
WAIT...WHO'S POSTING IN DEFENSE OF THE DOLLARS HERE?
KATATATATA (TAP-TAP)
Dunno.
It ain't me.
WHICH WOULD MEAN...
KATATA
...A REAL TEAM CALLED THE DOLLARS REALLY CAME TO BE!
Awesome!!
BA (LEAP)
Here we goooo!!
You know...

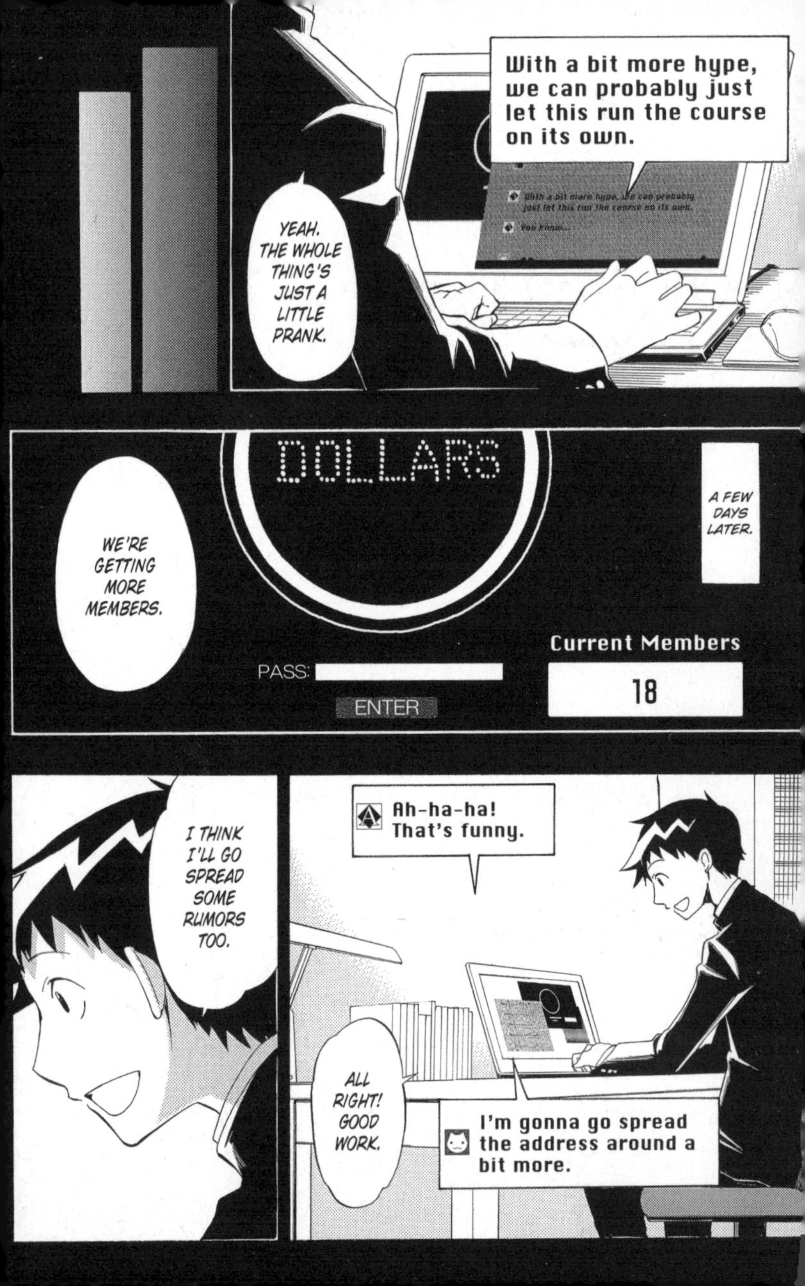
With a bit more hype, we can probably just let this run the course on its own.
YEAH. THE WHOLE THING'S JUST A LITTLE PRANK.
A FEW DAYS LATER.
DOLLARS
Current Members
18
WE'RE GETTING MORE MEMBERS.
PASS:
ENTER
Ah-ha-ha! That's funny.
I'm gonna go spread the address around a bit more.
ALL RIGHT! GOOD WORK.
I THINK I'LL GO SPREAD SOME RUMORS TOO.

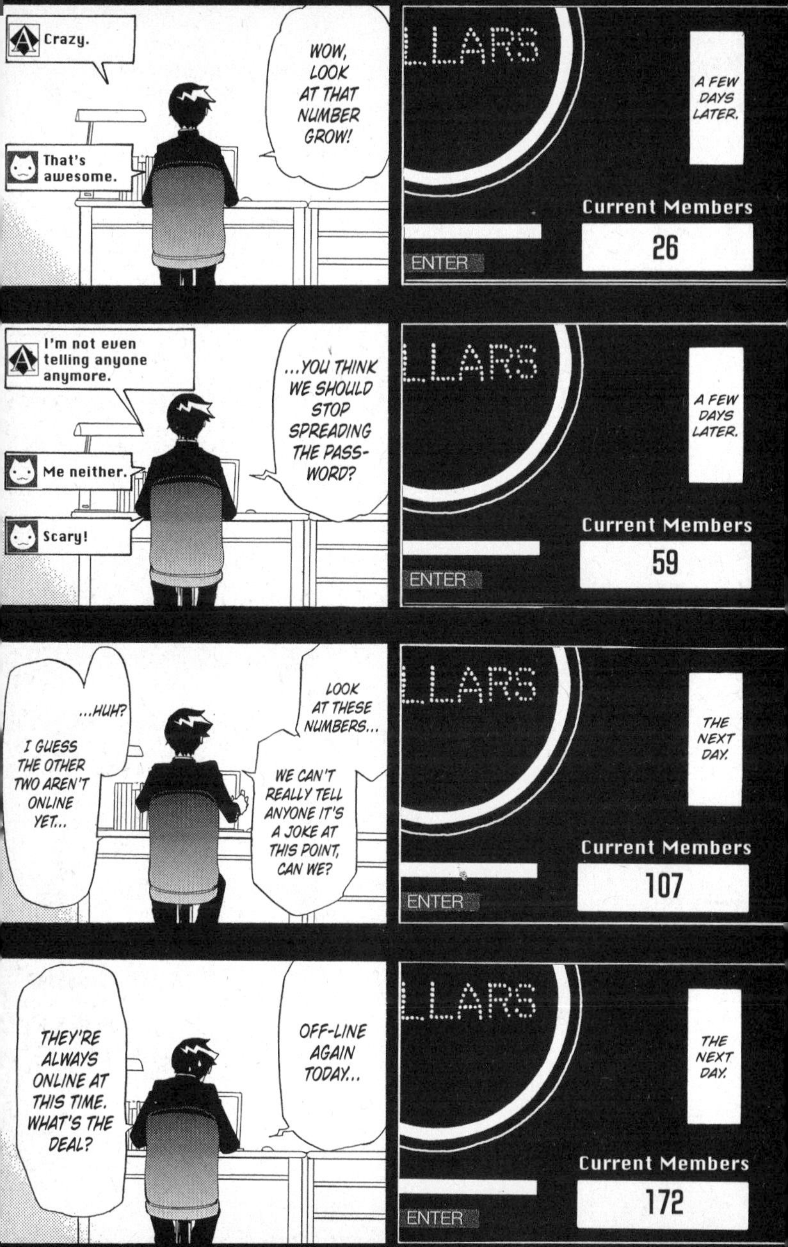
A FEW DAYS LATER.
Current Members
26
ENTER
WOW, LOOK AT THAT NUMBER GROW!
Crazy.
That's awesome.
A FEW DAYS LATER.
Current Members
59
ENTER
...YOU THINK WE SHOULD STOP SPREADING THE PASS-WORD?
I'm not even telling anyone anymore.
Me neither.
Scary!
THE NEXT DAY.
Current Members
107
ENTER
LOOK AT THESE NUMBERS...
WE CAN'T REALLY TELL ANYONE IT'S A JOKE AT THIS POINT, CAN WE?
...HUH?
I GUESS THE OTHER TWO AREN'T ONLINE YET...
THE NEXT DAY.
Current Members
172
ENTER
OFF-LINE AGAIN TODAY...
THEY'RE ALWAYS ONLINE AT THIS TIME. WHAT'S THE DEAL?

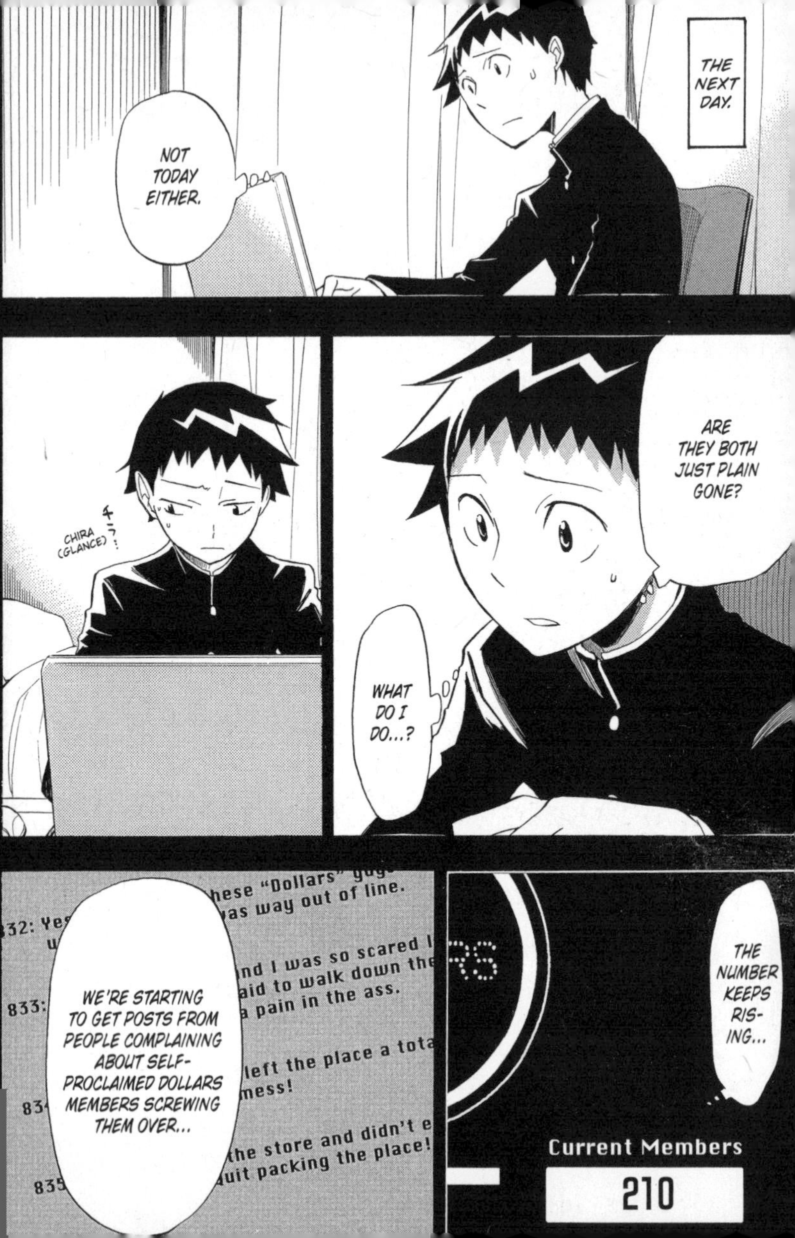
THE NEXT DAY.
NOT TODAY EITHER.
ARE THEY BOTH JUST PLAIN GONE?
WHAT DO I DO...?
チラ CHIRA (GLANCE)
THE NUMBER KEEPS RIS-ING...
Current Members
210
was way out of line.
832:
833:
a pain in the ass.
left the place a tota
mess!
834
the store and didn't e
quit packing the place!
835
WE'RE STARTING TO GET POSTS FROM PEOPLE COMPLAINING ABOUT SELF-PROCLAIMED DOLLARS MEMBERS SCREWING THEM OVER...

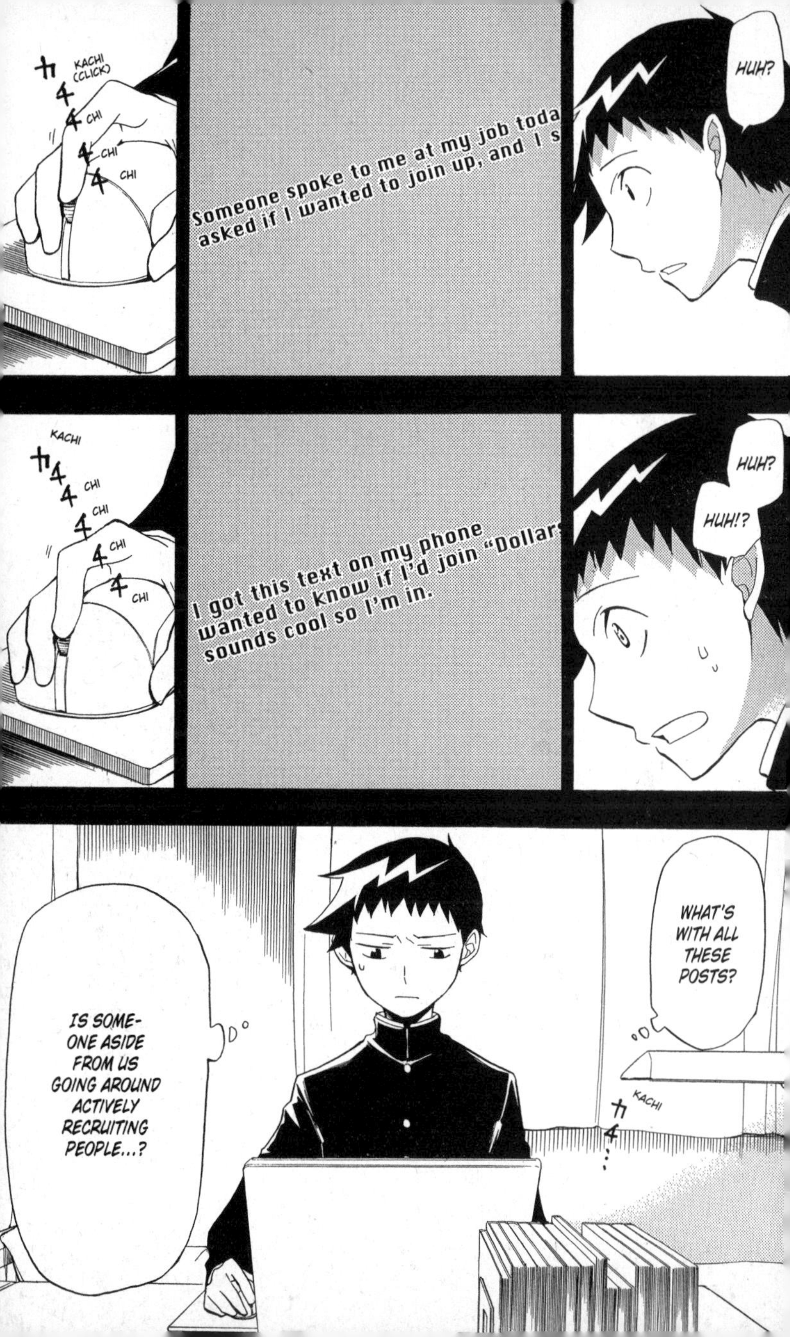
HUH?
Someone spoke to me at my job toda
asked if I wanted to join up, and I s
KACHI (CLICK)
CHI
CHI
CHI
HUH?
HUH!?
I got this text on my phone
wanted to know if I'd join "Dollars
sounds cool so I'm in.
KACHI
CHI
CHI
CHI
CHI
WHAT'S WITH ALL THESE POSTS?
IS SOME-ONE ASIDE FROM US GOING AROUND ACTIVELY RECRUITING PEOPLE...?
KACHI

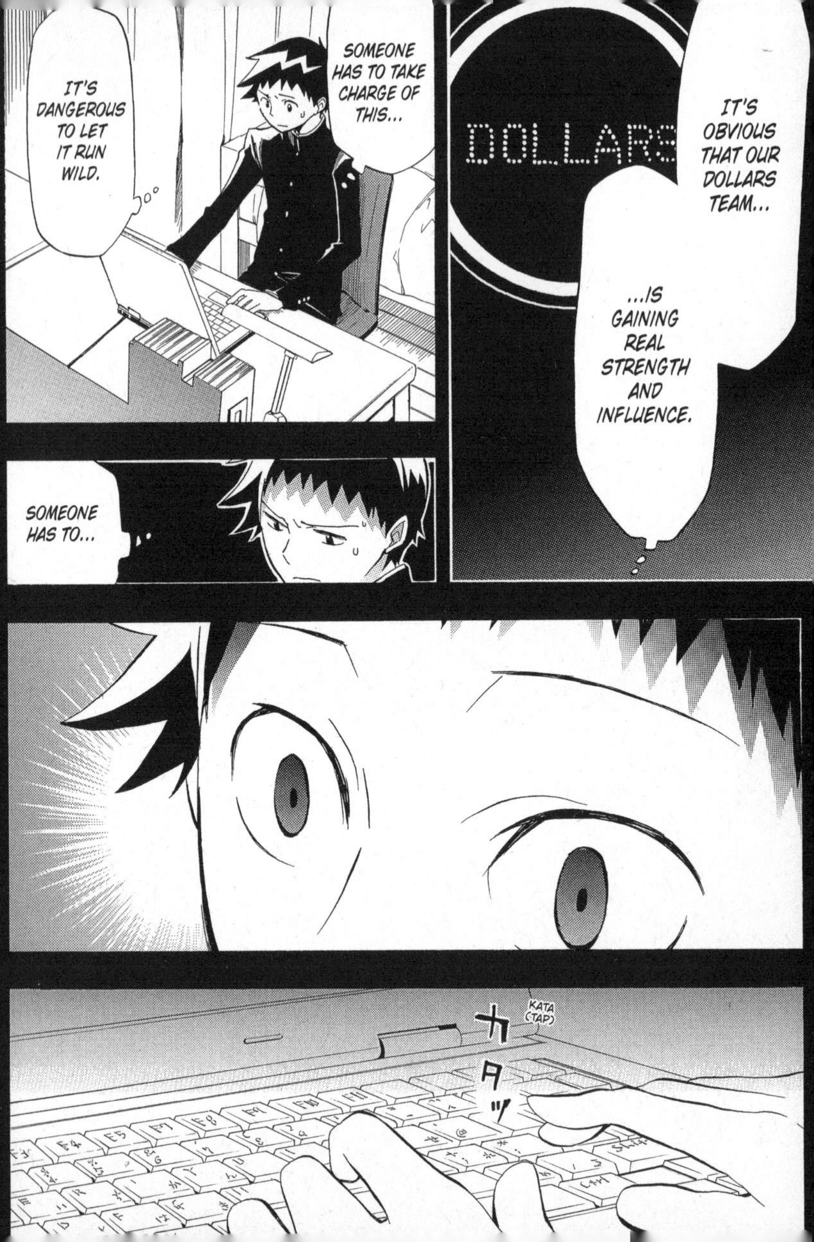
DOLLARS
IT'S OBVIOUS THAT OUR DOLLARS TEAM...
...IS GAINING REAL STRENGTH AND INFLUENCE.
SOMEONE HAS TO TAKE CHARGE OF THIS...
IT'S DANGEROUS TO LET IT RUN WILD.
SOMEONE HAS TO...
KATA (TAP)

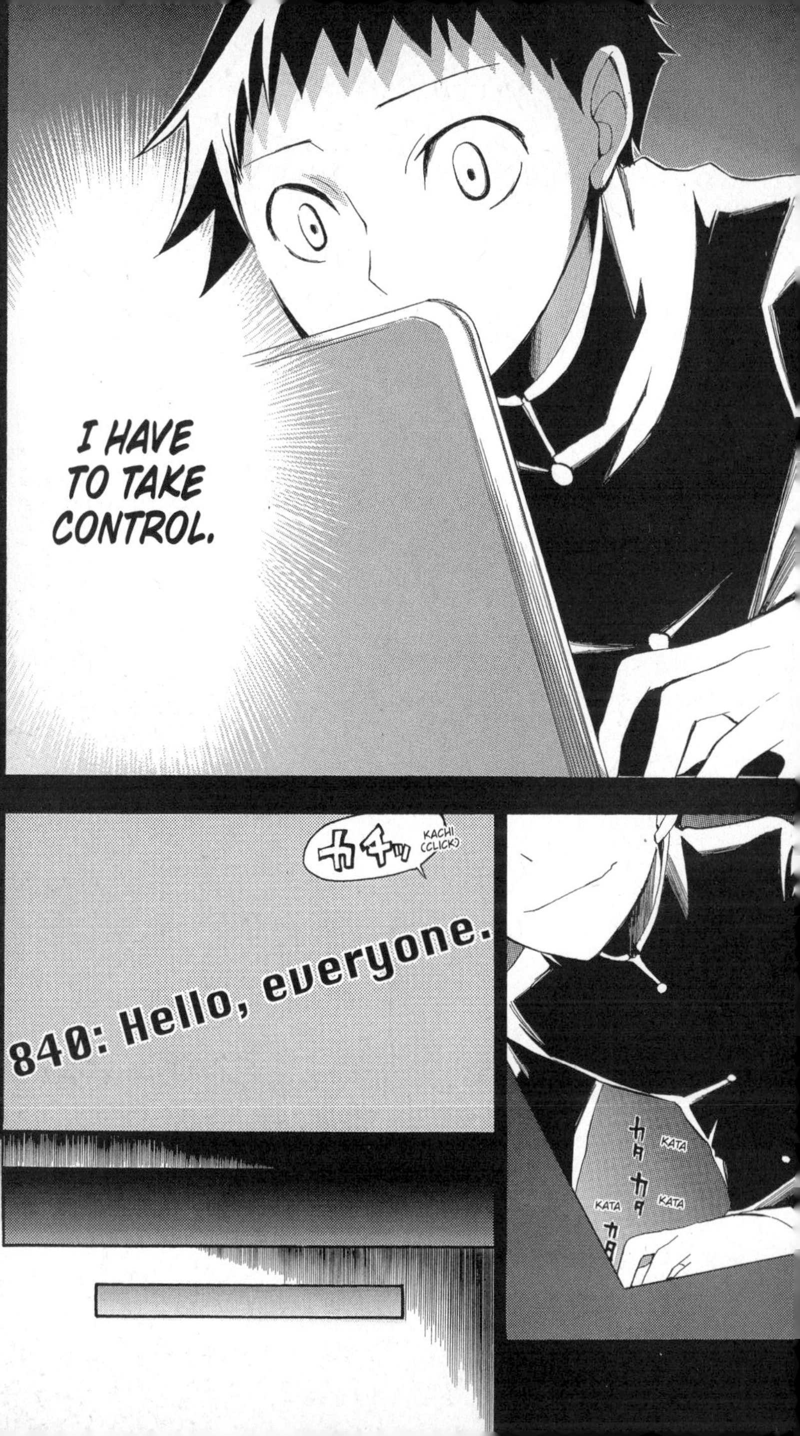
I HAVE TO TAKE CONTROL.
カタ KATA
カタ KATA
カタ KATA
カチッ KACHI (CLICK)
840: Hello, everyone.

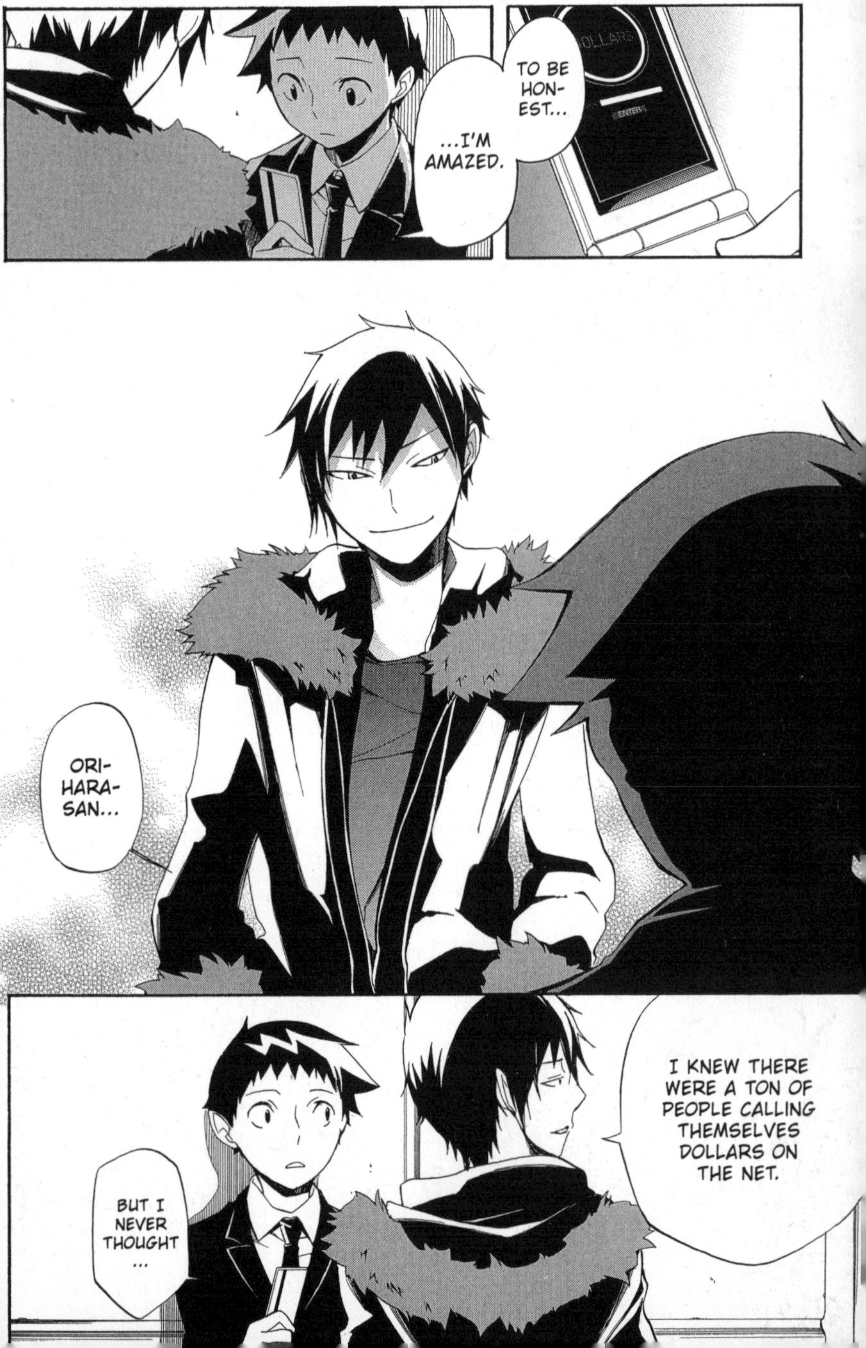
ENTER
TO BE HON-EST...
...I'M AMAZED.
ORI-HARA-SAN...
I KNEW THERE WERE A TON OF PEOPLE CALLING THEMSELVES DOLLARS ON THE NET.
BUT I NEVER THOUGHT ...

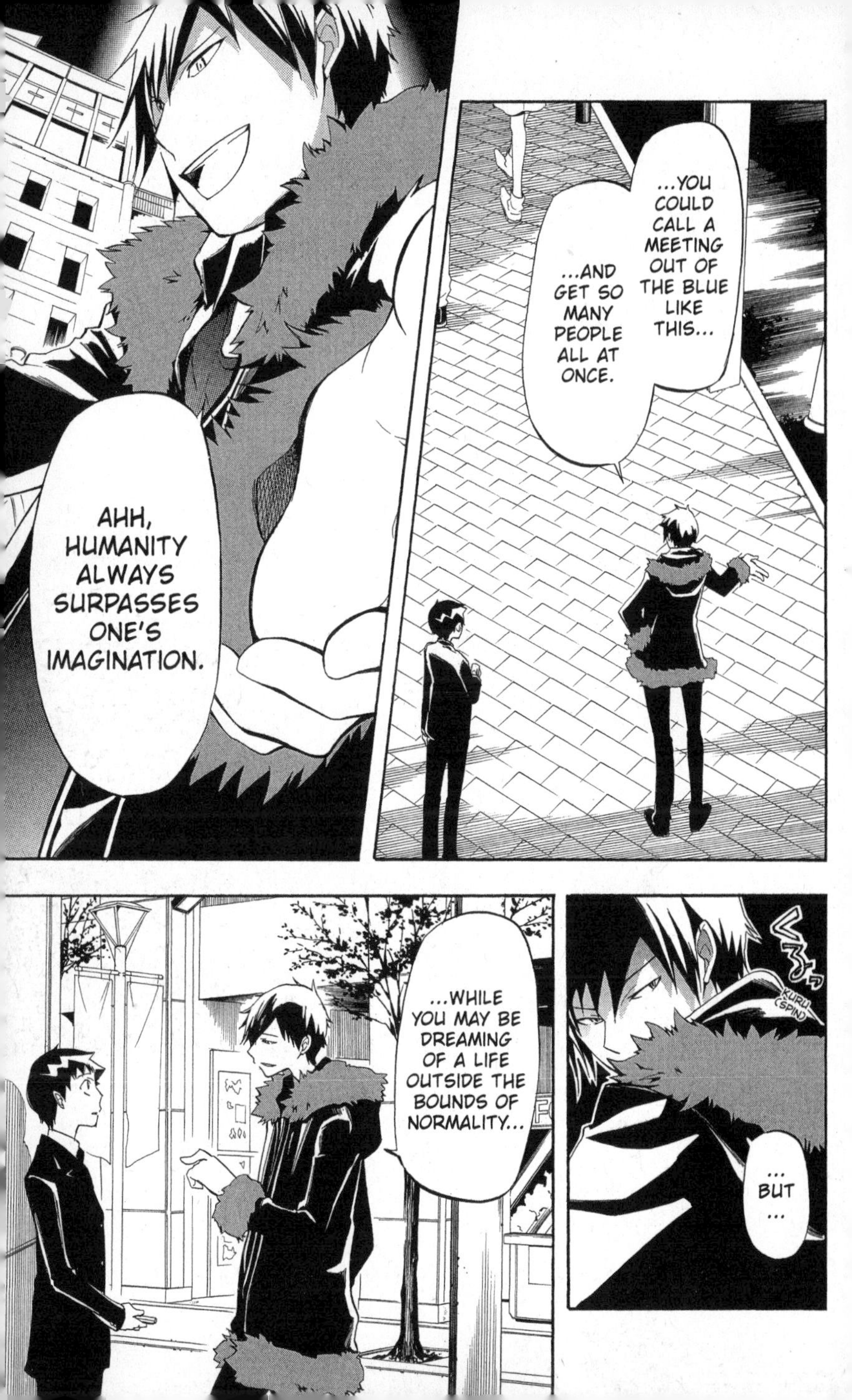
...YOU COULD CALL A MEETING OUT OF THE BLUE LIKE THIS...
...AND GET SO MANY PEOPLE ALL AT ONCE.
AHH, HUMANITY ALWAYS SURPASSES ONE'S IMAGINATION.
KURU (SPIN)
... BUT ...
...WHILE YOU MAY BE DREAMING OF A LIFE OUTSIDE THE BOUNDS OF NORMALITY...

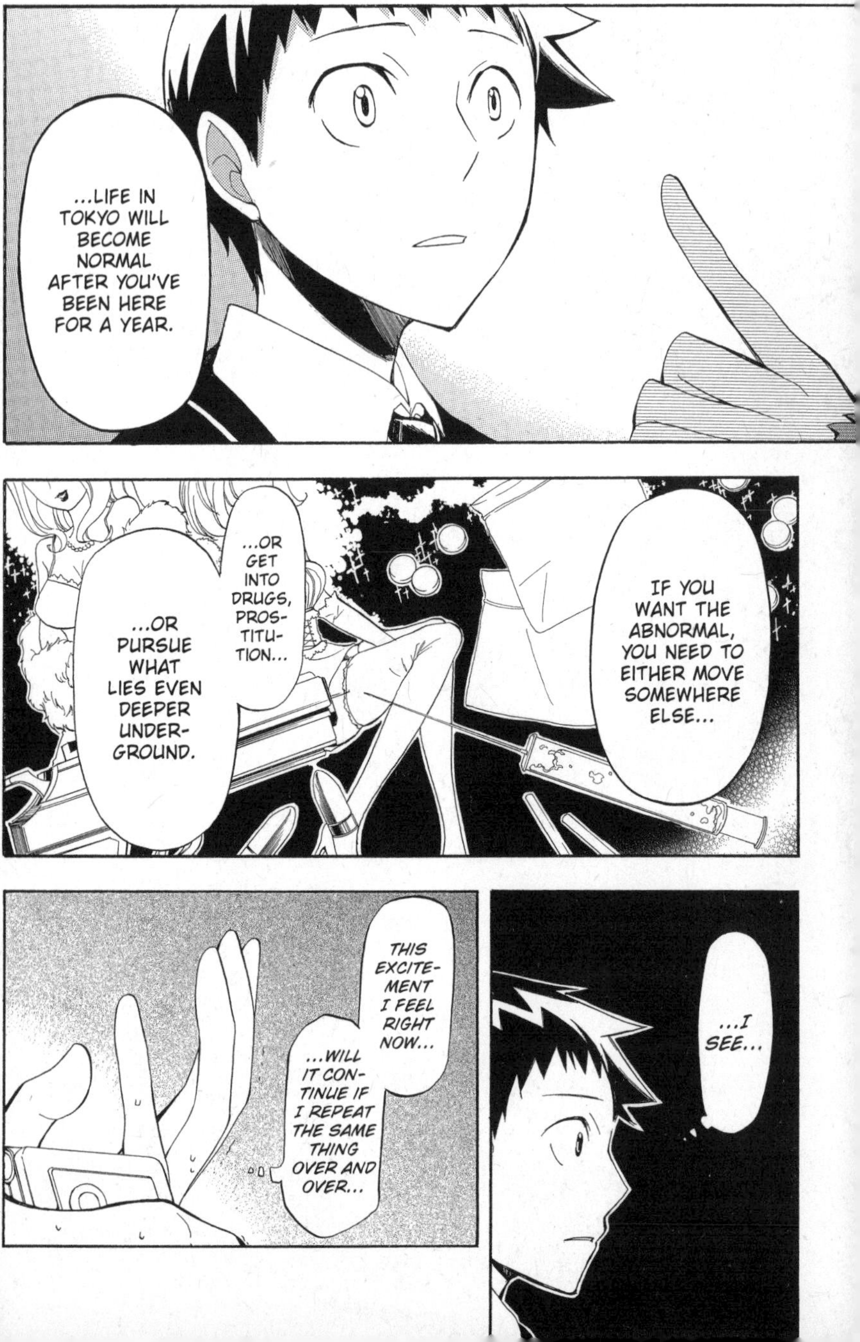
...LIFE IN TOKYO WILL BECOME NORMAL AFTER YOU'VE BEEN HERE FOR A YEAR.
IF YOU WANT THE ABNORMAL, YOU NEED TO EITHER MOVE SOMEWHERE ELSE...
...OR GET INTO DRUGS, PROS-TITU-TION...
...OR PURSUE WHAT LIES EVEN DEEPER UNDER-GROUND.
...I SEE...
THIS EXCITE-MENT I FEEL RIGHT NOW...
...WILL IT CON-TINUE IF I REPEAT THE SAME THING OVER AND OVER...

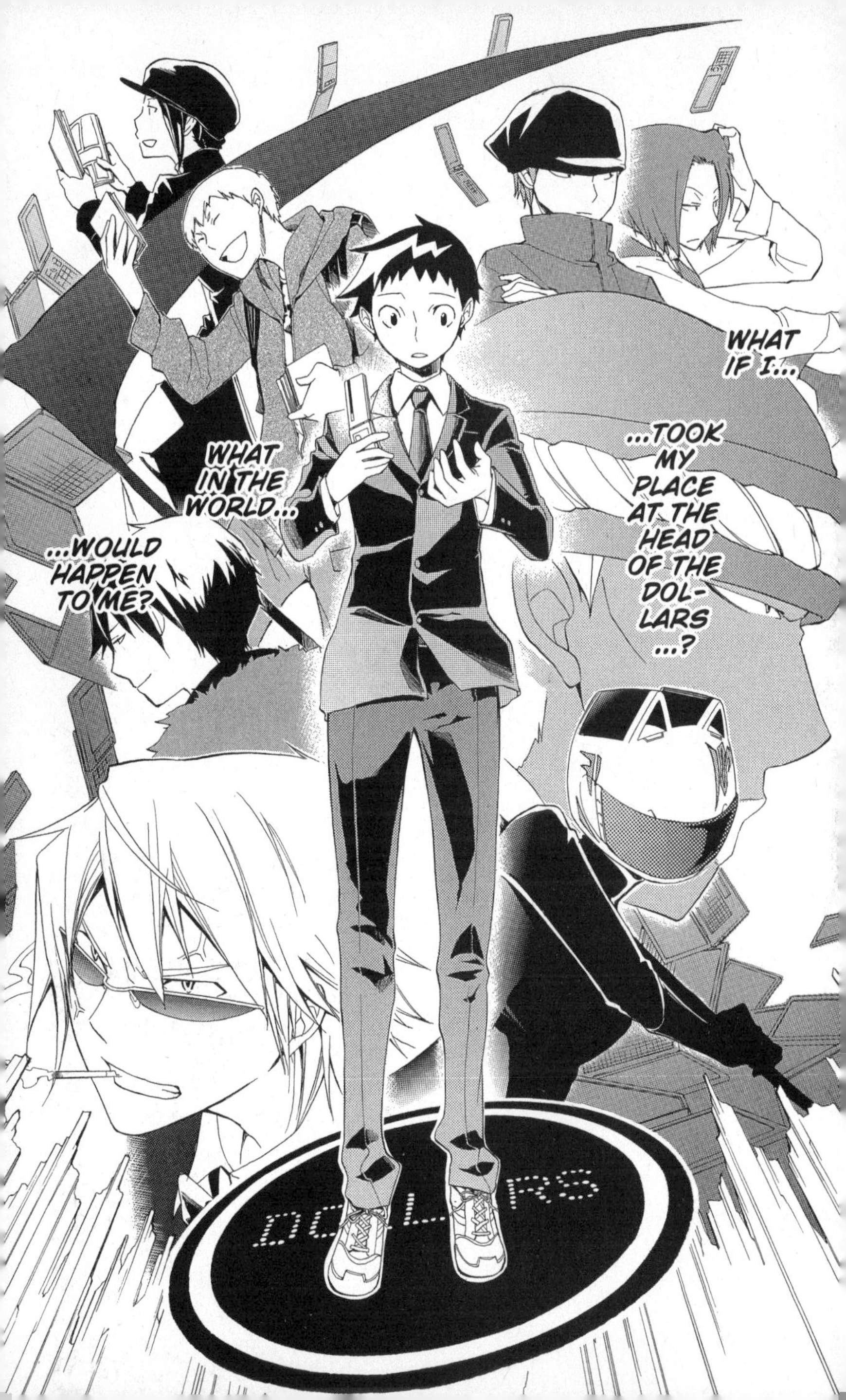
WHAT IF I...
...TOOK MY PLACE AT THE HEAD OF THE DOL-LARS ...?
WHAT IN THE WORLD...
...WOULD HAPPEN TO ME?

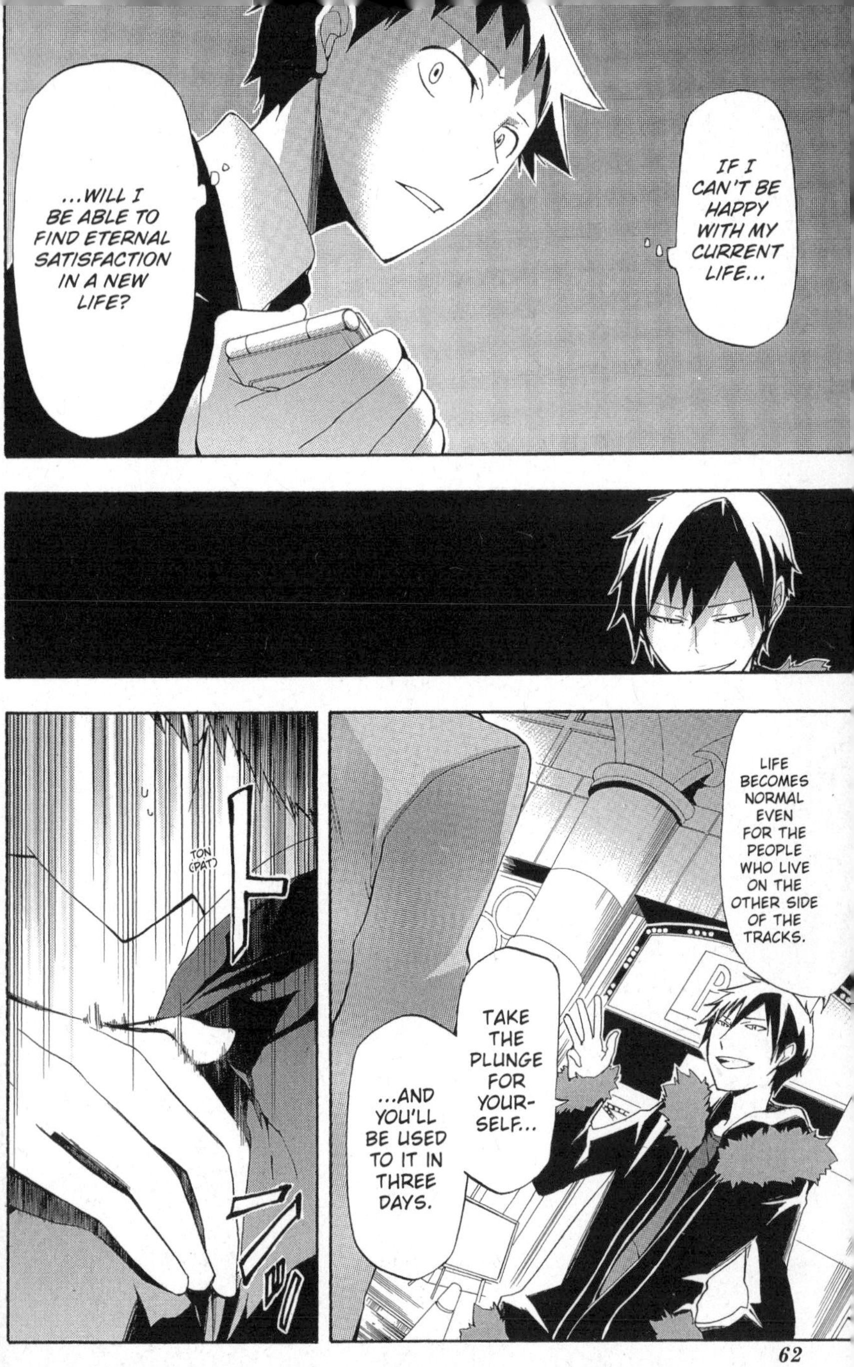
IF I CAN'T BE HAPPY WITH MY CURRENT LIFE...
...WILL I BE ABLE TO FIND ETERNAL SATISFACTION IN A NEW LIFE?
LIFE BECOMES NORMAL EVEN FOR THE PEOPLE WHO LIVE ON THE OTHER SIDE OF THE TRACKS.
TAKE THE PLUNGE FOR YOURSELF...
...AND YOU'LL BE USED TO IT IN THREE DAYS.
TON (PAT)

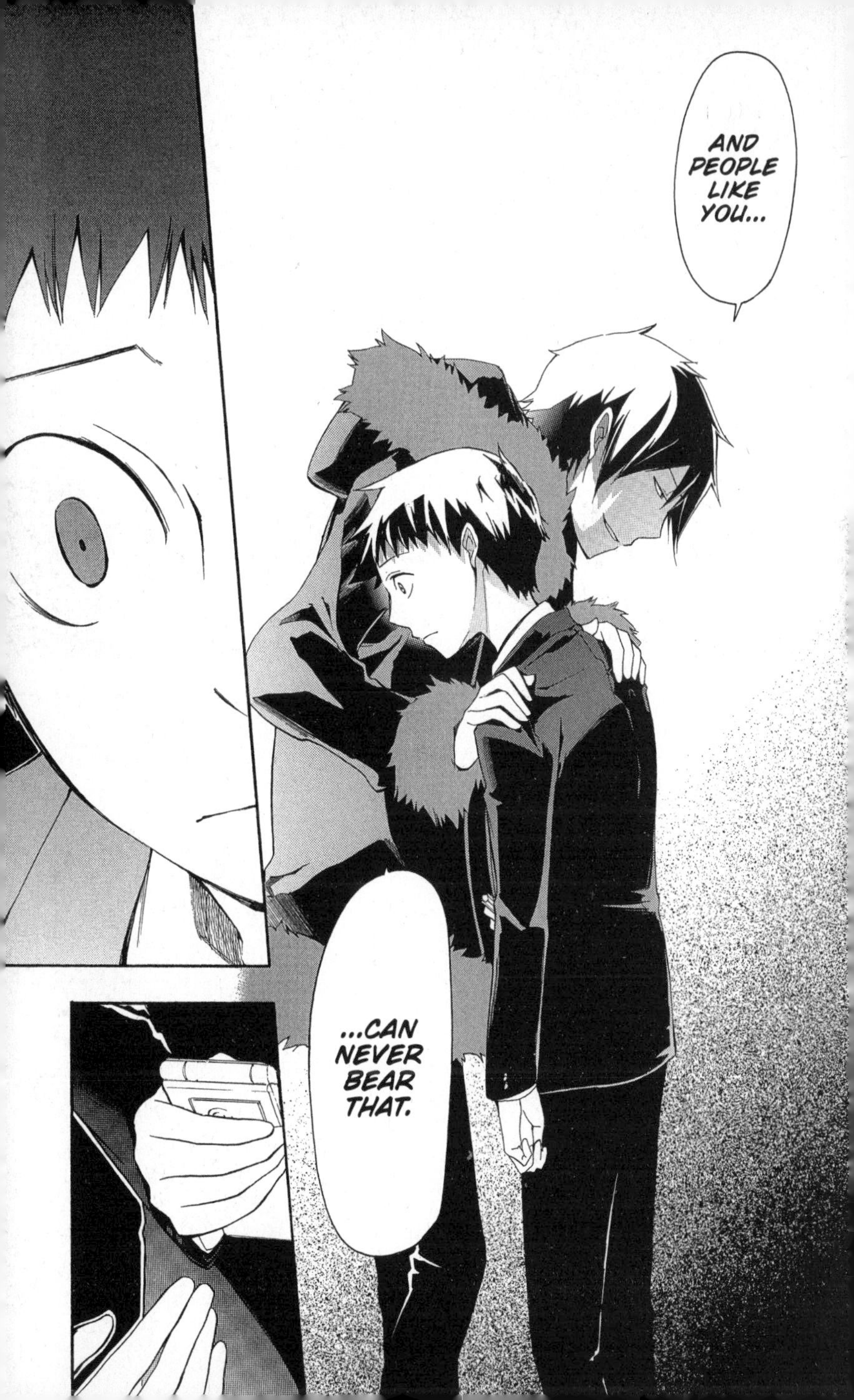
AND PEOPLE LIKE YOU...
...CAN NEVER BEAR THAT.

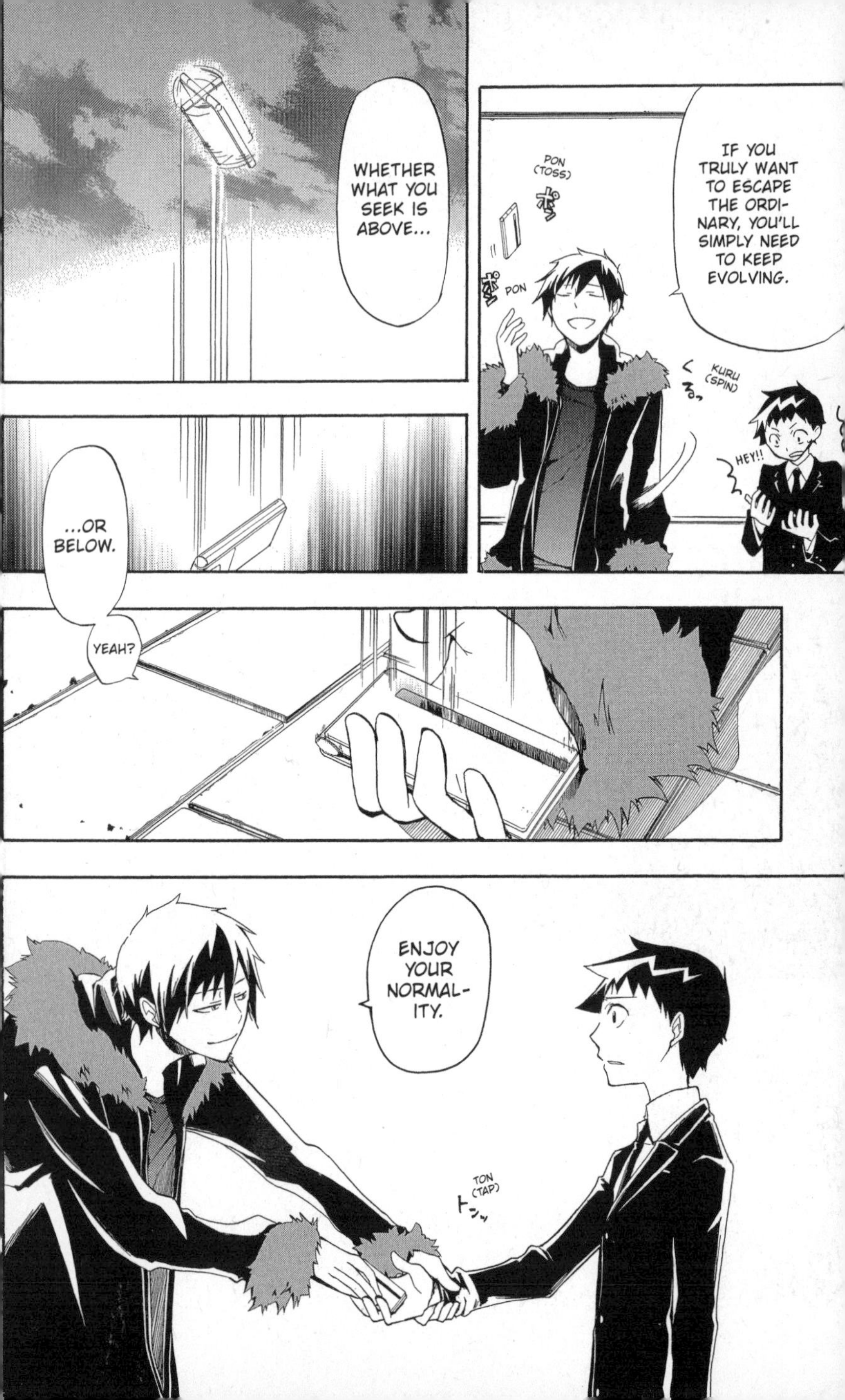
IF YOU TRULY WANT TO ESCAPE THE ORDINARY, YOU'LL SIMPLY NEED TO KEEP EVOLVING.
PON (TOSS)
PON
KURU (SPIN)
HEY!!
WHETHER WHAT YOU SEEK IS ABOVE...
...OR BELOW.
YEAH?
ENJOY YOUR NORMALITY.
TON (TAP)

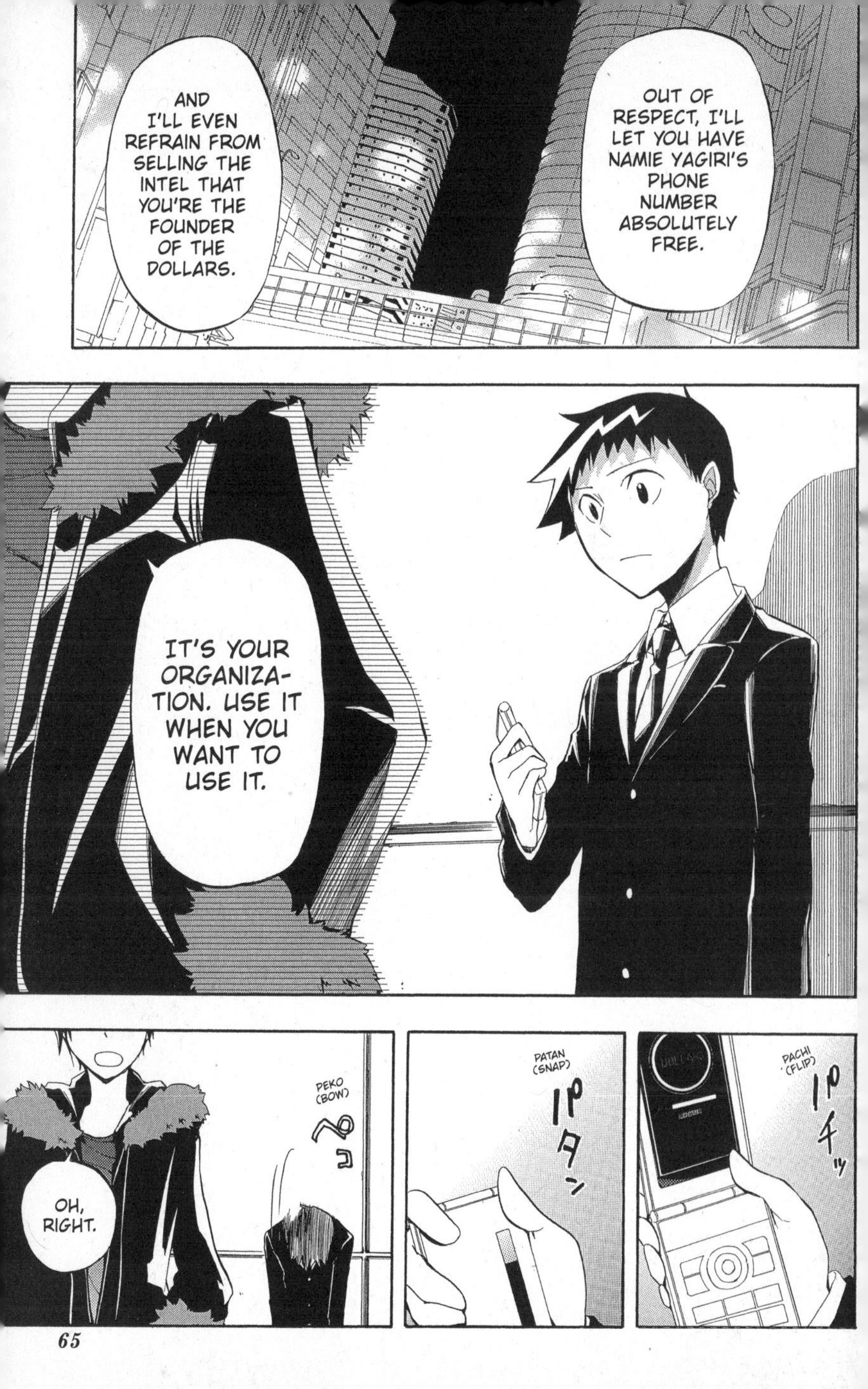
OUT OF RESPECT, I'LL LET YOU HAVE NAMIE YAGIRI'S PHONE NUMBER ABSOLUTELY FREE.
AND I'LL EVEN REFRAIN FROM SELLING THE INTEL THAT YOU'RE THE FOUNDER OF THE DOLLARS.
IT'S YOUR ORGANIZA-TION. USE IT WHEN YOU WANT TO USE IT.
PACHI (FLIP)
パチッ
PATAN (SNAP)
パタン
PEKO (BOW)
ペコ
OH, RIGHT.

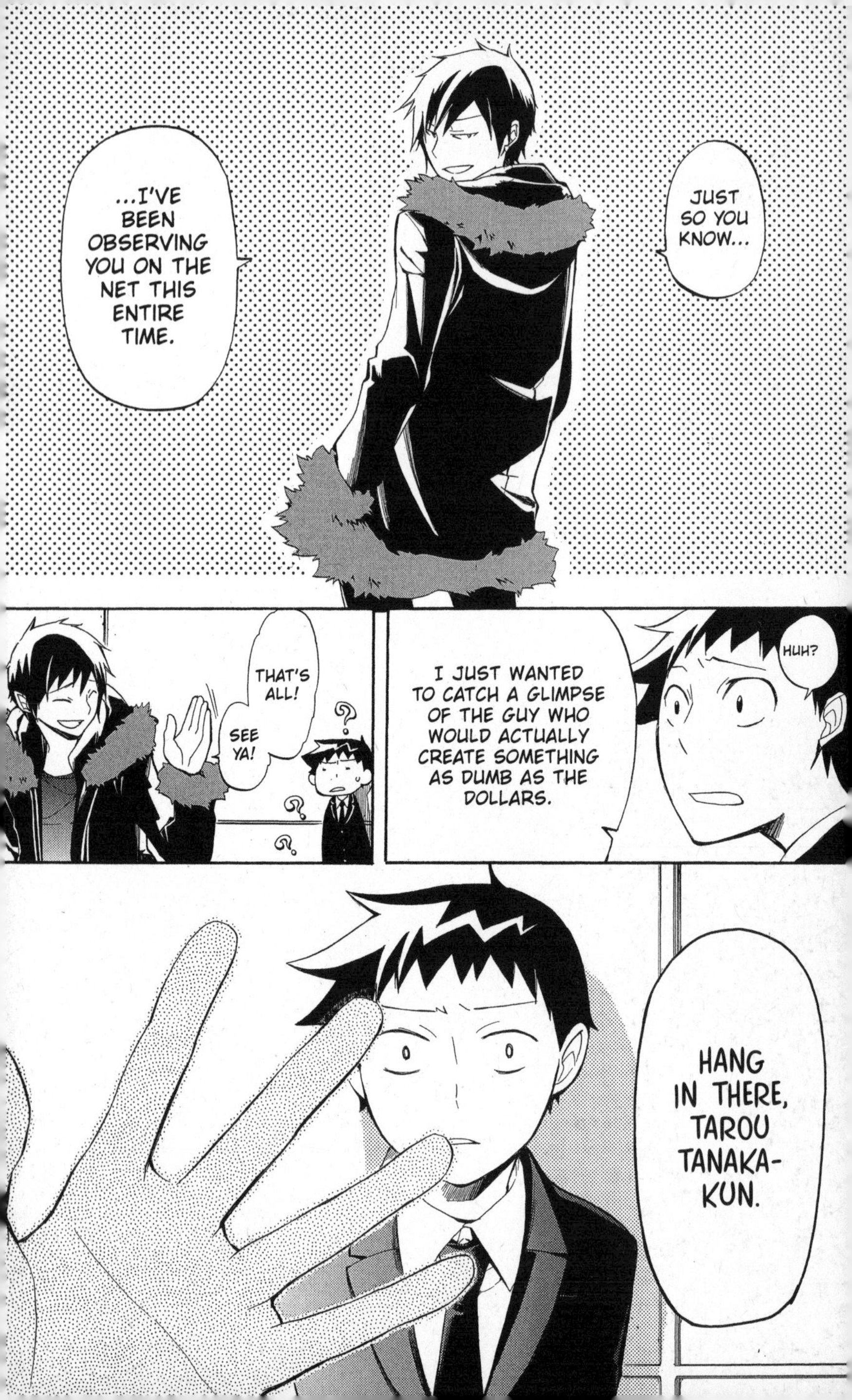
JUST SO YOU KNOW...
...I'VE BEEN OBSERVING YOU ON THE NET THIS ENTIRE TIME.
HUH?
I JUST WANTED TO CATCH A GLIMPSE OF THE GUY WHO WOULD ACTUALLY CREATE SOMETHING AS DUMB AS THE DOLLARS.
THAT'S ALL!
SEE YA!
HANG IN THERE, TAROU TANAKA-KUN.

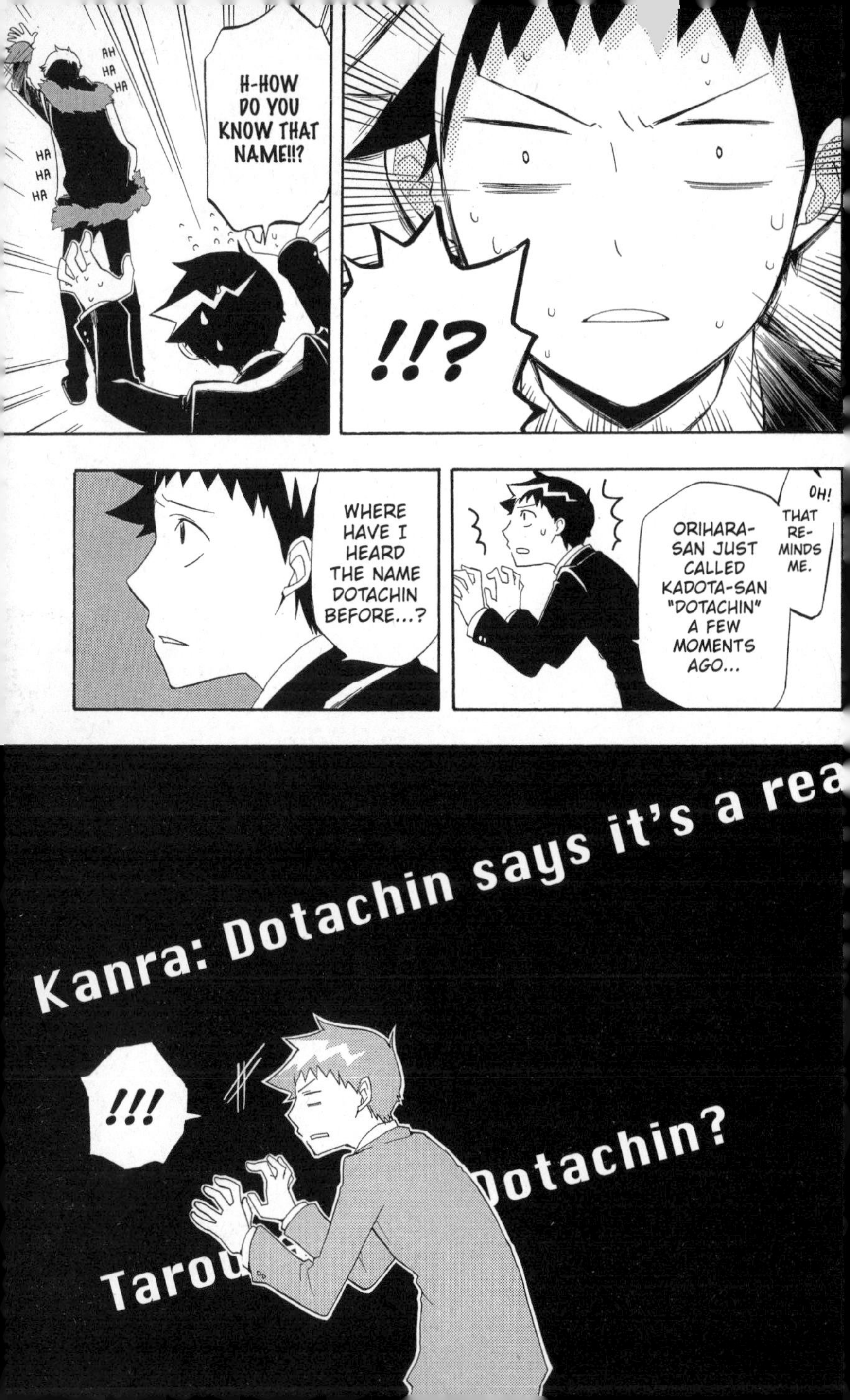
!!?
H-HOW DO YOU KNOW THAT NAME!!?
AH HA HA
HA HA HA
OH! THAT RE-MINDS ME.
ORIHARA-SAN JUST CALLED KADOTA-SAN "DOTACHIN" A FEW MOMENTS AGO...
WHERE HAVE I HEARD THE NAME DOTACHIN BEFORE...?
Kanra: Dotachin says it's a rea
!!!
Tarou
Dotachin?

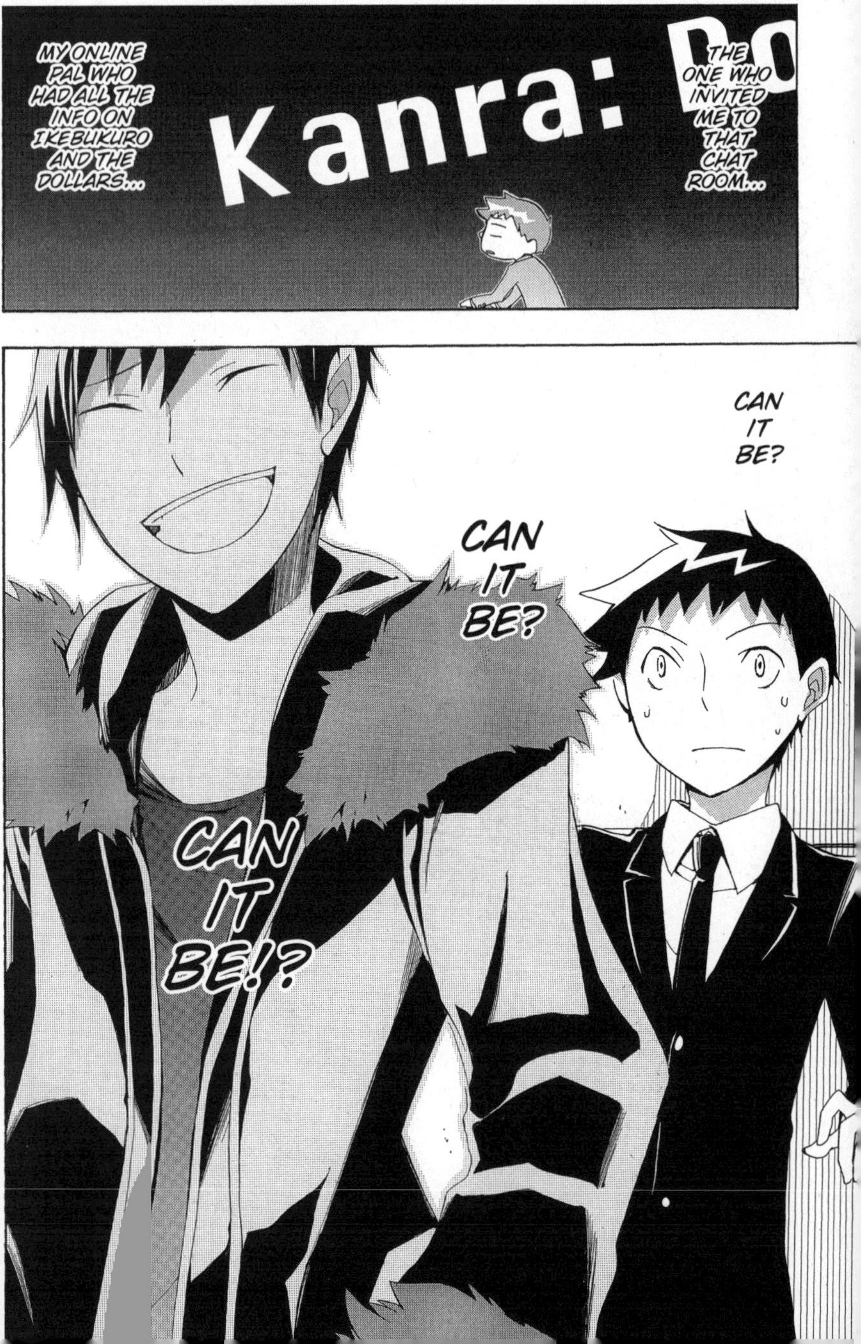
THE ONE WHO INVITED ME TO THAT CHAT ROOM...
Kanra: Do
MY ONLINE PAL WHO HAD ALL THE INFO ON IKEBUKURO AND THE DOLLARS...
CAN IT BE?
CAN IT BE?
CAN IT BE!?

20: WAWAWAWAWAWAWAWAWAWAWAWAWAWAWAWAWAWAWAWAWA!!

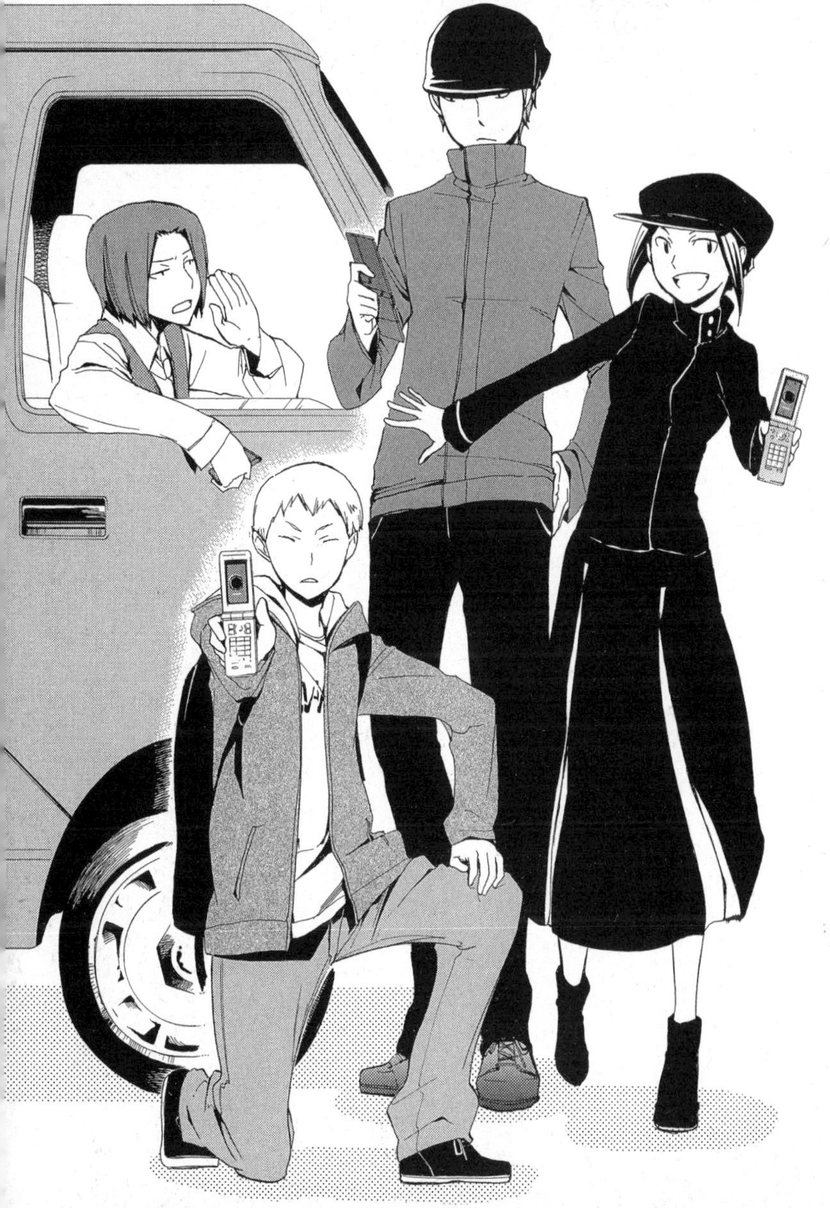

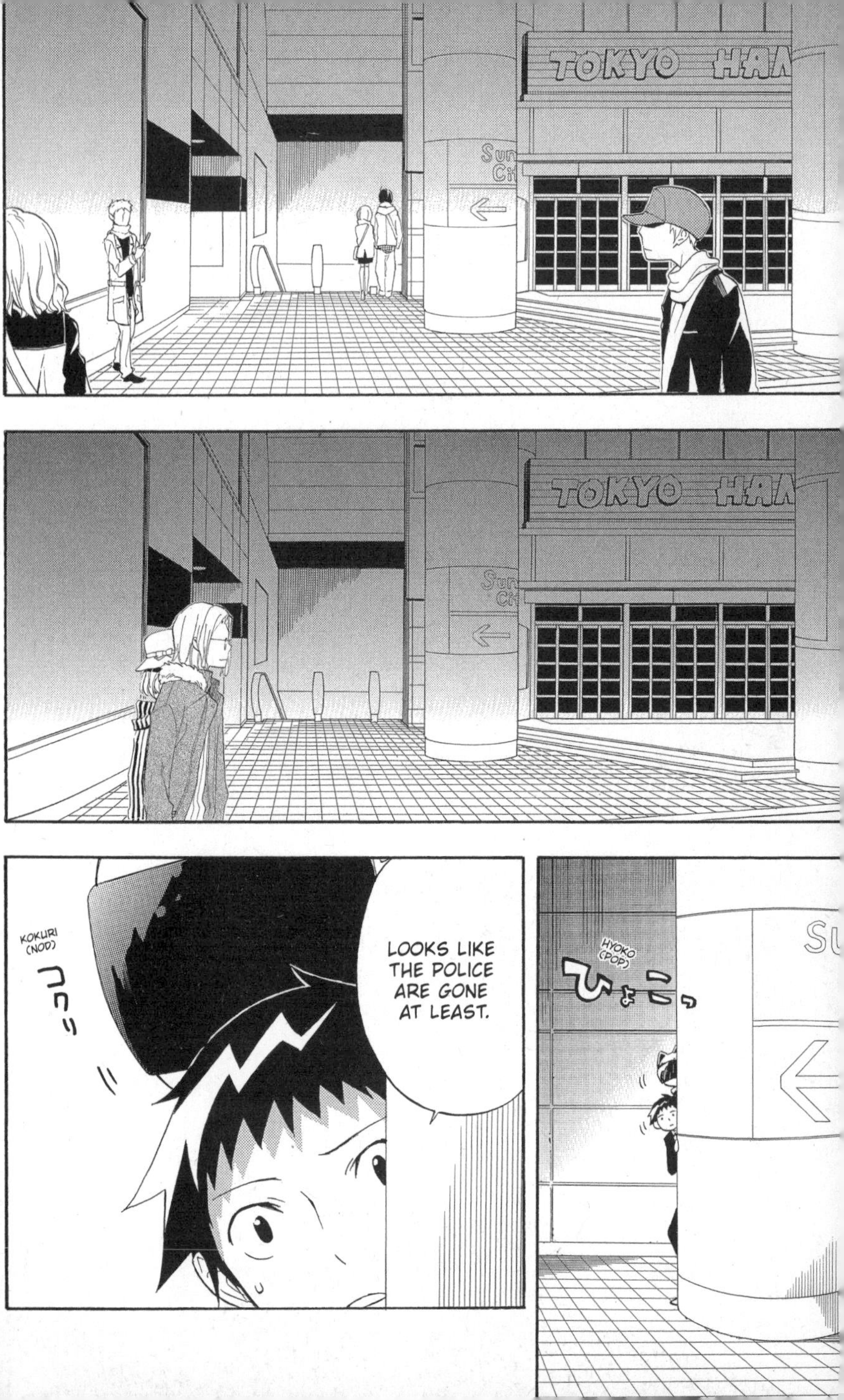
TOKYO
TOKYO
HYOKO (POP)
ひょこっ
KOKURI (NOD)
コクリ
LOOKS LIKE THE POLICE ARE GONE AT LEAST.

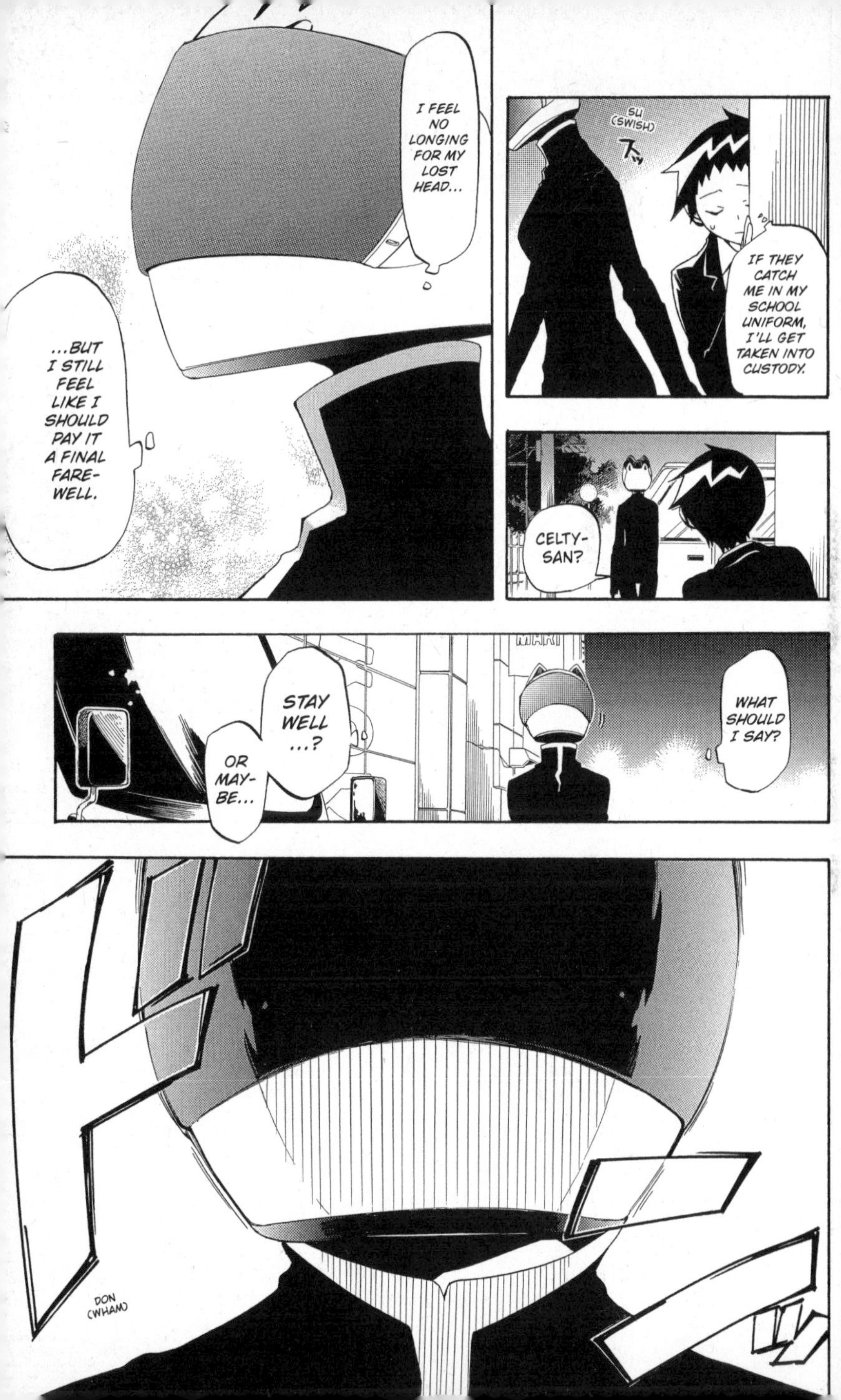
SU (SWISH)
IF THEY CATCH ME IN MY SCHOOL UNIFORM, I'LL GET TAKEN INTO CUSTODY.
CELTY-SAN?
I FEEL NO LONGING FOR MY LOST HEAD...
...BUT I STILL FEEL LIKE I SHOULD PAY IT A FINAL FARE-WELL.
WHAT SHOULD I SAY?
STAY WELL ...?
OR MAY-BE...
DON (WHAM)

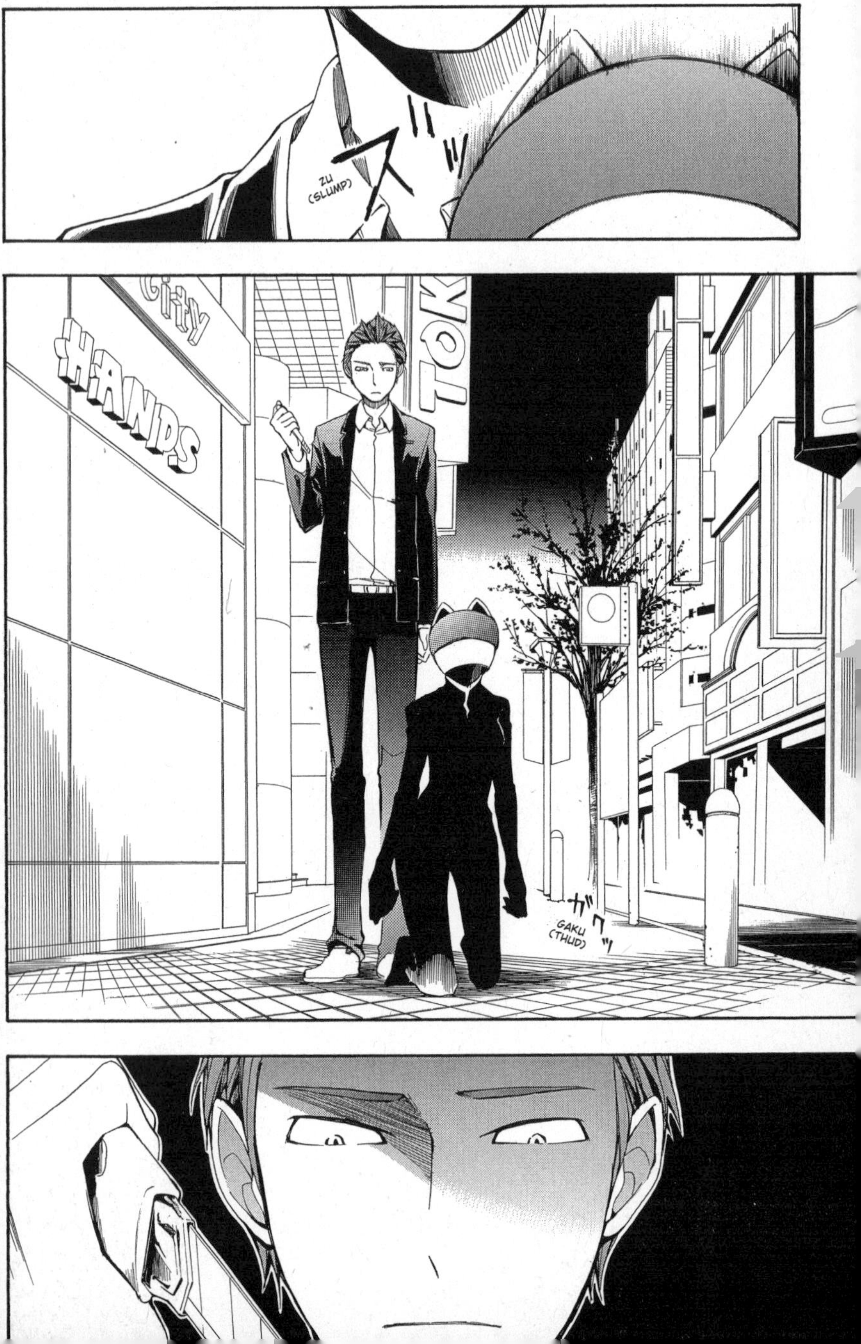
ZU
(SLUMP)
City
HANDS
TOK
GAKU
(THUD)

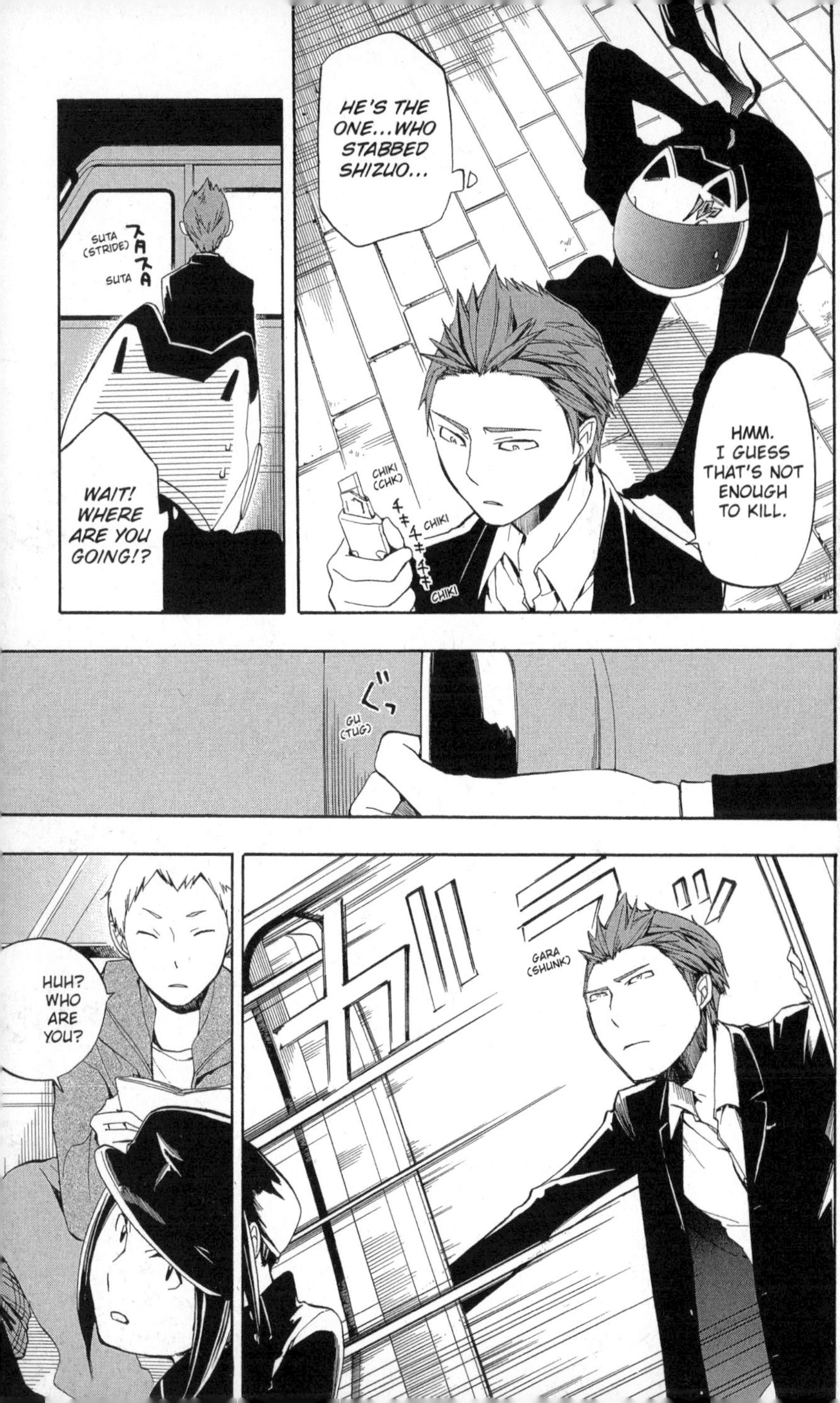
HE'S THE ONE...WHO STABBED SHIZUO...
HMM. I GUESS THAT'S NOT ENOUGH TO KILL.
CHIKI (CHK)
CHIKI
CHIKI
スタスタ
SUTA (STRIDE)
SUTA
WAIT! WHERE ARE YOU GOING!?
GU (TUG)
GARA (SHUNK)
HUH? WHO ARE YOU?

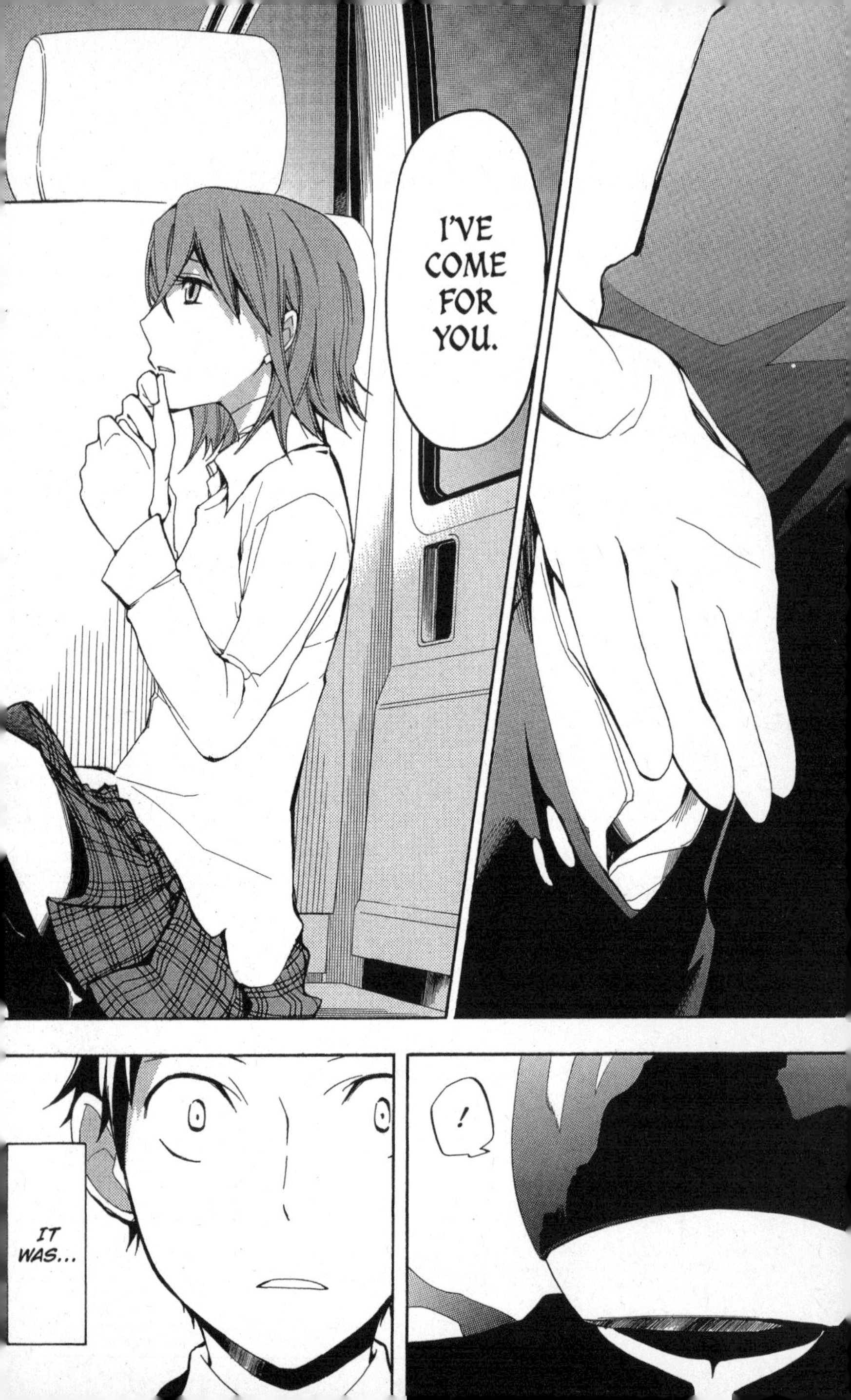
I'VE COME FOR YOU.
!
IT WAS...

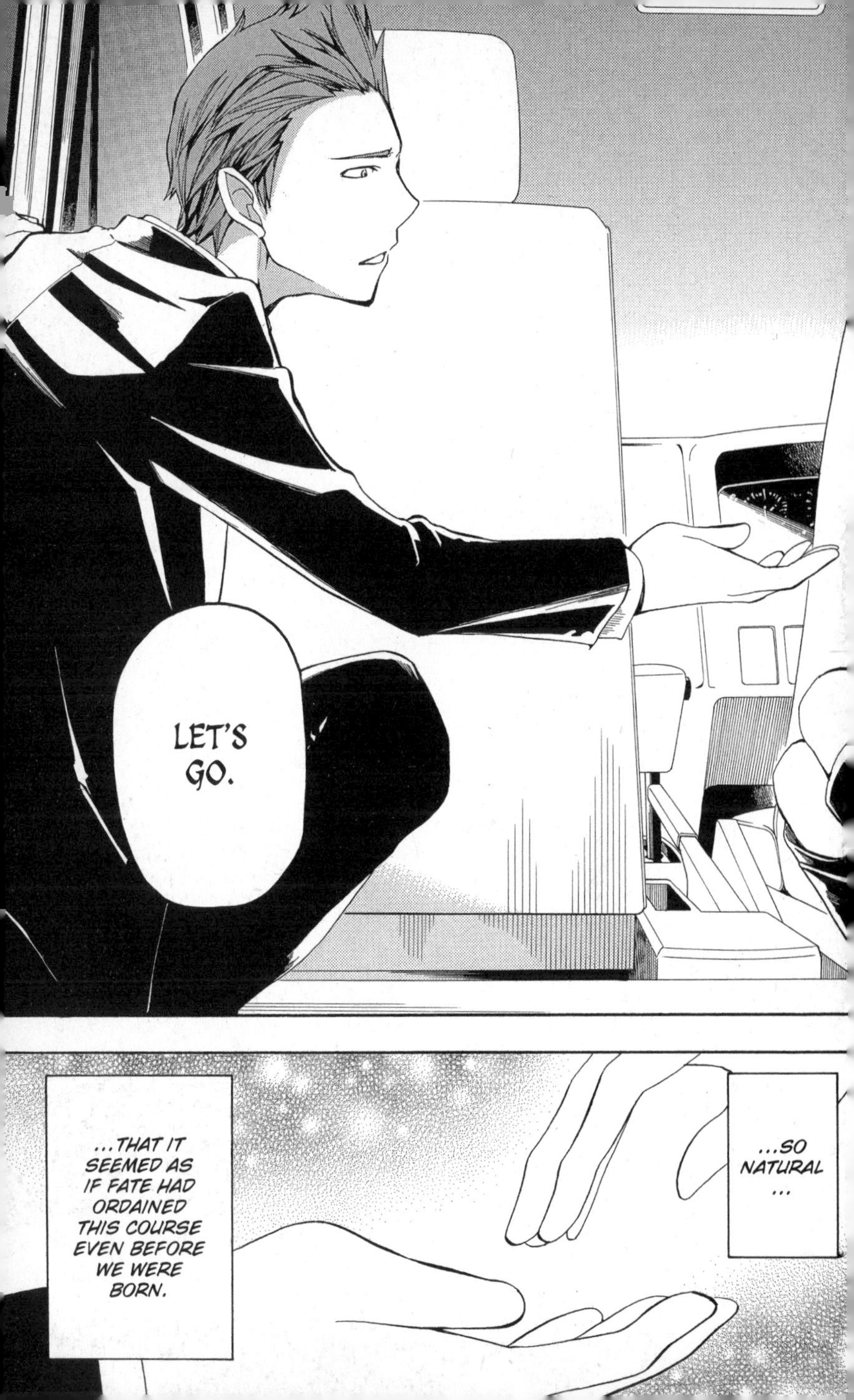
LET'S GO.
...SO NATURAL ...
...THAT IT SEEMED AS IF FATE HAD ORDAINED THIS COURSE EVEN BEFORE WE WERE BORN.

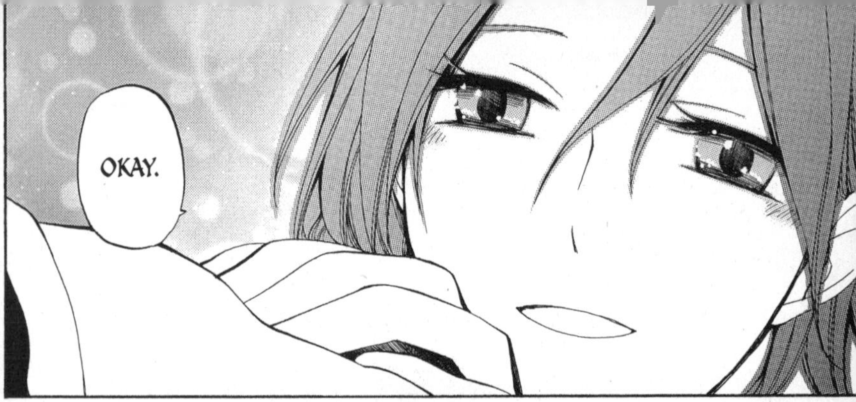
OKAY.

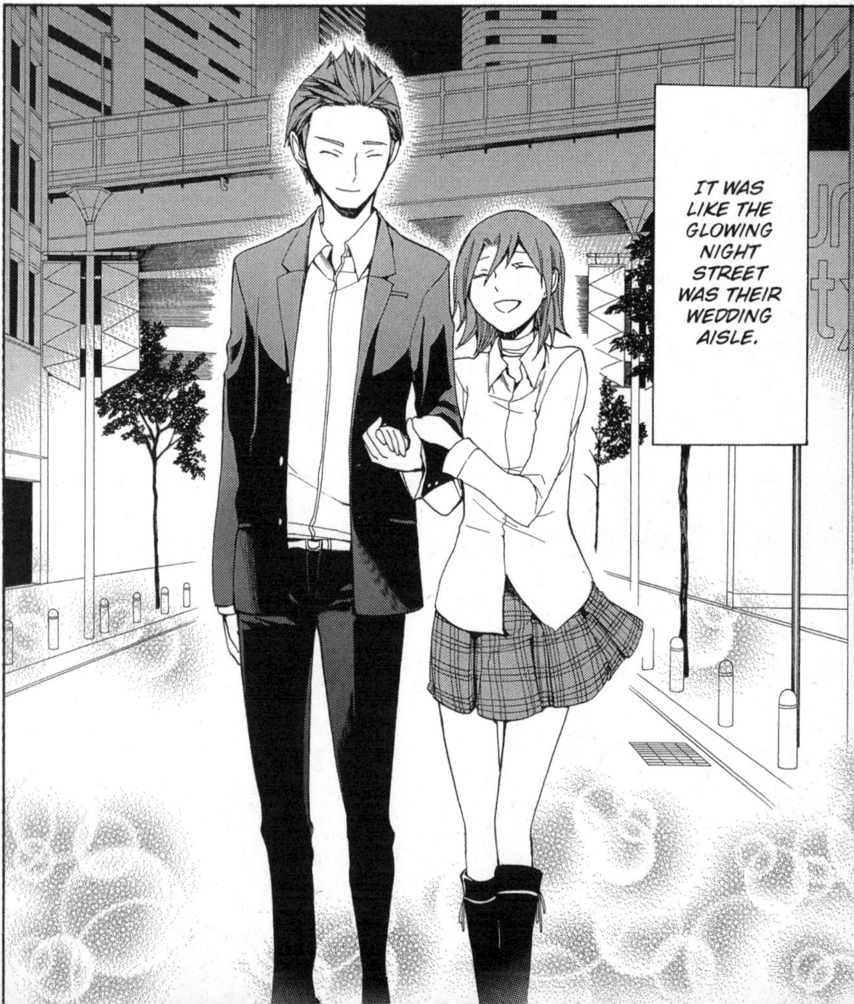
IT WAS LIKE THE GLOWING NIGHT STREET WAS THEIR WEDDING AISLE.

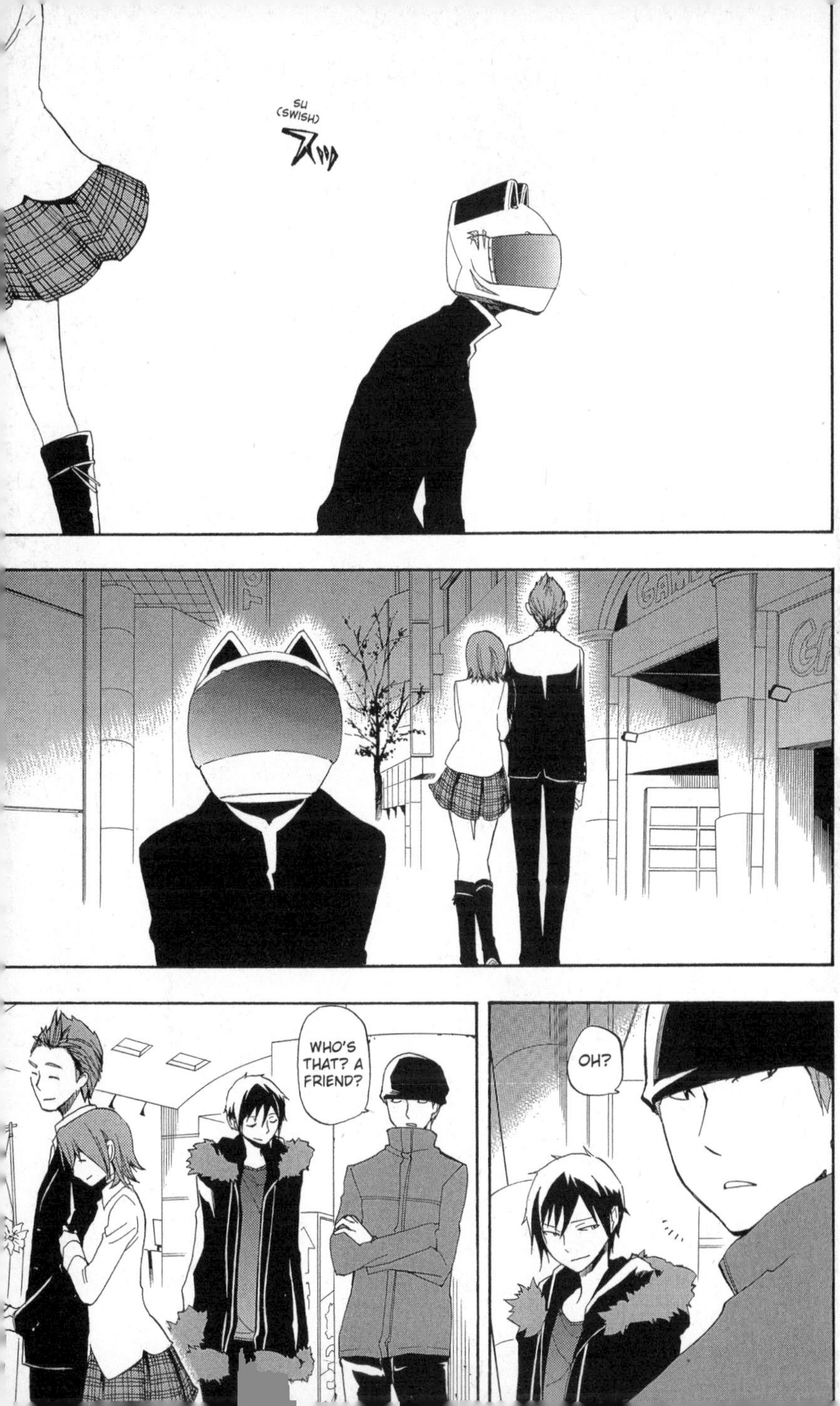
SU
(SWISH)
ス
OH?
WHO'S THAT? A FRIEND?

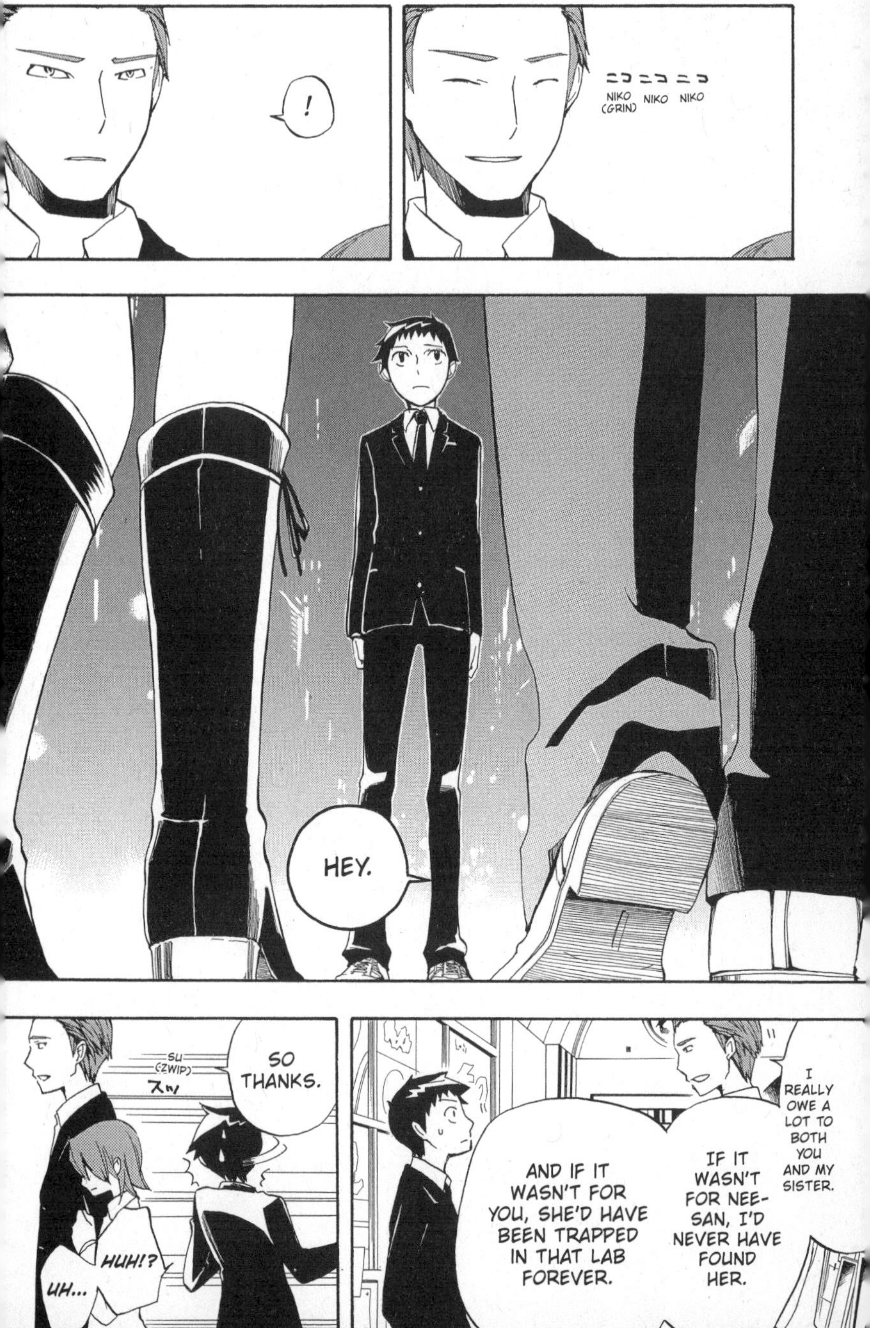
ニコ ニコ ニコ
NIKO (GRIN) NIKO NIKO
!
HEY.
I REALLY OWE A LOT TO BOTH YOU AND MY SISTER.
IF IT WASN'T FOR NEE-SAN, I'D NEVER HAVE FOUND HER.
AND IF IT WASN'T FOR YOU, SHE'D HAVE BEEN TRAPPED IN THAT LAB FOREVER.
SO THANKS.
スッ
SU (ZWIP)
HUH!?
UH...

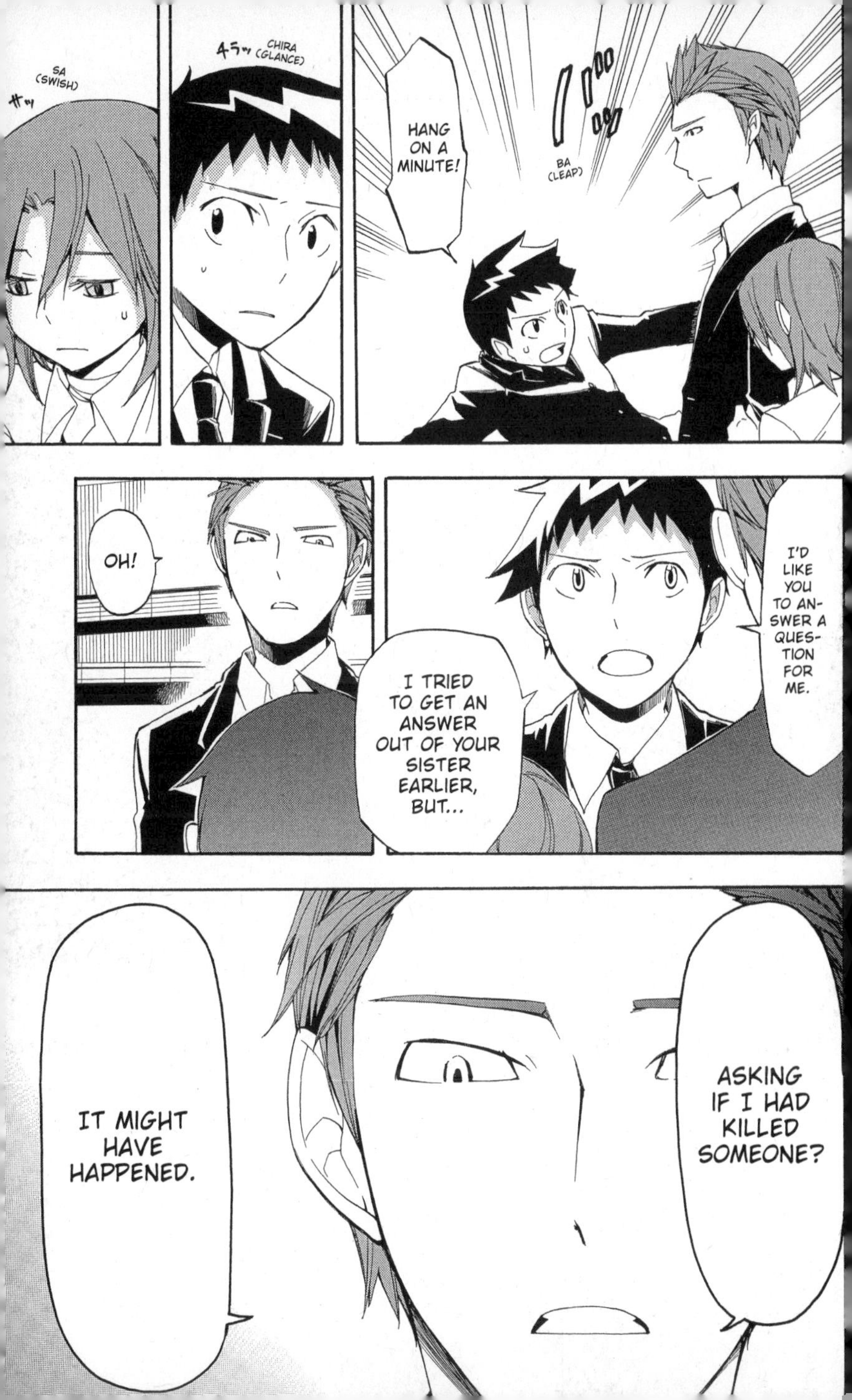
BA (LEAP)
HANG ON A MINUTE!
チラッ CHIRA (GLANCE)
サッ SA (SWISH)
I'D LIKE YOU TO AN-SWER A QUES-TION FOR ME.
I TRIED TO GET AN ANSWER OUT OF YOUR SISTER EARLIER, BUT...
OH!
ASKING IF I HAD KILLED SOMEONE?
IT MIGHT HAVE HAPPENED.

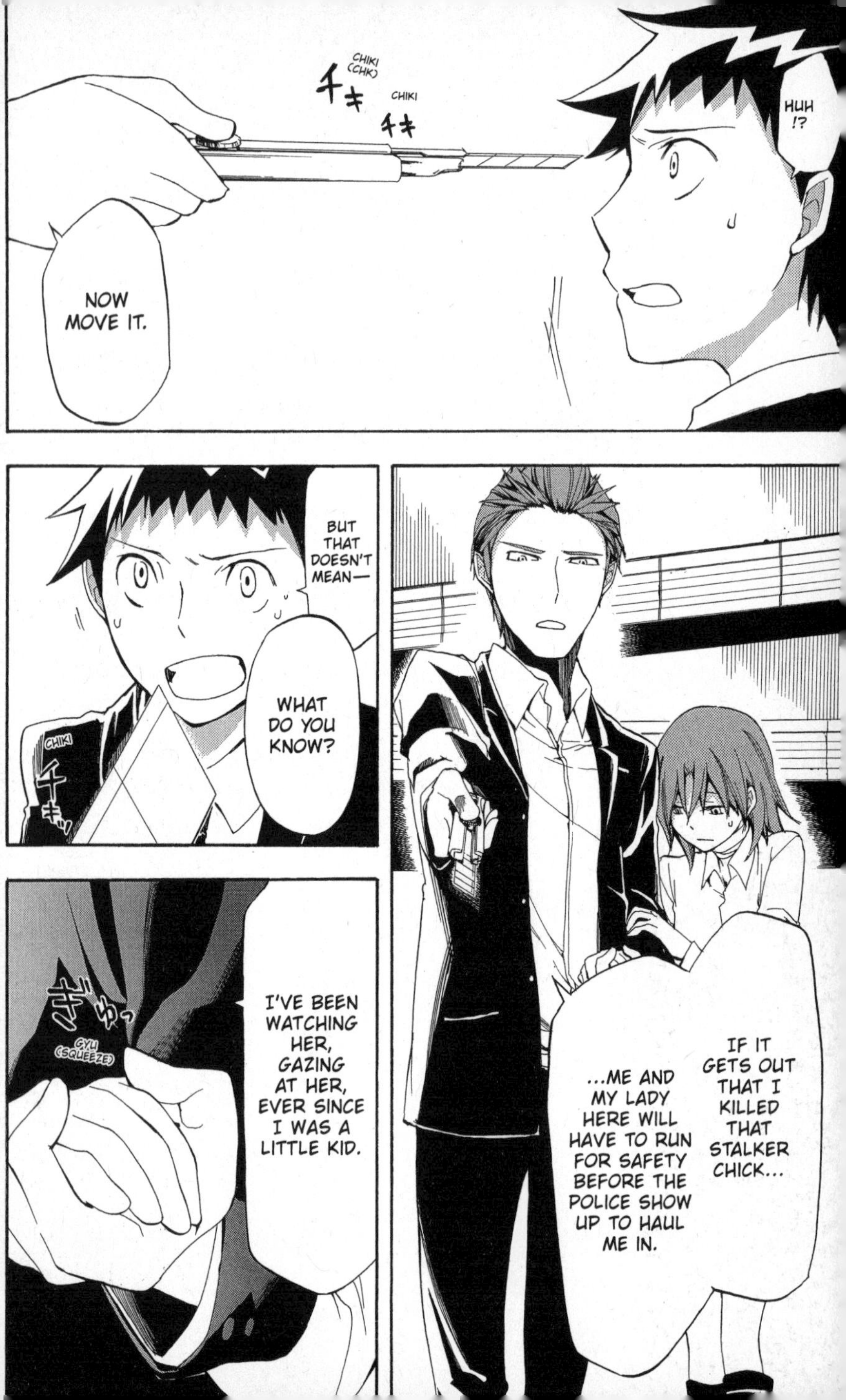
HUH !?
CHIKI (CHK)
チキ
CHIKI
チキ
NOW MOVE IT.
IF IT GETS OUT THAT I KILLED THAT STALKER CHICK...
...ME AND MY LADY HERE WILL HAVE TO RUN FOR SAFETY BEFORE THE POLICE SHOW UP TO HAUL ME IN.
BUT THAT DOESN'T MEAN—
WHAT DO YOU KNOW?
CHIKI
チキッ
I'VE BEEN WATCHING HER, GAZING AT HER, EVER SINCE I WAS A LITTLE KID.
ぎゅっ
GYU (SQUEEZE)

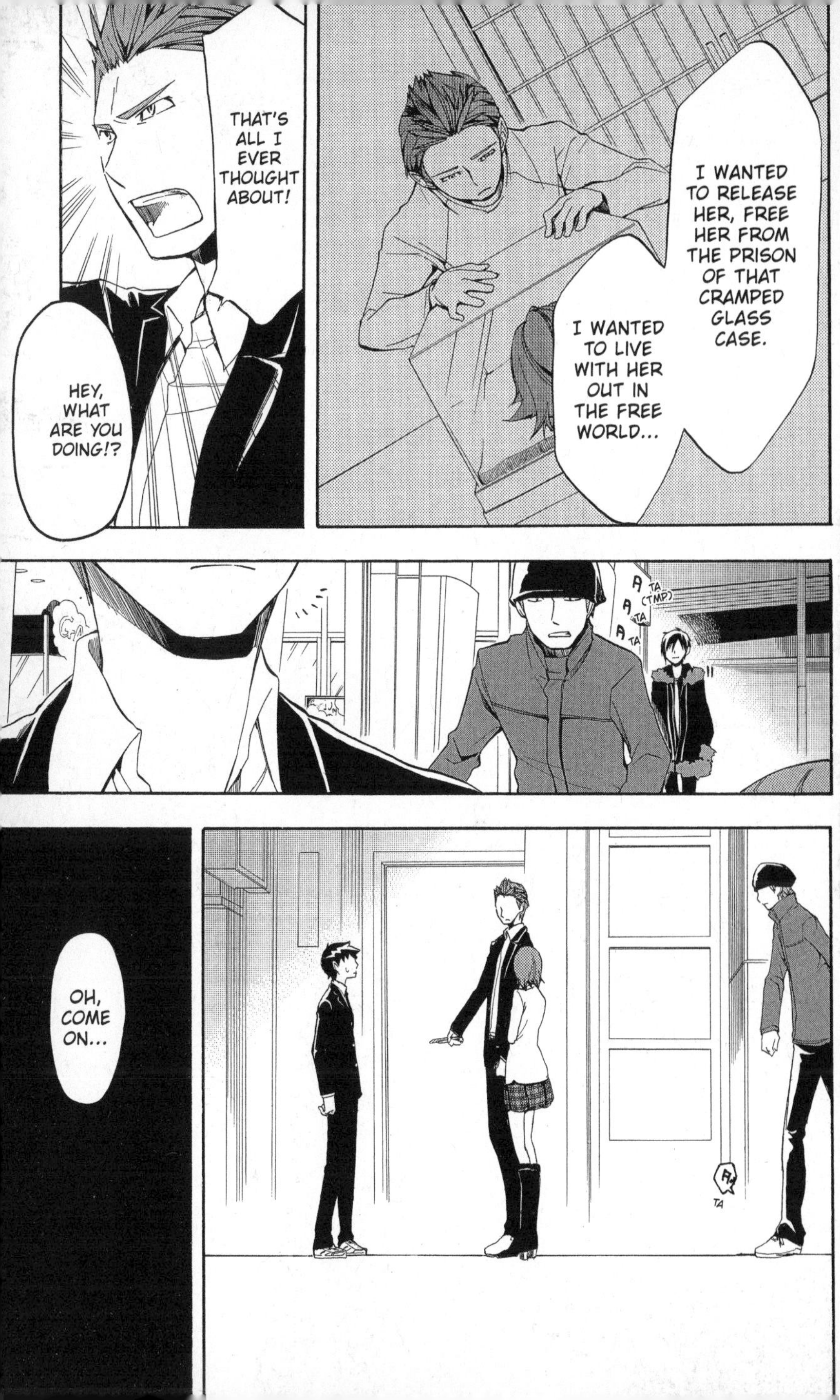
I WANTED TO RELEASE HER, FREE HER FROM THE PRISON OF THAT CRAMPED GLASS CASE.
I WANTED TO LIVE WITH HER OUT IN THE FREE WORLD...
THAT'S ALL I EVER THOUGHT ABOUT!
HEY, WHAT ARE YOU DOING!?
TA (TMP)
TA
TA
OH, COME ON...
TA

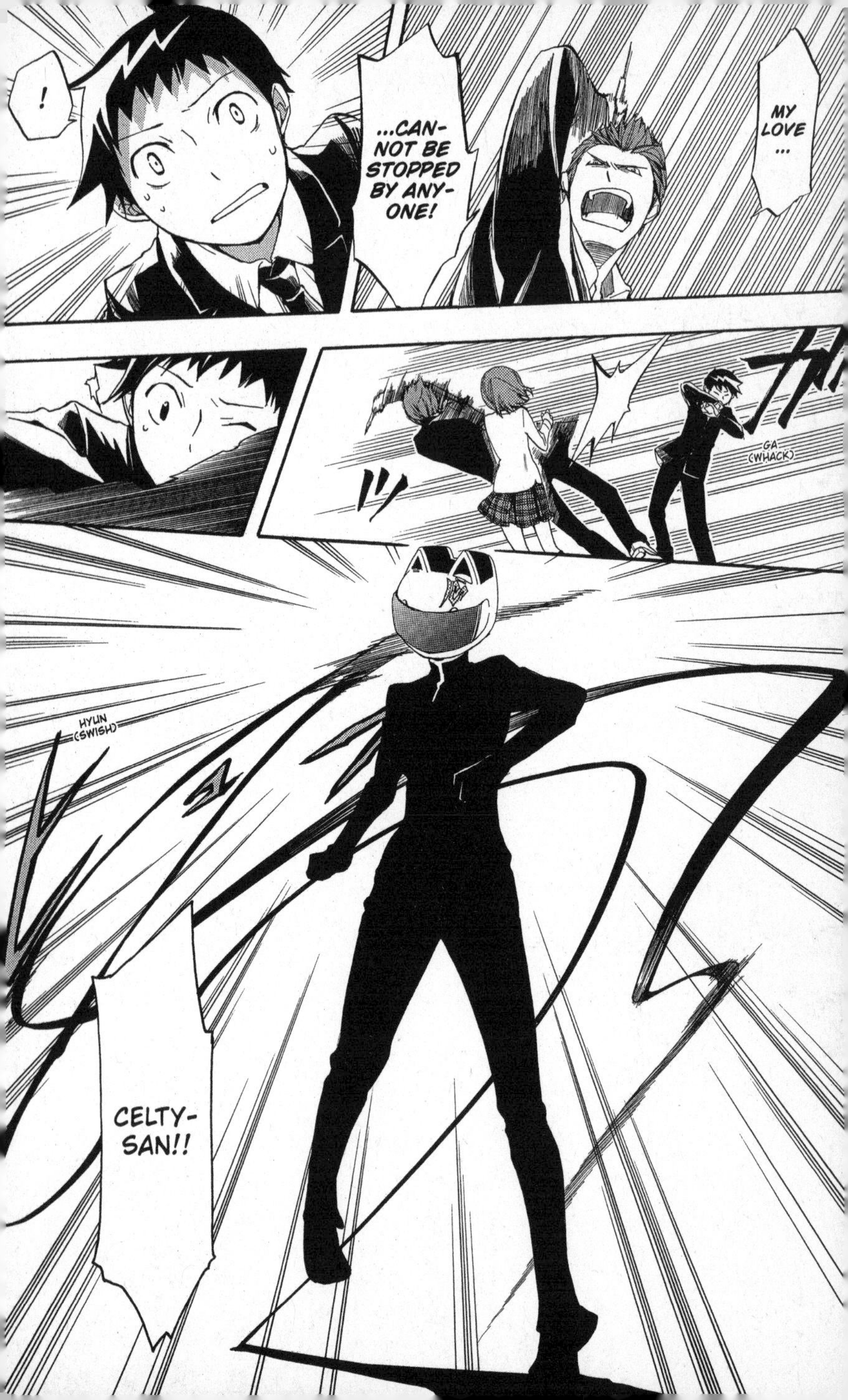
MY LOVE ...
...CAN-NOT BE STOPPED BY ANY-ONE!
!
GA (WHACK)
HYUN (SWISH)
CELTY-SAN!!

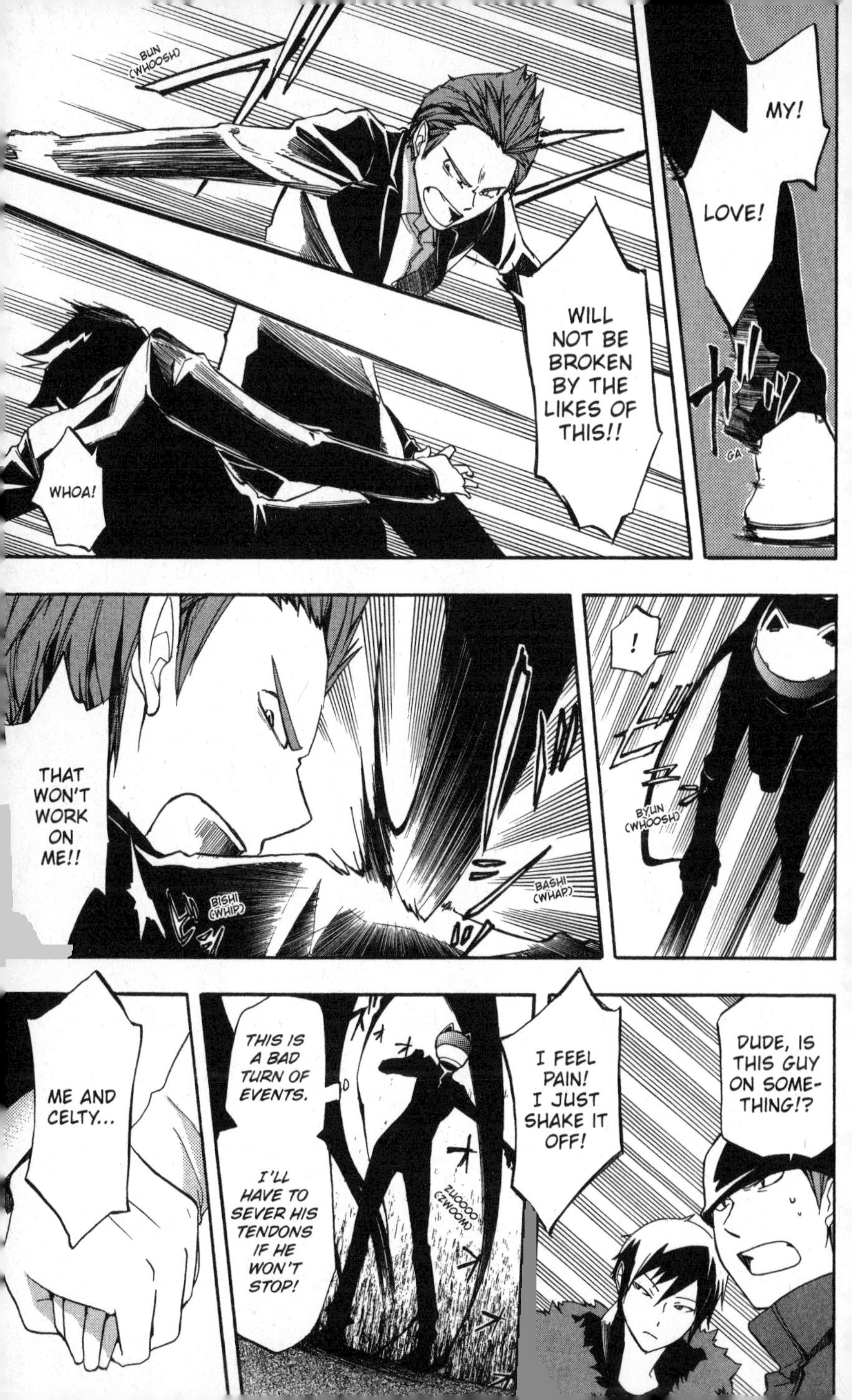
MY!
LOVE!
GA
WILL NOT BE BROKEN BY THE LIKES OF THIS!!
BUN (WHOOSH)
WHOA!
!
BYUN (WHOOSH)
THAT WON'T WORK ON ME!!
BASHI (WHAP)
BISHI (WHIP)
DUDE, IS THIS GUY ON SOME-THING!?
I FEEL PAIN! I JUST SHAKE IT OFF!
THIS IS A BAD TURN OF EVENTS.
I'LL HAVE TO SEVER HIS TENDONS IF HE WON'T STOP!
ZUOOOO (ZWOOM)
ME AND CELTY...

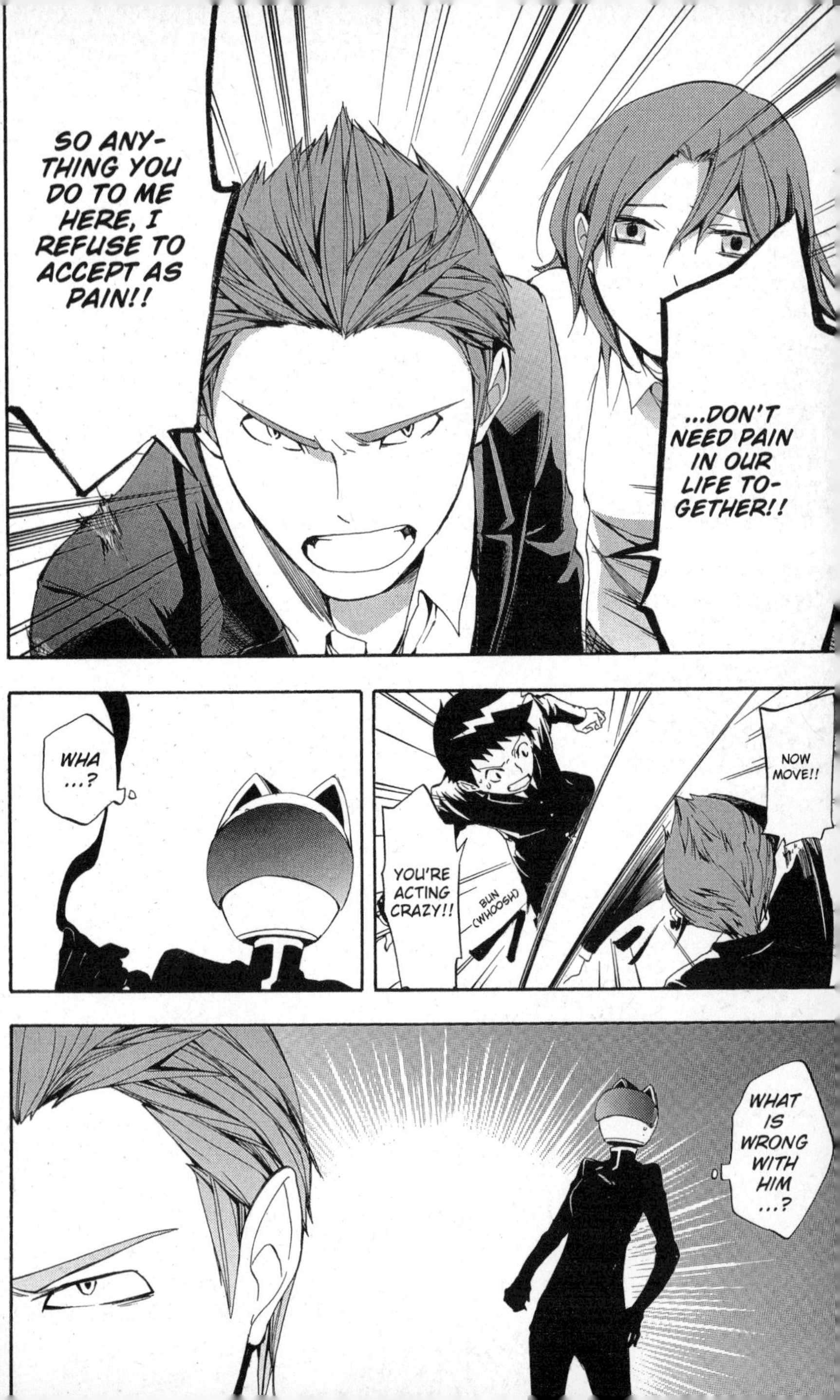
SO ANYTHING YOU DO TO ME HERE, I REFUSE TO ACCEPT AS PAIN!!
...DON'T NEED PAIN IN OUR LIFE TOGETHER!!
NOW MOVE!!
YOU'RE ACTING CRAZY!!
BUN (WHOOSH)
WHA ...?
WHAT IS WRONG WITH HIM ...?

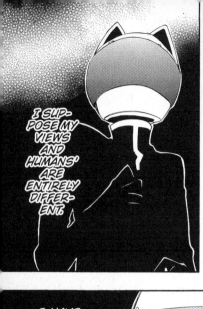

IS THIS THE FORM HIS LOVE TAKES?
WHAT IN THE WORLD ARE HIS VALUES?
I SUPPOSE MY VIEWS AND HUMANS' ARE ENTIRELY DIFFERENT.
I HAVE...
I HAVE MY OWN...
SURA (SWISH)
MY OWN...
ST...

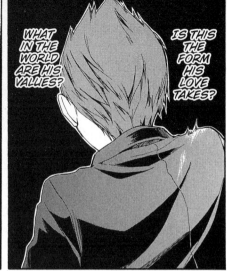

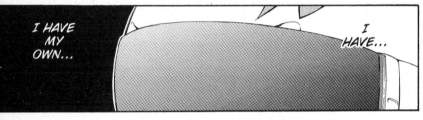

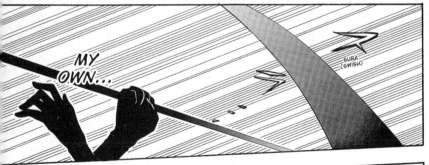

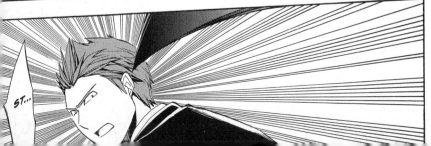

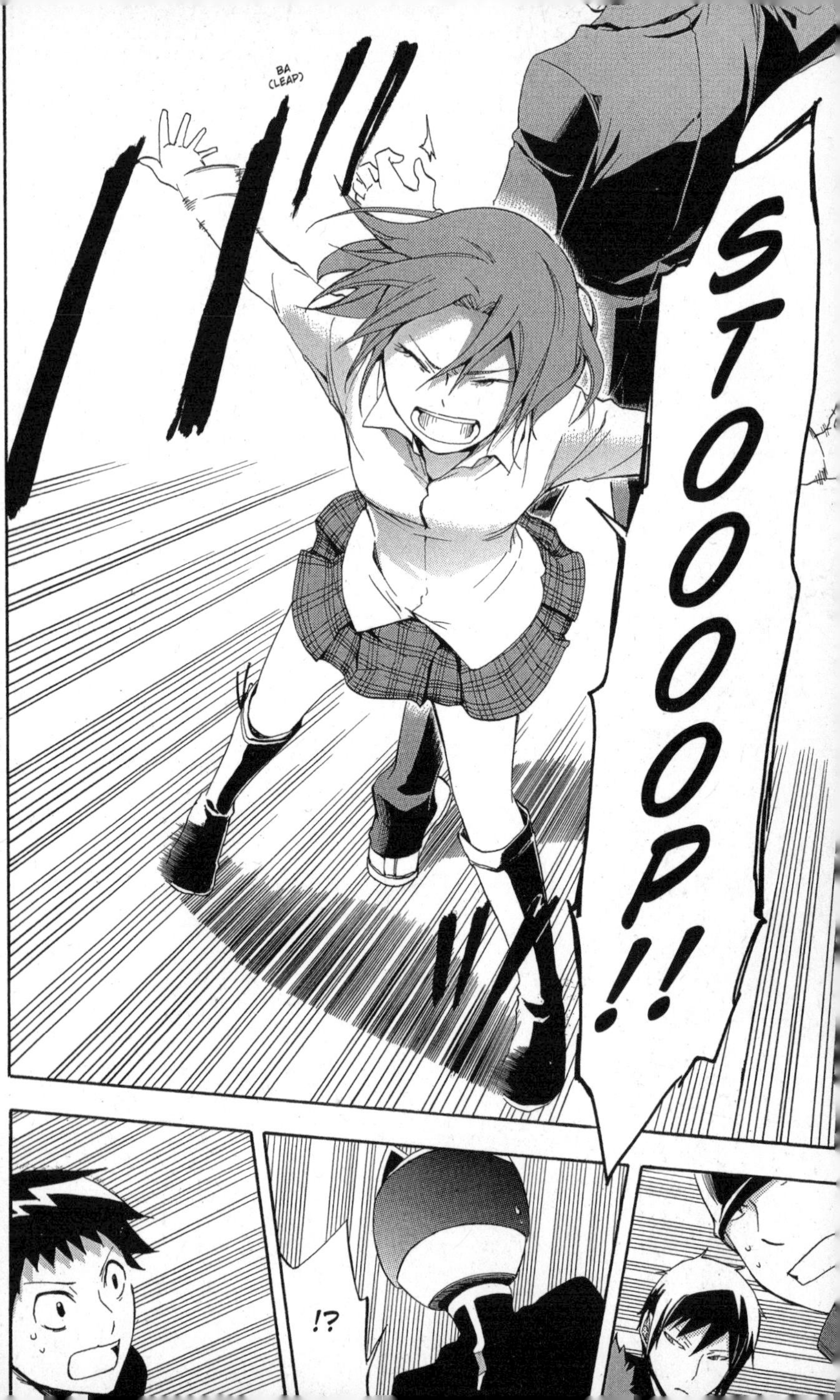
BA
(LEAP)
STOOOOP!!
!?

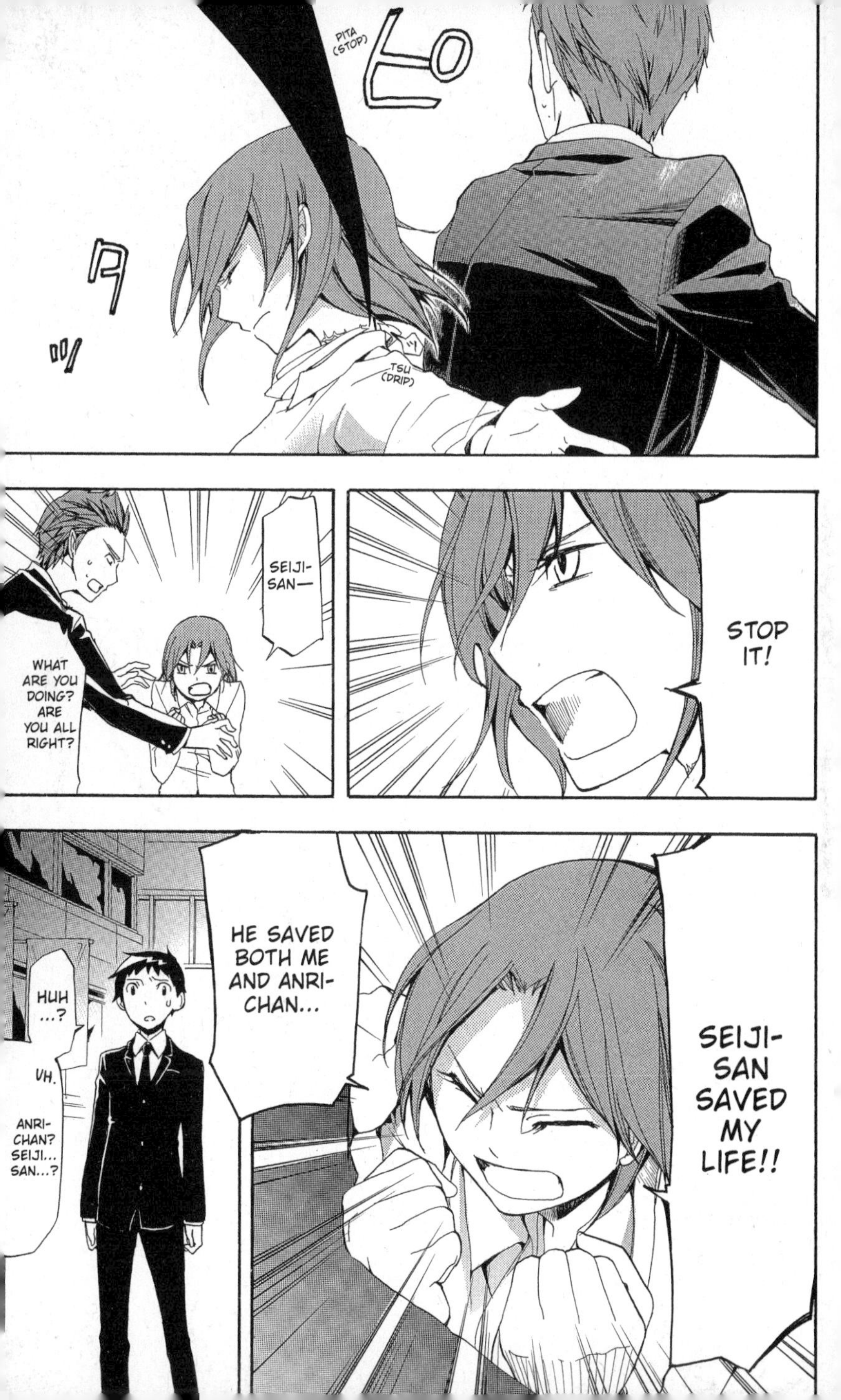
PITA (STOP)
TSU (DRIP)
STOP IT!
SEIJI-SAN—
WHAT ARE YOU DOING? ARE YOU ALL RIGHT?
SEIJI-SAN SAVED MY LIFE!!
HE SAVED BOTH ME AND ANRI-CHAN...
HUH ...?
UH.
ANRI-CHAN? SEIJI... SAN...?

COULD THAT BE...?

...HE ALREADY HAD SOMEONE HE'S IN LOVE WITH, YOU SEE?

YOU CAN'T KILL HIM...

BUT...

...EVEN THEN...

......

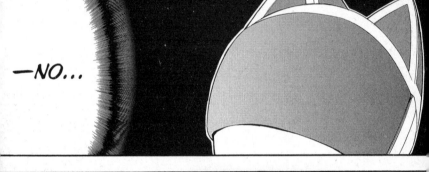

—NO...

THIS GIRL IS NOT MY HEAD!!

Y- YOU CAN'T...

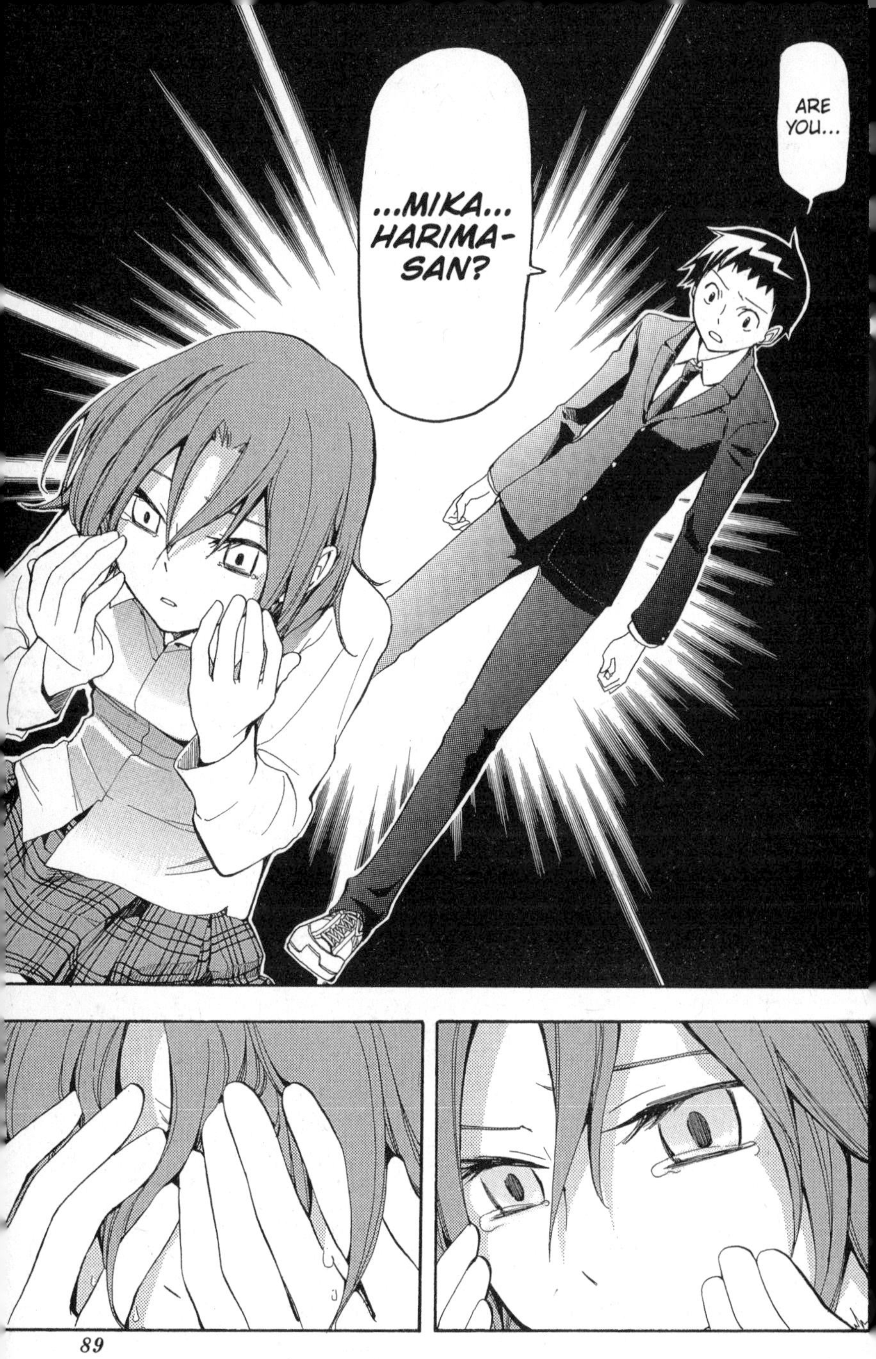
ARE YOU...
...MIKA... HARIMA-SAN?

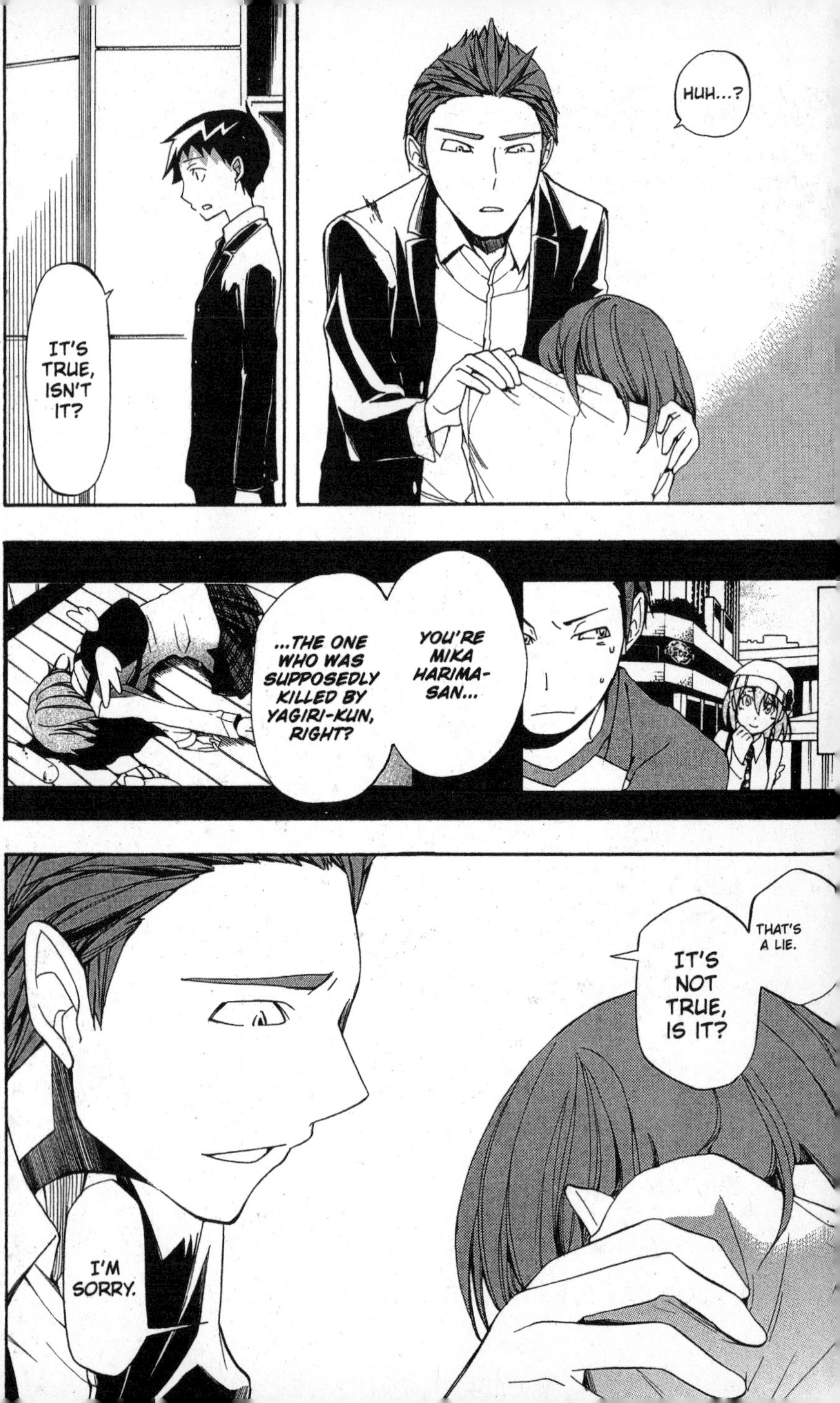
HUH...?
IT'S TRUE, ISN'T IT?
YOU'RE MIKA HARIMA-SAN...
...THE ONE WHO WAS SUPPOSEDLY KILLED BY YAGIRI-KUN, RIGHT?
THAT'S A LIE.
IT'S NOT TRUE, IS IT?
I'M SORRY.

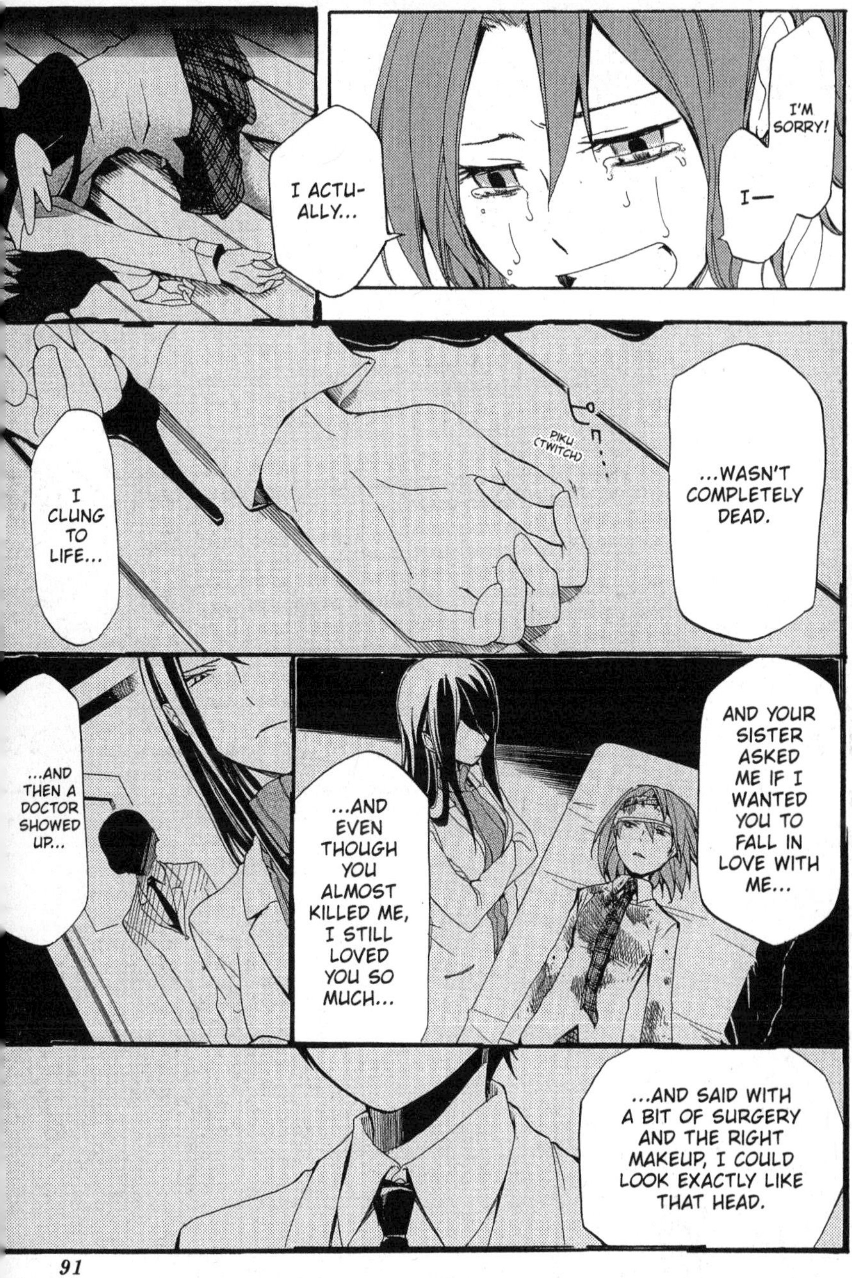
I'M SORRY!
I—
I ACTU-ALLY...
...WASN'T COMPLETELY DEAD.
PIKU (TWITCH)
I CLUNG TO LIFE...
AND YOUR SISTER ASKED ME IF I WANTED YOU TO FALL IN LOVE WITH ME...
...AND EVEN THOUGH YOU ALMOST KILLED ME, I STILL LOVED YOU SO MUCH...
...AND THEN A DOCTOR SHOWED UP...
...AND SAID WITH A BIT OF SURGERY AND THE RIGHT MAKEUP, I COULD LOOK EXACTLY LIKE THAT HEAD.

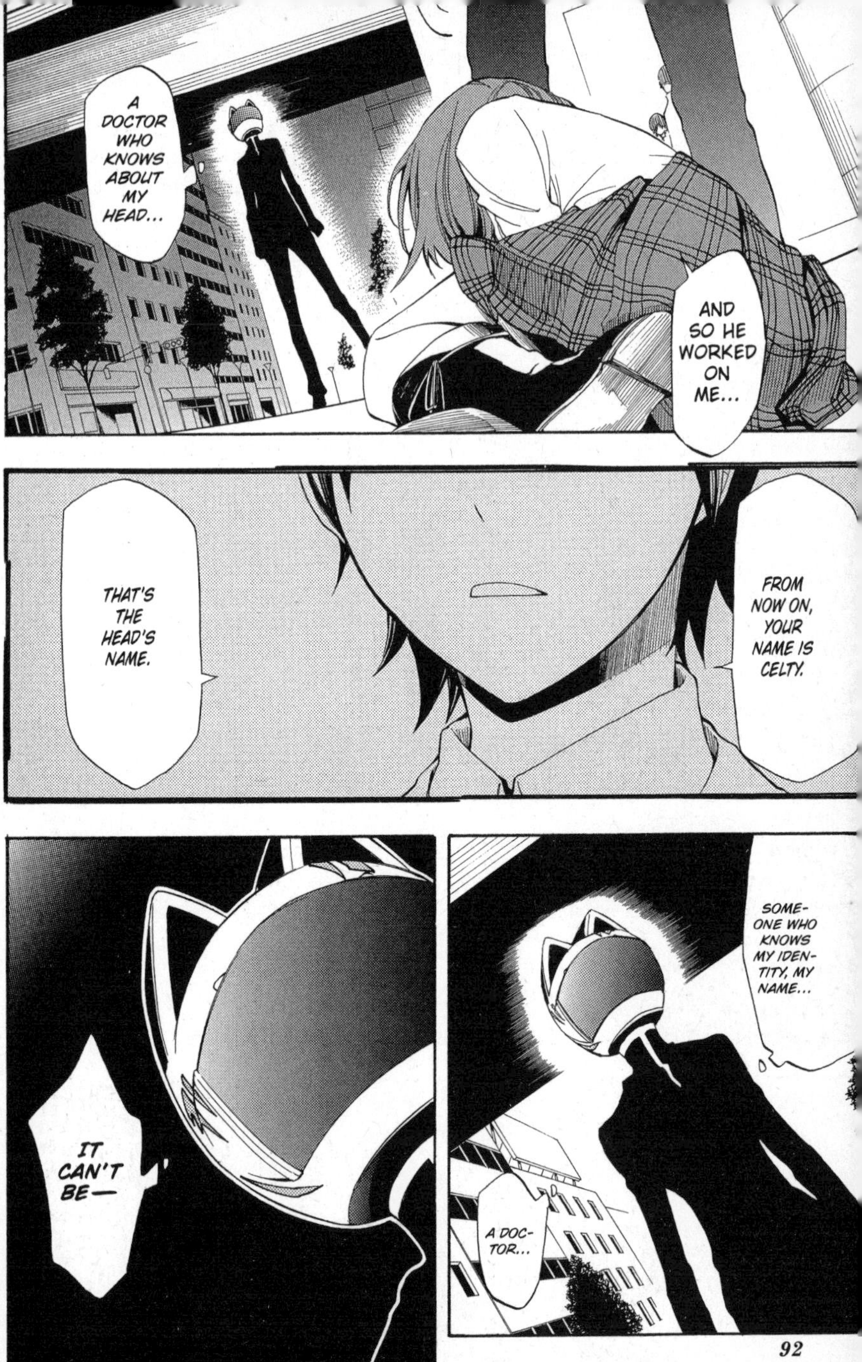
A DOCTOR WHO KNOWS ABOUT MY HEAD...
AND SO HE WORKED ON ME...
FROM NOW ON, YOUR NAME IS CELTY.
THAT'S THE HEAD'S NAME.
SOME-ONE WHO KNOWS MY IDEN-TITY, MY NAME...
A DOC-TOR...
IT CAN'T BE—

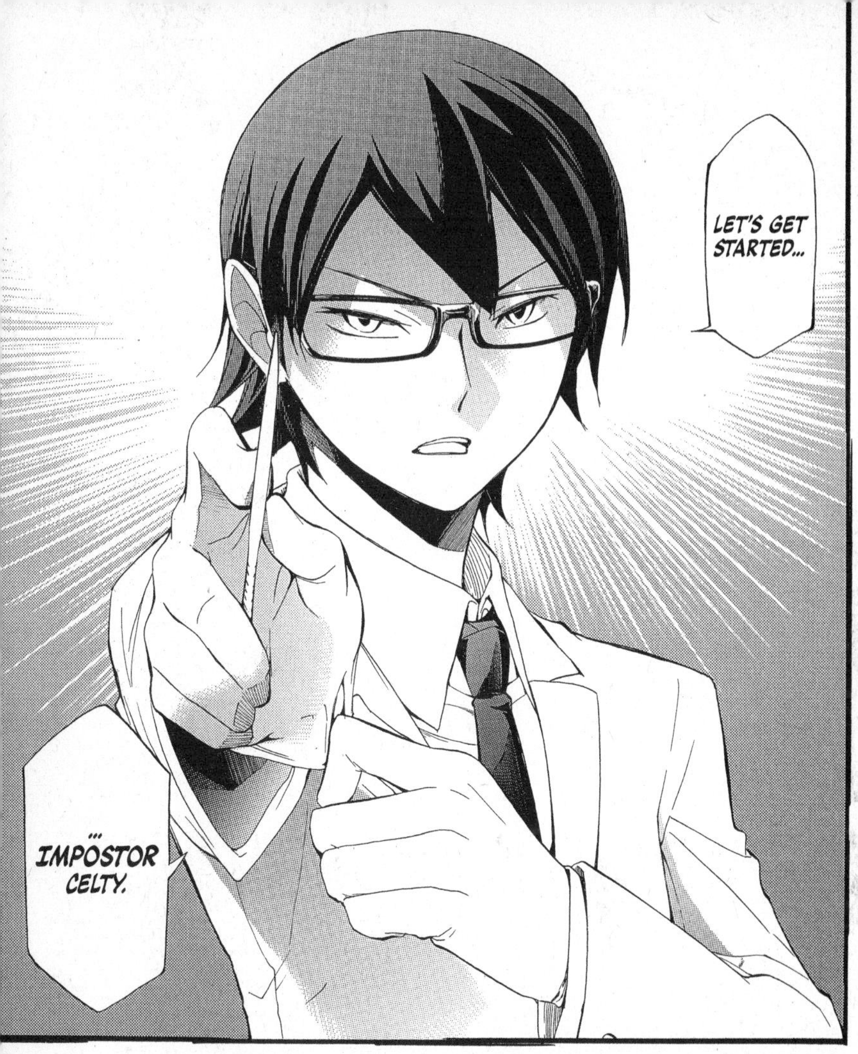
LET'S GET STARTED...
...IMPOSTOR CELTY.
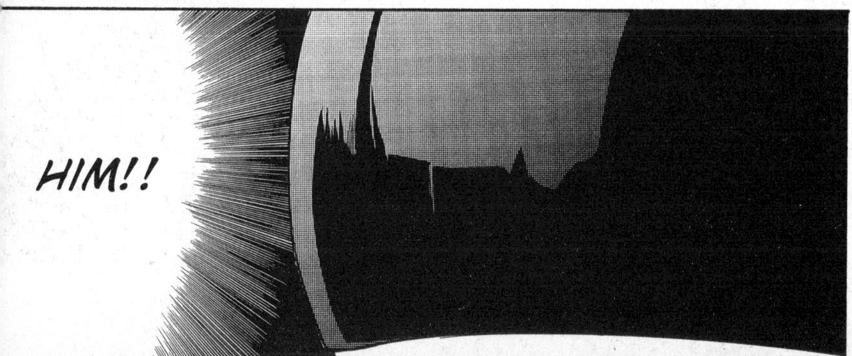
HIM!!

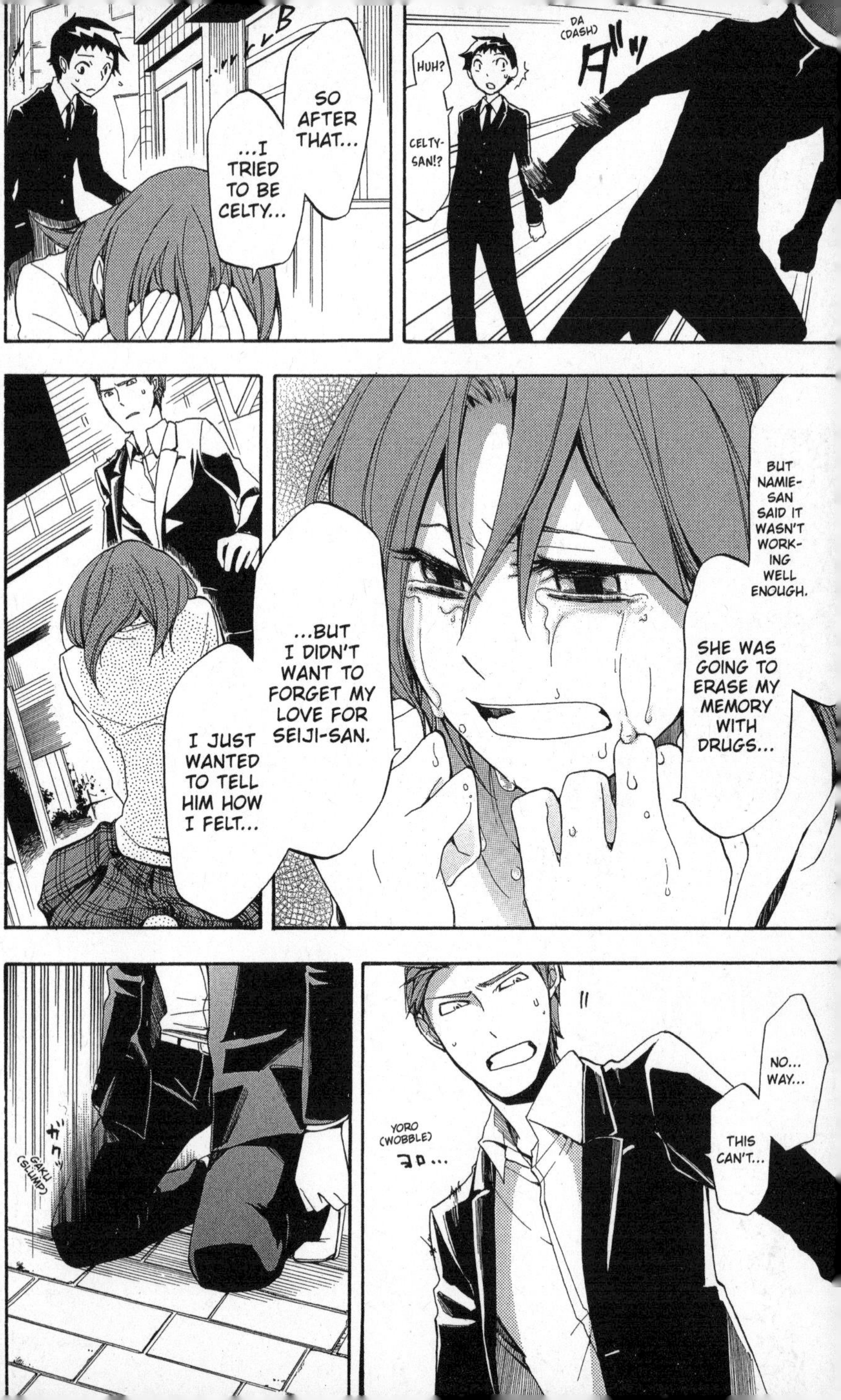
DA (DASH)
ダッ
HUH?
CELTY-SAN!?
SO AFTER THAT...
...I TRIED TO BE CELTY...
BUT NAMIE-SAN SAID IT WASN'T WORKING WELL ENOUGH.
SHE WAS GOING TO ERASE MY MEMORY WITH DRUGS...
...BUT I DIDN'T WANT TO FORGET MY LOVE FOR SEIJI-SAN.
I JUST WANTED TO TELL HIM HOW I FELT...
NO... WAY...
THIS CAN'T...
YORO (WOBBLE)
ヨロ...
GAKU (SLUMP)
ガクッ

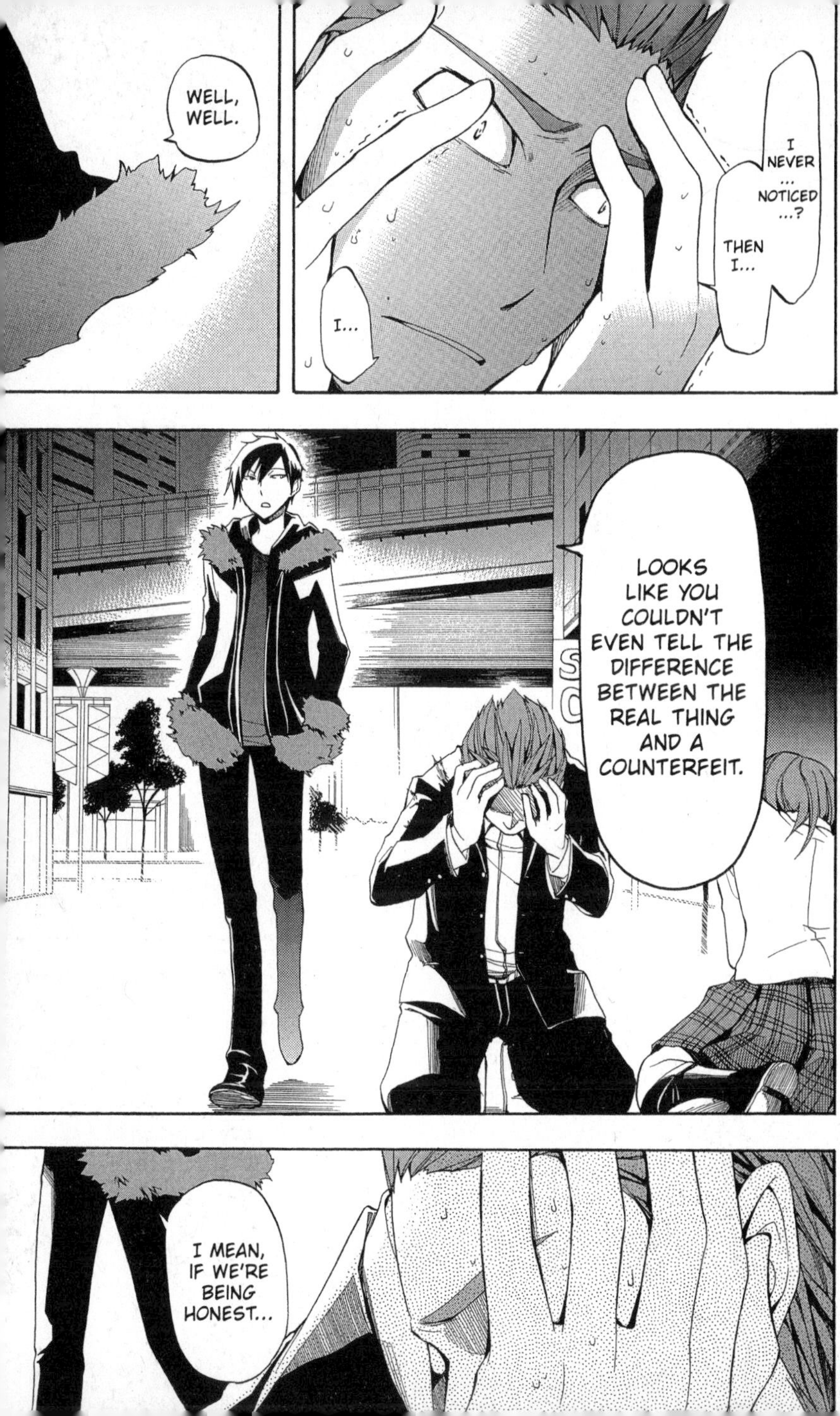
I NEVER ... NOTICED ...?
THEN I...
I...
WELL, WELL.
LOOKS LIKE YOU COULDN'T EVEN TELL THE DIFFERENCE BETWEEN THE REAL THING AND A COUNTERFEIT.
I MEAN, IF WE'RE BEING HONEST...

...THAT JUST SHOWS YOU HOW "REAL" YOUR LOVE FOR THAT HEAD IS.

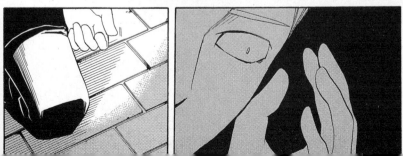

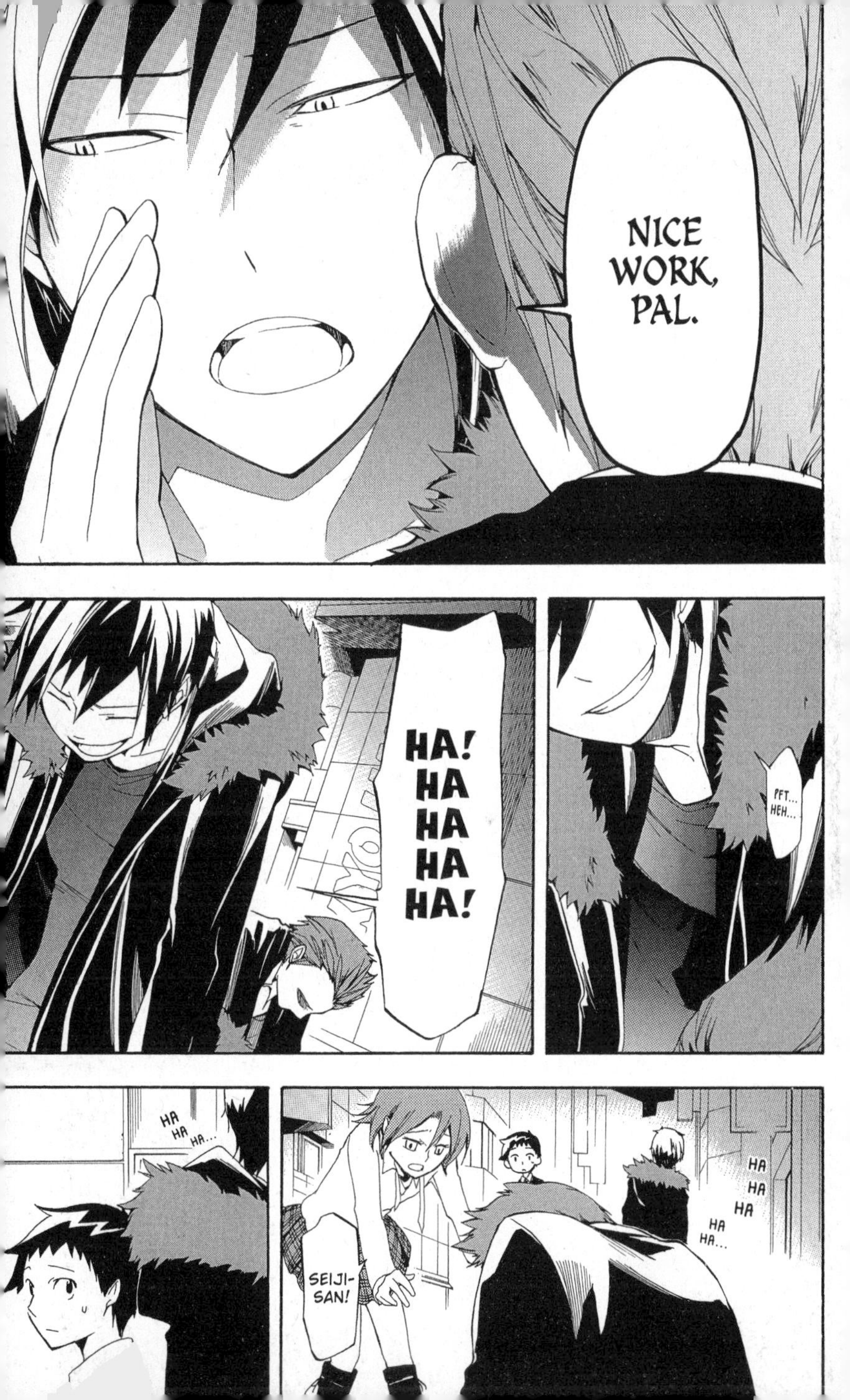
NICE WORK, PAL.
PFT... HEH...
HA! HA HA HA HA HA!
HA HA HA HA HA...
SEIJI-SAN!
HA HA HA...

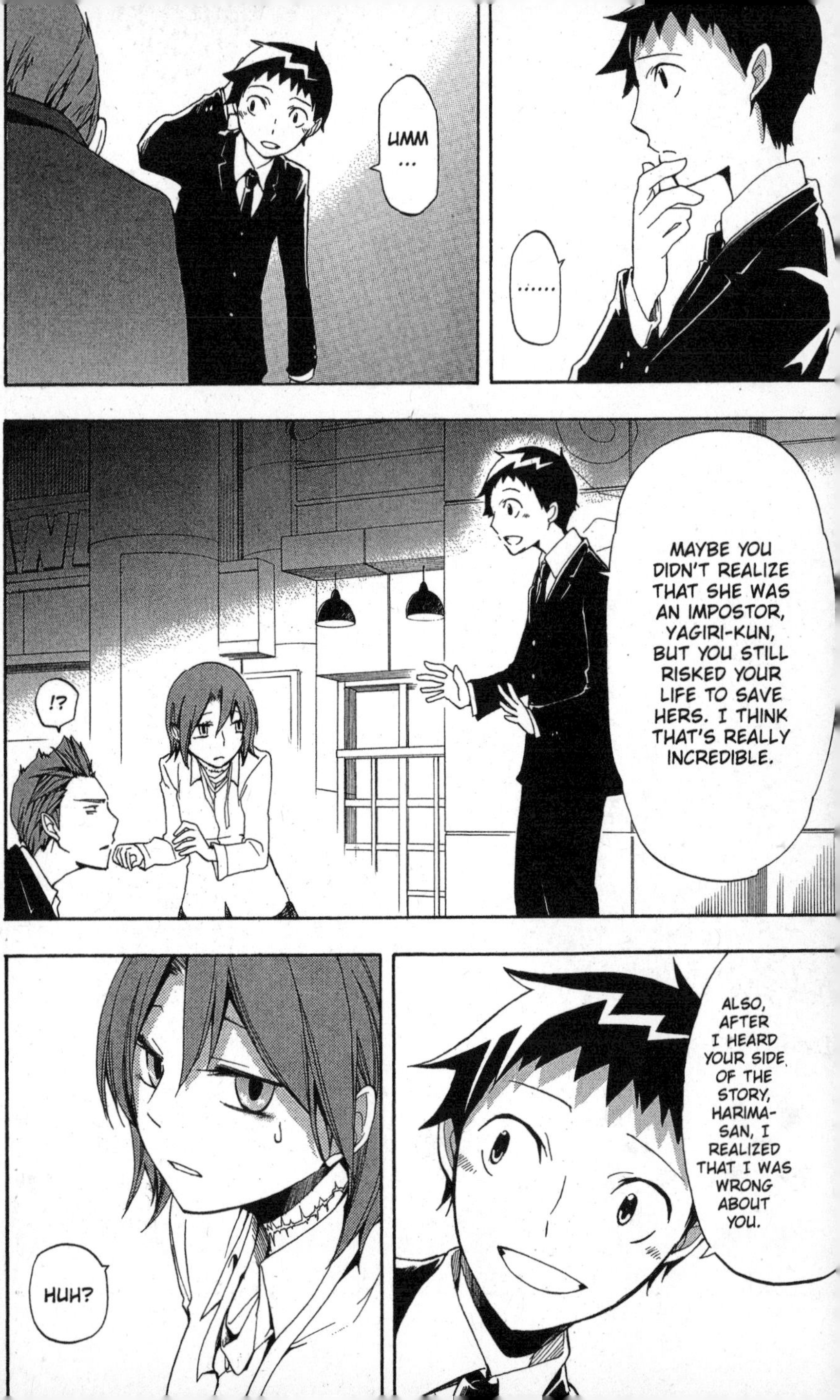
......
UMM ...
MAYBE YOU DIDN'T REALIZE THAT SHE WAS AN IMPOSTOR, YAGIRI-KUN, BUT YOU STILL RISKED YOUR LIFE TO SAVE HERS. I THINK THAT'S REALLY INCREDIBLE.
!?
ALSO, AFTER I HEARD YOUR SIDE OF THE STORY, HARIMA-SAN, I REALIZED THAT I WAS WRONG ABOUT YOU.
HUH?

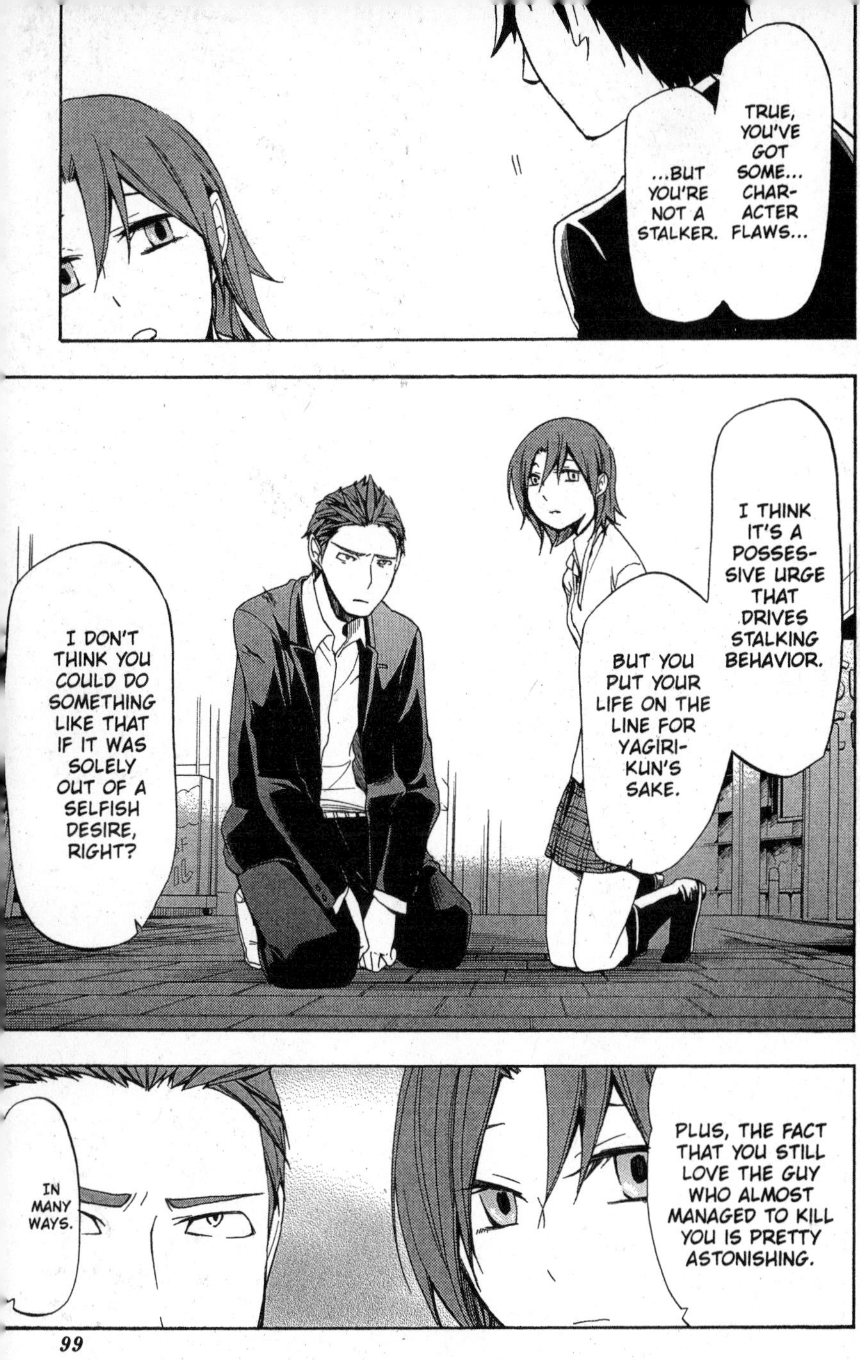
TRUE, YOU'VE GOT SOME... CHAR-ACTER FLAWS...
...BUT YOU'RE NOT A STALKER.
I THINK IT'S A POSSES-SIVE URGE THAT DRIVES STALKING BEHAVIOR.
BUT YOU PUT YOUR LIFE ON THE LINE FOR YAGIRI-KUN'S SAKE.
I DON'T THINK YOU COULD DO SOMETHING LIKE THAT IF IT WAS SOLELY OUT OF A SELFISH DESIRE, RIGHT?
PLUS, THE FACT THAT YOU STILL LOVE THE GUY WHO ALMOST MANAGED TO KILL YOU IS PRETTY ASTONISHING.
IN MANY WAYS.

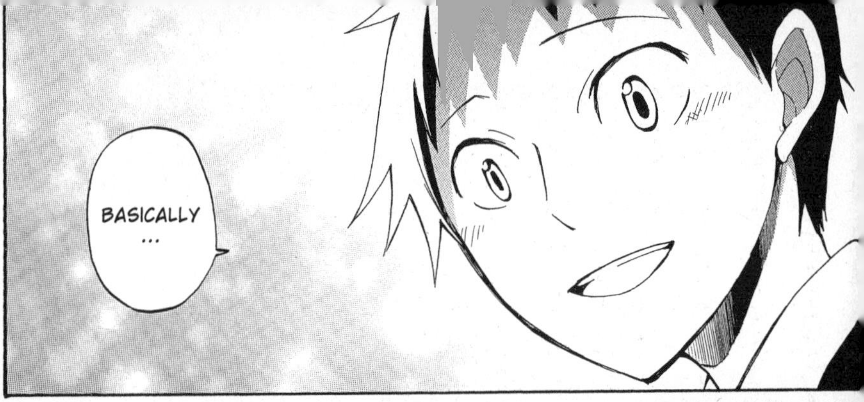
BASICALLY
...

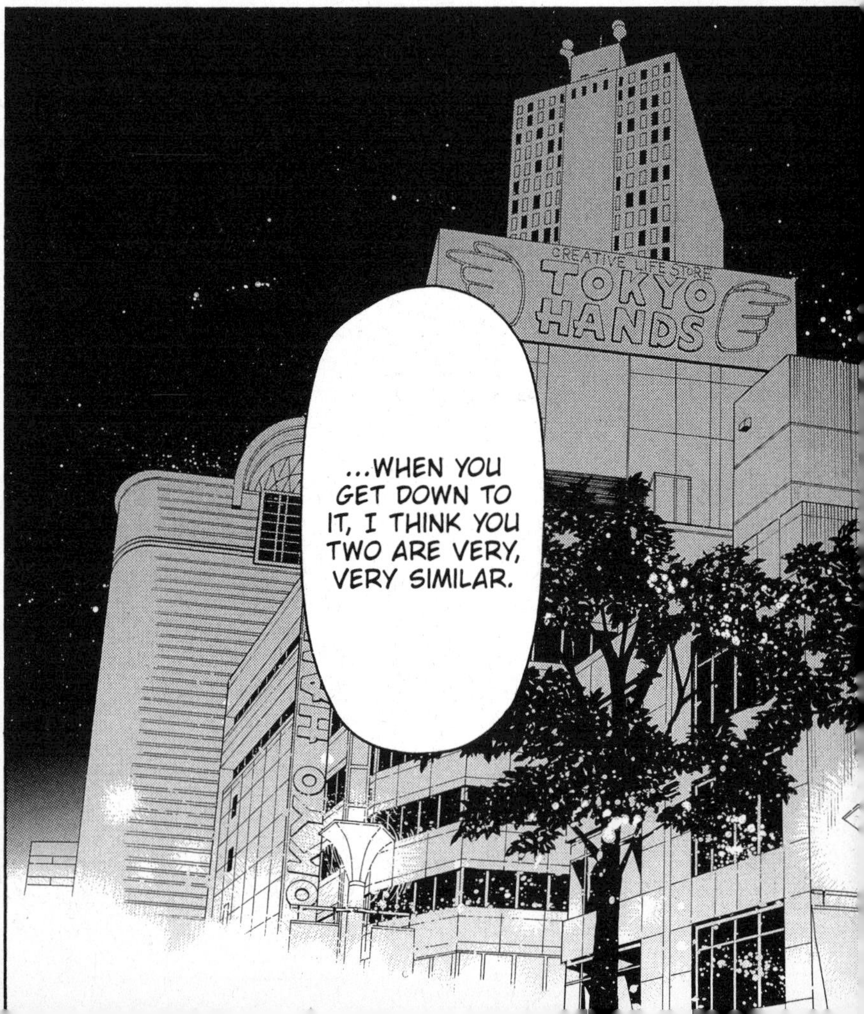
CREATIVE LIFE STORE
TOKYO HANDS
...WHEN YOU GET DOWN TO IT, I THINK YOU TWO ARE VERY, VERY SIMILAR.

21: WAWAWAWAWAWAWAWAWAWAWAWAWAWAWAWAWAWAWAWAWAWAWA!!

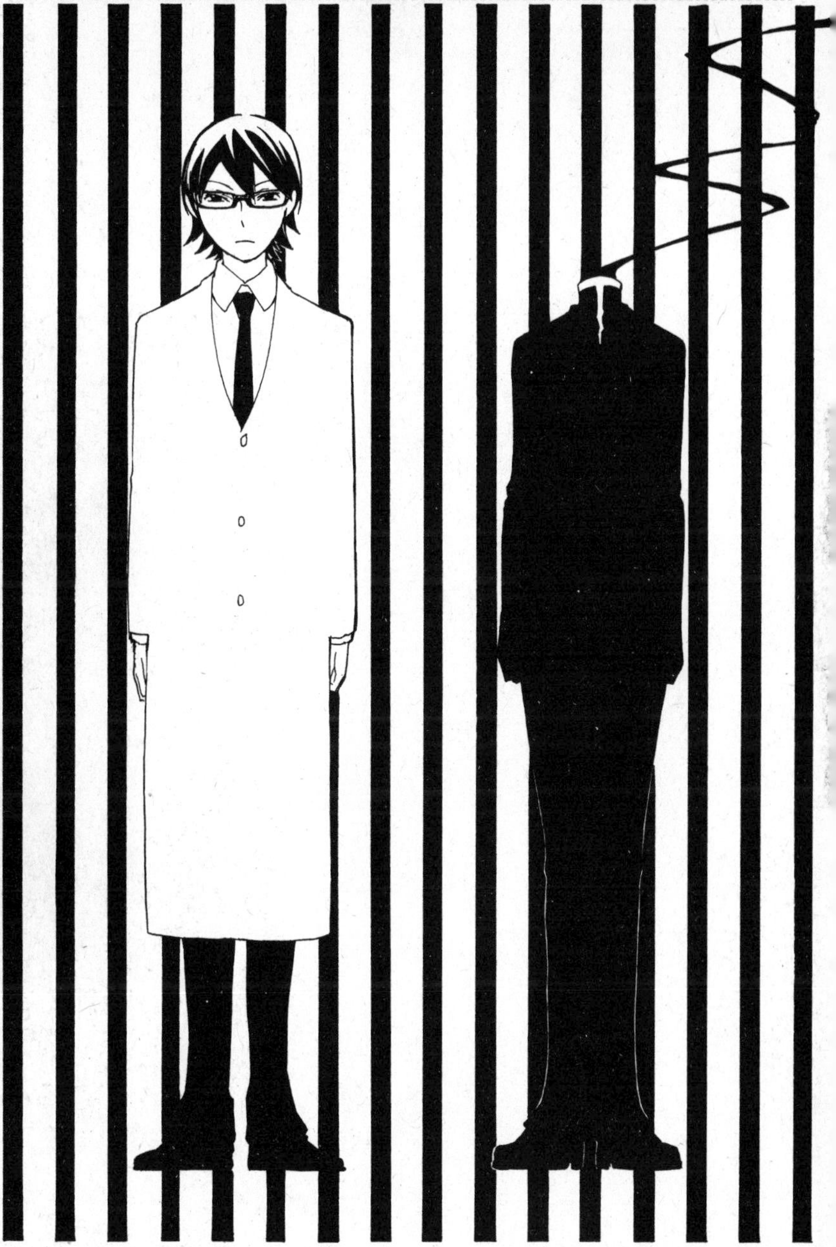

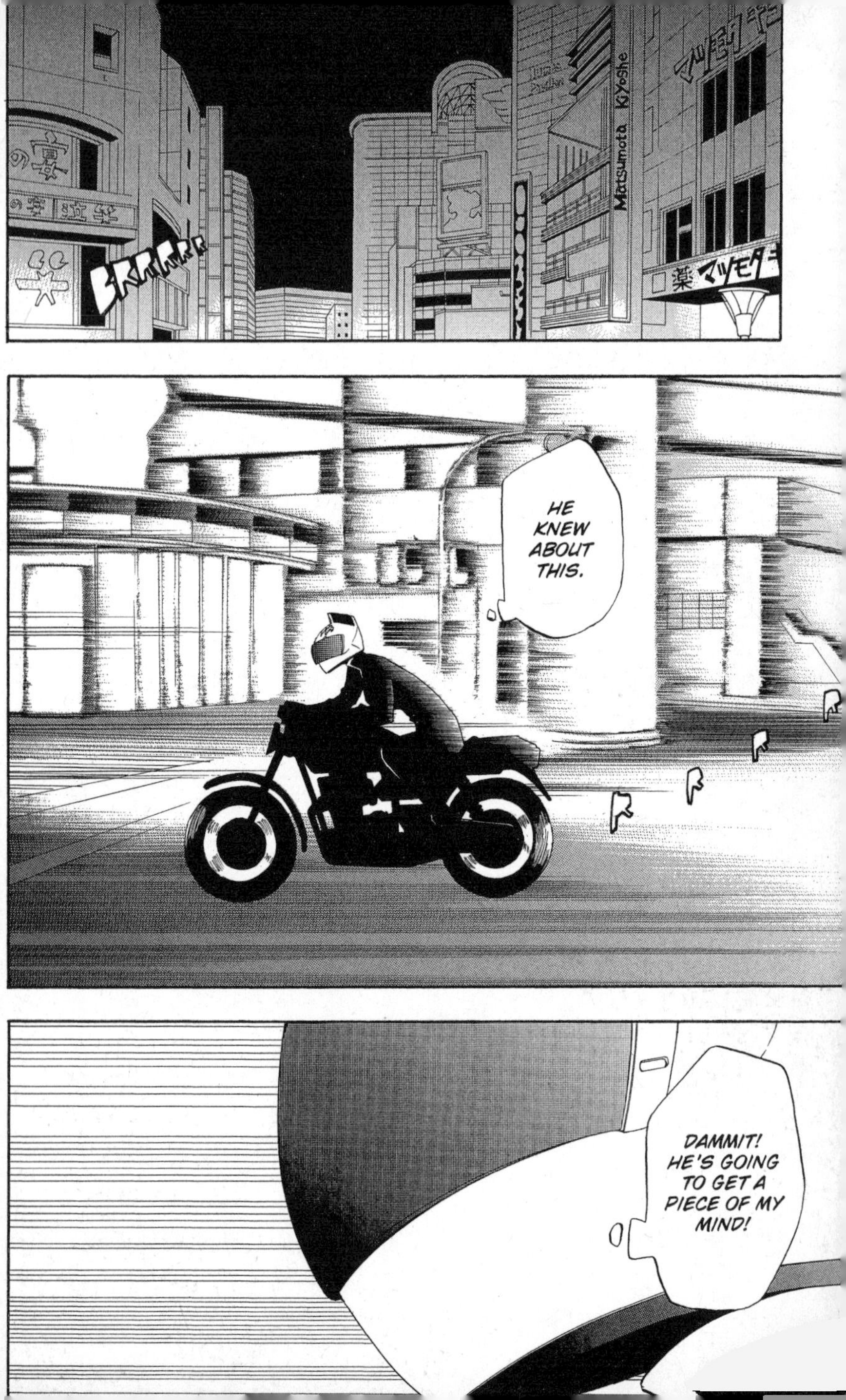
Matsumoto Kiyoshe
HE KNEW ABOUT THIS.
DAMMIT! HE'S GOING TO GET A PIECE OF MY MIND!

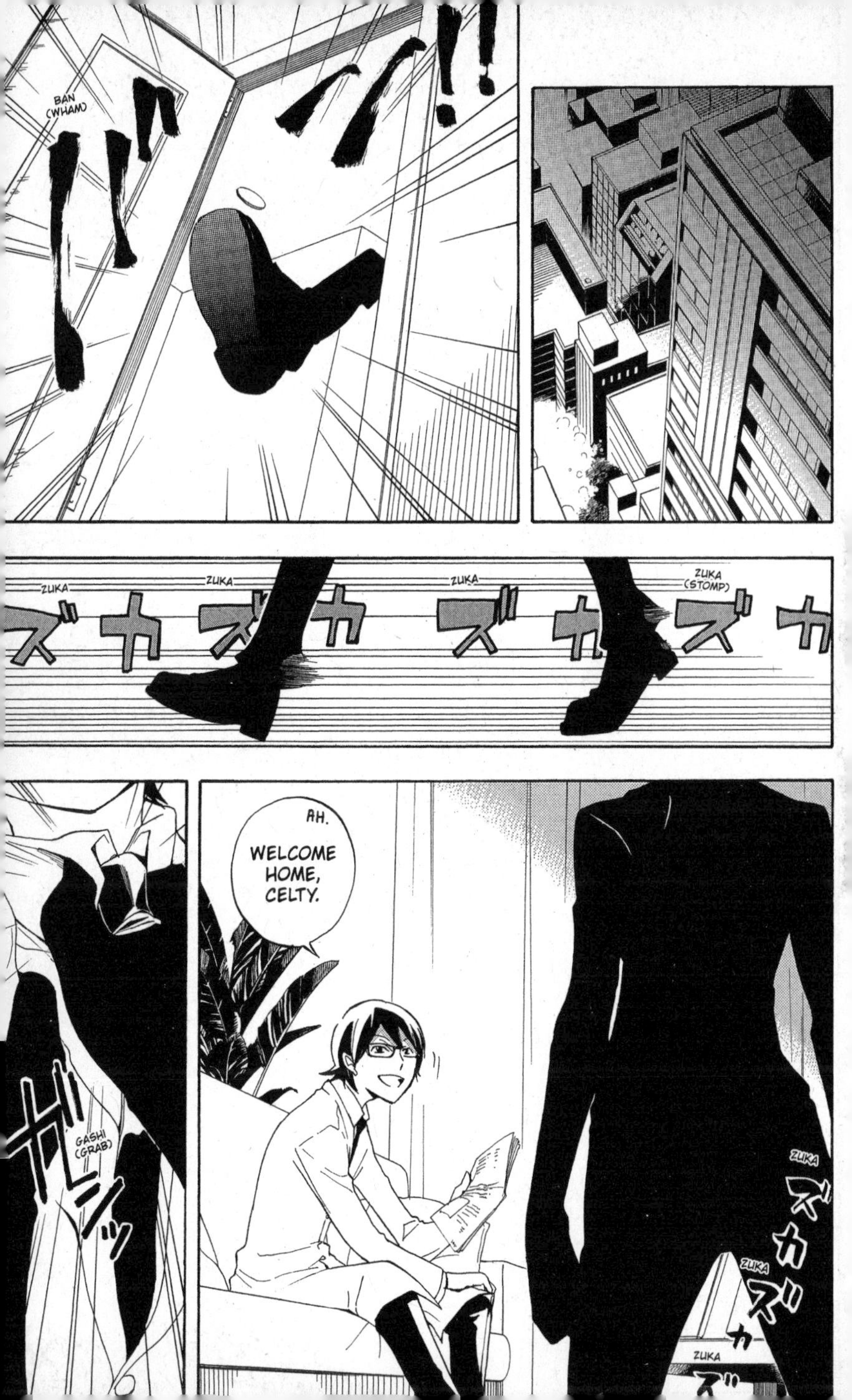
BAN (WHAM)
ZUKA (STOMP)
ZUKA
ZUKA
ZUKA
ZUKA
ZUKA
ZUKA
AH.
WELCOME HOME, CELTY.
GASHI (GRAB)

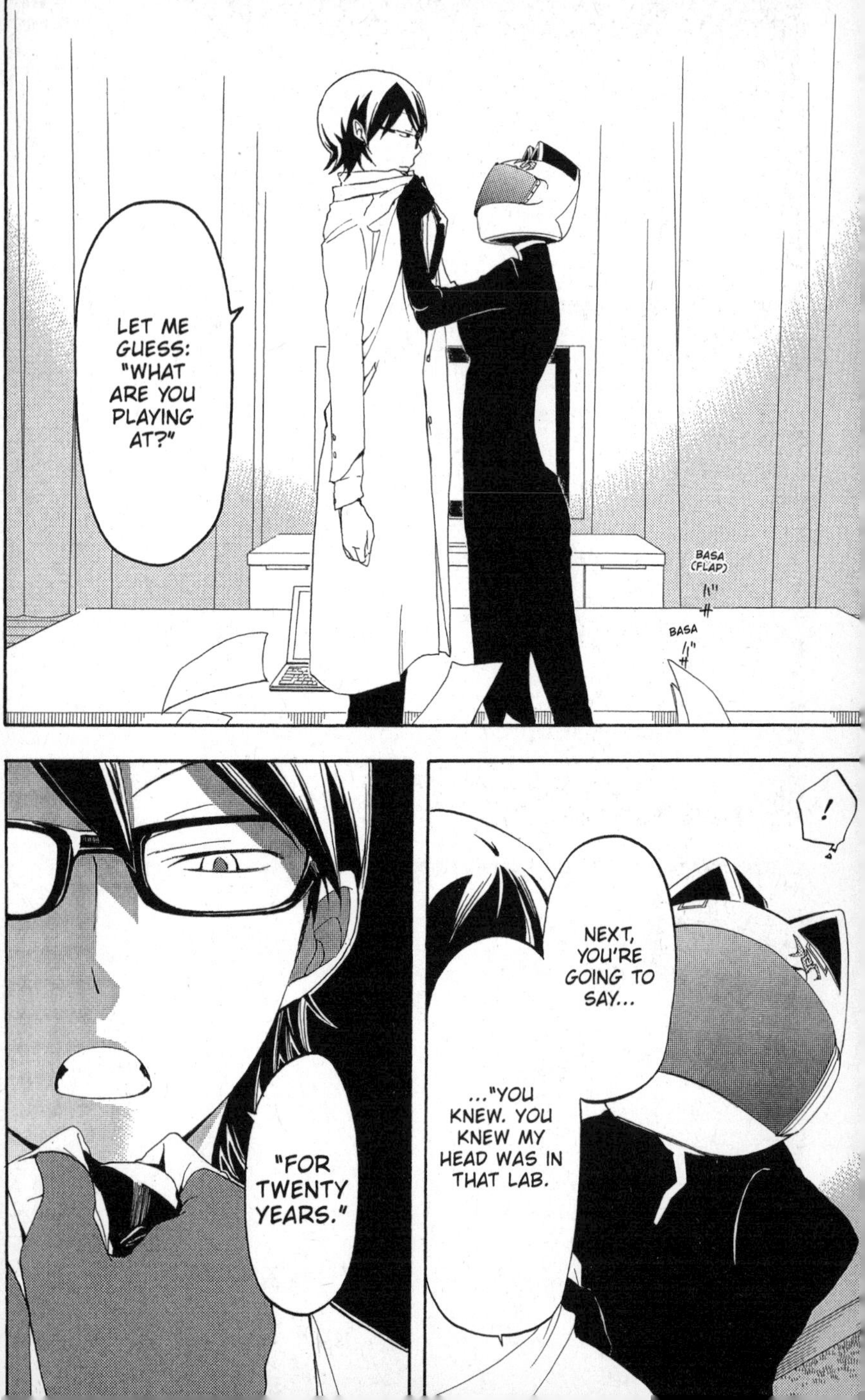
LET ME GUESS: "WHAT ARE YOU PLAYING AT?"
BASA (FLAP)
BASA
!
NEXT, YOU'RE GOING TO SAY...
..."YOU KNEW. YOU KNEW MY HEAD WAS IN THAT LAB.
"FOR TWENTY YEARS."

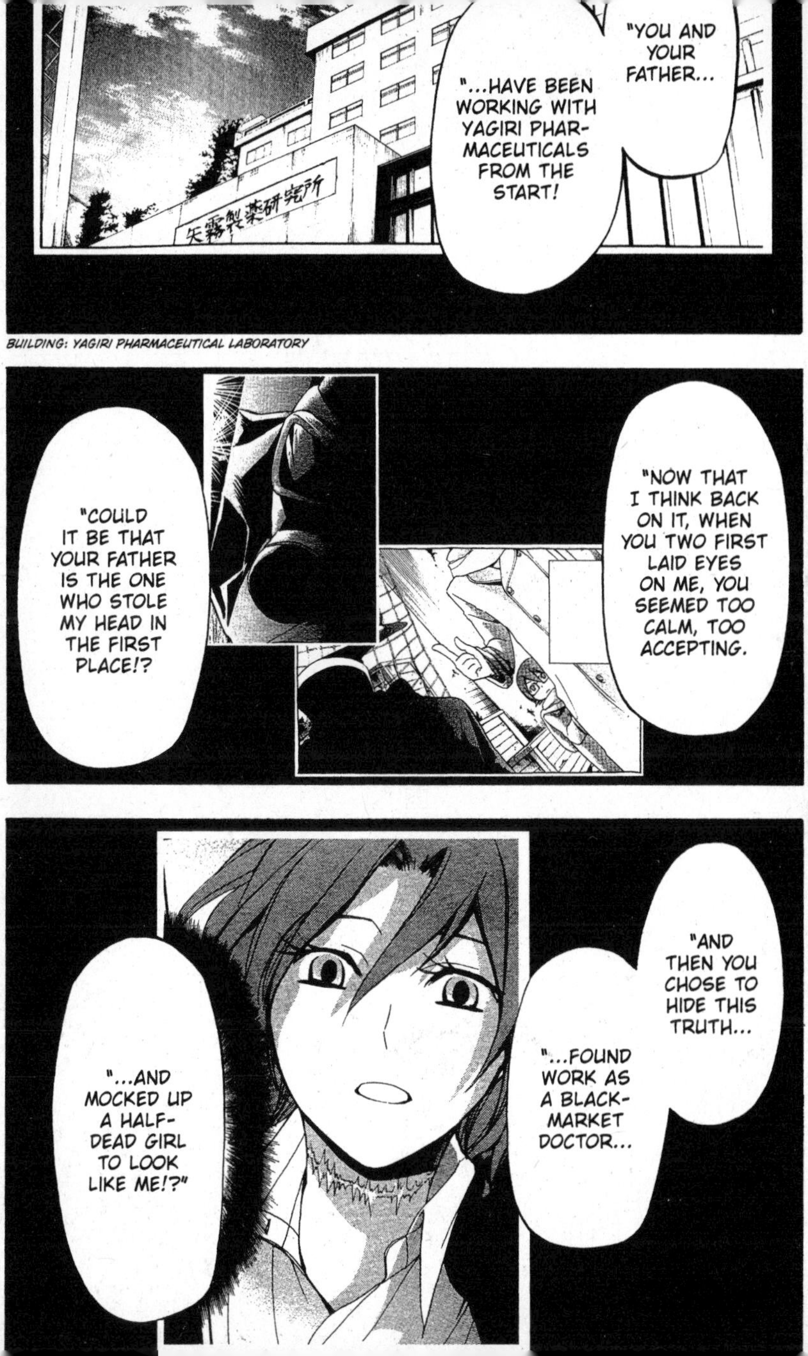
"YOU AND YOUR FATHER...
"...HAVE BEEN WORKING WITH YAGIRI PHAR-MACEUTICALS FROM THE START!
矢霧製薬研究所
BUILDING: YAGIRI PHARMACEUTICAL LABORATORY
"NOW THAT I THINK BACK ON IT, WHEN YOU TWO FIRST LAID EYES ON ME, YOU SEEMED TOO CALM, TOO ACCEPTING.
"COULD IT BE THAT YOUR FATHER IS THE ONE WHO STOLE MY HEAD IN THE FIRST PLACE!?
"AND THEN YOU CHOSE TO HIDE THIS TRUTH...
"...FOUND WORK AS A BLACK-MARKET DOCTOR...
"...AND MOCKED UP A HALF-DEAD GIRL TO LOOK LIKE ME!?"

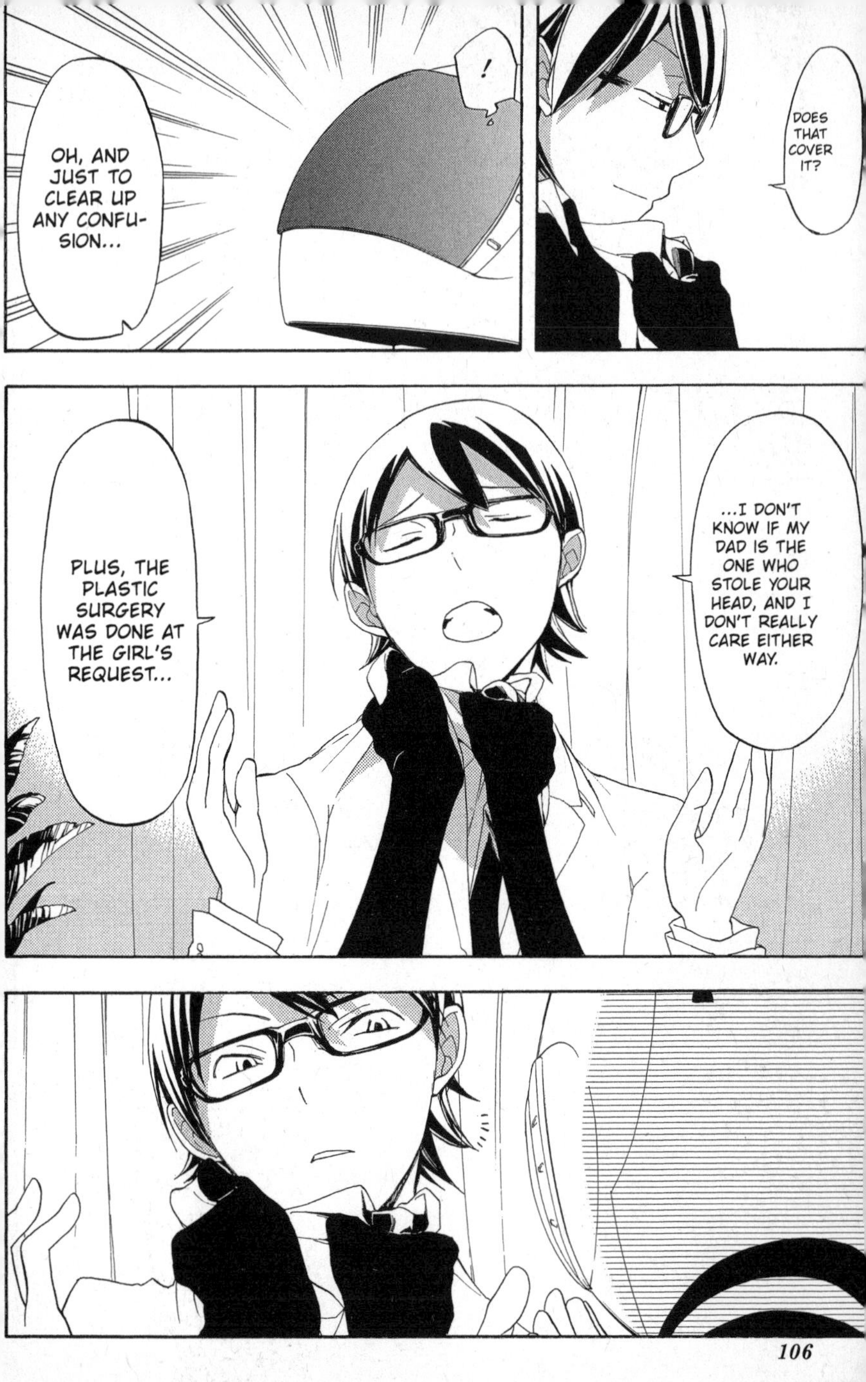
DOES THAT COVER IT?
!
OH, AND JUST TO CLEAR UP ANY CONFUSION...
...I DON'T KNOW IF MY DAD IS THE ONE WHO STOLE YOUR HEAD, AND I DON'T REALLY CARE EITHER WAY.
PLUS, THE PLASTIC SURGERY WAS DONE AT THE GIRL'S REQUEST...

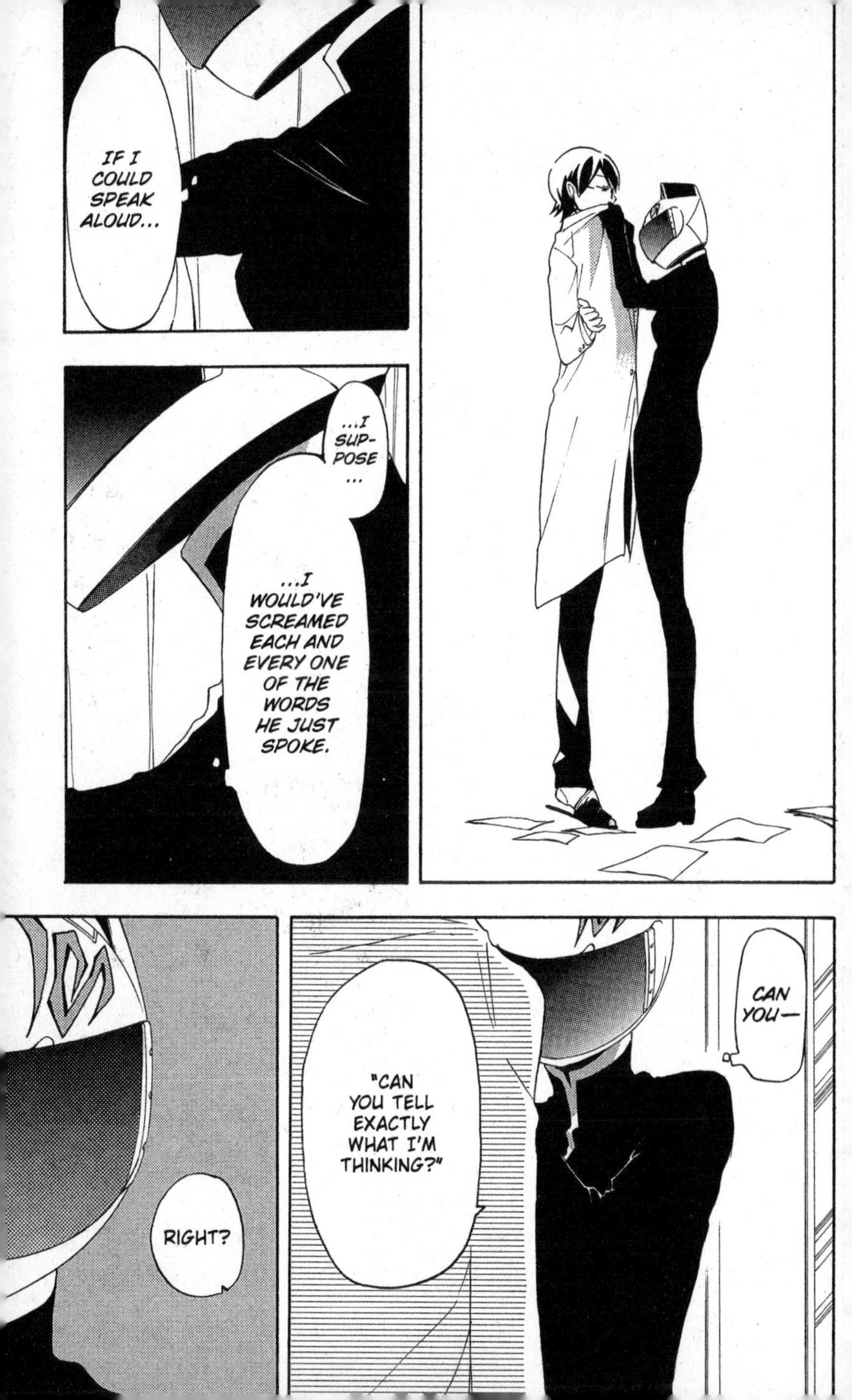
IF I COULD SPEAK ALOUD...
...I SUP-POSE...
...I WOULD'VE SCREAMED EACH AND EVERY ONE OF THE WORDS HE JUST SPOKE.
CAN YOU—
"CAN YOU TELL EXACTLY WHAT I'M THINKING?"
RIGHT?

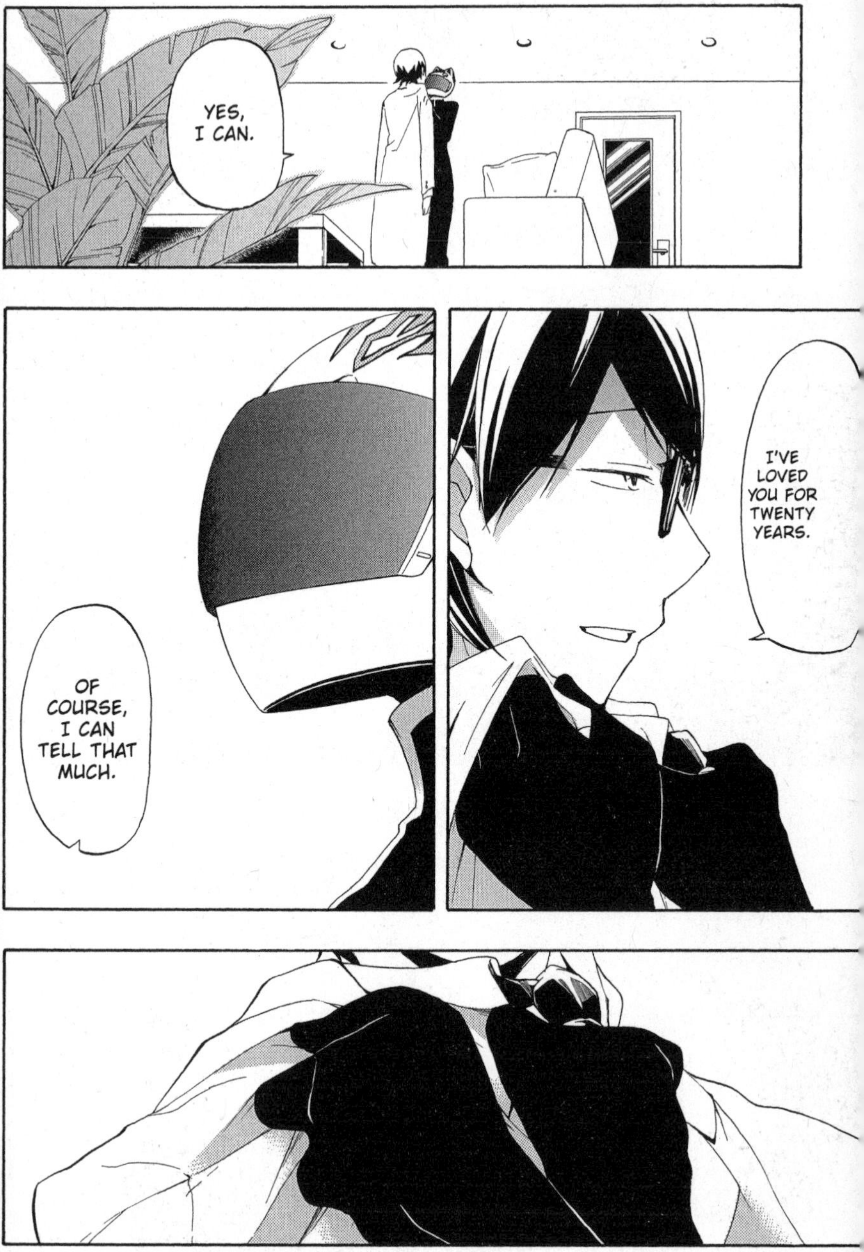
YES, I CAN.
I'VE LOVED YOU FOR TWENTY YEARS.
OF COURSE, I CAN TELL THAT MUCH.

SUTON
(PLOP)

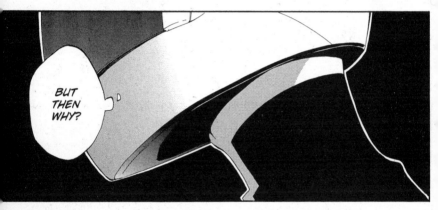

BUT
THEN
WHY?

WHY
WOULD
YOU KEEP
QUIET
ABOUT
THE
WHERE-
ABOUTS
OF MY
HEAD
UNTIL
NOW?

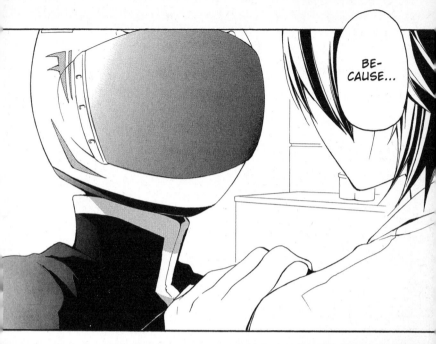

BE-
CAUSE...

...I LOVE
YOU.

110

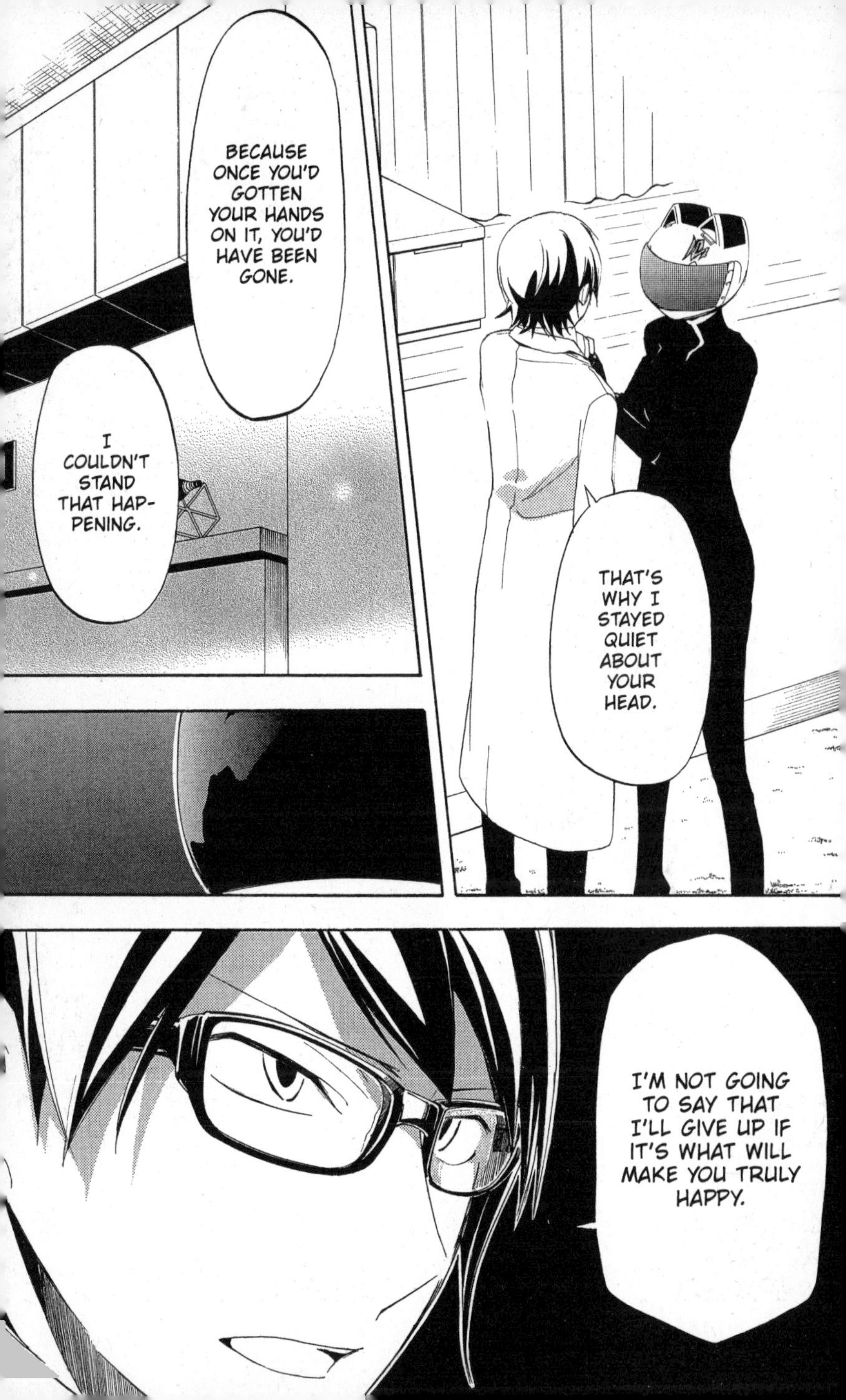
THAT'S WHY I STAYED QUIET ABOUT YOUR HEAD.
BECAUSE ONCE YOU'D GOTTEN YOUR HANDS ON IT, YOU'D HAVE BEEN GONE.
I COULDN'T STAND THAT HAP-PENING.
I'M NOT GOING TO SAY THAT I'LL GIVE UP IF IT'S WHAT WILL MAKE YOU TRULY HAPPY.

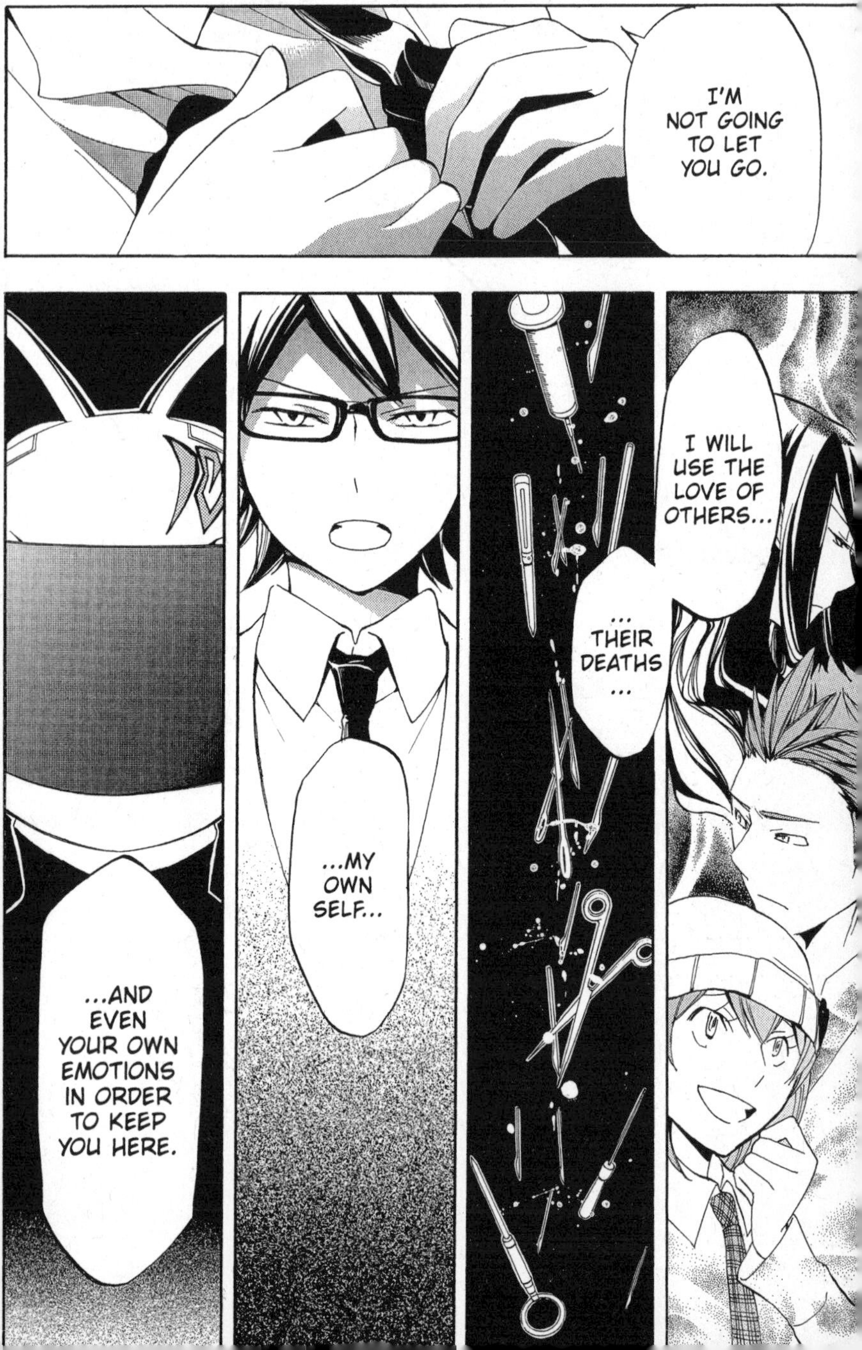
I'M NOT GOING TO LET YOU GO.
I WILL USE THE LOVE OF OTHERS...
...THEIR DEATHS...
...MY OWN SELF...
...AND EVEN YOUR OWN EMOTIONS IN ORDER TO KEEP YOU HERE.

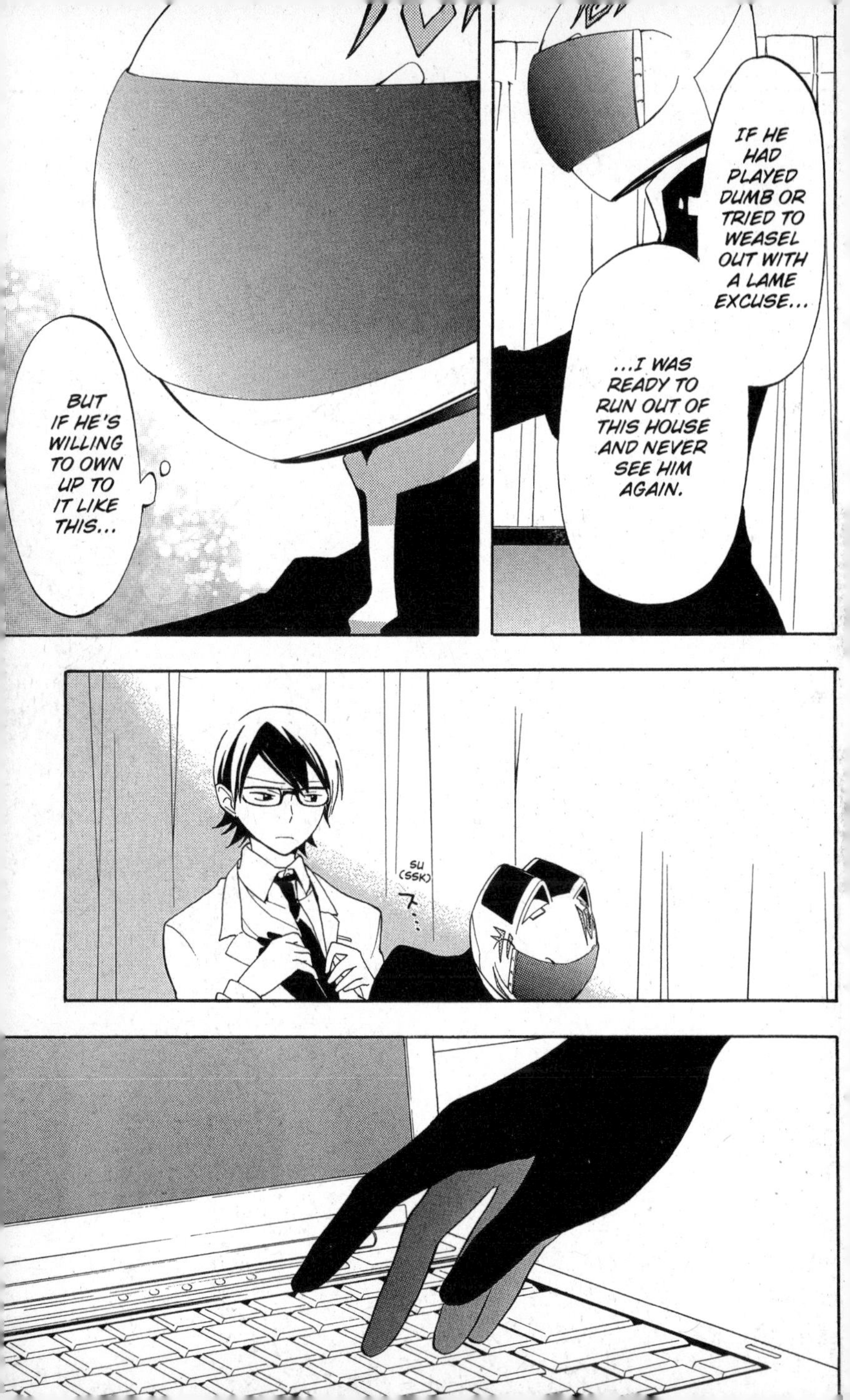
IF HE HAD PLAYED DUMB OR TRIED TO WEASEL OUT WITH A LAME EXCUSE...
...I WAS READY TO RUN OUT OF THIS HOUSE AND NEVER SEE HIM AGAIN.
BUT IF HE'S WILLING TO OWN UP TO IT LIKE THIS...
SU (SSK)

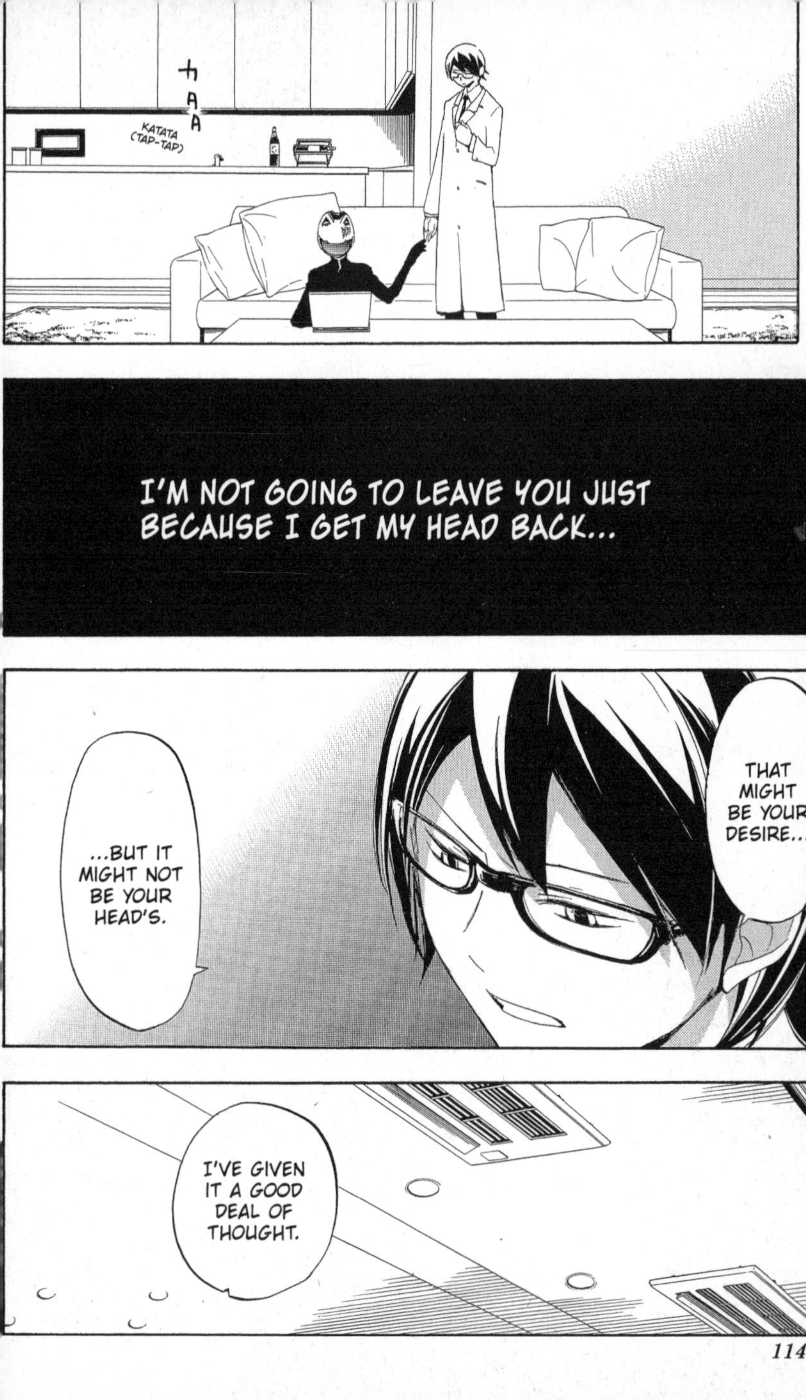
KATATA (TAP-TAP)
I'M NOT GOING TO LEAVE YOU JUST BECAUSE I GET MY HEAD BACK...
THAT MIGHT BE YOUR DESIRE...
...BUT IT MIGHT NOT BE YOUR HEAD'S.
I'VE GIVEN IT A GOOD DEAL OF THOUGHT.

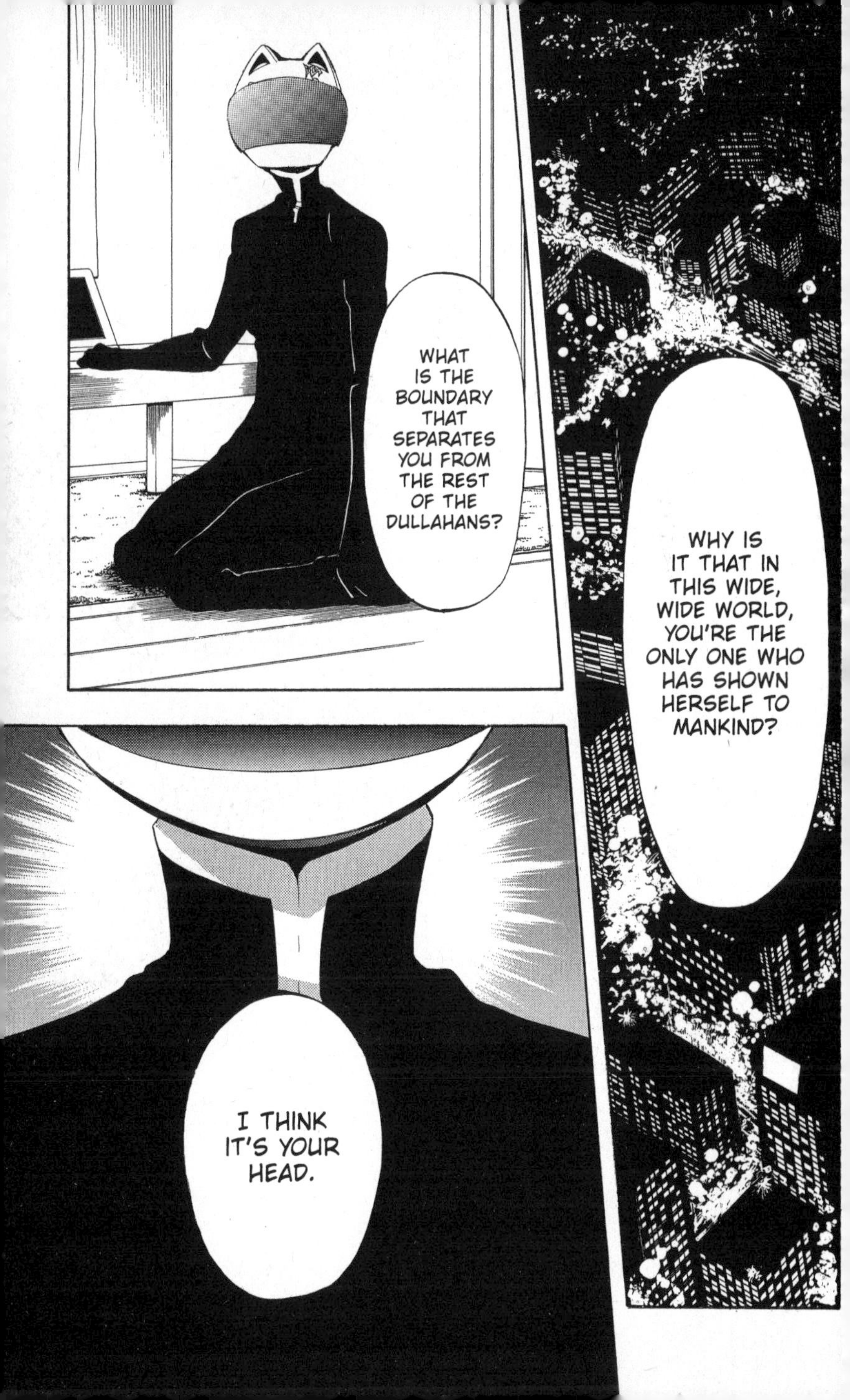
WHY IS IT THAT IN THIS WIDE, WIDE WORLD, YOU'RE THE ONLY ONE WHO HAS SHOWN HERSELF TO MANKIND?
WHAT IS THE BOUNDARY THAT SEPARATES YOU FROM THE REST OF THE DULLAHANS?
I THINK IT'S YOUR HEAD.

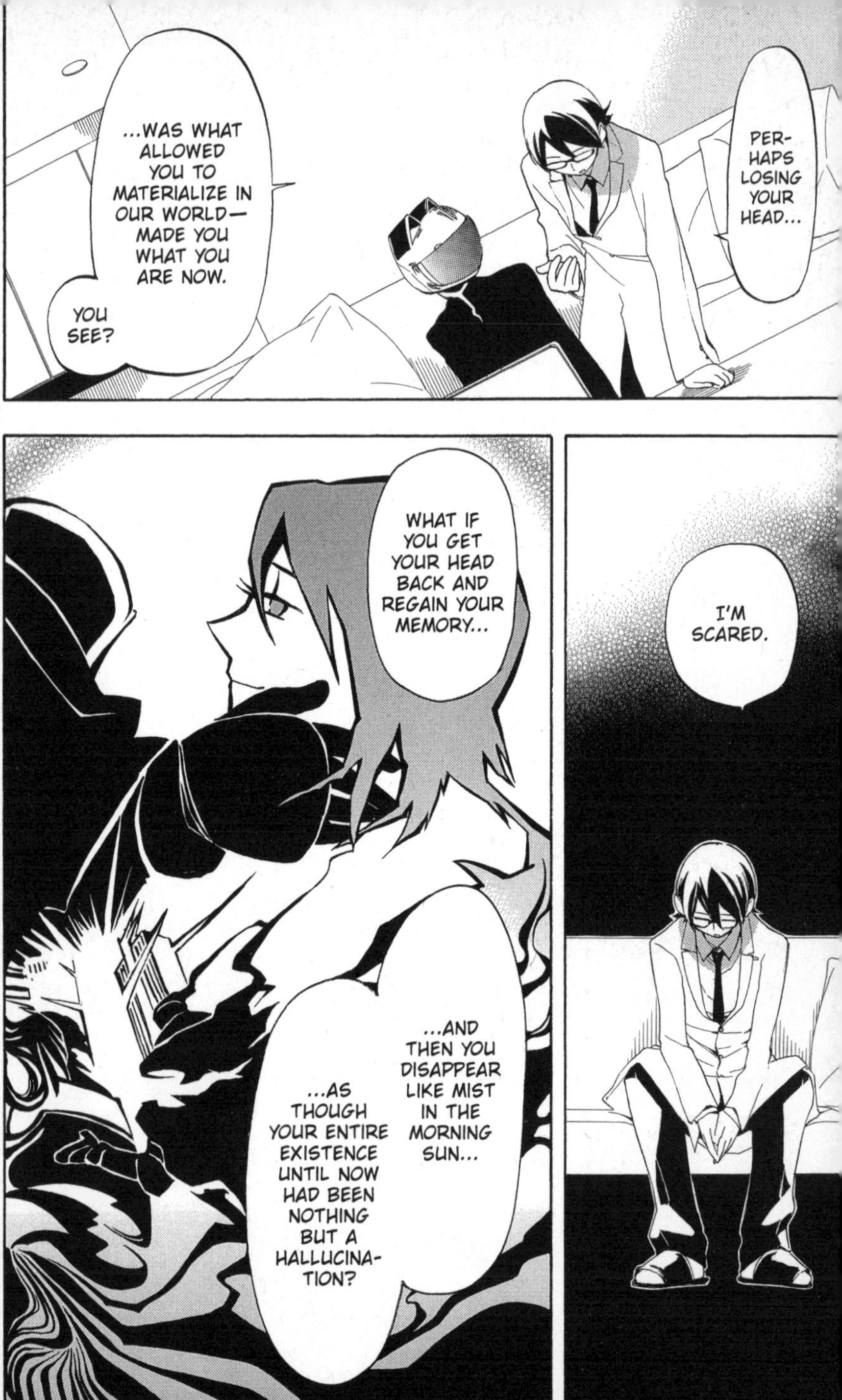
PER-HAPS LOSING YOUR HEAD...
...WAS WHAT ALLOWED YOU TO MATERIALIZE IN OUR WORLD—MADE YOU WHAT YOU ARE NOW.
YOU SEE?
I'M SCARED.
WHAT IF YOU GET YOUR HEAD BACK AND REGAIN YOUR MEMORY...
...AND THEN YOU DISAPPEAR LIKE MIST IN THE MORNING SUN...
...AS THOUGH YOUR ENTIRE EXISTENCE UNTIL NOW HAD BEEN NOTHING BUT A HALLUCINA-TION?

THAT'S WHAT I'M AFRAID OF.

KATA KATA KATA KATA KATA KATA (TAP)

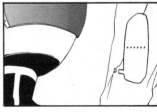

....

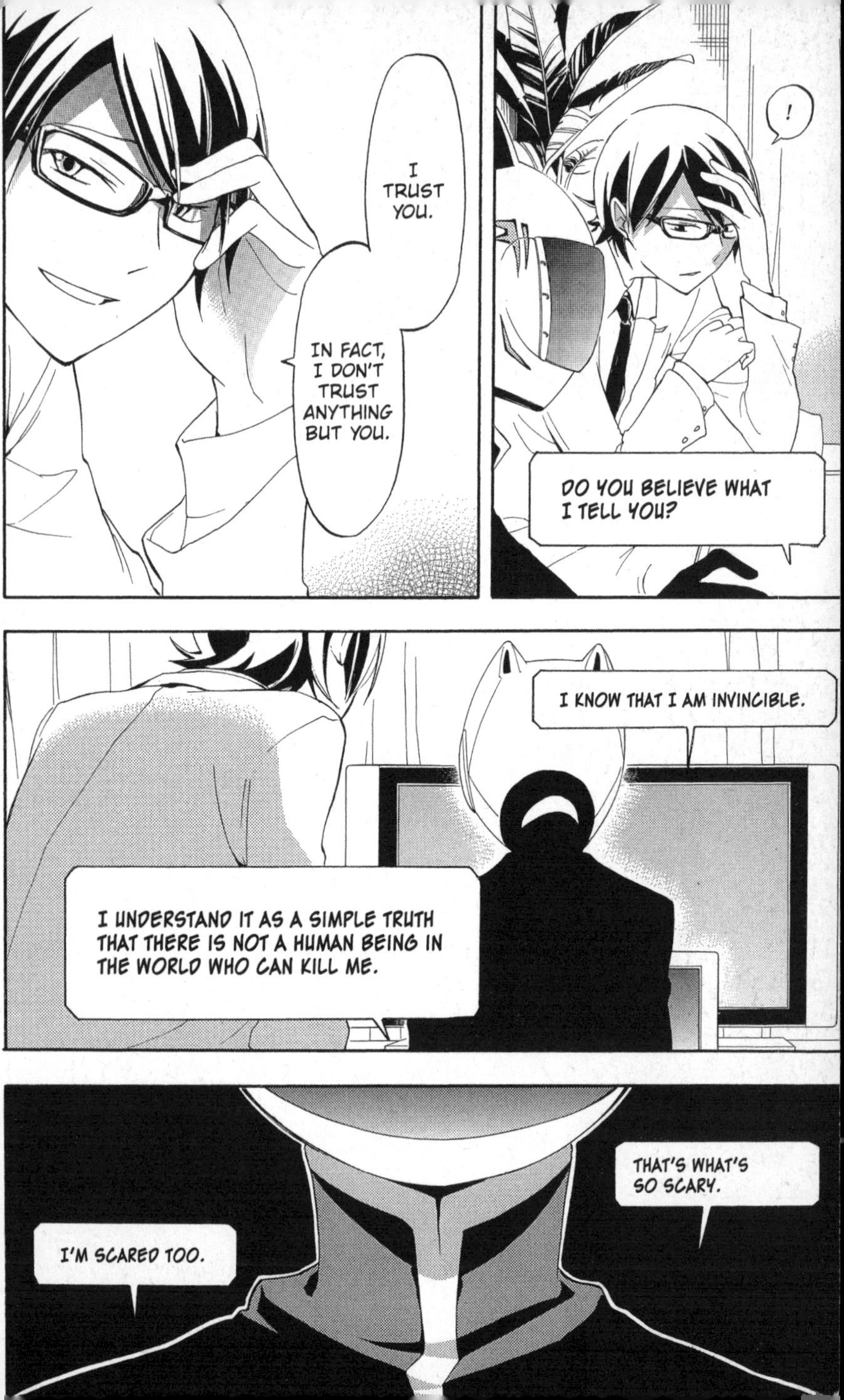
!
DO YOU BELIEVE WHAT I TELL YOU?
I TRUST YOU.
IN FACT, I DON'T TRUST ANYTHING BUT YOU.
I KNOW THAT I AM INVINCIBLE.
I UNDERSTAND IT AS A SIMPLE TRUTH THAT THERE IS NOT A HUMAN BEING IN THE WORLD WHO CAN KILL ME.
THAT'S WHAT'S SO SCARY.
I'M SCARED TOO.

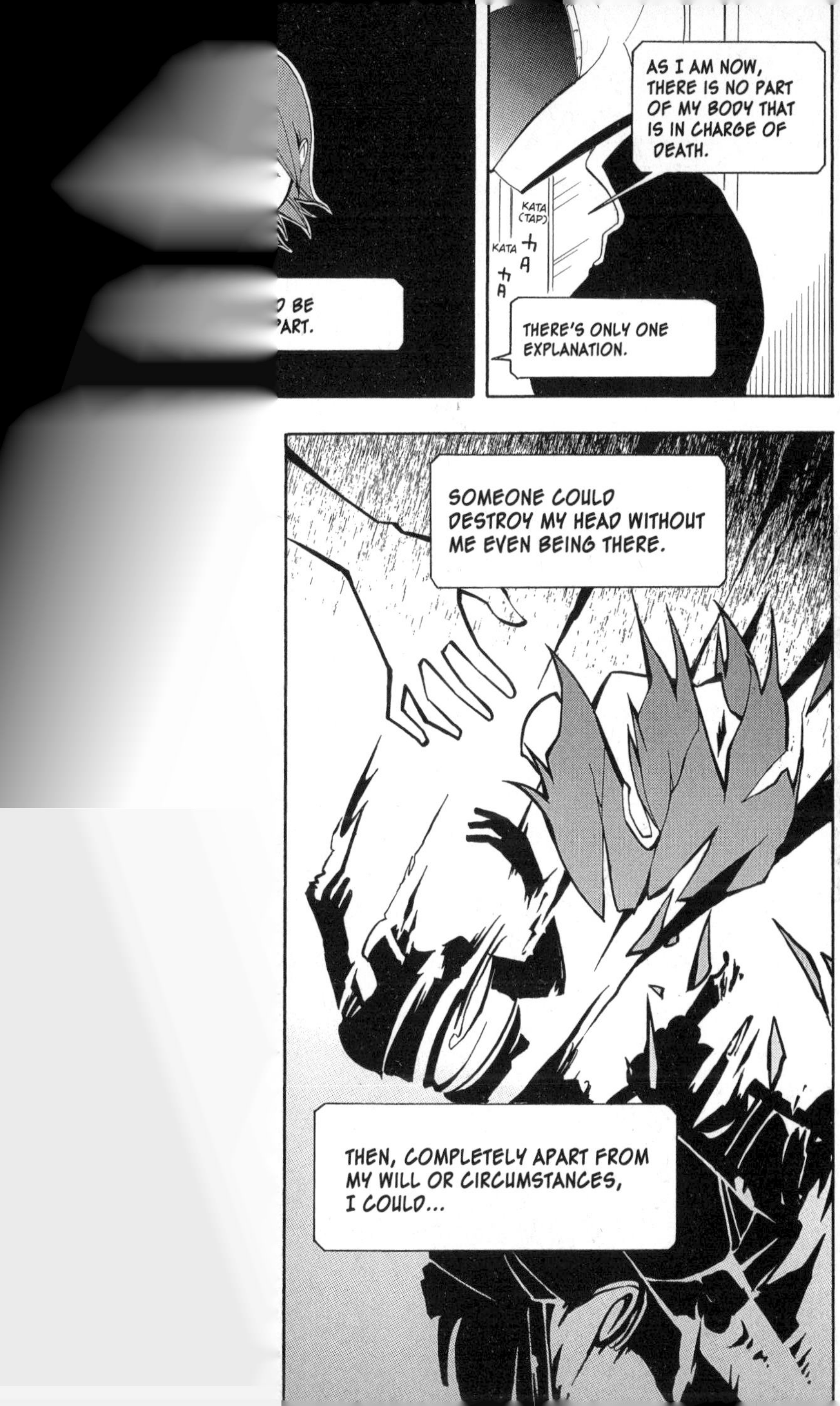
AS I AM NOW, THERE IS NO PART OF MY BODY THAT IS IN CHARGE OF DEATH.
KATA (TAP)
KATA
THERE'S ONLY ONE EXPLANATION.
BE
ART.
SOMEONE COULD DESTROY MY HEAD WITHOUT ME EVEN BEING THERE.
THEN, COMPLETELY APART FROM MY WILL OR CIRCUMSTANCES, I COULD...

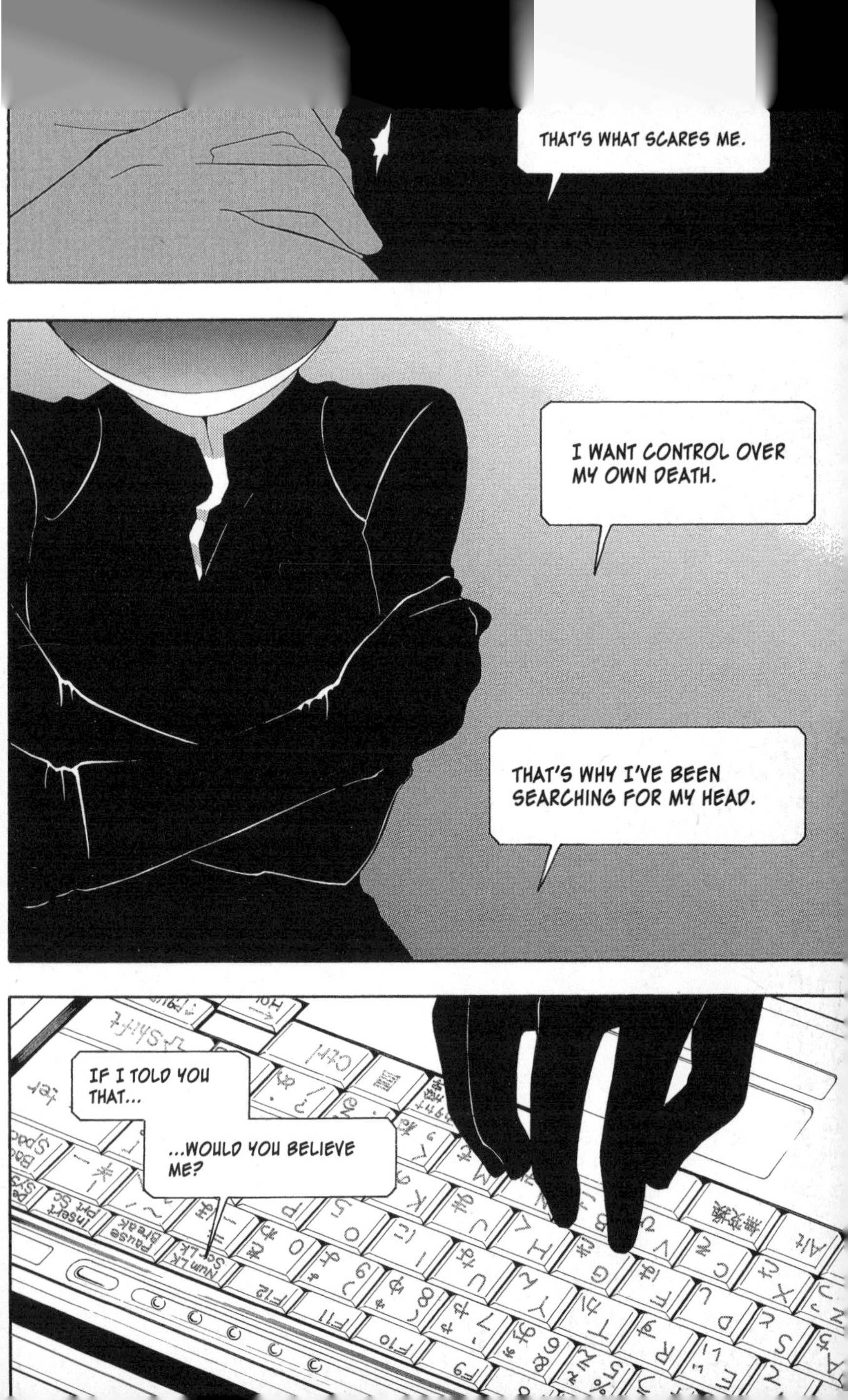
THAT'S WHAT SCARES ME.
I WANT CONTROL OVER MY OWN DEATH.
THAT'S WHY I'VE BEEN SEARCHING FOR MY HEAD.
IF I TOLD YOU THAT...
...WOULD YOU BELIEVE ME?

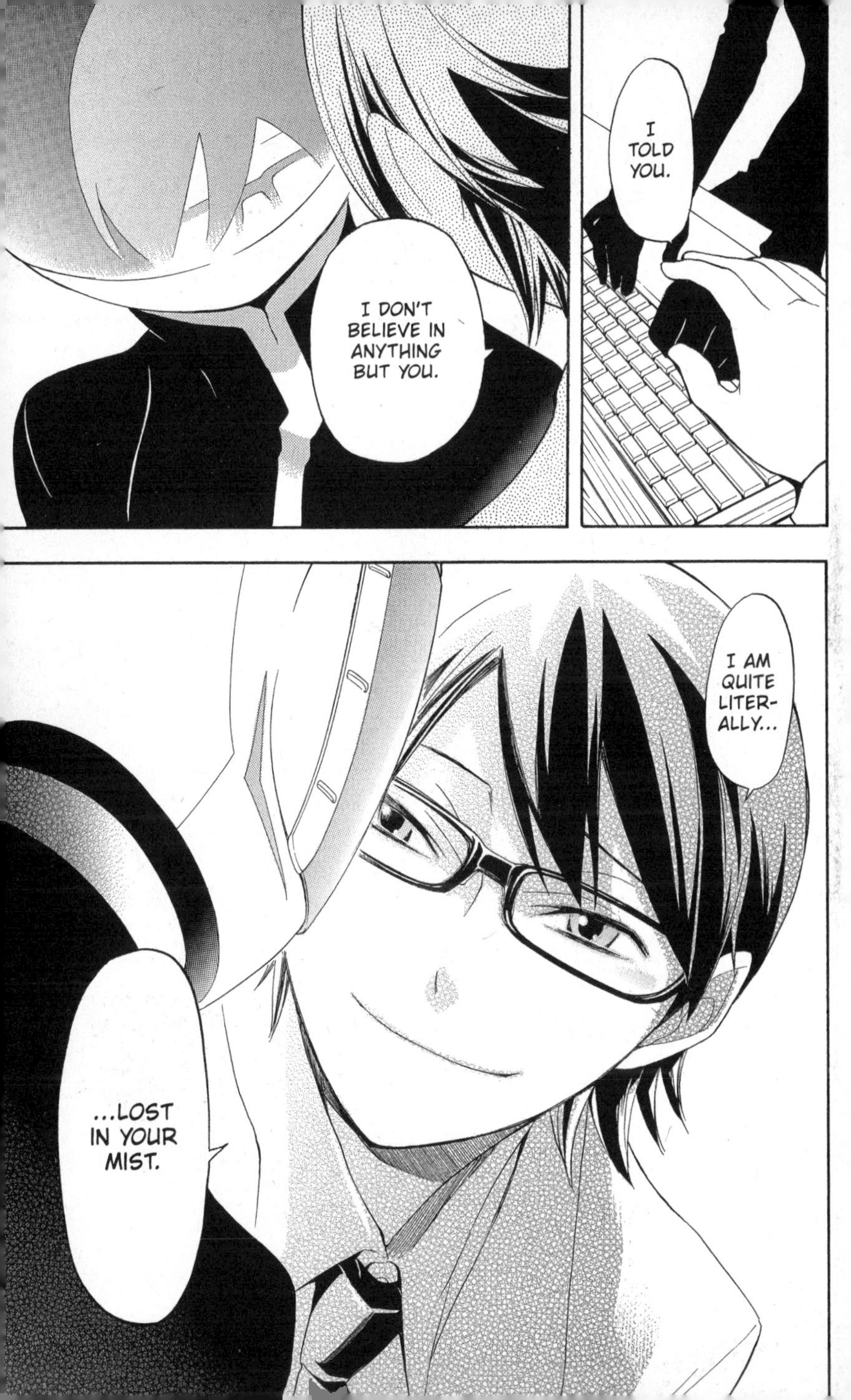
I TOLD YOU.
I DON'T BELIEVE IN ANYTHING BUT YOU.
I AM QUITE LITER-ALLY...
...LOST IN YOUR MIST.

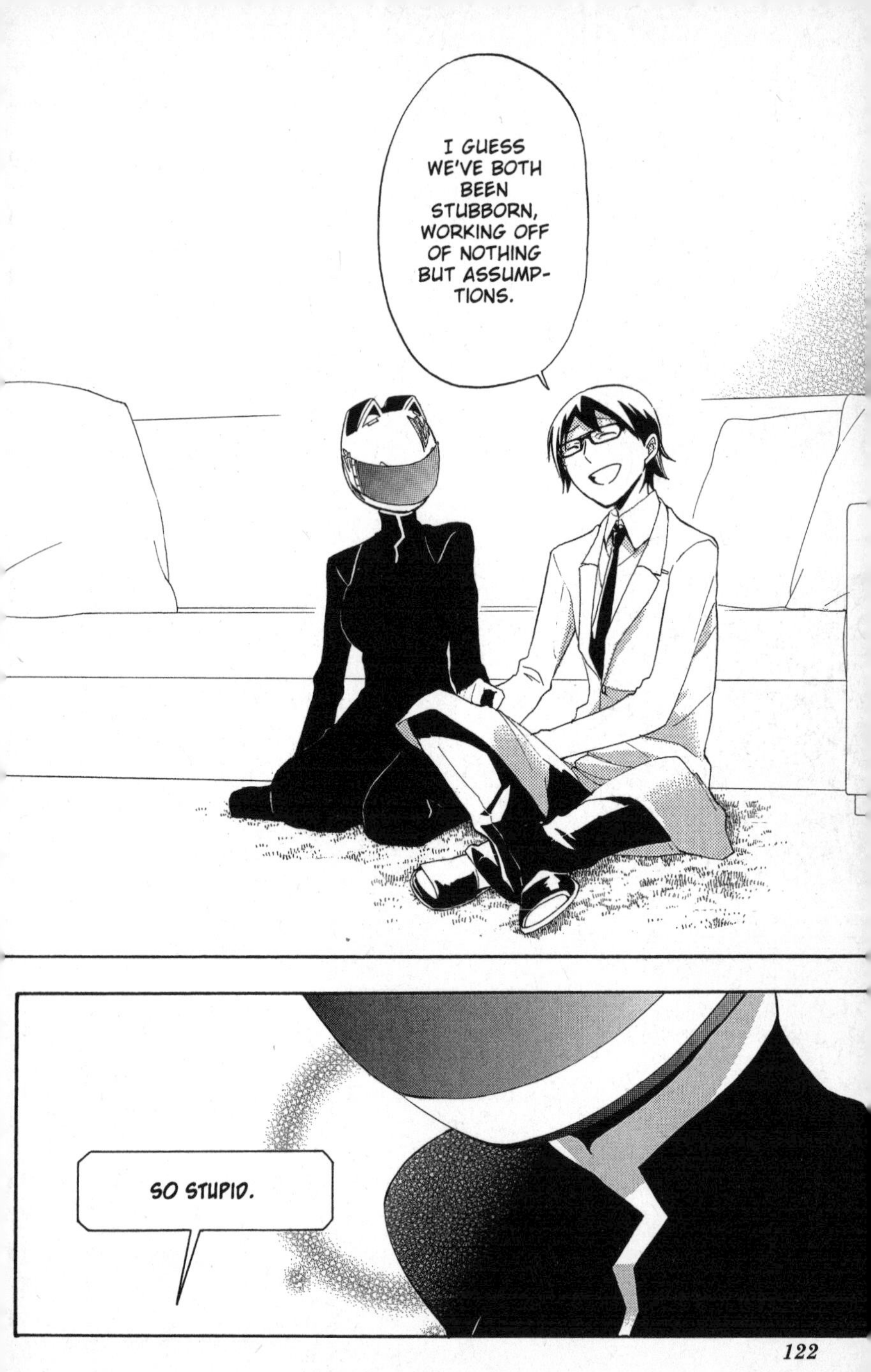
I GUESS WE'VE BOTH BEEN STUBBORN, WORKING OFF OF NOTHING BUT ASSUMPTIONS.
SO STUPID.

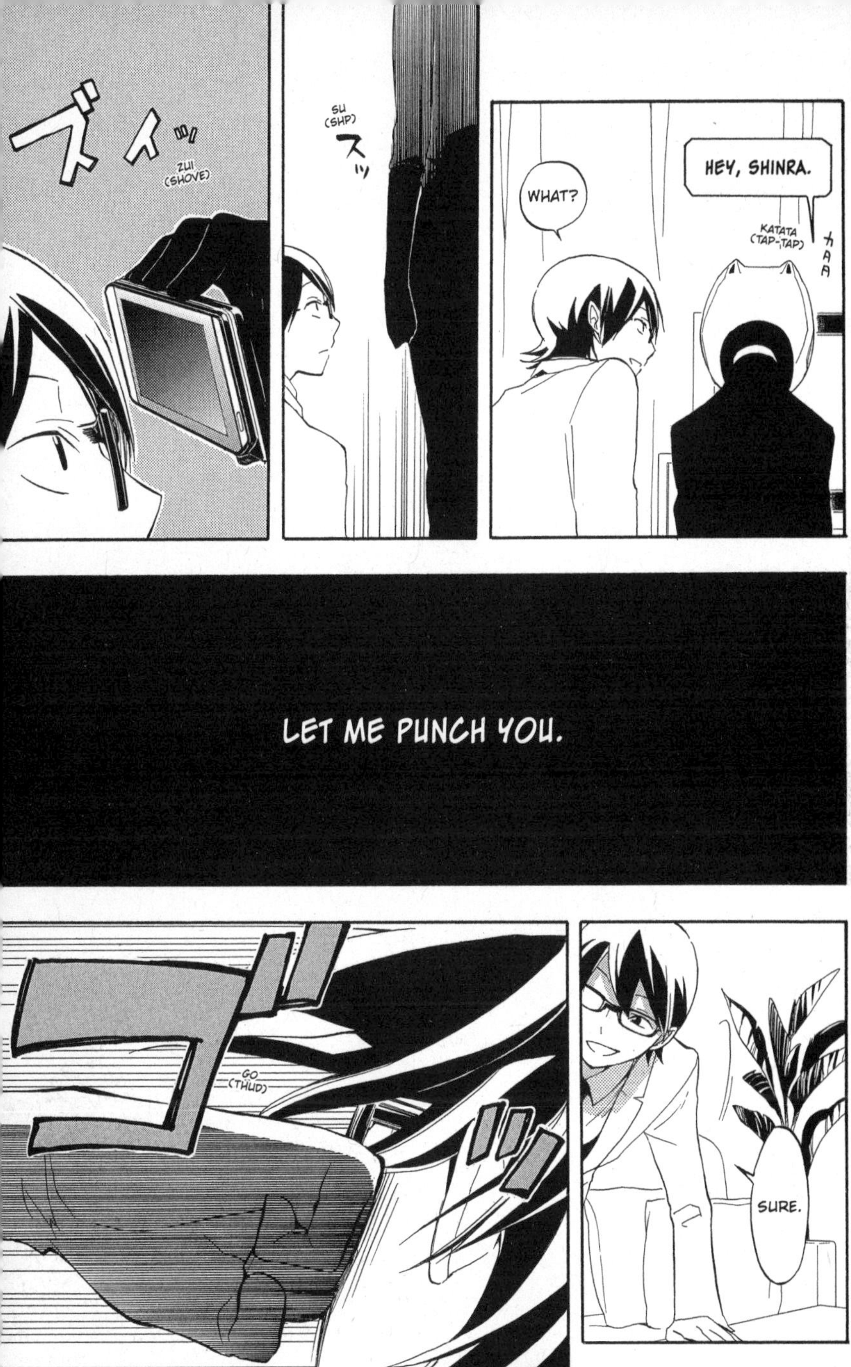
HEY, SHINRA.
KATATA (TAP-TAP)
カタタ
WHAT?
SU (SHP)
スッ
ズイッ
ZUI (SHOVE)
LET ME PUNCH YOU.
SURE.
ゴッ
GO (THUD)

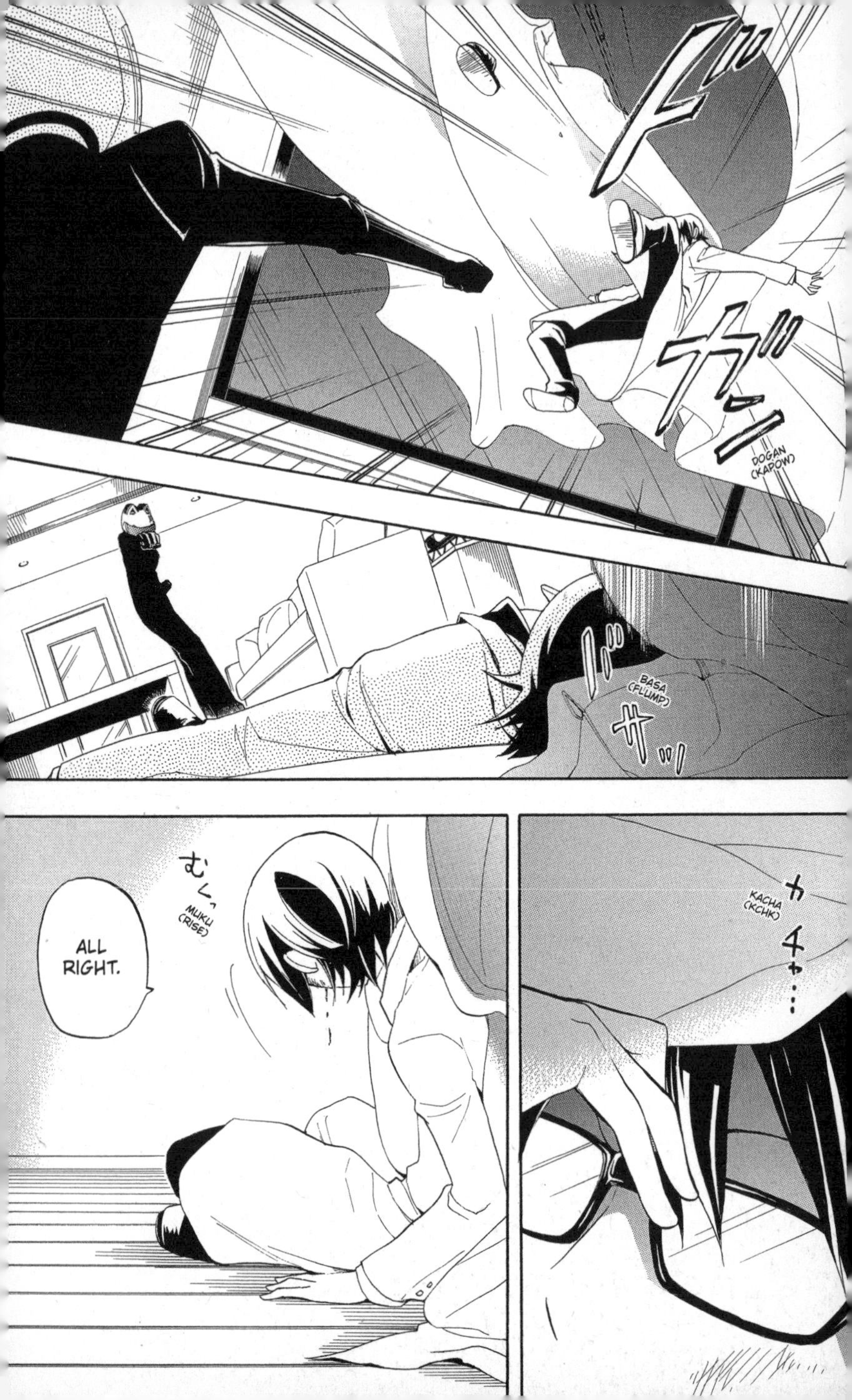
DOGAN (KAPOW)
BASA (FLUMP)
カチャ…
KACHA (KCHK)
むくっ
MUKU (RISE)
ALL RIGHT.

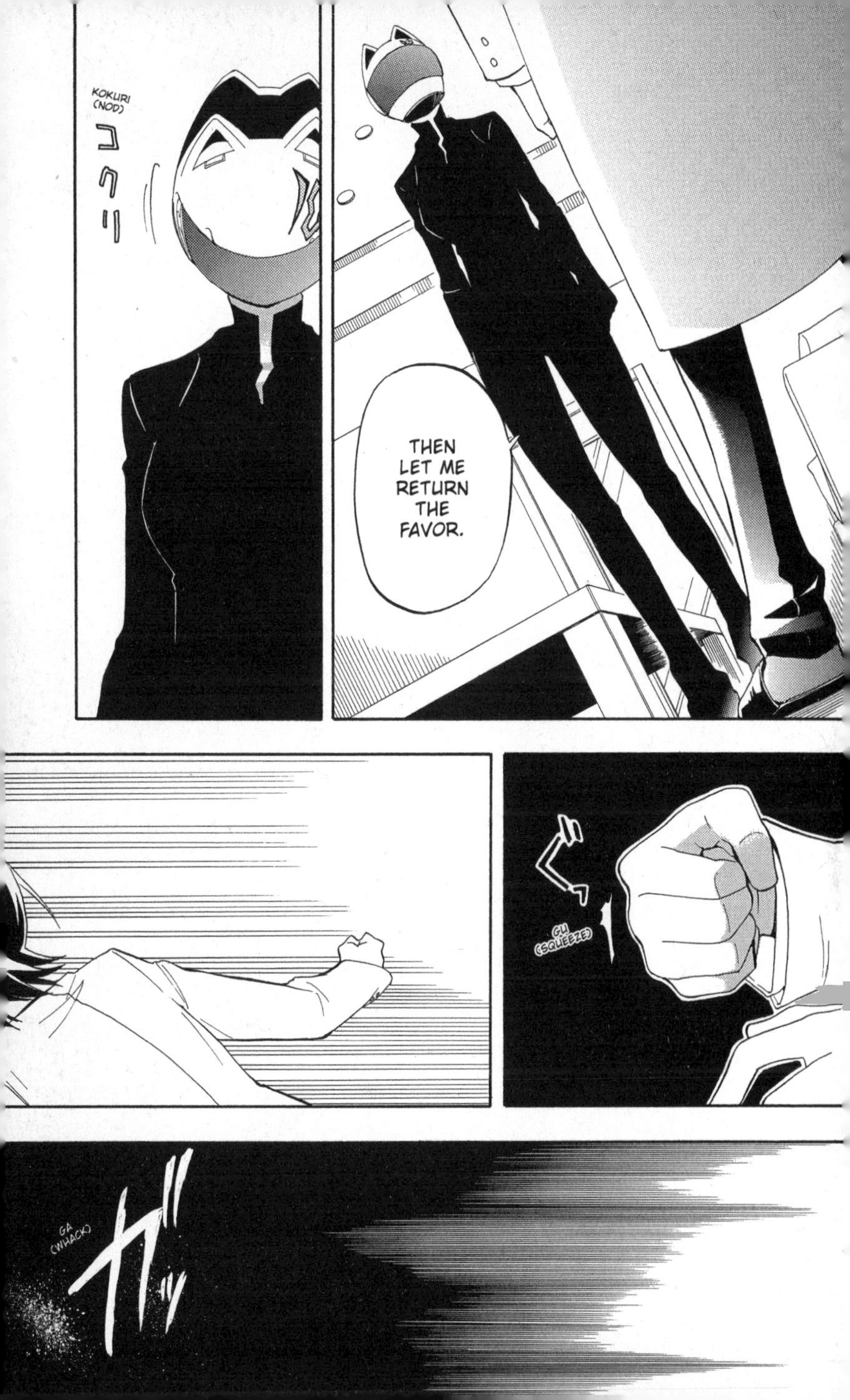
THEN LET ME RETURN THE FAVOR.
KOKURI (NOD)
コクリ
GU (SQUEEZE)
グッ
GA (WHACK)
ガッ

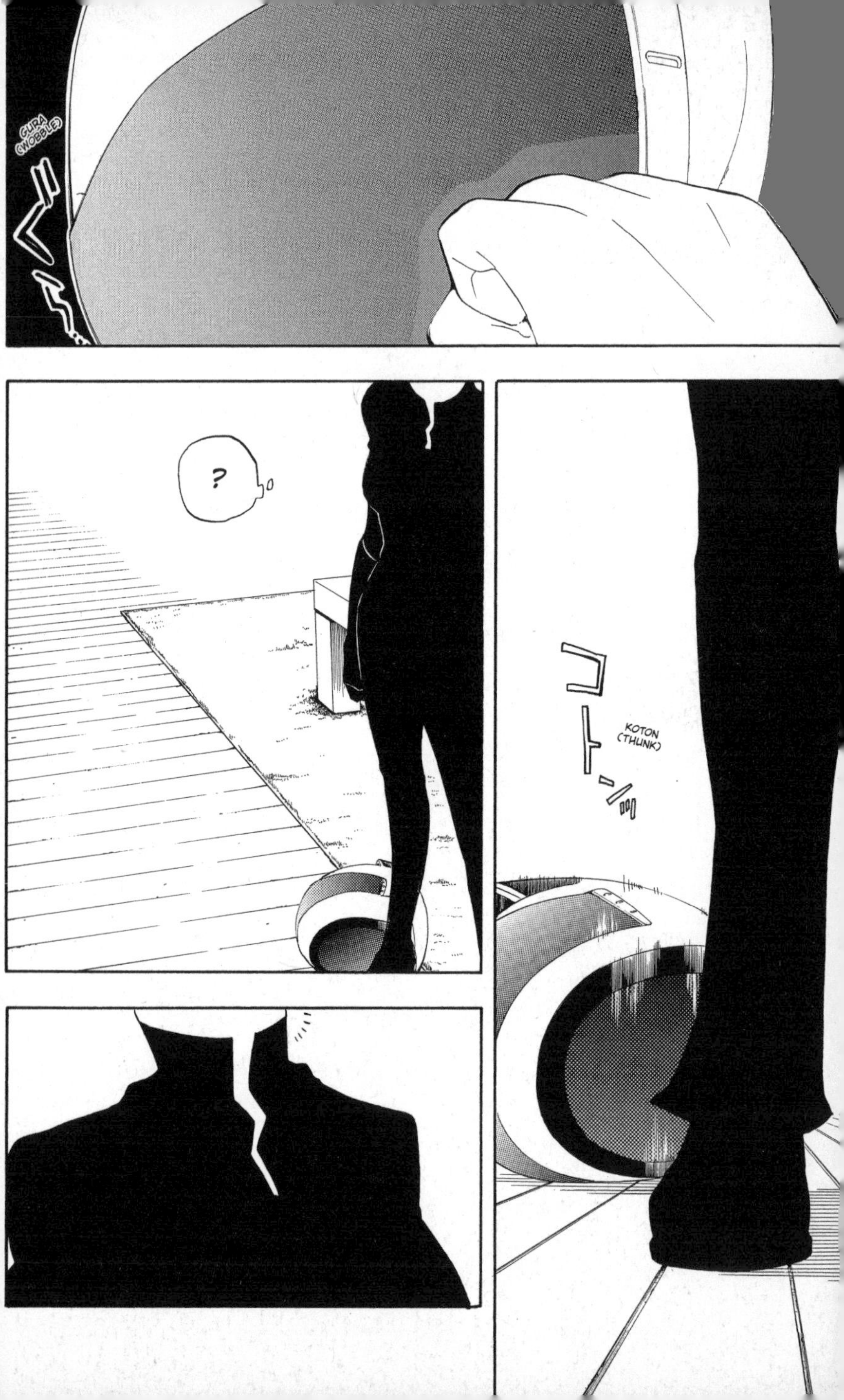
GURA (WOBBLE)
KOTON (THUNK)
?

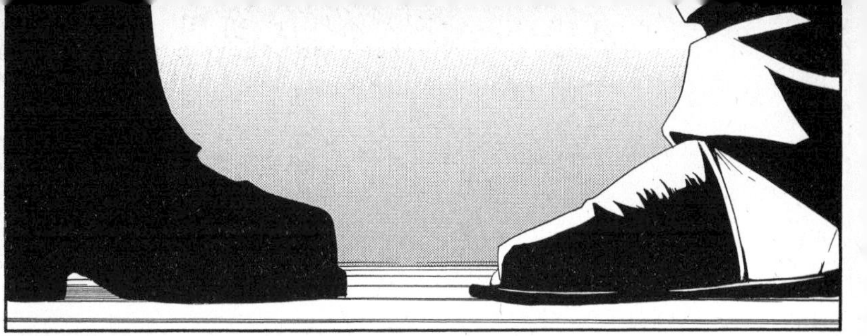

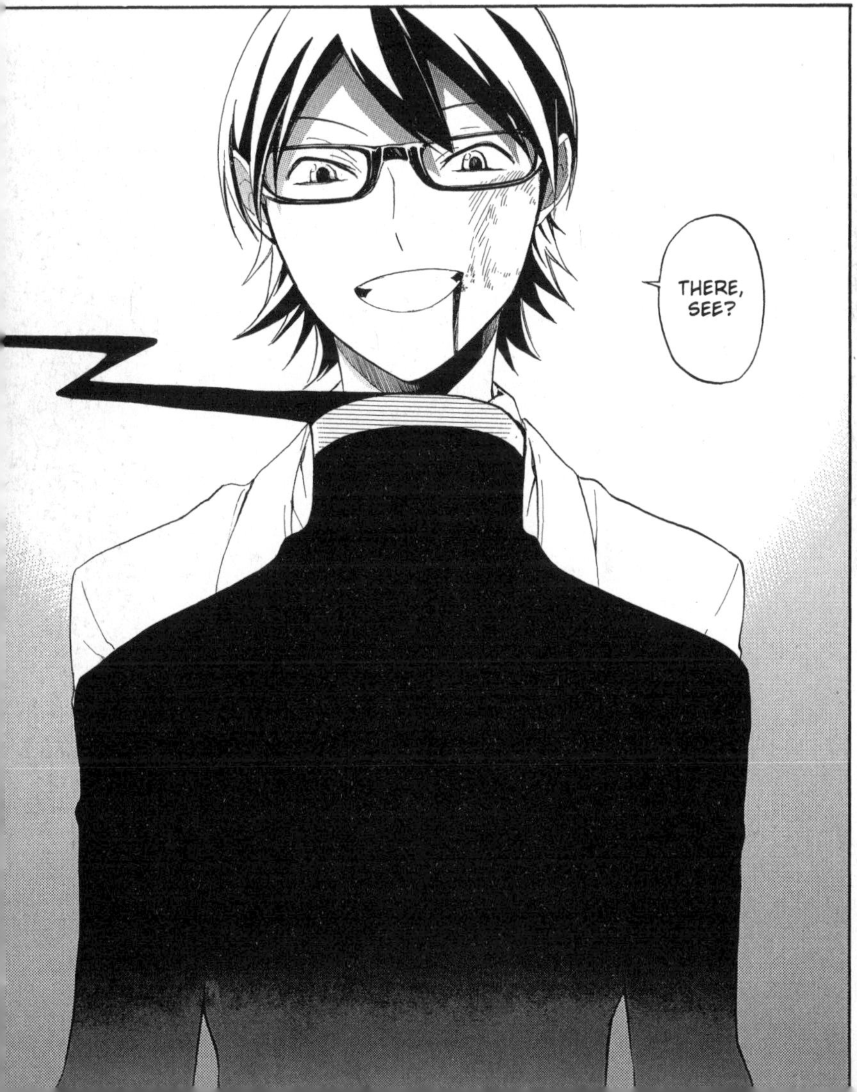
THERE, SEE?

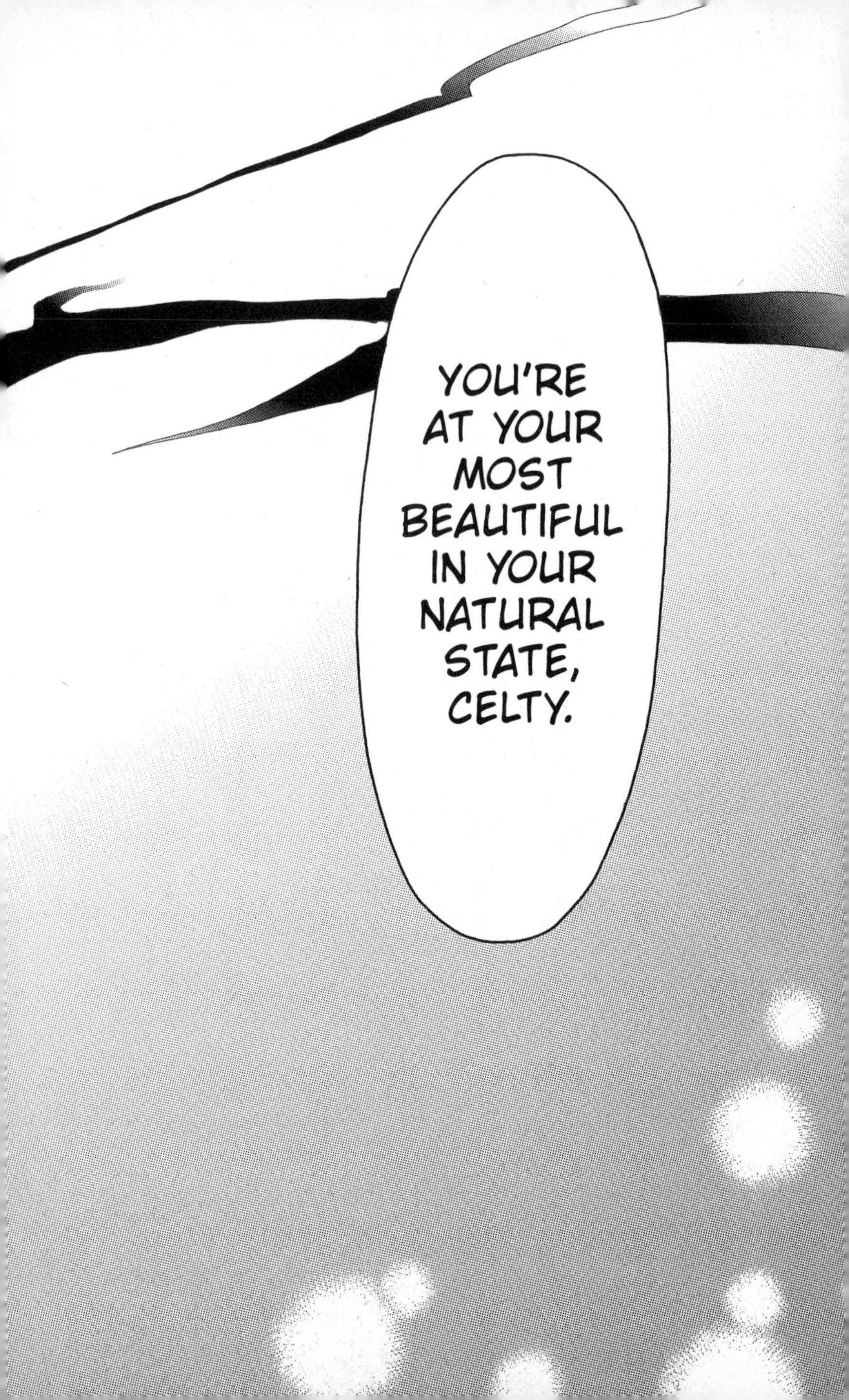
YOU'RE AT YOUR MOST BEAUTIFUL IN YOUR NATURAL STATE, CELTY.

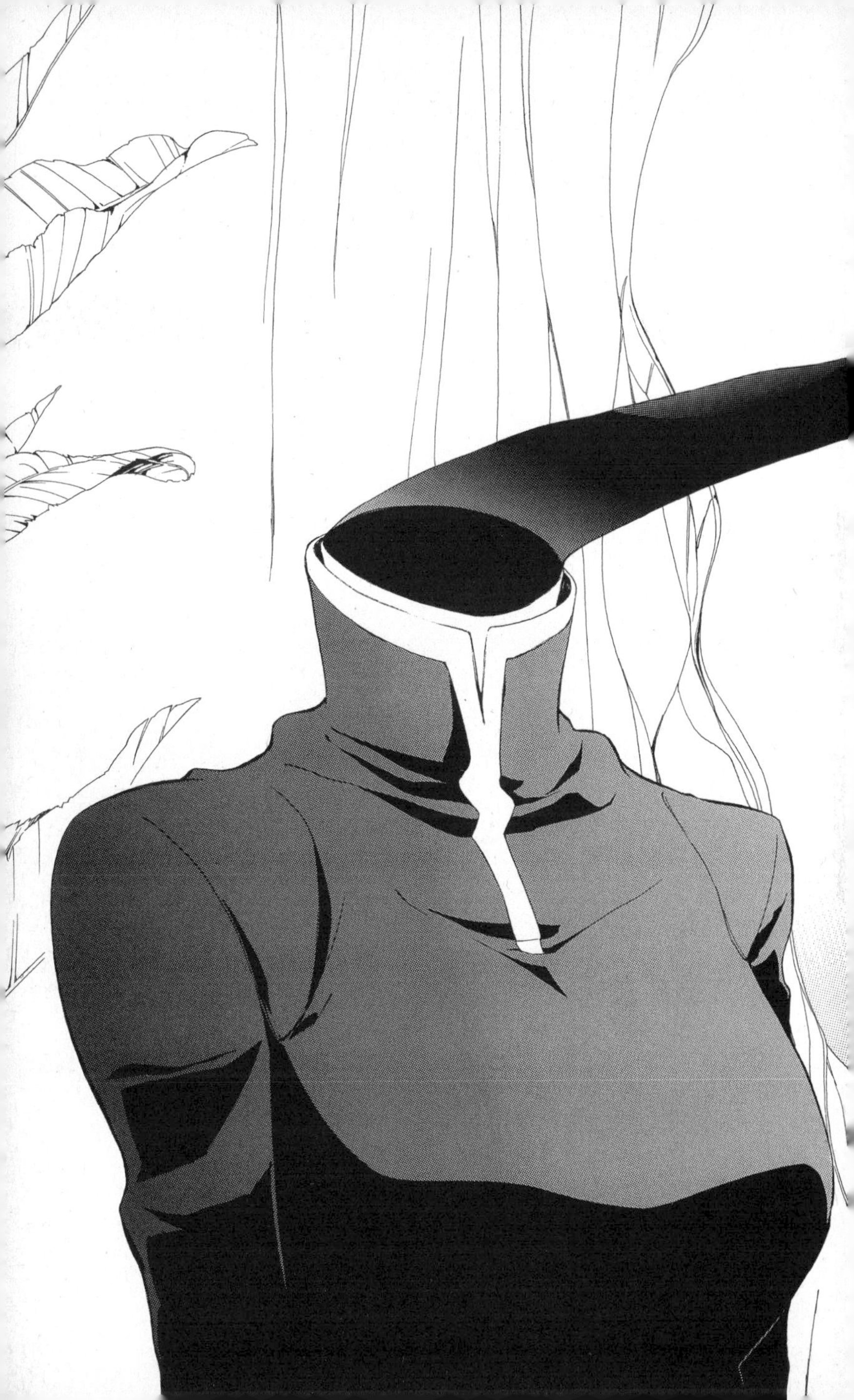

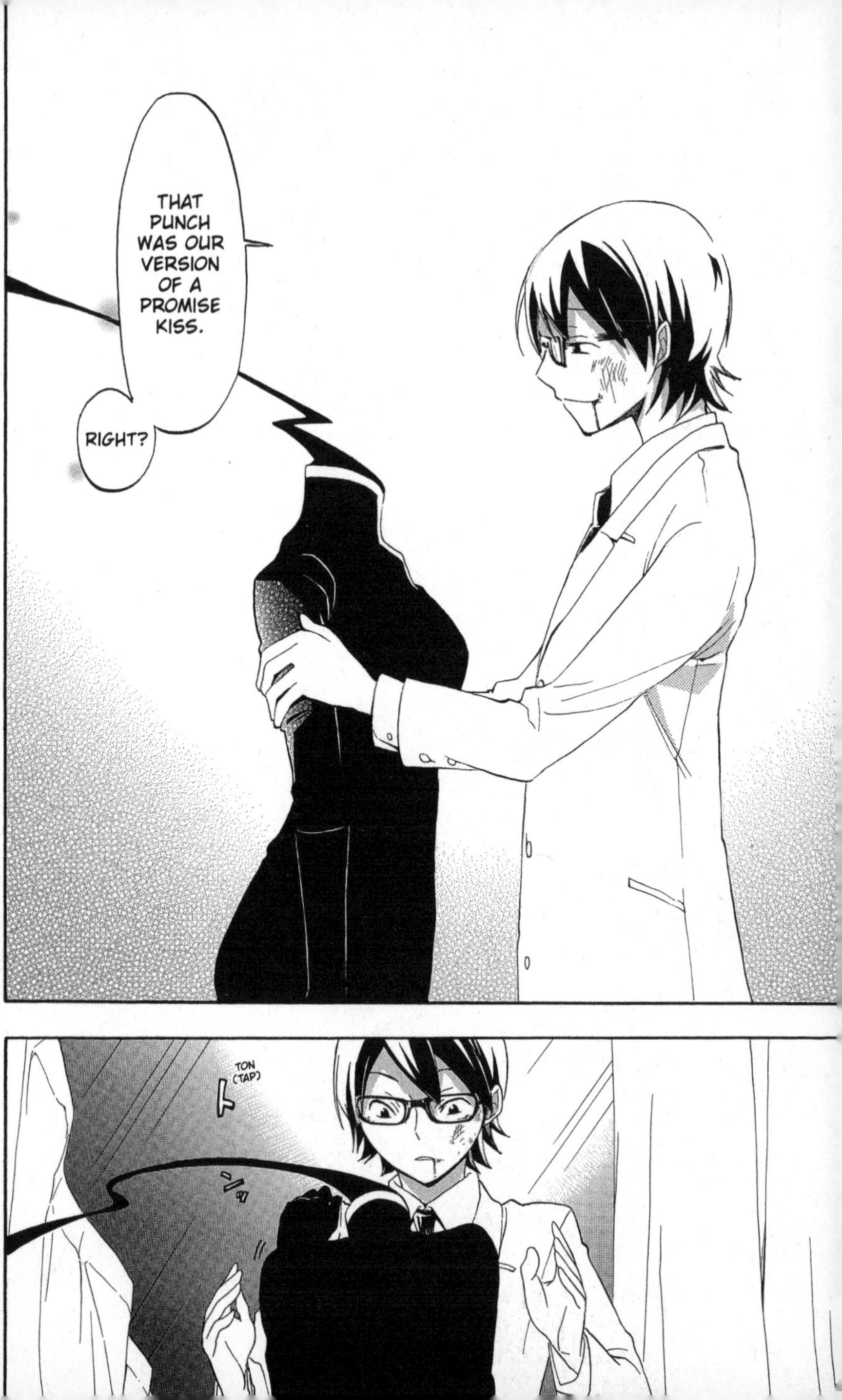
THAT PUNCH WAS OUR VERSION OF A PROMISE KISS.
RIGHT?
ト
TON (TAP)

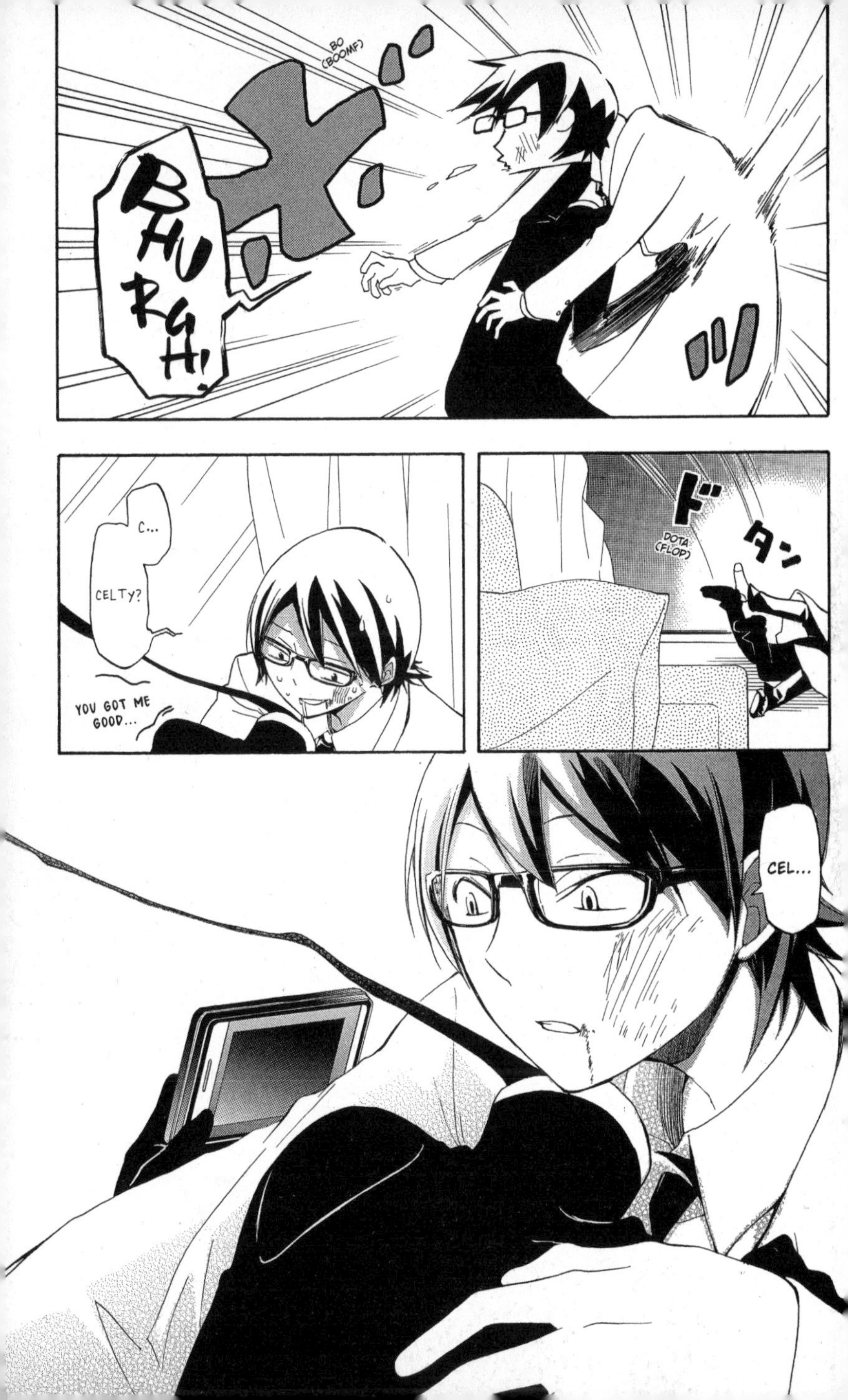

BO (BOOMF)
BHURGH!
ドタン
DOTA (FLOP)
C...
CELTY?
YOU GOT ME GOOD...
CEL...

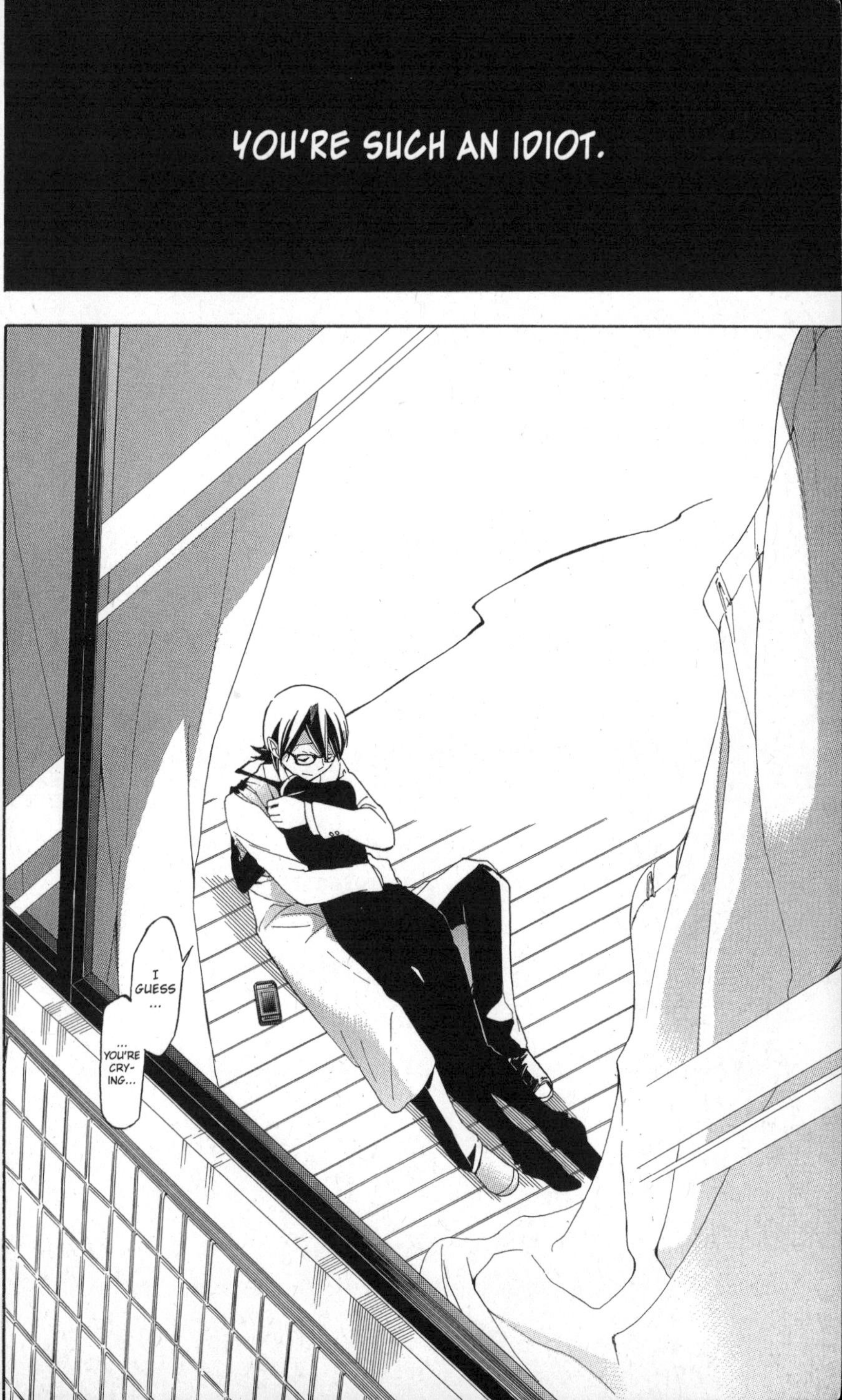
YOU'RE SUCH AN IDIOT.
I GUESS ...
... YOU'RE CRY-ING...

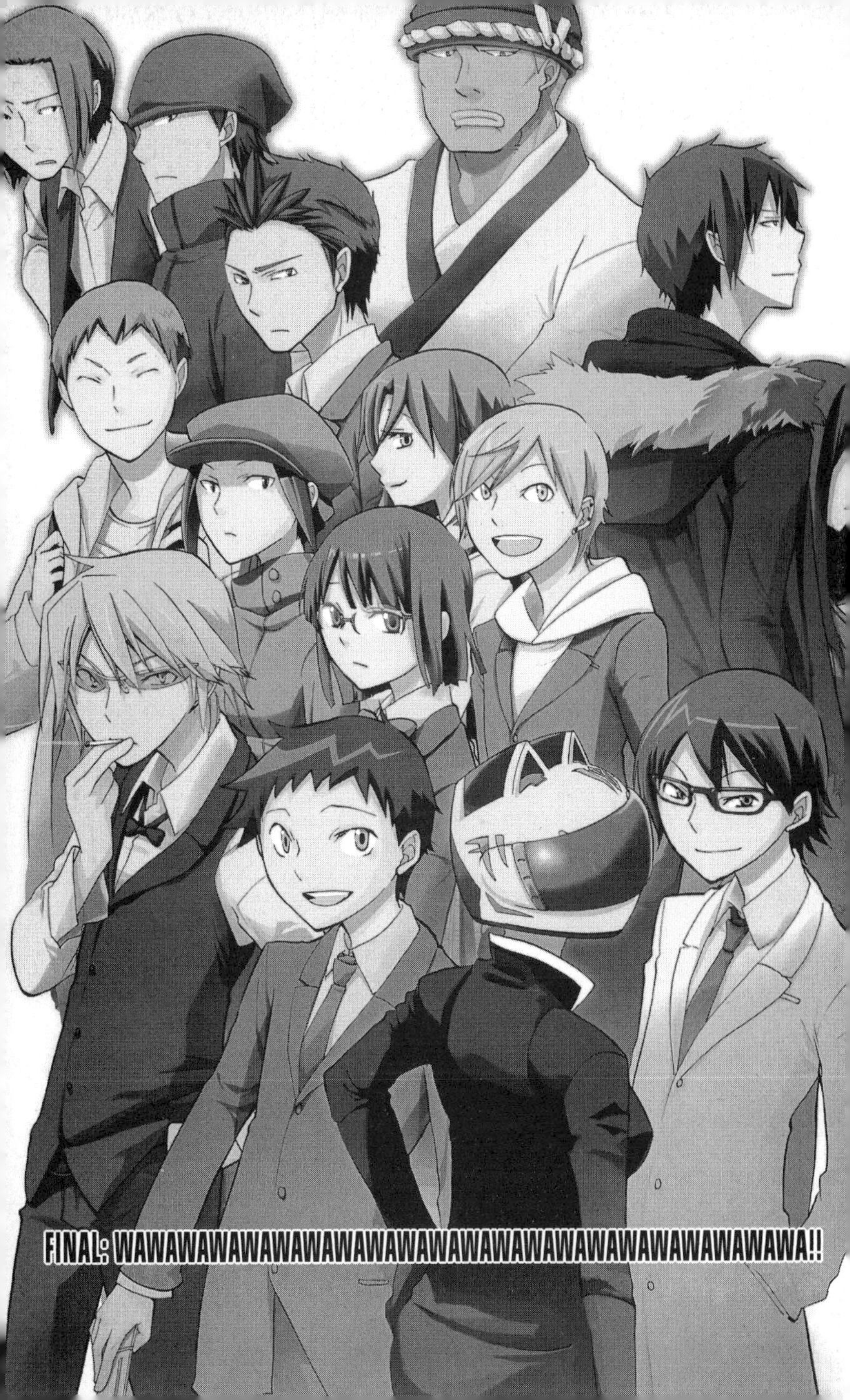
FINAL: WAWAWAWAWAWAWAWAWAWAWAWAWAWAWAWAWAWAWAWAWAWA!!

DRRR!!

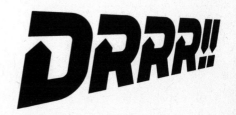

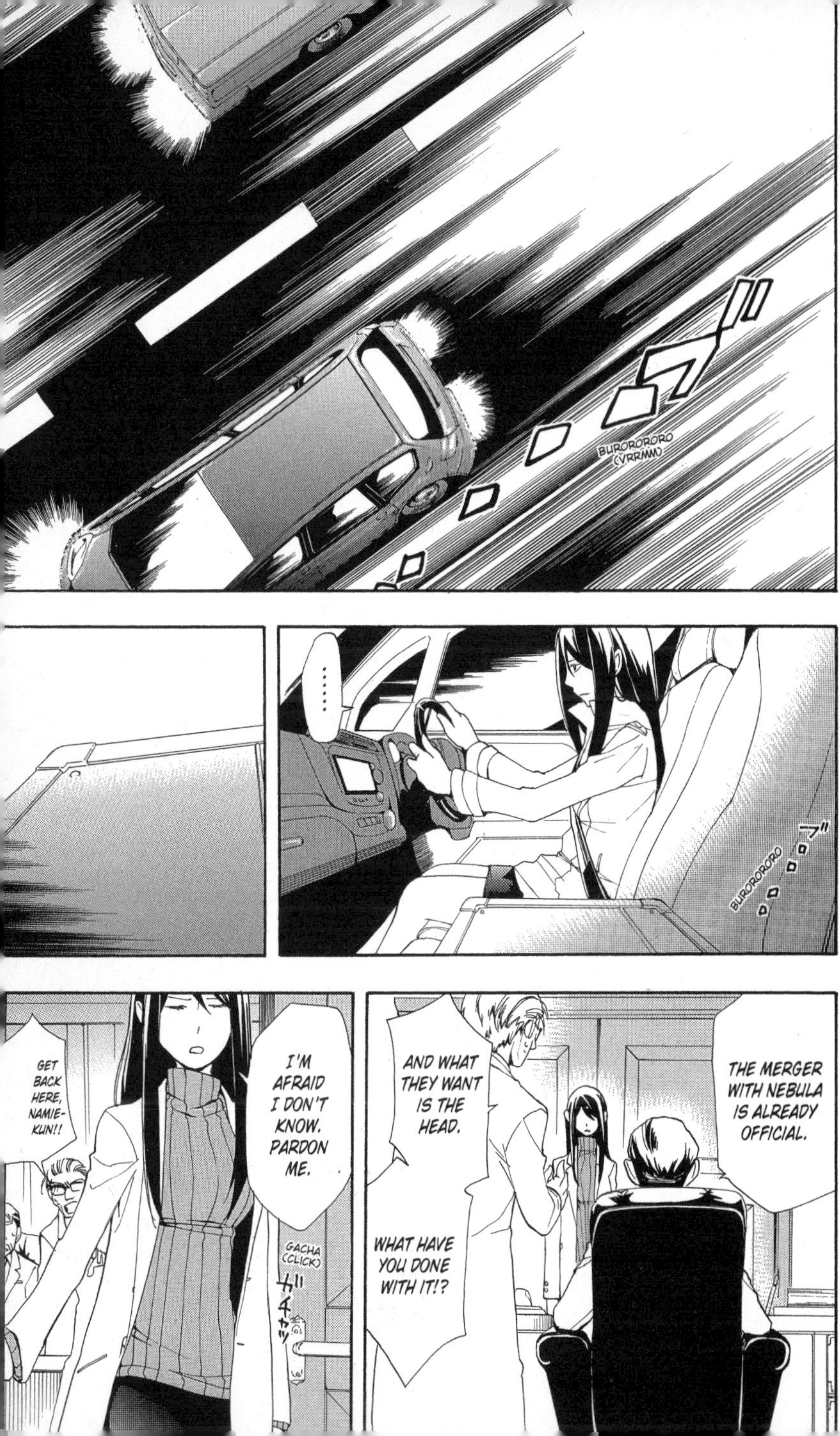
BUROROROR
(VRRMM)
......
BUROROROR
THE MERGER WITH NEBULA IS ALREADY OFFICIAL.
AND WHAT THEY WANT IS THE HEAD.
WHAT HAVE YOU DONE WITH IT!?
I'M AFRAID I DON'T KNOW. PARDON ME.
GACHA
(CLICK)
GET BACK HERE, NAMIE-KUN!!

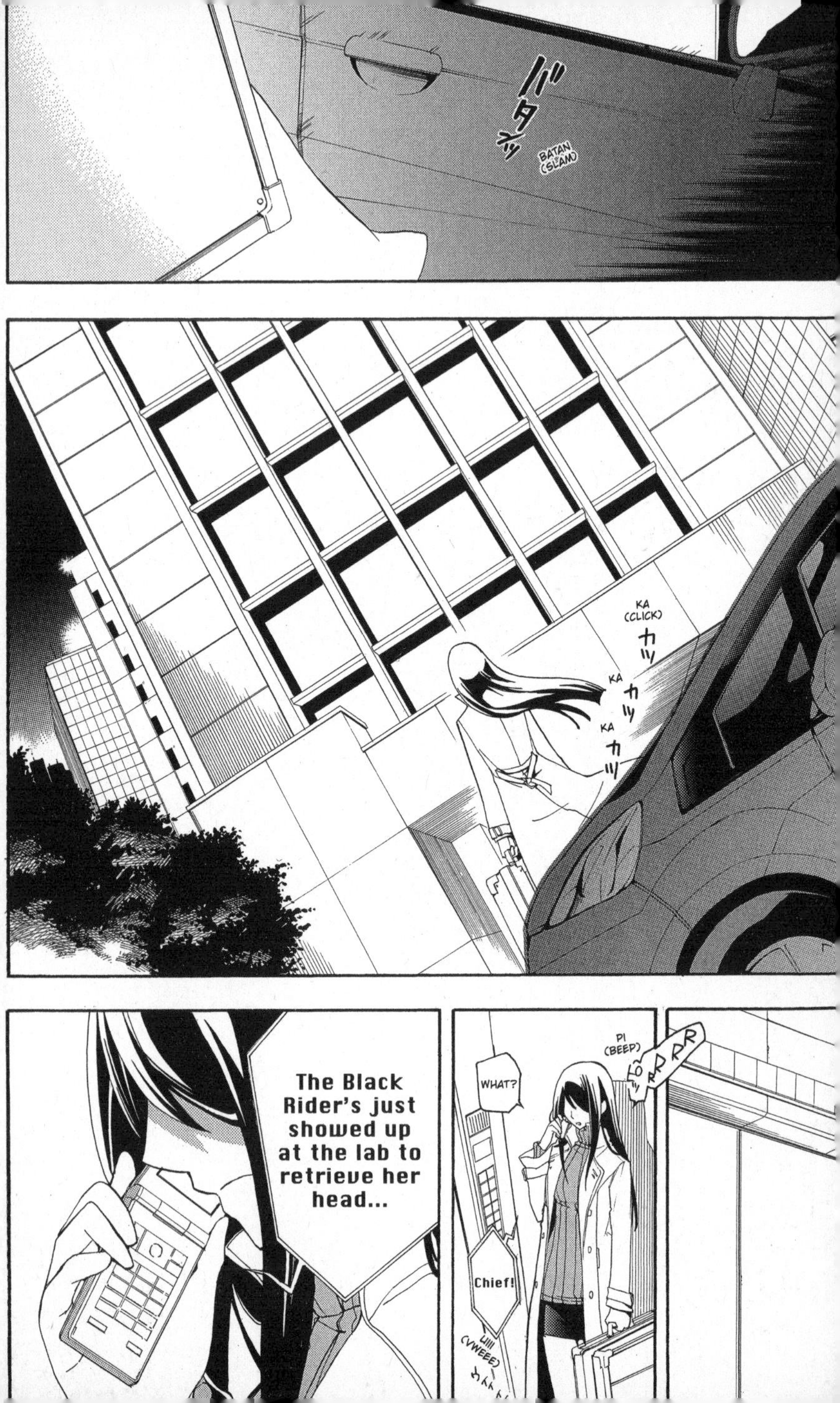

バタッ
BATAN (SLAM)
KA (CLICK)
カッ
KA
カッ
KA
カッ
PI (BEEP)
WHAT?
Chief!
UIII (VWEEE)
The Black Rider's just showed up at the lab to retrieve her head...

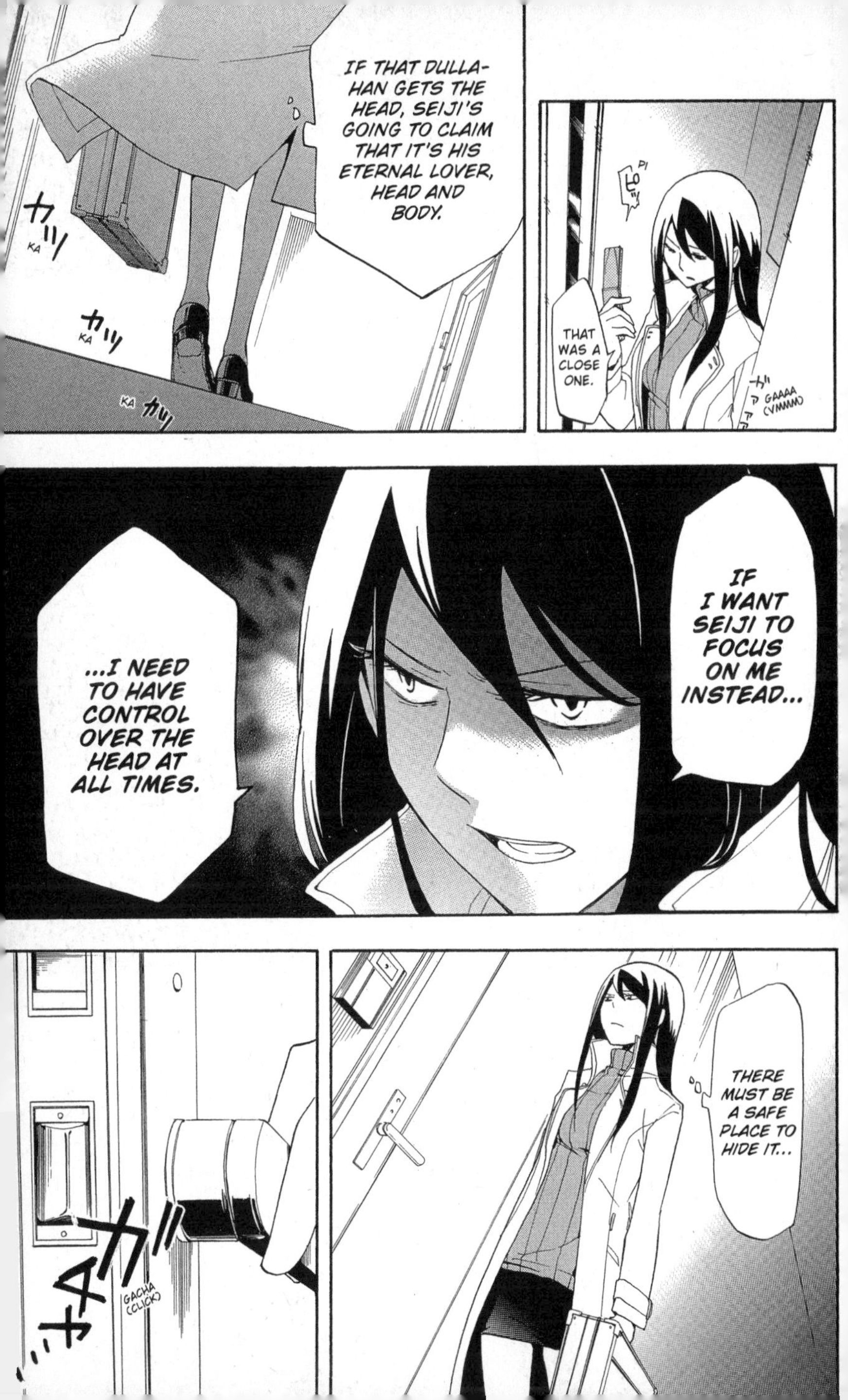
PI
THAT WAS A CLOSE ONE.
GAAAA (VMMM)
IF THAT DULLA-HAN GETS THE HEAD, SEIJI'S GOING TO CLAIM THAT IT'S HIS ETERNAL LOVER, HEAD AND BODY.
KA
KA
KA
IF I WANT SEIJI TO FOCUS ON ME INSTEAD...
...I NEED TO HAVE CONTROL OVER THE HEAD AT ALL TIMES.
THERE MUST BE A SAFE PLACE TO HIDE IT...
GACHA (CLICK)

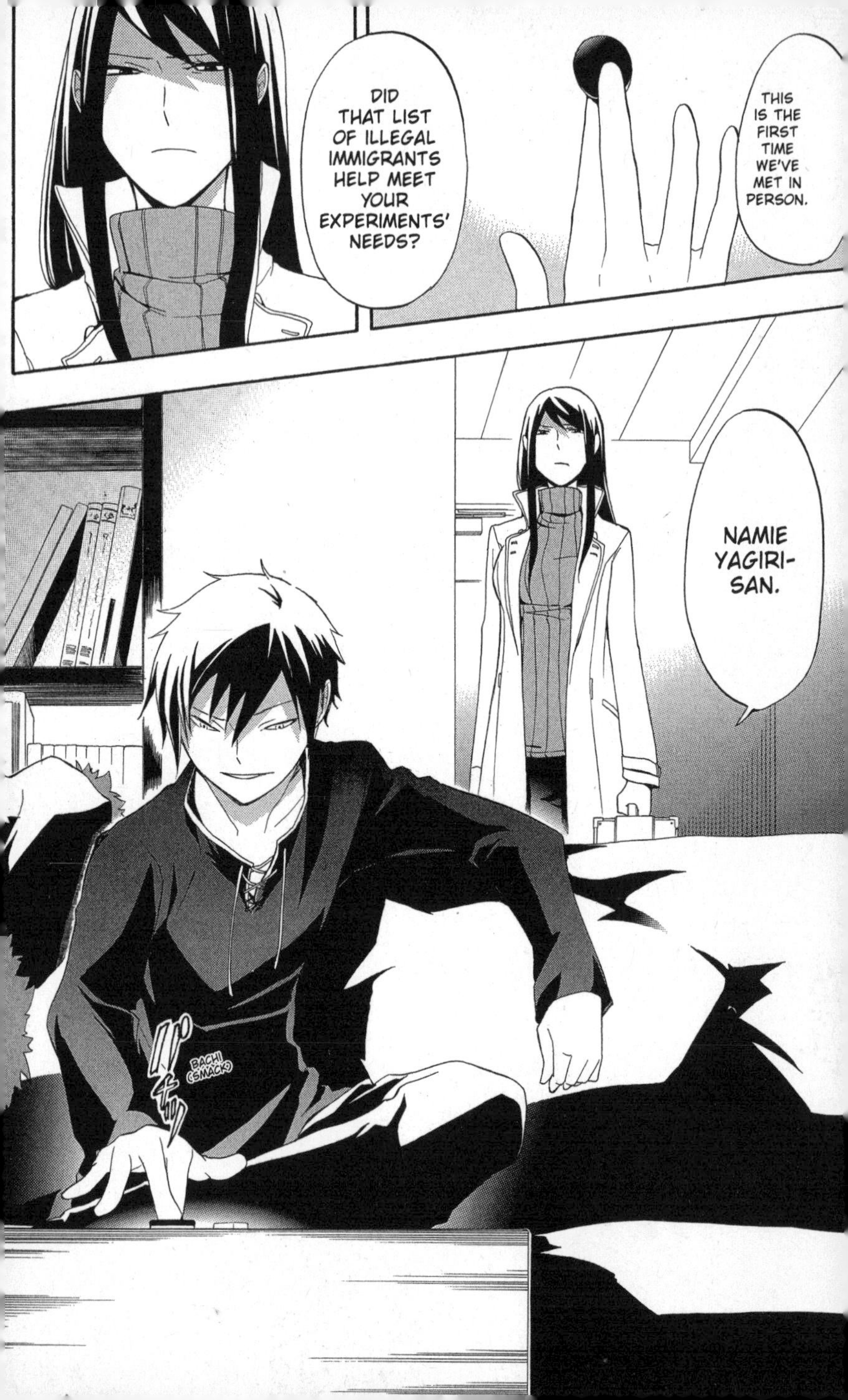
THIS IS THE FIRST TIME WE'VE MET IN PERSON.
DID THAT LIST OF ILLEGAL IMMIGRANTS HELP MEET YOUR EXPERIMENTS' NEEDS?
NAMIE YAGIRI-SAN.
BACHI (SMACK)

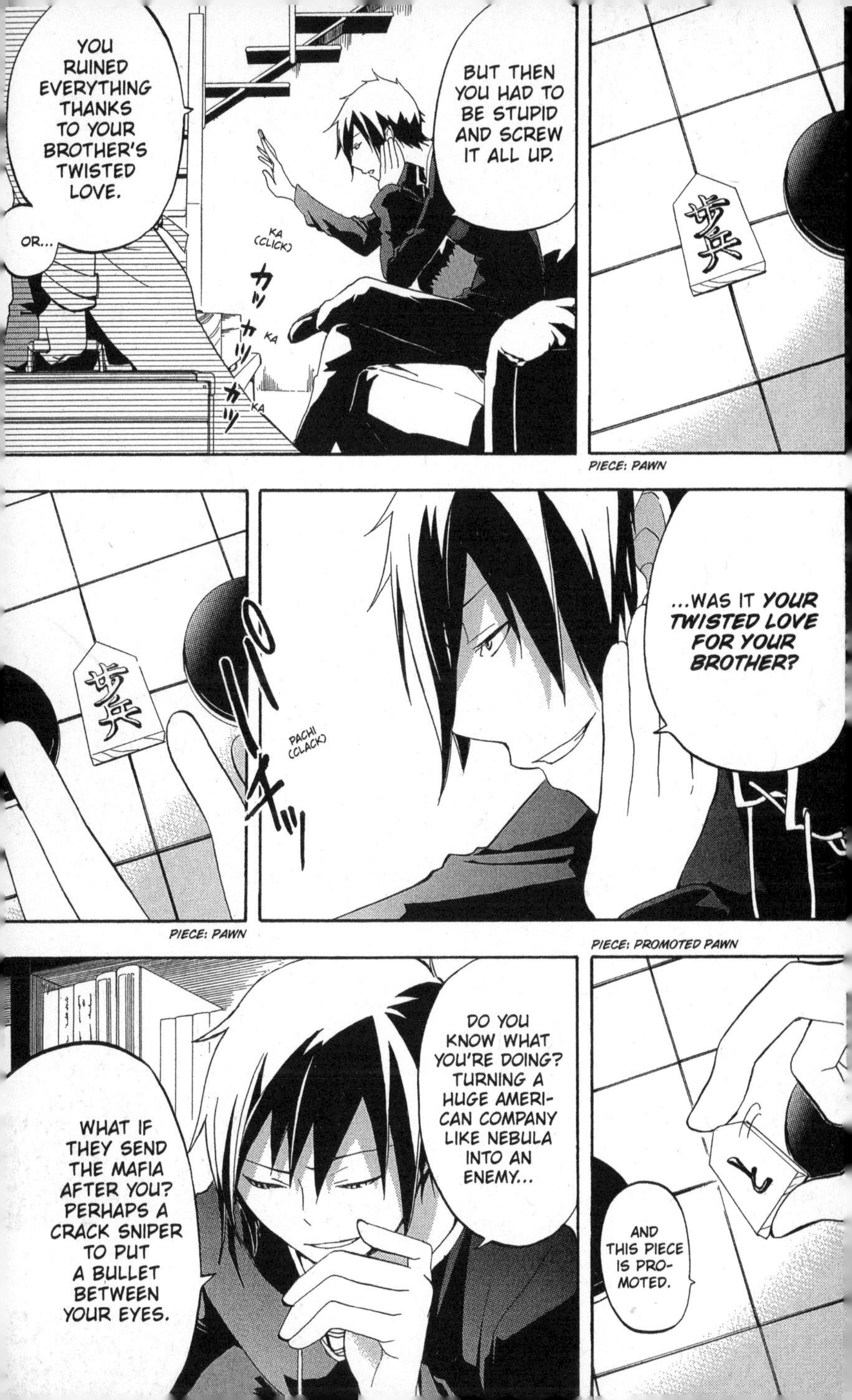
PIECE: PAWN
BUT THEN YOU HAD TO BE STUPID AND SCREW IT ALL UP.
YOU RUINED EVERYTHING THANKS TO YOUR BROTHER'S TWISTED LOVE.
OR...
KA (CLICK)
KA
KA
...WAS IT *YOUR TWISTED LOVE FOR YOUR BROTHER?*
PACHI (CLACK)
PIECE: PAWN
PIECE: PROMOTED PAWN
AND THIS PIECE IS PRO-MOTED.
DO YOU KNOW WHAT YOU'RE DOING? TURNING A HUGE AMERI-CAN COMPANY LIKE NEBULA INTO AN ENEMY...
WHAT IF THEY SEND THE MAFIA AFTER YOU? PERHAPS A CRACK SNIPER TO PUT A BULLET BETWEEN YOUR EYES.

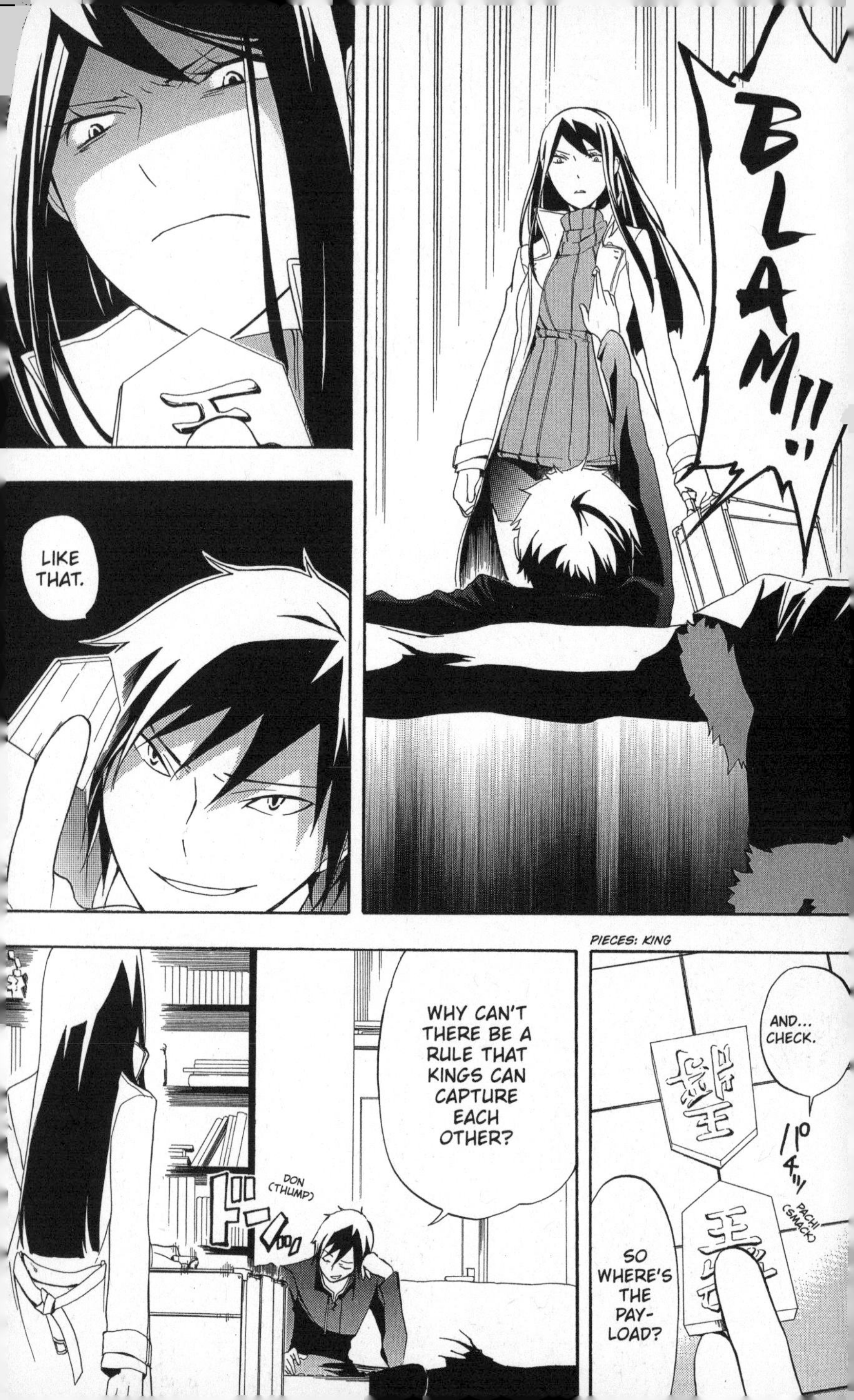
BLAM!!
LIKE THAT.
PIECES: KING
AND... CHECK.
PACHI (SMACK)
SO WHERE'S THE PAY-LOAD?
WHY CAN'T THERE BE A RULE THAT KINGS CAN CAPTURE EACH OTHER?
DON (THUMP)

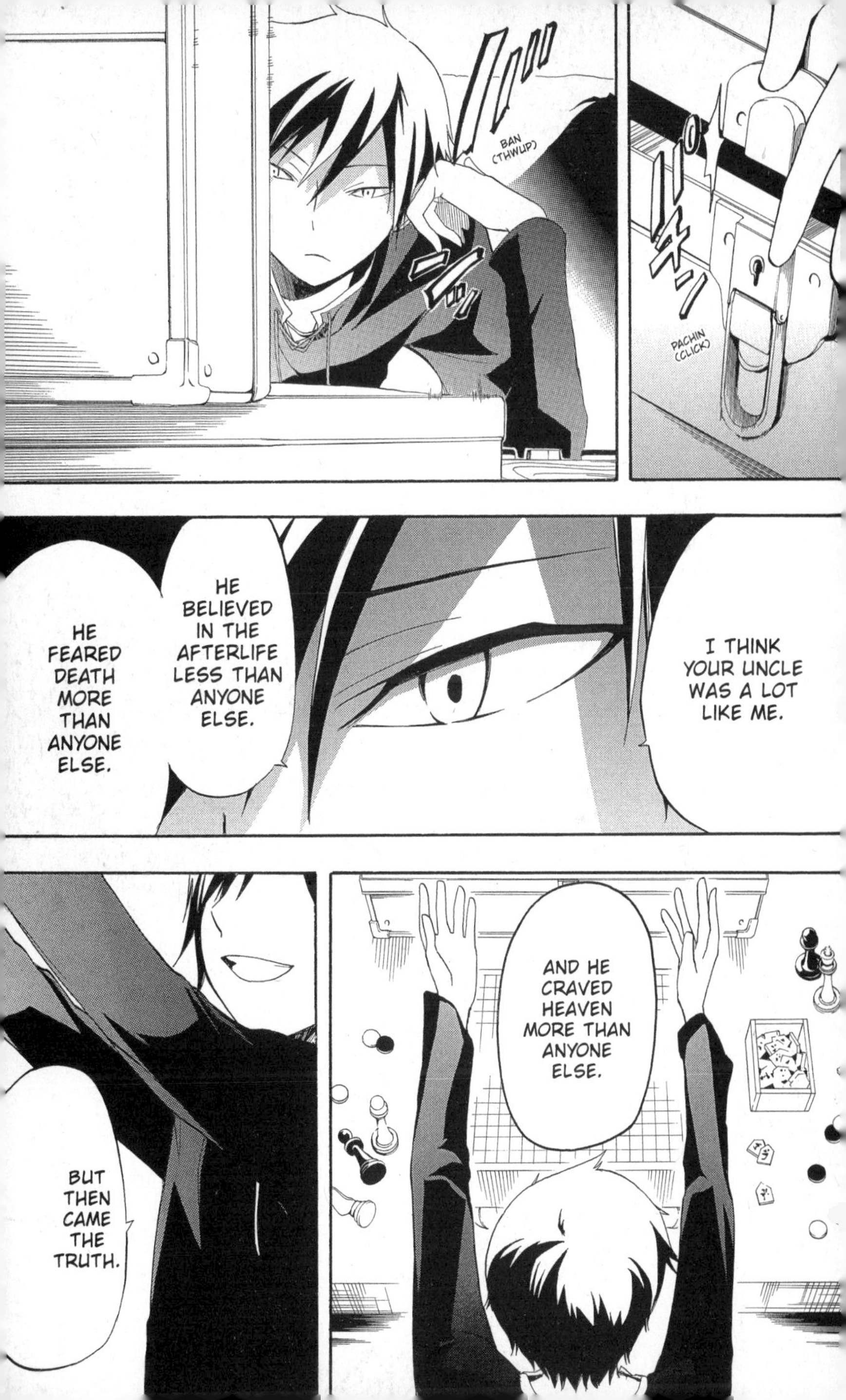
PACHIN (CLICK)
BAN (THWUP)
I THINK YOUR UNCLE WAS A LOT LIKE ME.
HE BELIEVED IN THE AFTERLIFE LESS THAN ANYONE ELSE.
HE FEARED DEATH MORE THAN ANYONE ELSE.
AND HE CRAVED HEAVEN MORE THAN ANYONE ELSE.
BUT THEN CAME THE TRUTH.

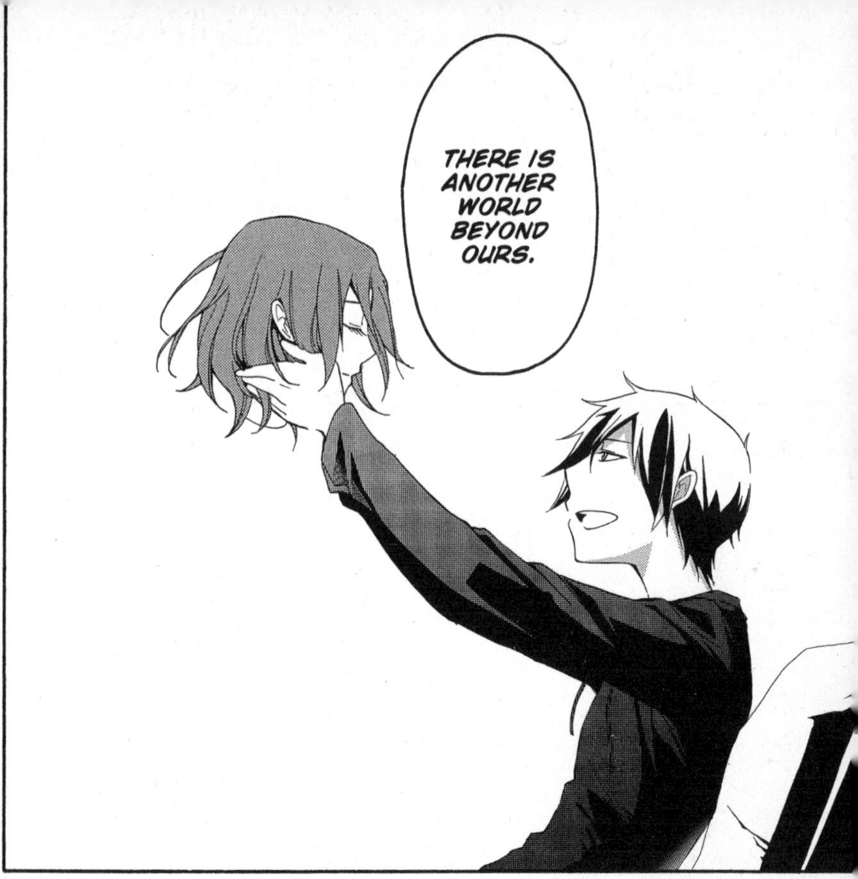
THERE IS ANOTHER WORLD BEYOND OURS.
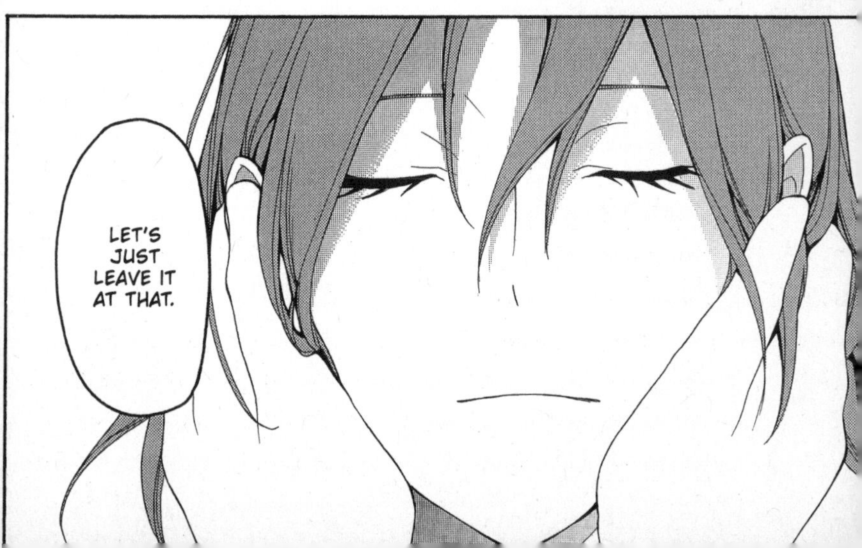
LET'S JUST LEAVE IT AT THAT.

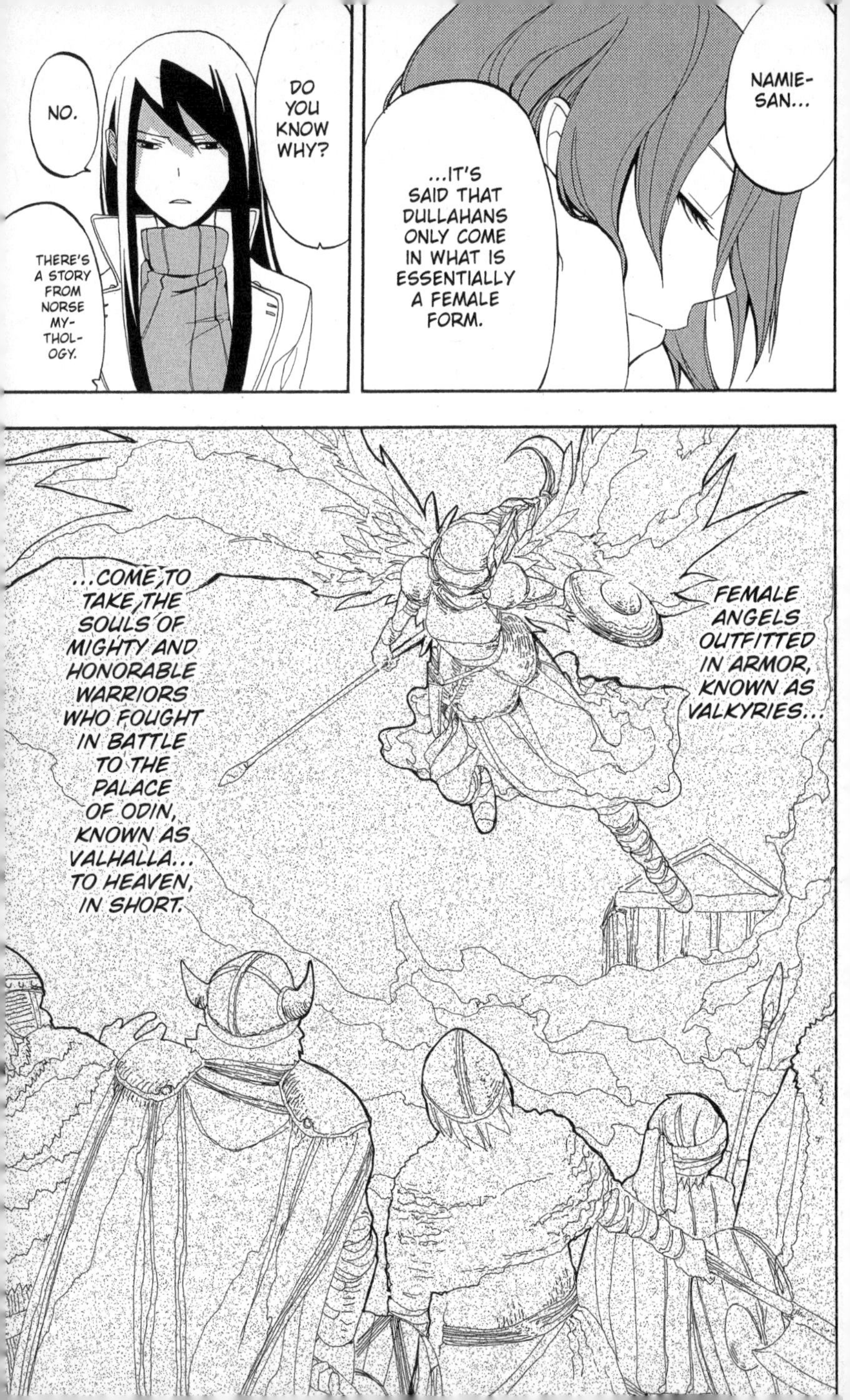
NAMIE-SAN...
...IT'S SAID THAT DULLAHANS ONLY COME IN WHAT IS ESSENTIALLY A FEMALE FORM.
DO YOU KNOW WHY?
NO.
THERE'S A STORY FROM NORSE MYTHOLOGY.
FEMALE ANGELS OUTFITTED IN ARMOR, KNOWN AS VALKYRIES...
...COME TO TAKE THE SOULS OF MIGHTY AND HONORABLE WARRIORS WHO FOUGHT IN BATTLE TO THE PALACE OF ODIN, KNOWN AS VALHALLA... TO HEAVEN, IN SHORT.

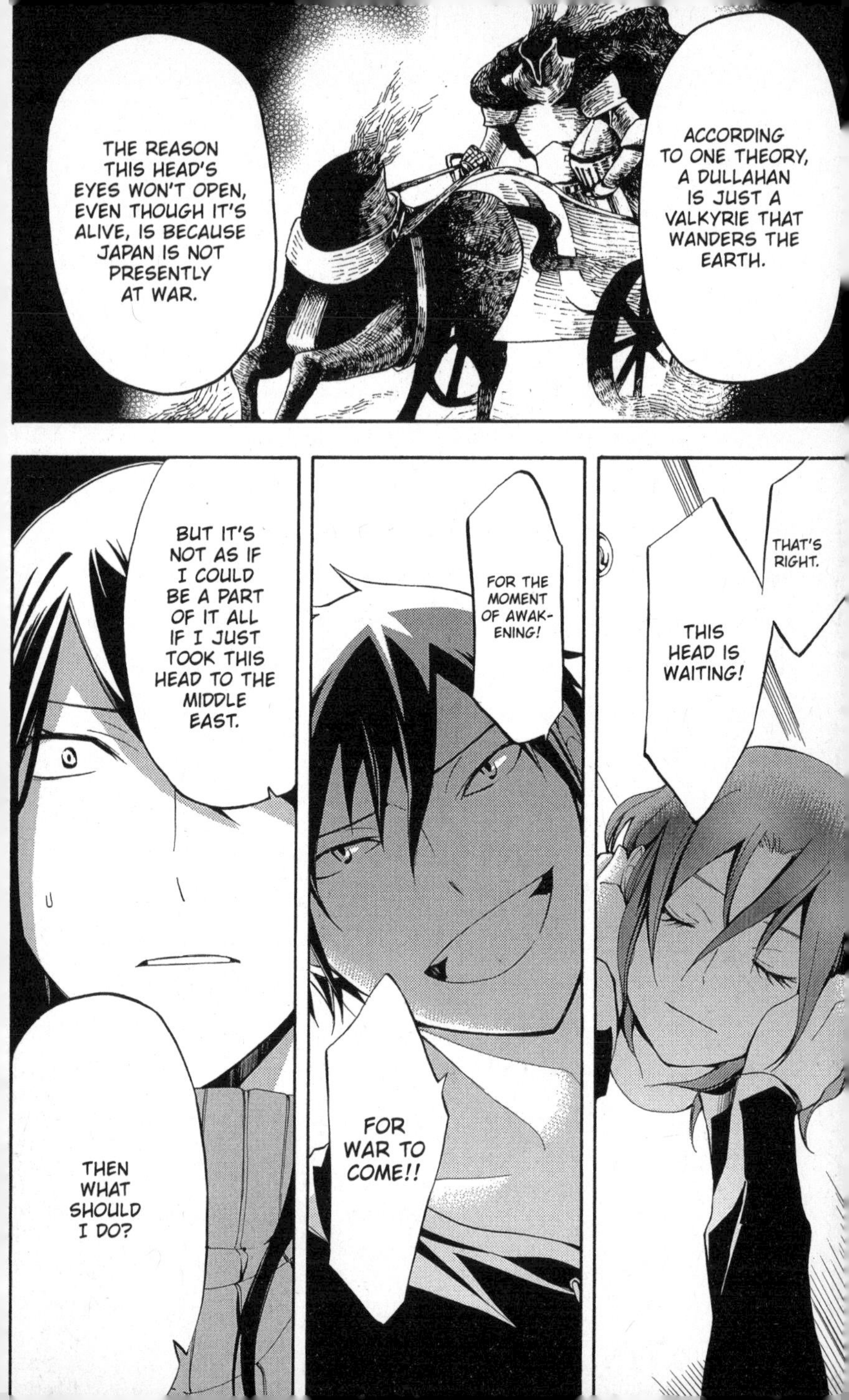
ACCORDING TO ONE THEORY, A DULLAHAN IS JUST A VALKYRIE THAT WANDERS THE EARTH.
THE REASON THIS HEAD'S EYES WON'T OPEN, EVEN THOUGH IT'S ALIVE, IS BECAUSE JAPAN IS NOT PRESENTLY AT WAR.
THAT'S RIGHT.
THIS HEAD IS WAITING!
FOR THE MOMENT OF AWAKENING!
FOR WAR TO COME!!
BUT IT'S NOT AS IF I COULD BE A PART OF IT ALL IF I JUST TOOK THIS HEAD TO THE MIDDLE EAST.
THEN WHAT SHOULD I DO?

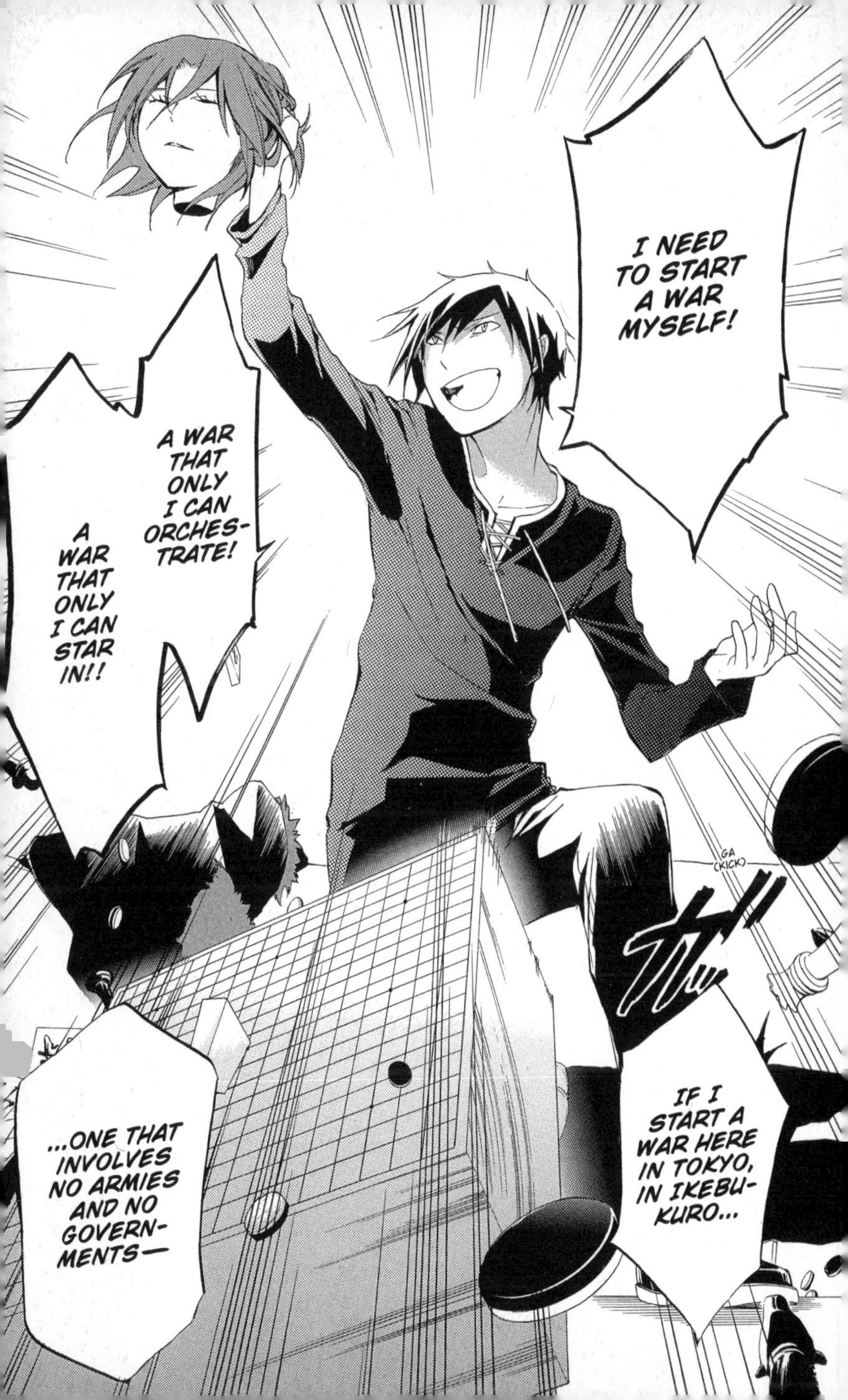
I NEED TO START A WAR MYSELF!
A WAR THAT ONLY I CAN ORCHES-TRATE!
A WAR THAT ONLY I CAN STAR IN!!
GA (KICK)
IF I START A WAR HERE IN TOKYO, IN IKEBU-KURO...
...ONE THAT INVOLVES NO ARMIES AND NO GOVERN-MENTS—

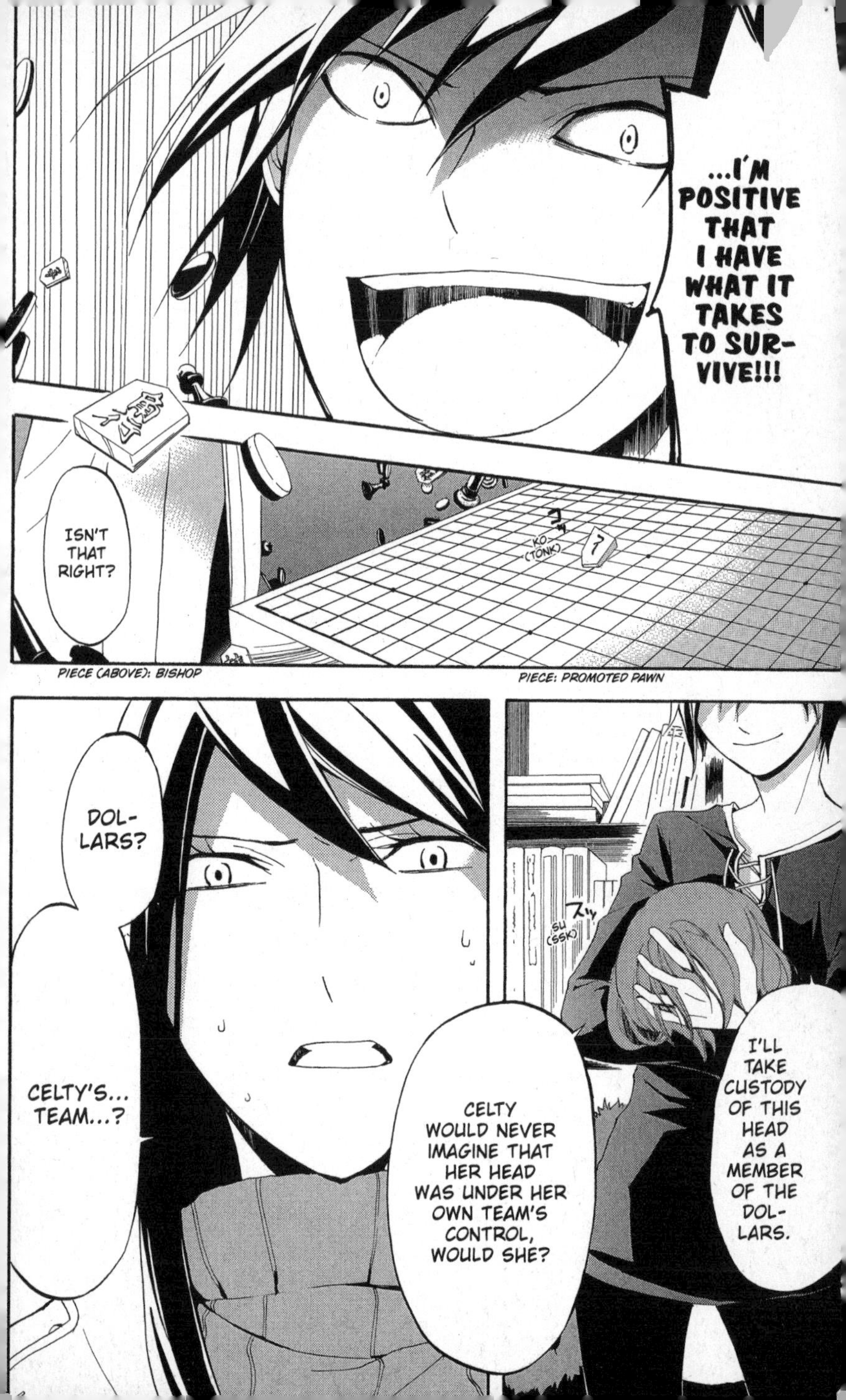
...I'M POSITIVE THAT I HAVE WHAT IT TAKES TO SUR-VIVE!!!
ISN'T THAT RIGHT?
KO (TONK)
PIECE (ABOVE): BISHOP
PIECE: PROMOTED PAWN
SU (SSK)
I'LL TAKE CUSTODY OF THIS HEAD AS A MEMBER OF THE DOL-LARS.
DOL-LARS?
CELTY'S... TEAM...?
CELTY WOULD NEVER IMAGINE THAT HER HEAD WAS UNDER HER OWN TEAM'S CONTROL, WOULD SHE?

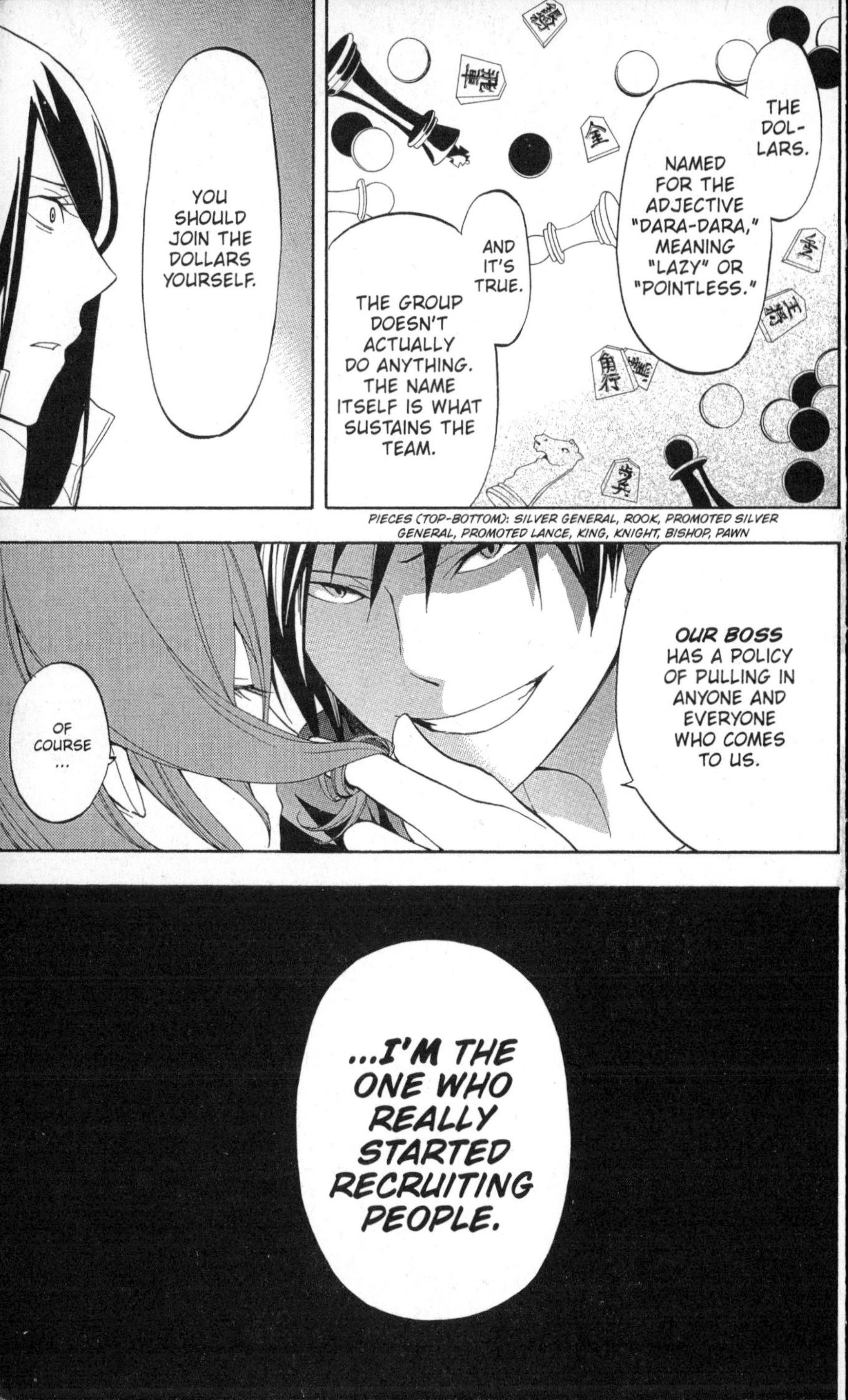
THE DOLLARS.
NAMED FOR THE ADJECTIVE "DARA-DARA," MEANING "LAZY" OR "POINTLESS."
AND IT'S TRUE.
THE GROUP DOESN'T ACTUALLY DO ANYTHING. THE NAME ITSELF IS WHAT SUSTAINS THE TEAM.
YOU SHOULD JOIN THE DOLLARS YOURSELF.
PIECES (TOP-BOTTOM): SILVER GENERAL, ROOK, PROMOTED SILVER GENERAL, PROMOTED LANCE, KING, KNIGHT, BISHOP, PAWN
OUR BOSS HAS A POLICY OF PULLING IN ANYONE AND EVERYONE WHO COMES TO US.
OF COURSE...
...I'M THE ONE WHO REALLY STARTED RECRUITING PEOPLE.

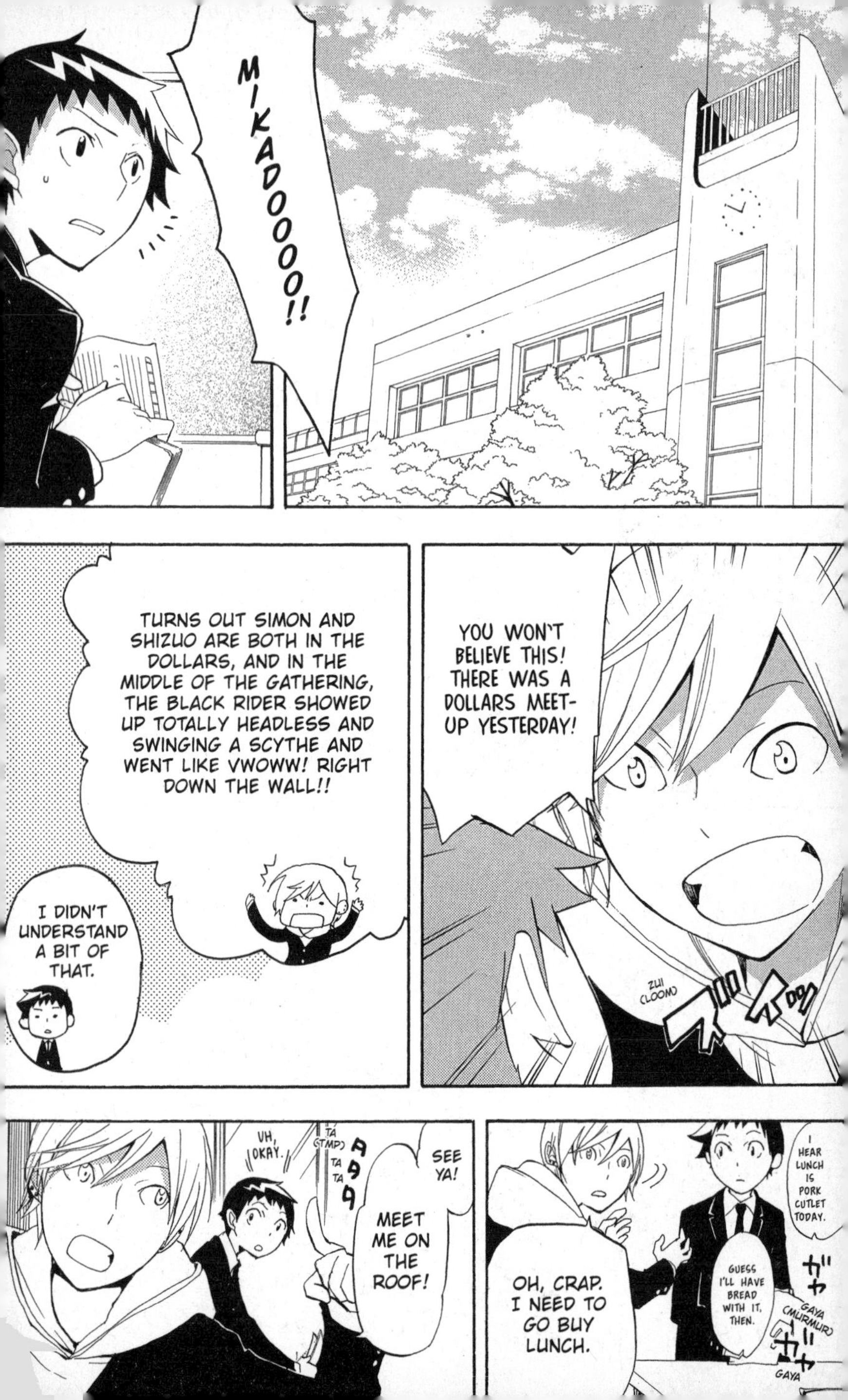
MIKADOOOOO!!
YOU WON'T BELIEVE THIS! THERE WAS A DOLLARS MEET-UP YESTERDAY!
ZUI (LOOM)
TURNS OUT SIMON AND SHIZUO ARE BOTH IN THE DOLLARS, AND IN THE MIDDLE OF THE GATHERING, THE BLACK RIDER SHOWED UP TOTALLY HEADLESS AND SWINGING A SCYTHE AND WENT LIKE VWOWW! RIGHT DOWN THE WALL!!
I DIDN'T UNDERSTAND A BIT OF THAT.
I HEAR LUNCH IS PORK CUTLET TODAY.
GUESS I'LL HAVE BREAD WITH IT, THEN.
OH, CRAP. I NEED TO GO BUY LUNCH.
GAYA (MURMUR) GAYA
SEE YA!
MEET ME ON THE ROOF!
TA (TMP) TA TA
UH, OKAY.

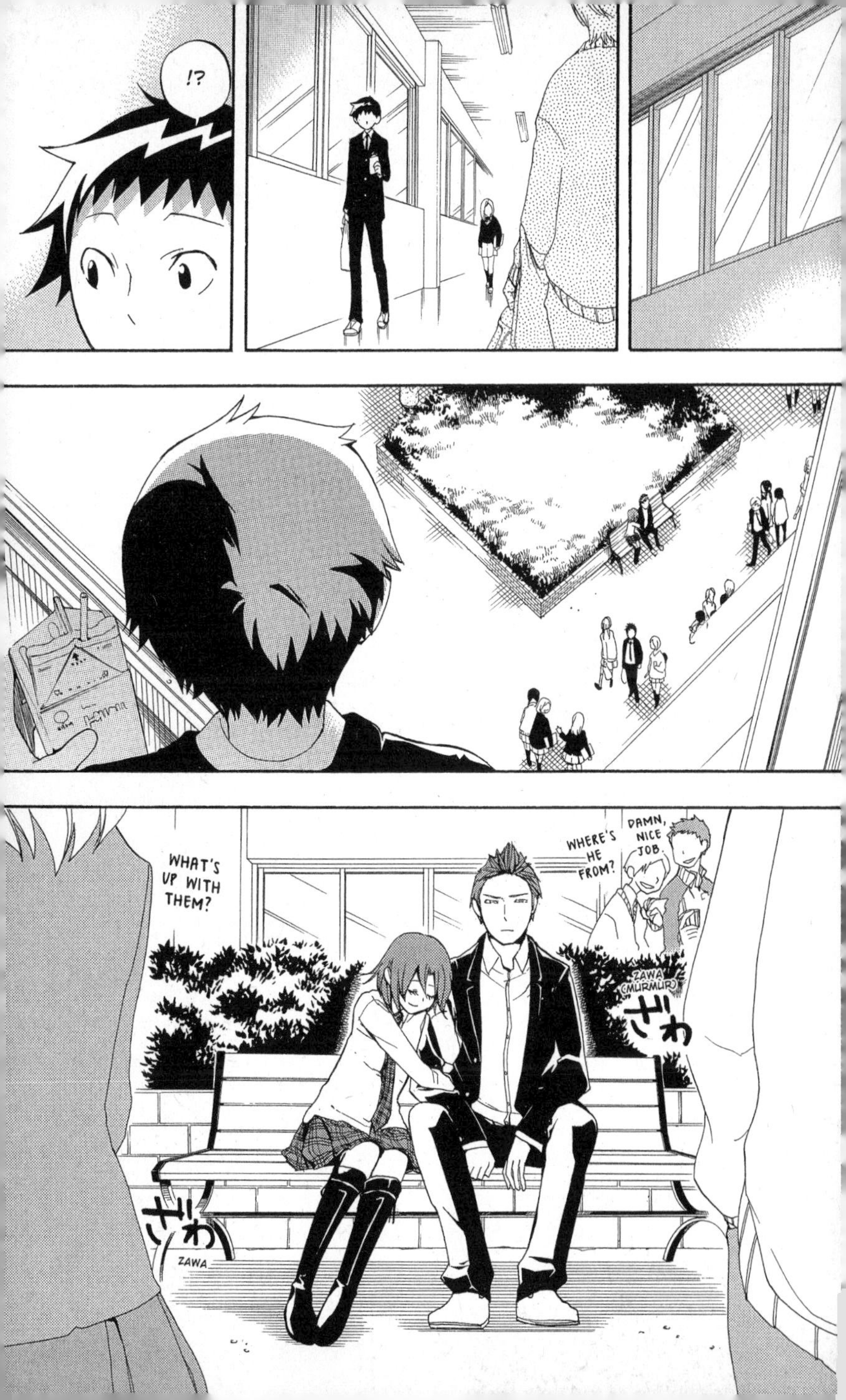
!?
DAMN, NICE JOB.
WHERE'S HE FROM?
ZAWA (MURMUR)
ざわ
WHAT'S UP WITH THEM?
ざわ
ZAWA

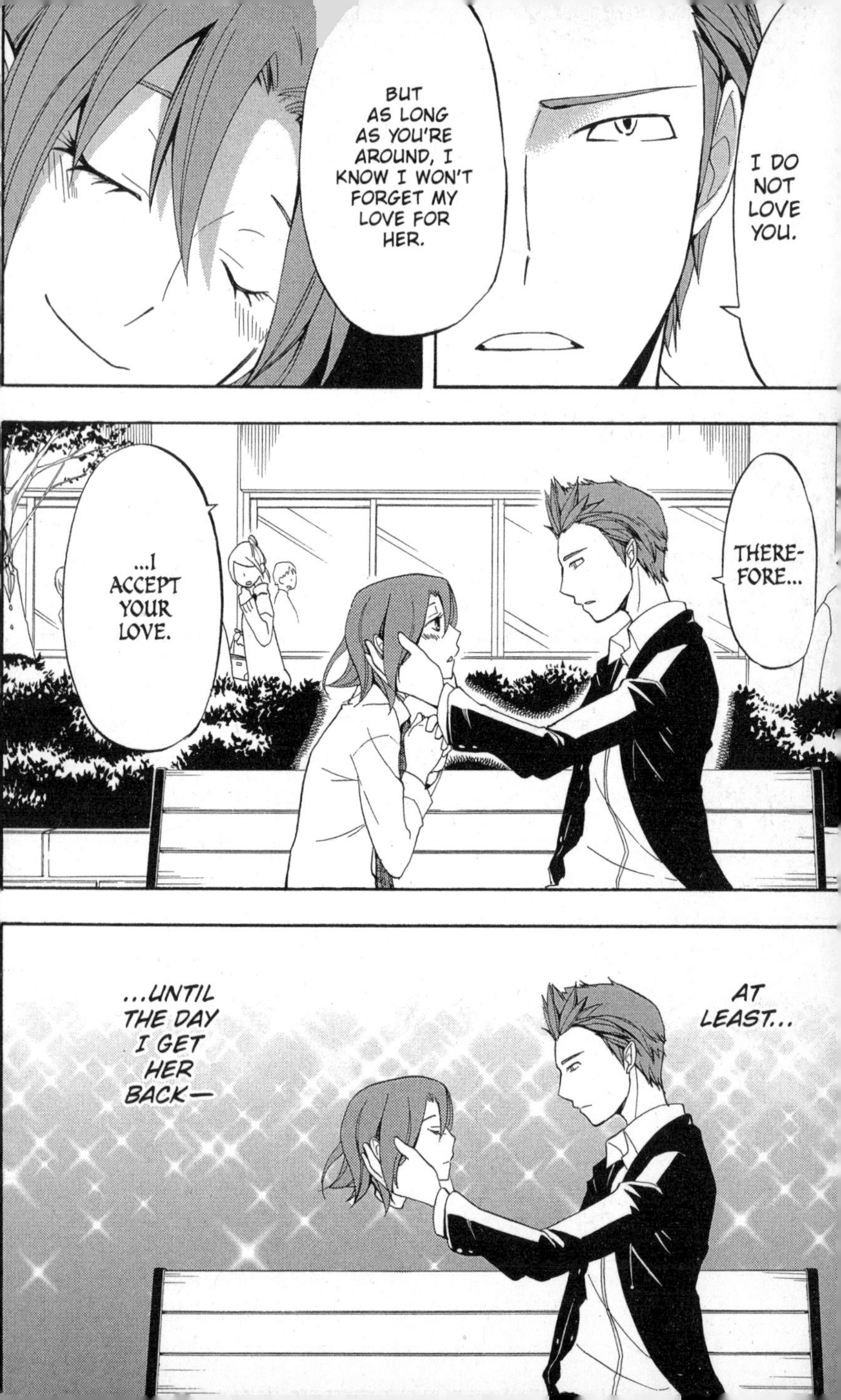
I DO NOT LOVE YOU.
BUT AS LONG AS YOU'RE AROUND, I KNOW I WON'T FORGET MY LOVE FOR HER.
THEREFORE...
...I ACCEPT YOUR LOVE.
AT LEAST...
...UNTIL THE DAY I GET HER BACK—

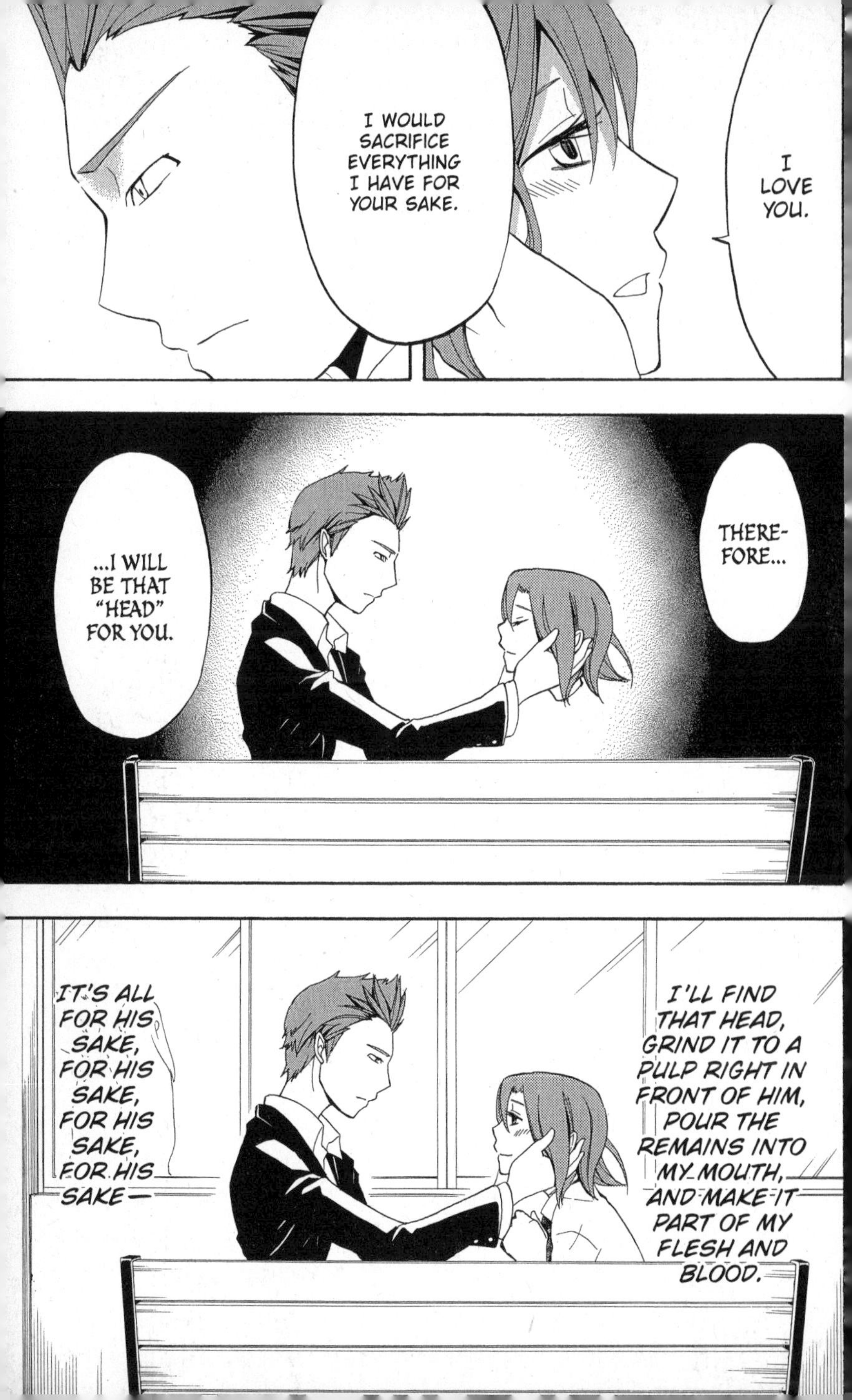
I LOVE YOU.
I WOULD SACRIFICE EVERYTHING I HAVE FOR YOUR SAKE.
THEREFORE...
...I WILL BE THAT "HEAD" FOR YOU.
I'LL FIND THAT HEAD, GRIND IT TO A PULP RIGHT IN FRONT OF HIM, POUR THE REMAINS INTO MY MOUTH, AND MAKE IT PART OF MY FLESH AND BLOOD.
IT'S ALL FOR HIS SAKE, FOR HIS SAKE, FOR HIS SAKE, FOR HIS SAKE—

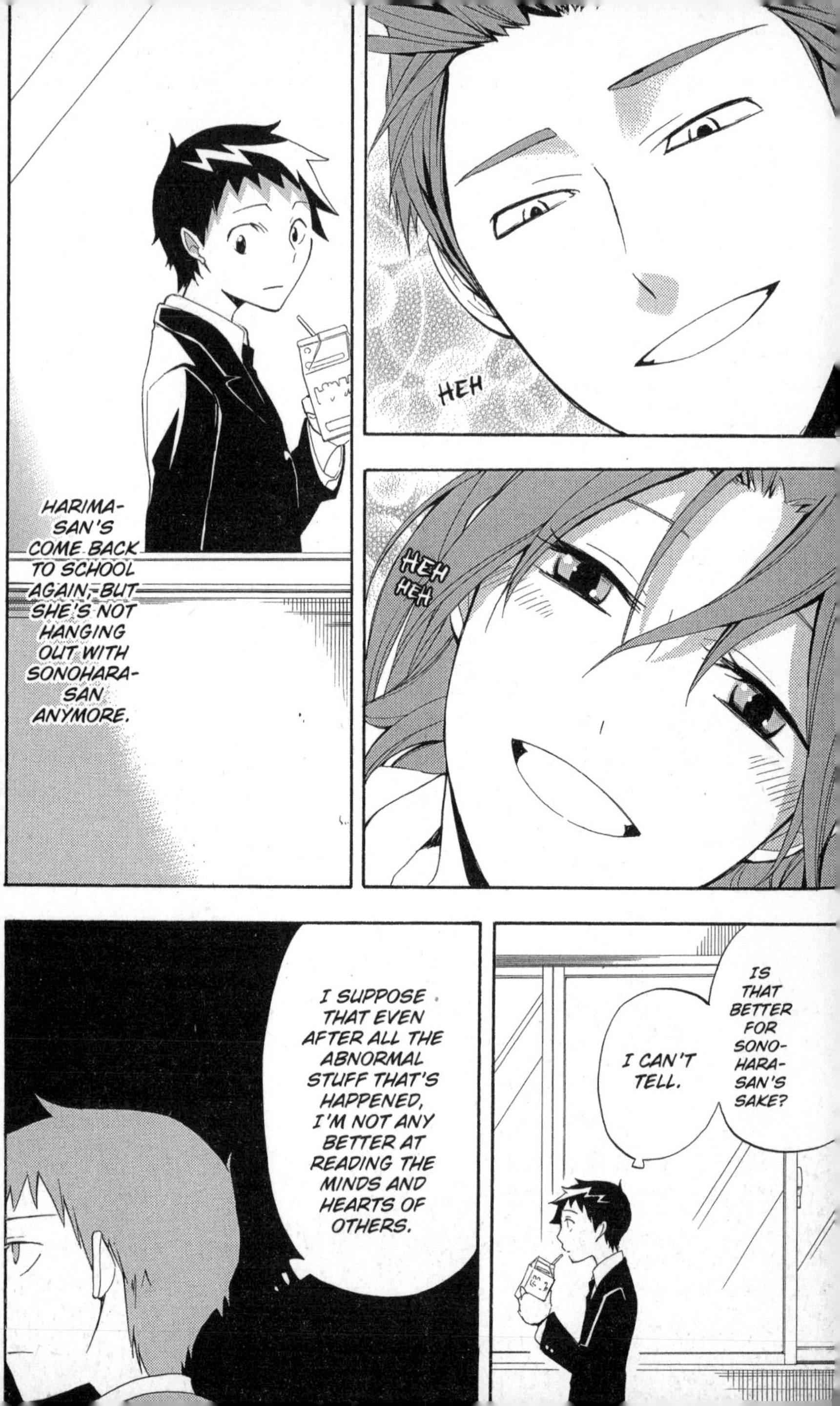
HEH
HEH HEH
HARIMA-SAN'S COME BACK TO SCHOOL AGAIN, BUT SHE'S NOT HANGING OUT WITH SONOHARA-SAN ANYMORE.
IS THAT BETTER FOR SONOHARA-SAN'S SAKE?
I CAN'T TELL.
I SUPPOSE THAT EVEN AFTER ALL THE ABNORMAL STUFF THAT'S HAPPENED, I'M NOT ANY BETTER AT READING THE MINDS AND HEARTS OF OTHERS.

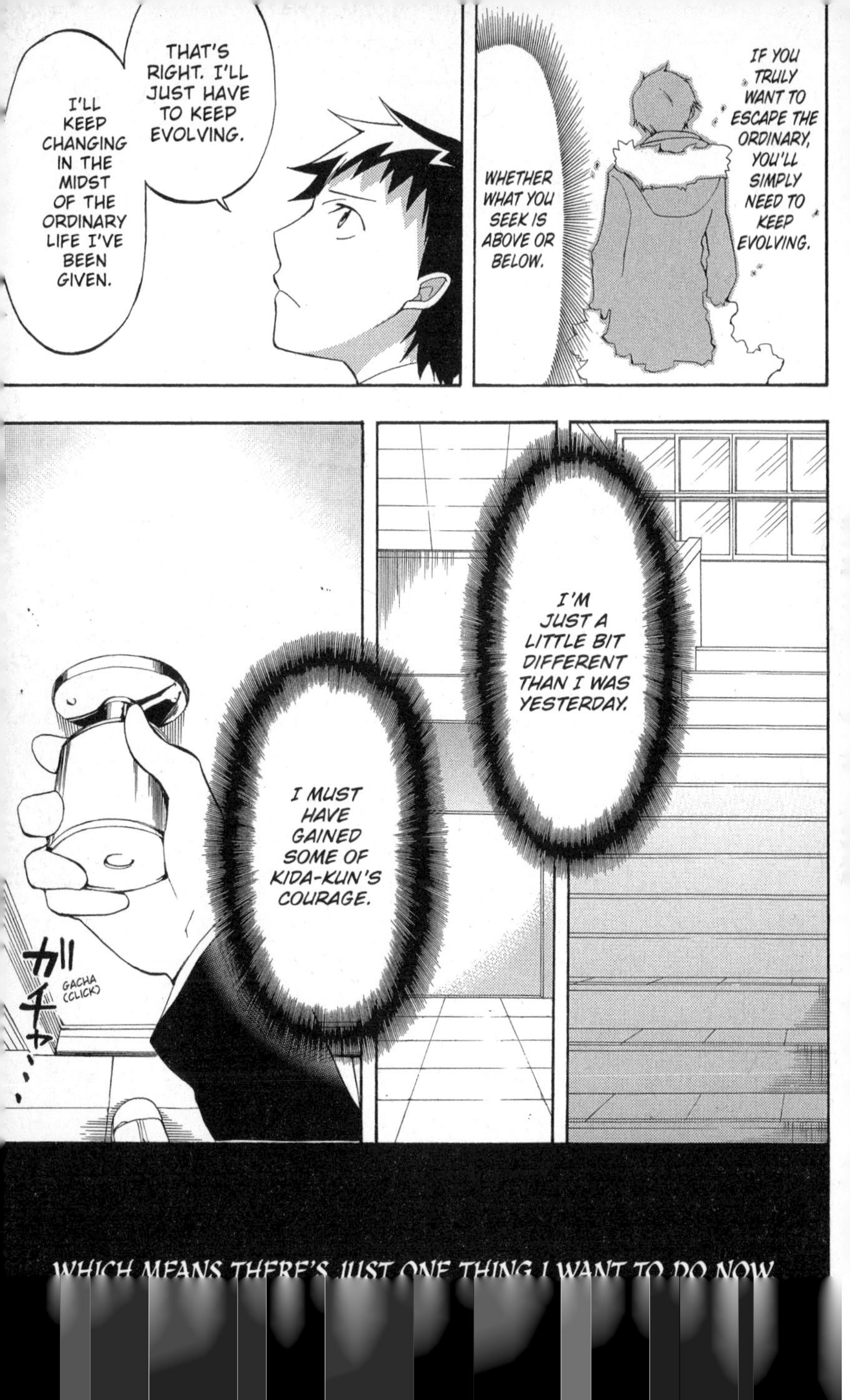
IF YOU TRULY WANT TO ESCAPE THE ORDINARY, YOU'LL SIMPLY NEED TO KEEP EVOLVING.
WHETHER WHAT YOU SEEK IS ABOVE OR BELOW.
THAT'S RIGHT. I'LL JUST HAVE TO KEEP EVOLVING.
I'LL KEEP CHANGING IN THE MIDST OF THE ORDINARY LIFE I'VE BEEN GIVEN.
I'M JUST A LITTLE BIT DIFFERENT THAN I WAS YESTERDAY.
I MUST HAVE GAINED SOME OF KIDA-KUN'S COURAGE.
カチャ
GACHA (CLICK)
WHICH MEANS THERE'S JUST ONE THING I WANT TO DO NOW

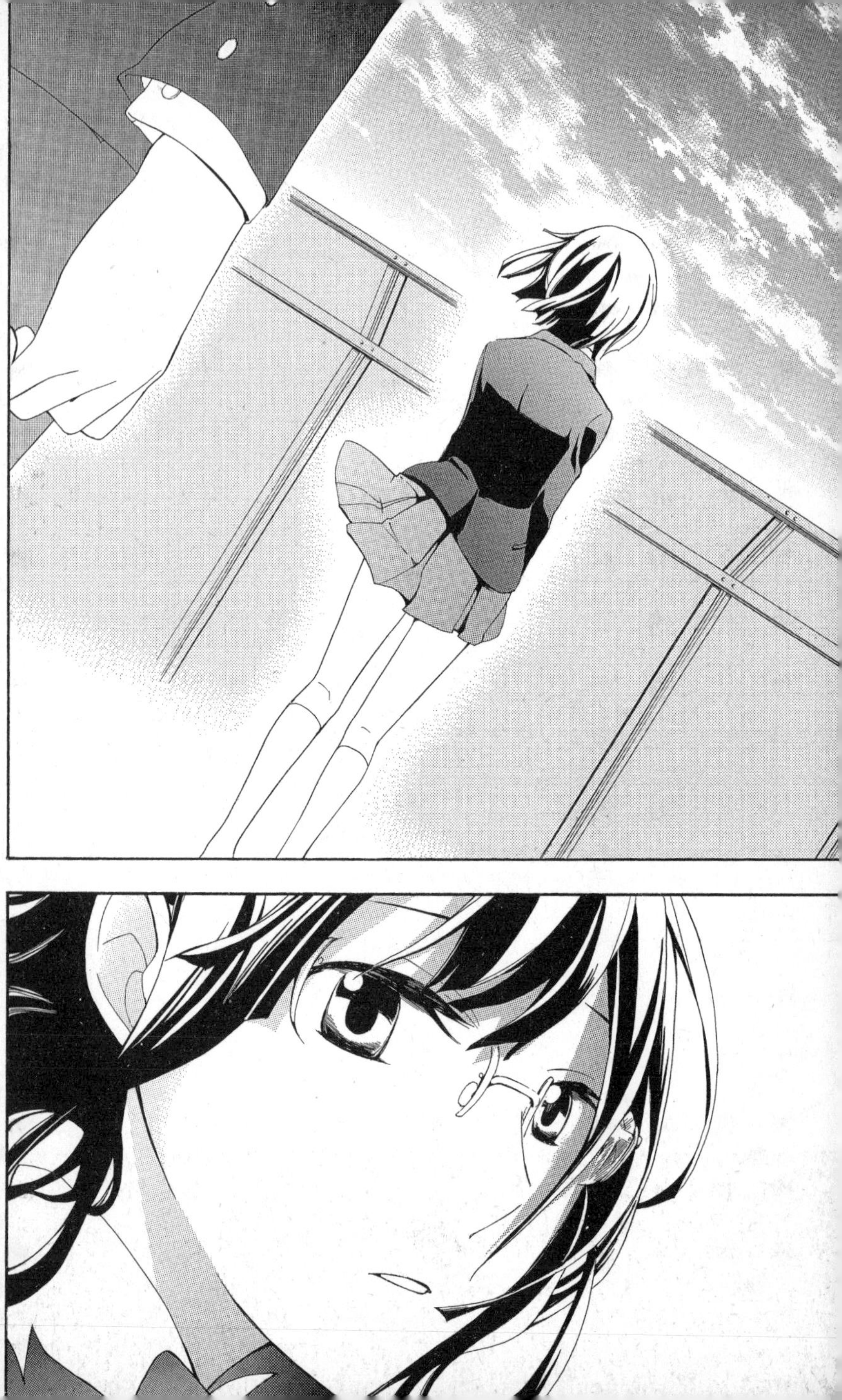

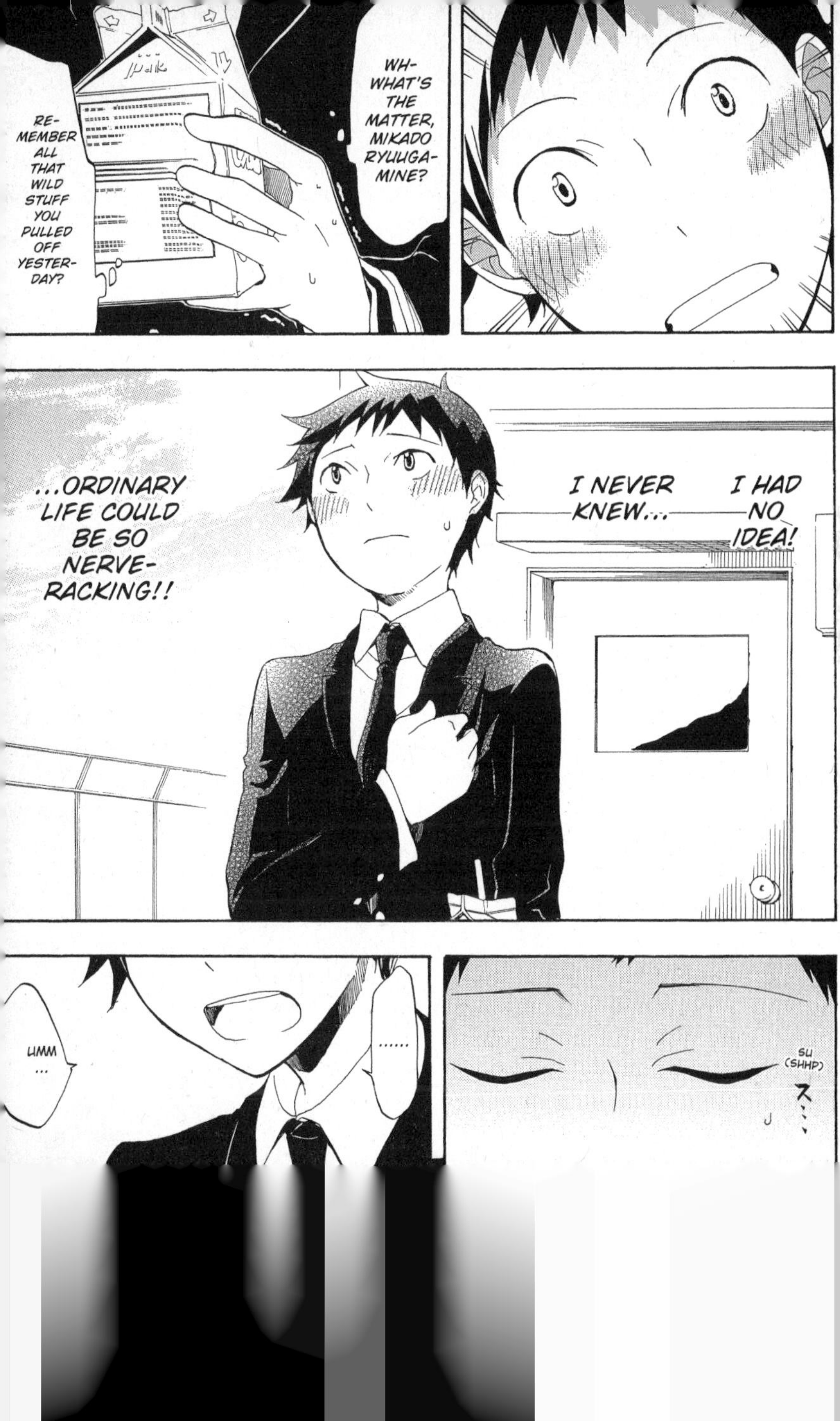
WH- WHAT'S THE MATTER, MIKADO RYUUGAMINE?
RE- MEMBER ALL THAT WILD STUFF YOU PULLED OFF YESTER- DAY?
I HAD NO IDEA!
I NEVER KNEW...
...ORDINARY LIFE COULD BE SO NERVE- RACKING!!
SU (SHHP)
ス・・・
......
UMM ...

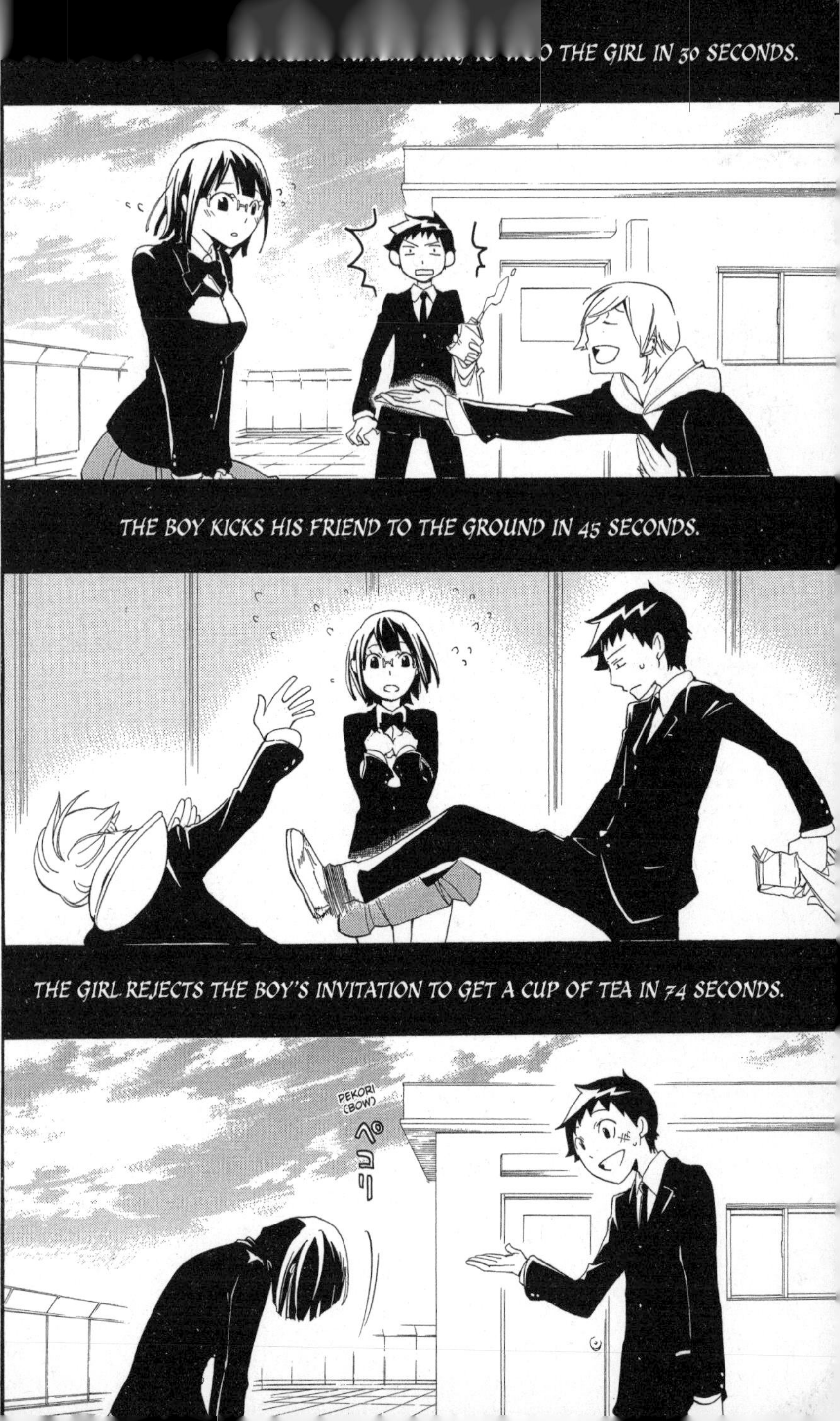
THE GIRL IN 30 SECONDS.
THE BOY KICKS HIS FRIEND TO THE GROUND IN 45 SECONDS.
THE GIRL REJECTS THE BOY'S INVITATION TO GET A CUP OF TEA IN 74 SECONDS.
PEKORI (BOW)
ペコリ

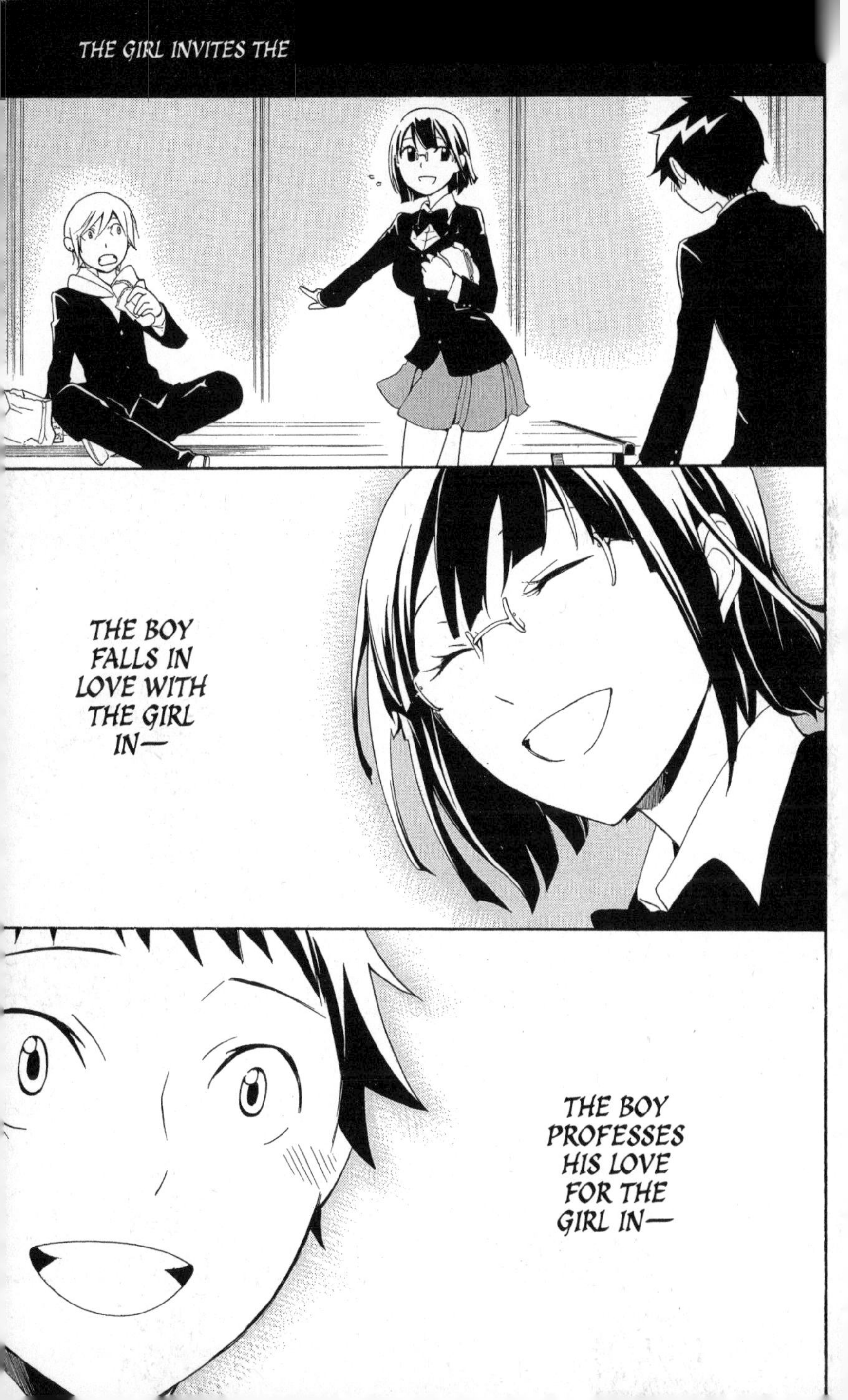
THE GIRL INVITES THE
THE BOY FALLS IN LOVE WITH THE GIRL IN—
THE BOY PROFESSES HIS LOVE FOR THE GIRL IN—

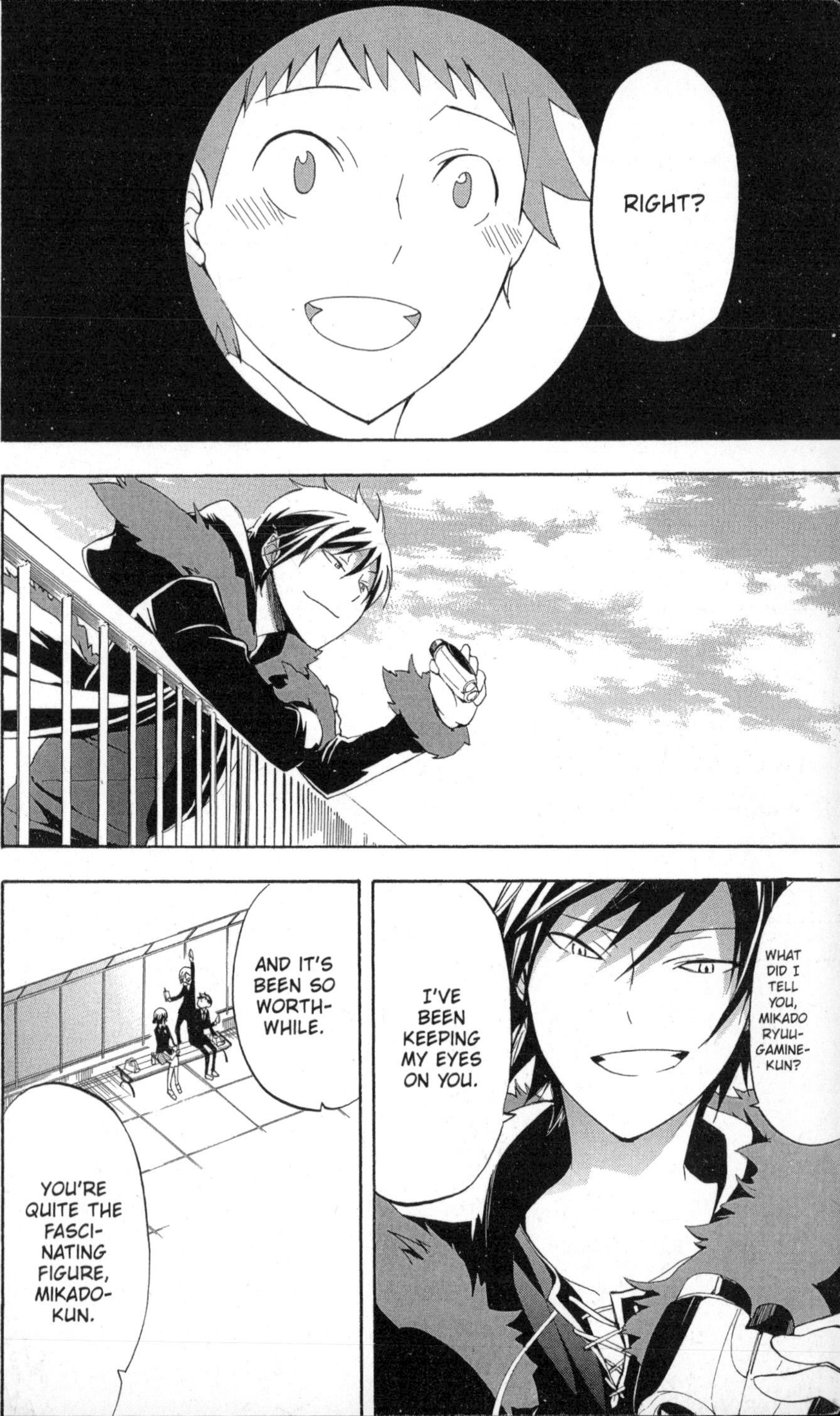
RIGHT?
WHAT DID I TELL YOU, MIKADO RYUU-GAMINE-KUN?
I'VE BEEN KEEPING MY EYES ON YOU.
AND IT'S BEEN SO WORTH-WHILE.
YOU'RE QUITE THE FASCI-NATING FIGURE, MIKADO-KUN.

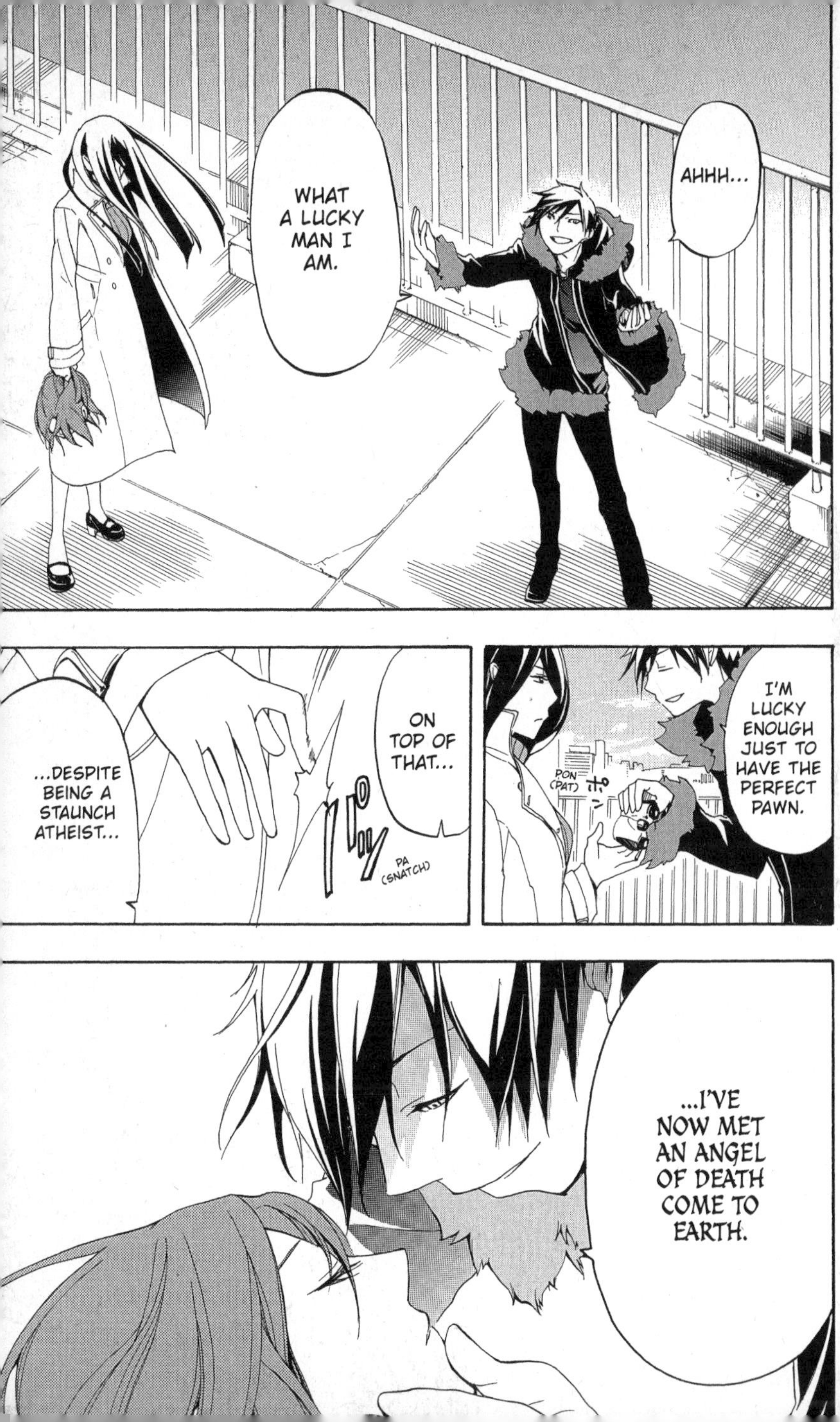
AHHH...
WHAT A LUCKY MAN I AM.
I'M LUCKY ENOUGH JUST TO HAVE THE PERFECT PAWN.
PON (PAT)
ON TOP OF THAT...
PA (SNATCH)
...DESPITE BEING A STAUNCH ATHEIST...
...I'VE NOW MET AN ANGEL OF DEATH COME TO EARTH.

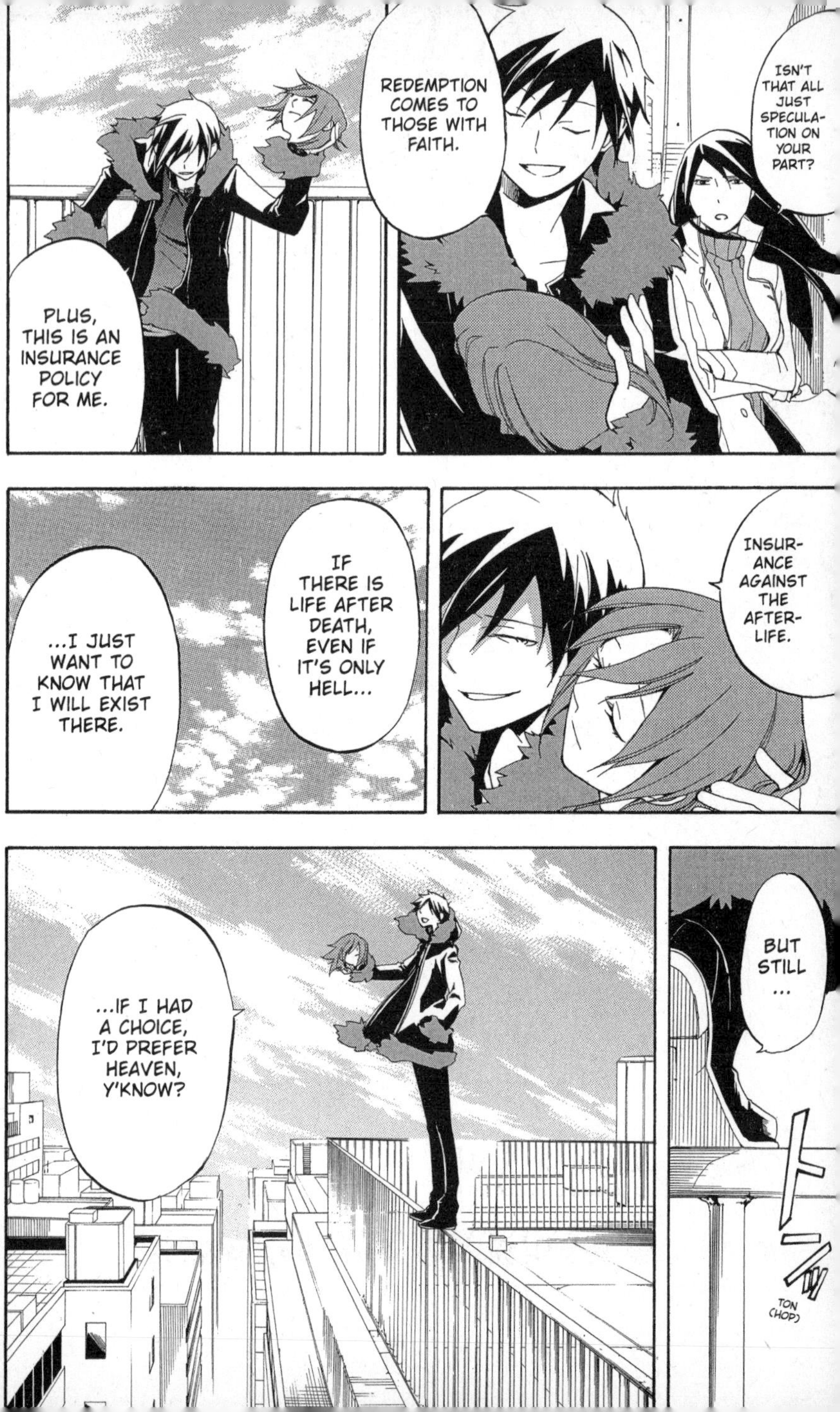
ISN'T THAT ALL JUST SPECULATION ON YOUR PART?
REDEMPTION COMES TO THOSE WITH FAITH.
PLUS, THIS IS AN INSURANCE POLICY FOR ME.
INSURANCE AGAINST THE AFTERLIFE.
IF THERE IS LIFE AFTER DEATH, EVEN IF IT'S ONLY HELL...
...I JUST WANT TO KNOW THAT I WILL EXIST THERE.
BUT STILL ...
TON (HOP)
...IF I HAD A CHOICE, I'D PREFER HEAVEN, Y'KNOW?

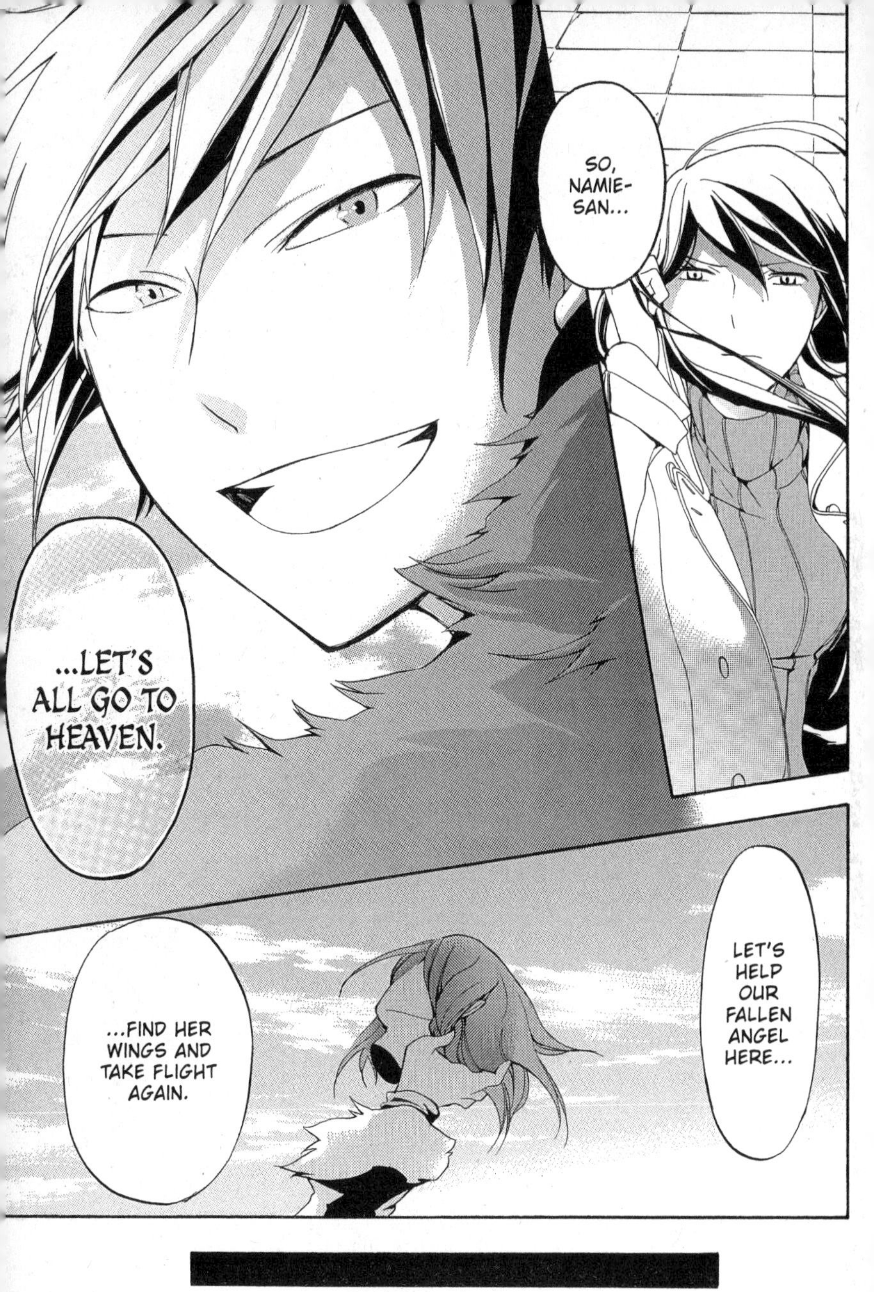
SO, NAMIE-SAN...
...LET'S ALL GO TO HEAVEN.
LET'S HELP OUR FALLEN ANGEL HERE...
...FIND HER WINGS AND TAKE FLIGHT AGAIN.

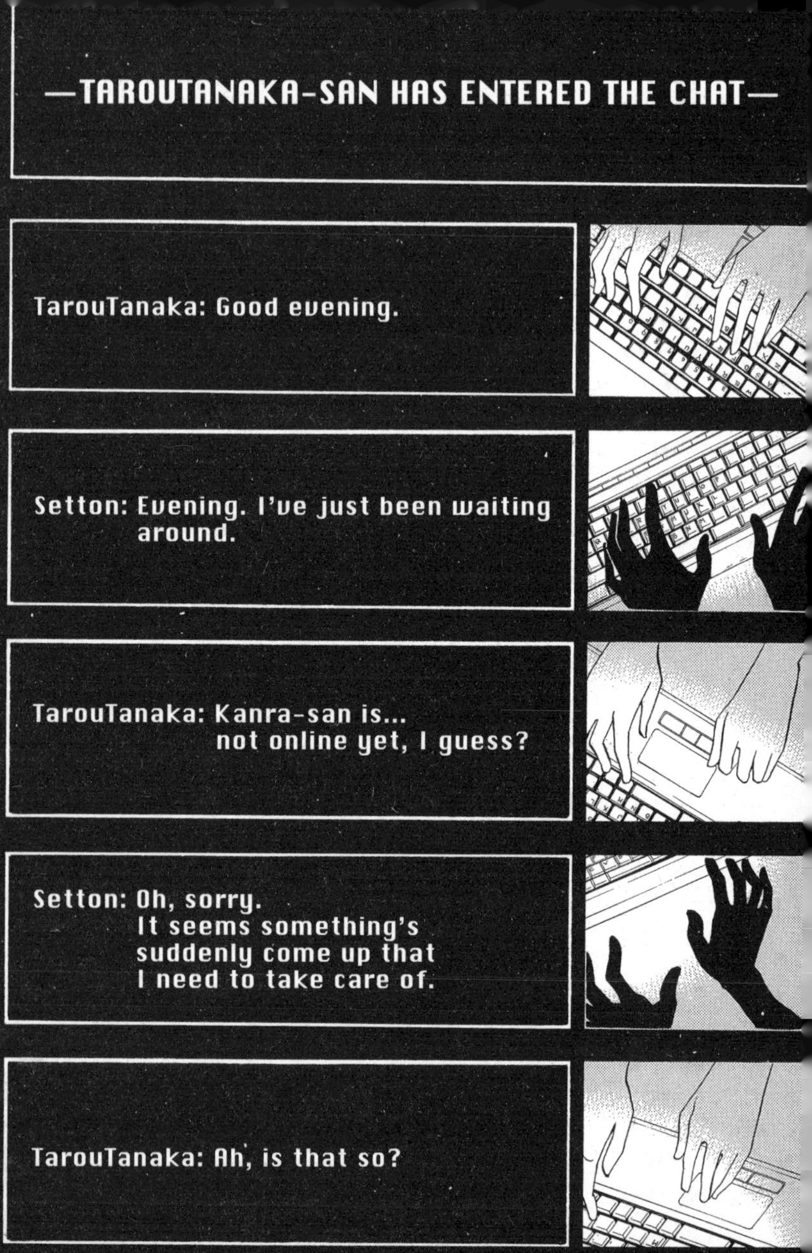
—TAROUTANAKA-SAN HAS ENTERED THE CHAT—
TarouTanaka: Good evening.
Setton: Evening. I've just been waiting around.
TarouTanaka: Kanra-san is... not online yet, I guess?
Setton: Oh, sorry. It seems something's suddenly come up that I need to take care of.
TarouTanaka: Ah, is that so?

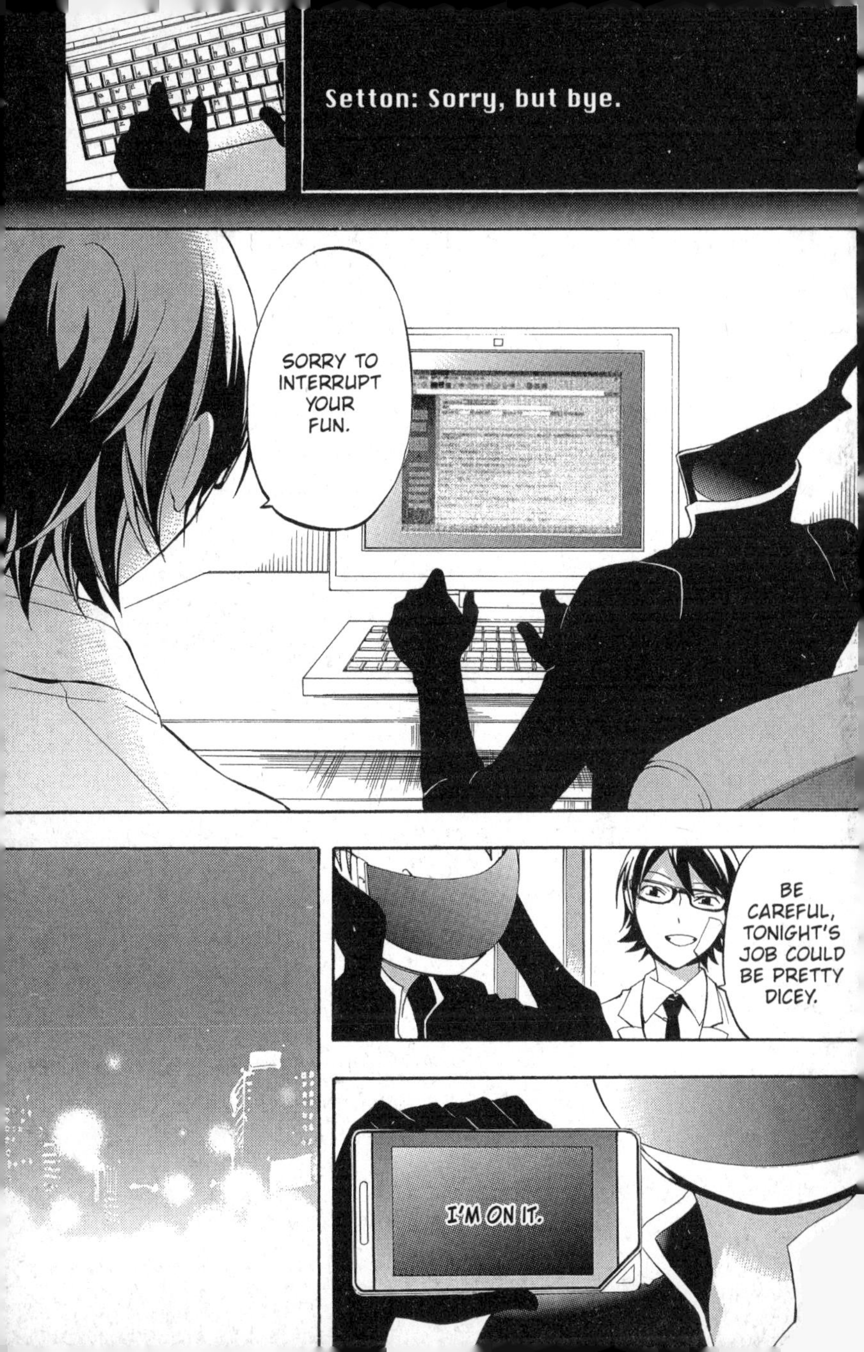
Setton: Sorry, but bye.
SORRY TO INTERRUPT YOUR FUN.
BE CAREFUL, TONIGHT'S JOB COULD BE PRETTY DICEY.
I'M ON IT.

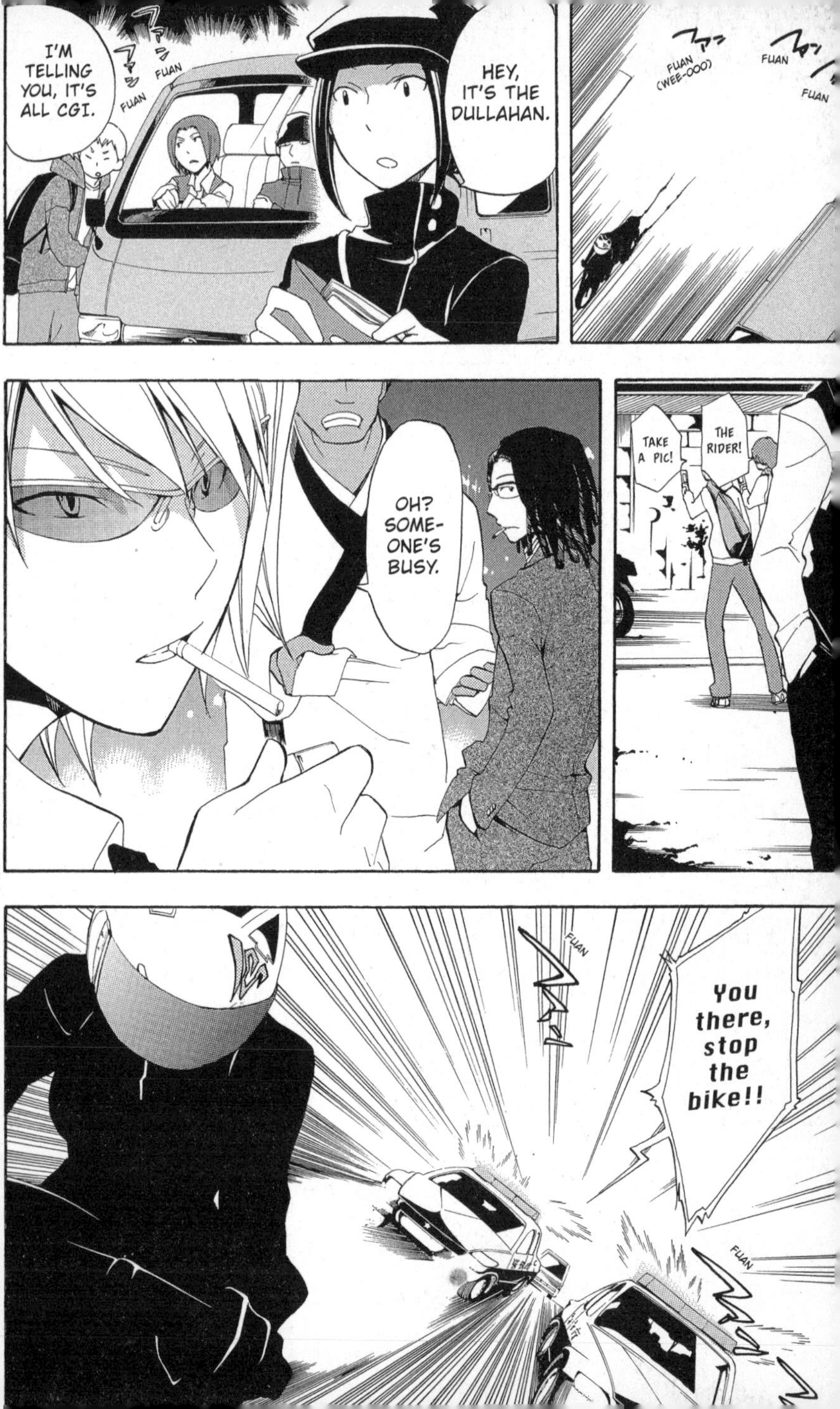
FUAN (WEE-OOO)
FUAN
FUAN
HEY, IT'S THE DULLAHAN.
FUAN
FUAN
I'M TELLING YOU, IT'S ALL CGI.
THE RIDER!
TAKE A PIC!
OH? SOME-ONE'S BUSY.
FUAN
You there, stop the bike!!
FUAN

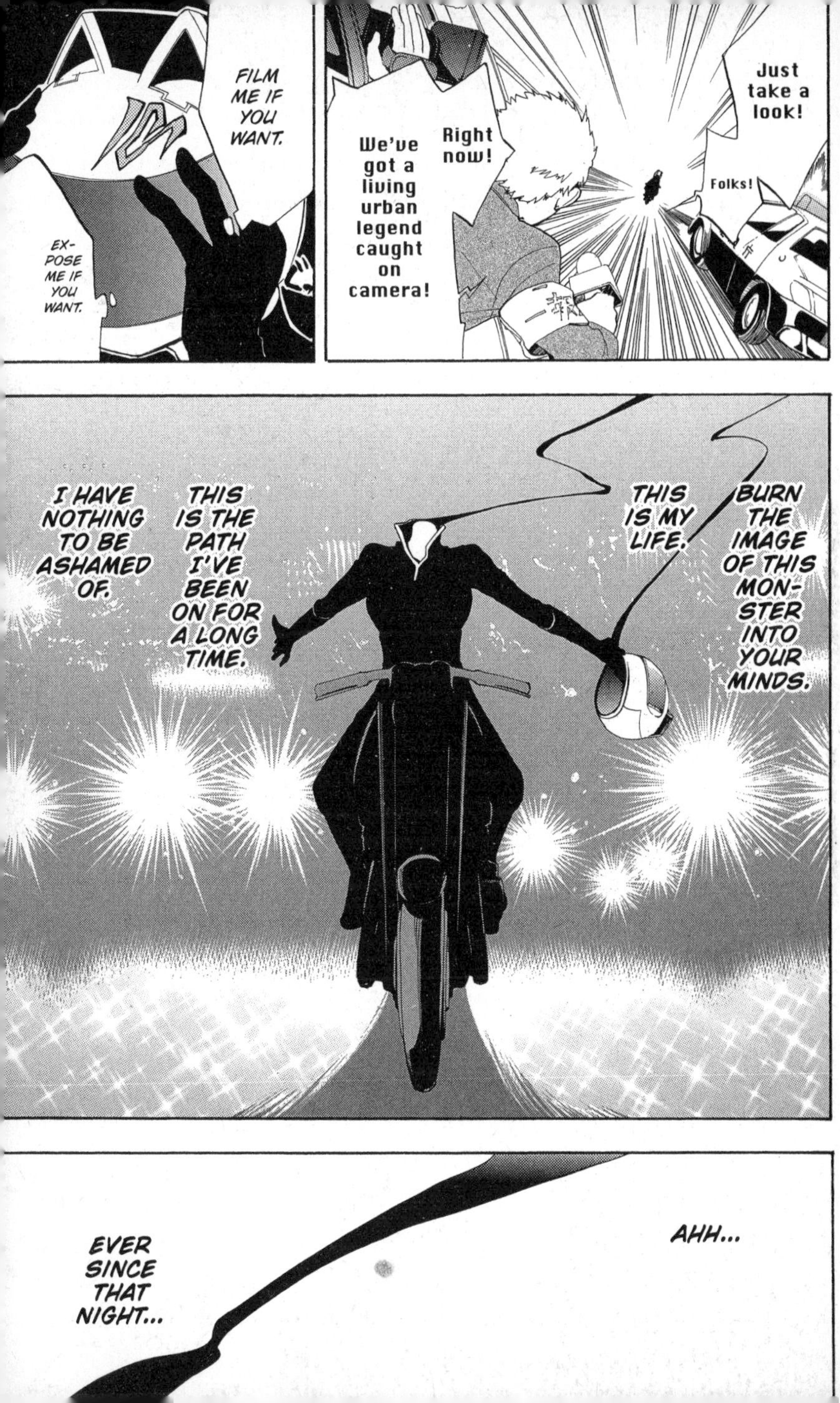
Just take a look!
Folks!
Right now!
We've got a living urban legend caught on camera!
FILM ME IF YOU WANT.
EXPOSE ME IF YOU WANT.
BURN THE IMAGE OF THIS MONSTER INTO YOUR MINDS.
THIS IS MY LIFE.
THIS IS THE PATH I'VE BEEN ON FOR A LONG TIME.
I HAVE NOTHING TO BE ASHAMED OF.
AHH...
EVER SINCE THAT NIGHT...

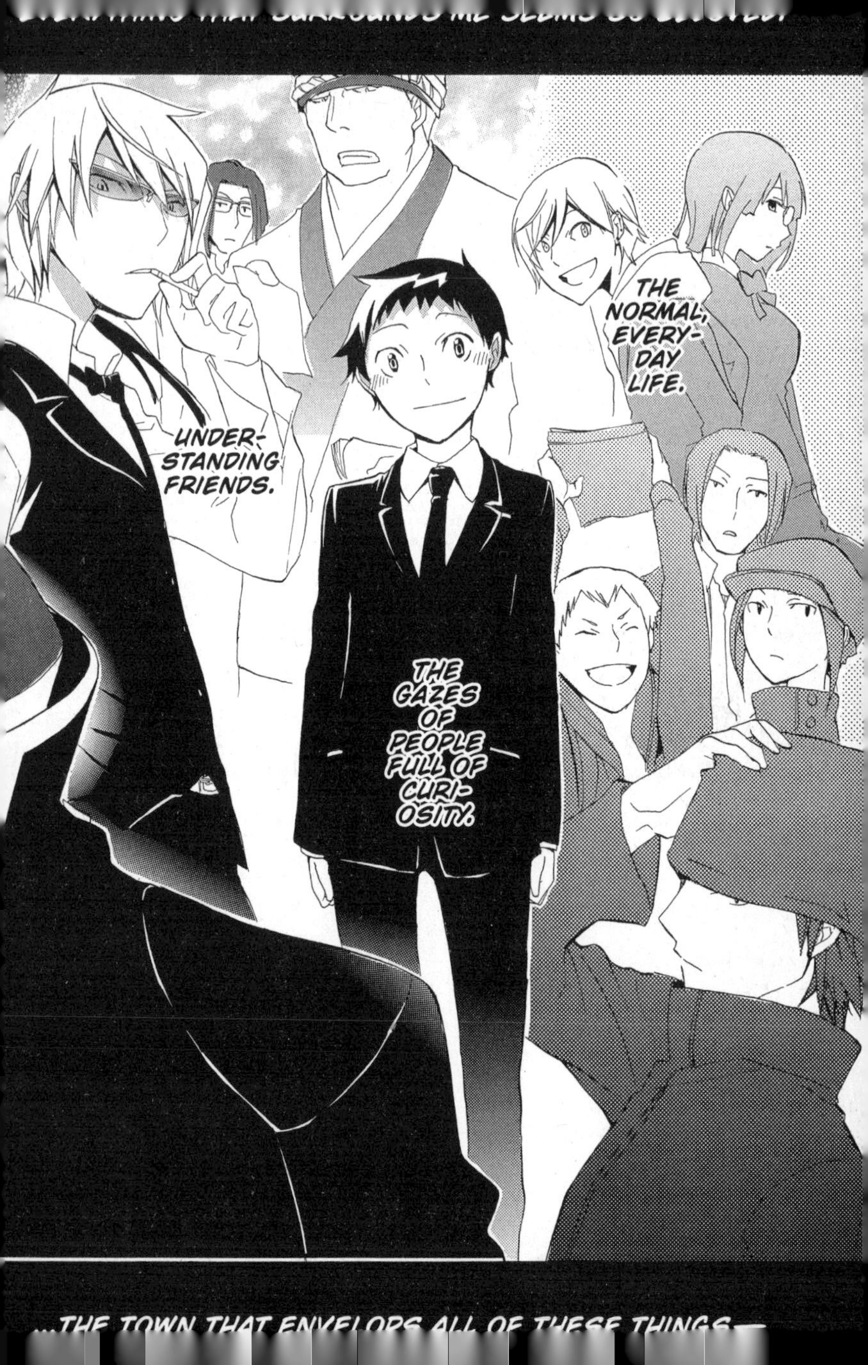
THE NORMAL, EVERY-DAY LIFE.
UNDER-STANDING FRIENDS.
THE GAZES OF PEOPLE FULL OF CURI-OSITY.
...THE TOWN THAT ENVELOPS ALL OF THESE THINGS—

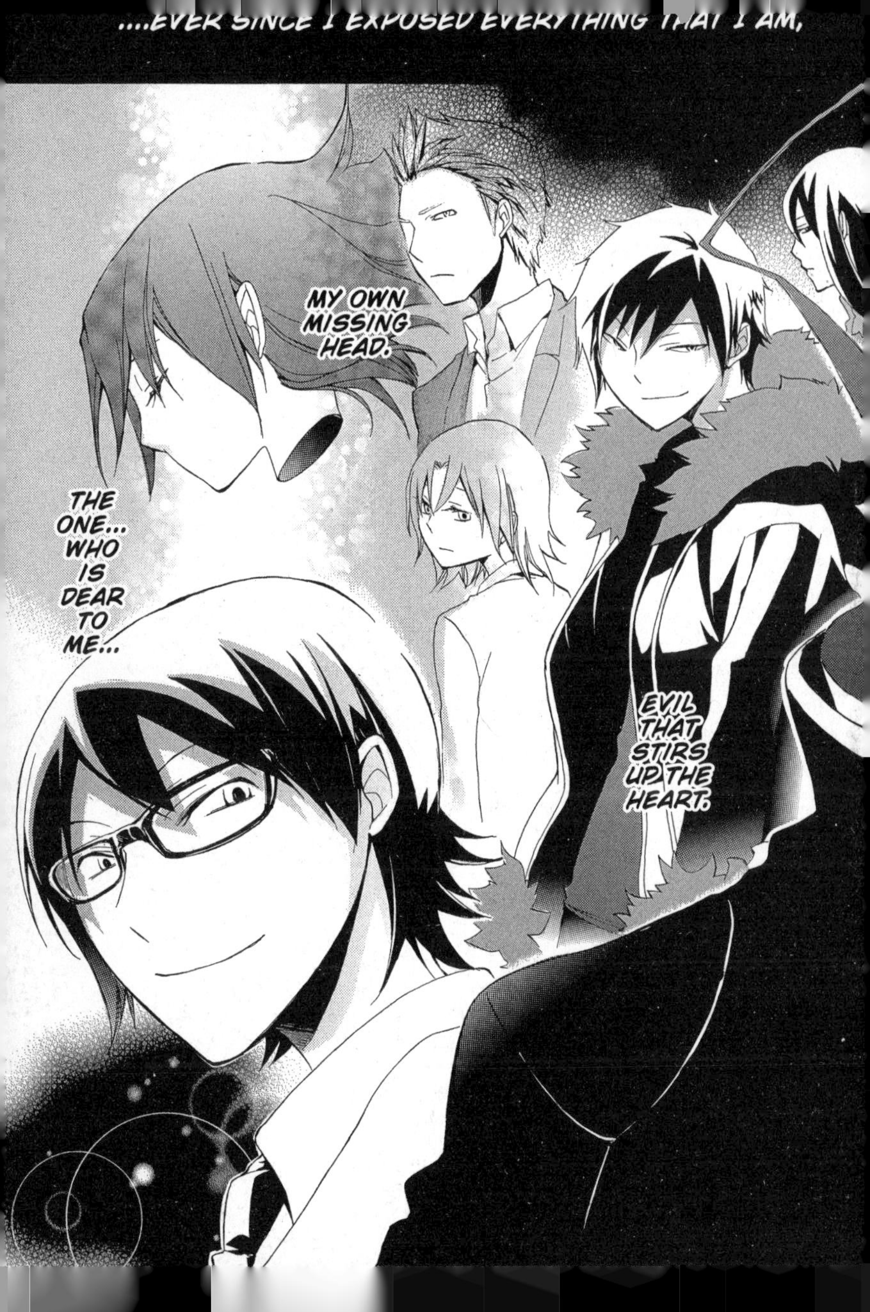
....EVER SINCE I EXPOSED EVERYTHING THAT I AM,
MY OWN MISSING HEAD.
EVIL THAT STIRS UP THE HEART.
THE ONE... WHO IS DEAR TO ME...

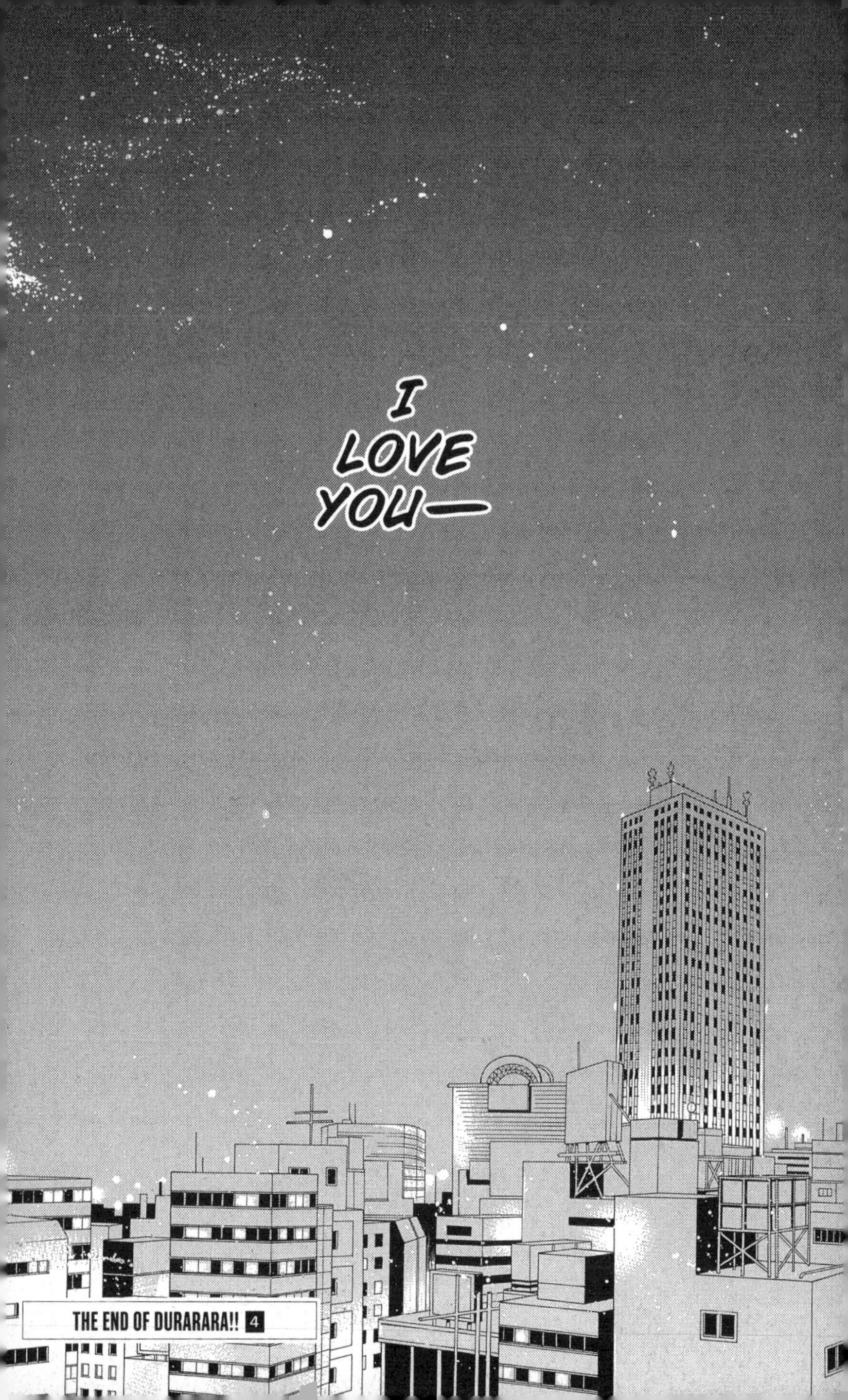
I LOVE YOU—
THE END OF DURARARA!! 4

TRANSLATION NOTES

COMMON HONORIFICS

No honorific: Indicates familiarity or closeness; if used without permission or reason, addressing someone this way would constitute an insult.

san: The Japanese equivalent of Mr./Mrs./Miss. If a situation calls for politeness, this is the fail-safe honorific.

kun: Used most often when referring to boys, this indicates affection or familiarity. Occasionally used by older men among their peers, but it may also be used by anyone referring to a person of lower standing.

chan: An affectionate honorific indicating familiarity used mostly in reference to girls; also used in reference to cute persons or animals of either gender.

PAGE 139

Shogi: A Japanese board game similar to chess. Many of the recognizable international chess pieces are included and move according to the same rules—such as the king, rook, and bishop—but others are unique to shogi. One major difference is that nearly all of the pieces can be promoted by crossing the board, not just the pawn. Additionally, captured pieces can be returned to the board as though they were your own.

PAGE 147

Dollars: The source of this name is the Japanese adjective *dara-dara*, which means "lazy," "pointless," or "endless." Even though the longtime Japanese pronunciation of dollar is *doru*, the pronunciation of the Dollars gang in the story is *daraazu* (hence the connection to *dara*).

Cast:

Mikado Ryugamine

Masaomi Kida

Anri Sonohara

Namie Yagiri

Seiji Yagiri

Mika Harima

Izaya Orihara

Shizuo Heiwajima

Tom Tanaka

Simon Brezhnev

Walker Yumasaki

Erika Karisawa

Saburo Togusa

Kyouhei Kadota

Shinra Kishitani

Celty Sturluson

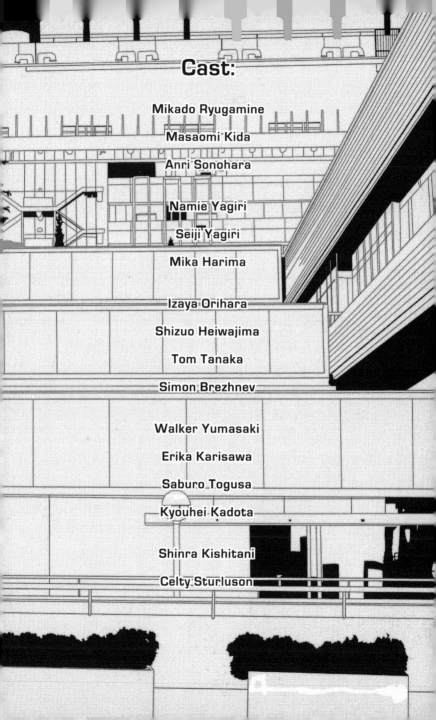

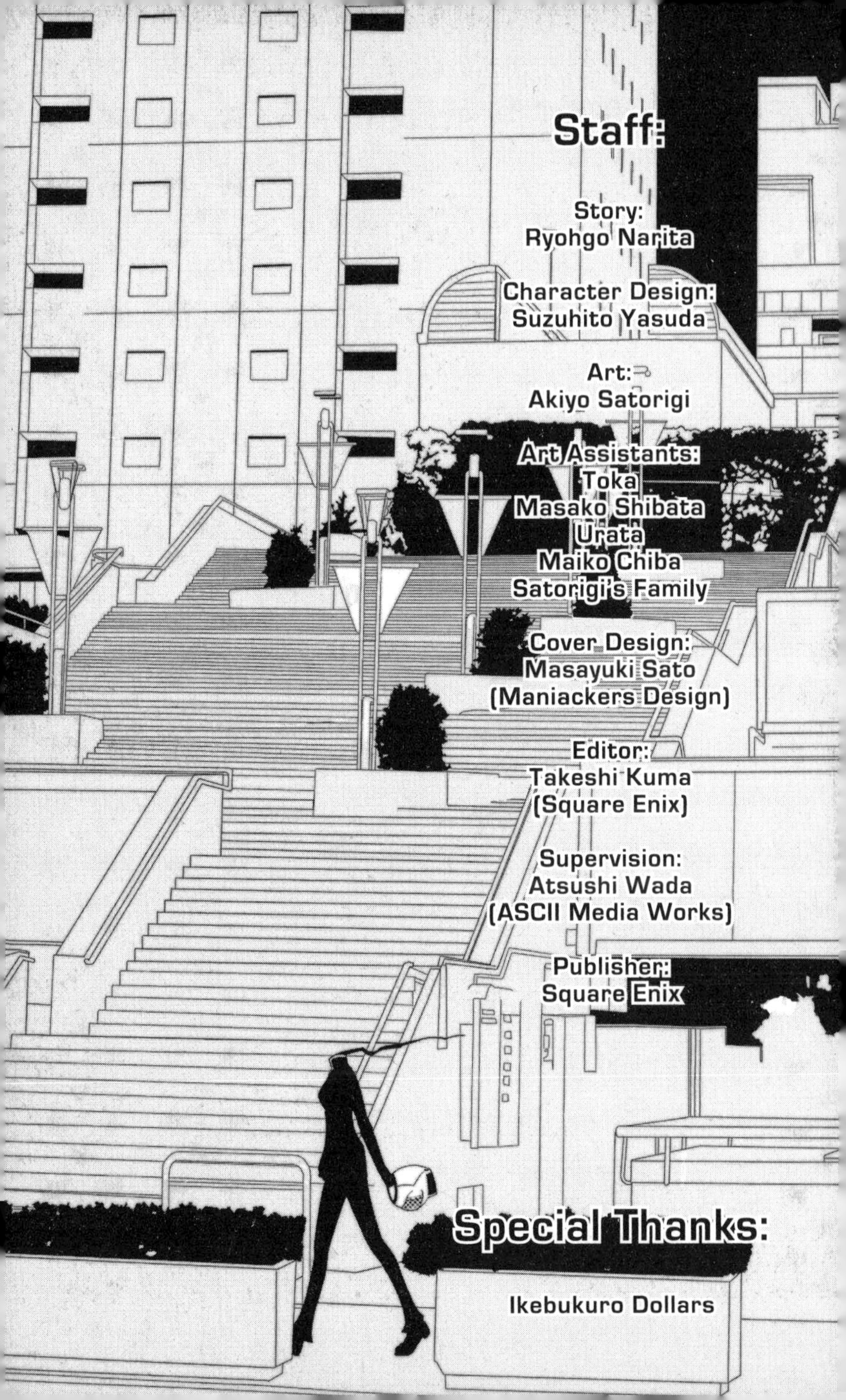

Staff:

Story:
Ryohgo Narita

Character Design:
Suzuhito Yasuda

Art:
Akiyo Satorigi

Art Assistants:
Toka
Masako Shibata
Urata
Maiko Chiba
Satorigi's Family

Cover Design:
Masayuki Sato
(Maniackers Design)

Editor:
Takeshi Kuma
(Square Enix)

Supervision:
Atsushi Wada
(ASCII Media Works)

Publisher:
Square Enix

Special Thanks:

Ikebukuro Dollars

Hello, I am Ryohgo Narita, the so-called "creator" of this mixed-media project called *Durarara!!*

This is the fourth time I've given this introduction, and it's also time to place a temporary hold on this comic adaptation.

These four volumes make up the story described in the very first volume of the novel series.

Now, there are nine novels in the *Durarara!!* series at the time of this writing, so in the future you'll see this character and that character make a splash, a character will show off a secret side, a character's past will be exposed, a new non-human character will be introduced, Ikebukuro will be ruled by vampires, the Ikebukuro vigilante force will fight back, matching blood with blood—wait, sorry, part of that wasn't true. The vampires are in a different story of mine, called *Vamp!* However, if you read both *Durarara!!* and *Vamp!* you'll notice some funny little details, so if you ever get the chance————(redacted)————Oops, close one! I very nearly advertised another product again.

So anyway, *Durarara!!* is a wild and fantastical story featuring a heroine and principal character known as Celty Sturluson, a headless monster. But how did this story appear to you? In Satorigi-san's hands, the story features a Celty who is a bit more human (which is weird in itself) and a lot more adorable. If you enjoyed this character and the Ikebukuro she lives in, I could not be more

Illustration: Suzuhito Yasuda

Of course, not only is this fiction, but I originally started this story eight years ago, and I assure you that modern Ikebukuro doesn't have any color gangs or men who throw vending machines, so don't get the wrong idea!

(However, color gangs were a real thing there years ago. In fact, they still exist in Saitama Prefecture now. I'm serious!)

Finally, as a reader like the rest of you, I've truly enjoyed this comic adaptation! Satorigi-san's version of *Durarara!!* has such a wonderful vibe, I couldn't wait to read the newest chapter every month. In fact, many of the fan letters I receive say, "I got into the story through the manga," so I think there's a great relationship between the novels and the manga!

The anime's gotten huge on the Internet, where many people have had the chance to see it for themselves. I hope that novel, manga, and anime continue to coexist in a relationship of mutual inspiration, and I intend to utilize that inspiration in my writing!

To Satorigi-san; Kuma-san, the manga editor; all the artists who participated in the anthology; Yana Toboso-san, who drew the illustrations for the *Durarara* and *Black Butler* collaboration—thank you for all of your support.

And most of all, thank you to all of the readers who have kept this story alive! Keep your eyes peeled for the manga continuation of the story, *Durarara!!*

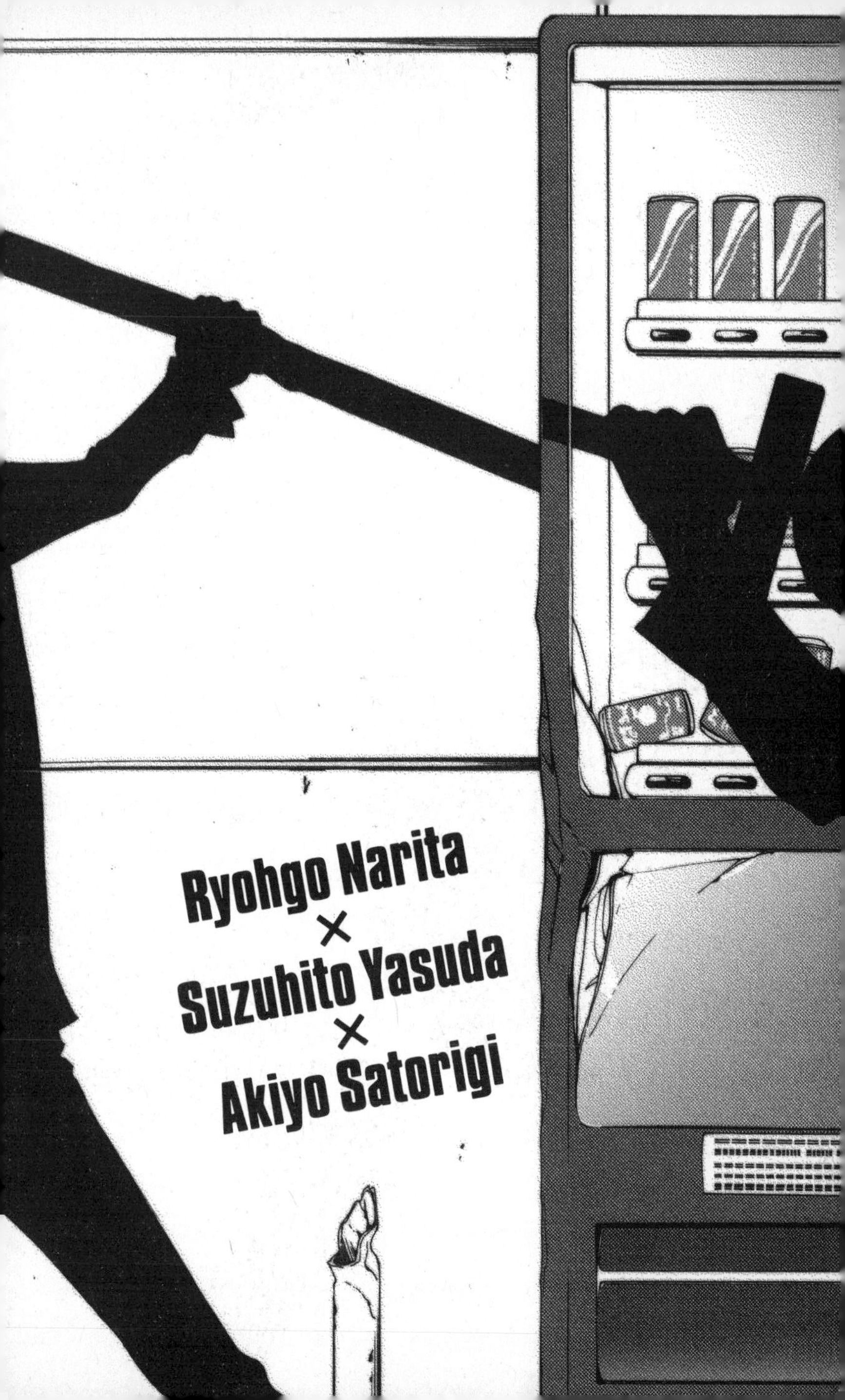
Ryohgo Narita
×
Suzuhito Yasuda
×
Akiyo Satorigi

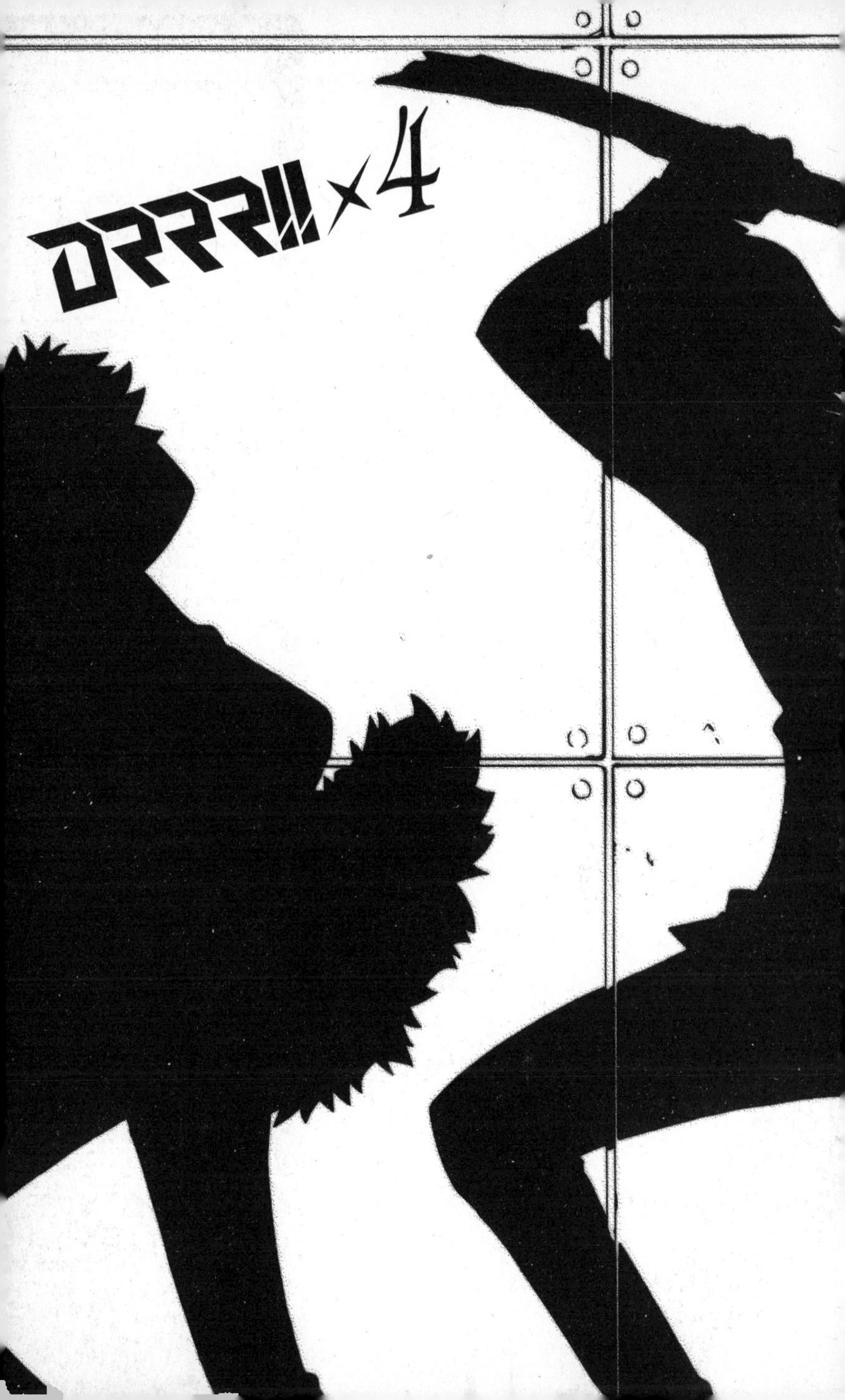
DRRR!! ×4

DURARARA!! ④

**RYOHGO NARITA
SUZUHITO YASUDA
AKIYO SATORIGI**

Translation: Stephen Paul

Lettering: Lys Blakeslee

DURARARA!! Vol. 4 © Ryohgo Narita / ASCII MEDIA WORKS
© 2011 Akiyo Satorigi / SQUARE ENIX CO., LTD. All rights reserved. First published in Japan in 2011 by SQUARE ENIX CO., LTD. English translation rights arranged with SQUARE ENIX CO., LTD. and Hachette Book Group through Tuttle-Mori Agency, Inc.

Translation © 2012 by SQUARE ENIX CO., LTD.

Yen Press
Hachette Book Group
237 Park Avenue, New York, NY 10017

www.HachetteBookGroup.com
www.YenPress.com

Yen Press is an imprint of Hachette Book Group, Inc. The Yen Press name and logo are trademarks of Hachette Book Group, Inc.

First Yen Press Edition: October 2012

ISBN: 978-0-316-20933-5

10 9 8 7 6 5 4 3

BVG

Printed in the United States of America